Communication in

Transdisciplinary Teams

Gaetano R. Lotrecchiano & Shalini Misra
(Editors)

Communication in Transdisciplinary Teams

Gaetano R. Lotrecchiano & Shalini Misra
(Editors)

Informing Science Press

Communication in Transdisciplinary Teams

Copyright © 2020 Informing Science Press

Cover illustration from Vikiss.
https://www.istockphoto.com/vector/neo-abstract-style-illustration-gm1144772976-307902789

Cover design: Gaetano R. Lotrecchiano, EdD, PhD

ISBN: 978-1-68110-052-4

Published by
Informing Science Press
publishing arm of the Informing Science Institute:
131 Brookhill Court
Santa Rosa
California
95409
USA
Phone: +1 707 537-2211
ISPress.org
InformingScience.org

Printed in the USA

Gaetano R. Lotrecchiano & Shalini Misra (Editors). 2020
Communication in Transdisciplinary Teams
Santa Rosa, CA: Informing Science Press

Table of Contents

CHAPTER 3: COMMUNICATIVE PROCESSES IN TRANS-SECTOR TRANSDISCIPLINARY COLLABORATIONS.. **91**

Chitvan Trivedi, Shalini Misra

CHAPTER 4: A NEW PARADIGM FOR RESEARCH ORGANIZATION: ACADEMIC LEADERSHIP IN TRANSDISCIPLINARY SCIENCE TEAMS **123**

Elina I. Mäkinen

CHAPTER 8: CHALLENGES AND OPPORTUNITIES IN CONDUCTING COLLABORATIVE TRANSDISCIPLINARY RESEARCH (TDR): A CASE FROM A SMALL ACADEMIC INSTITUTION IN PUERTO RICO.. 227
Nilda G. Medina, Loggina S. Báez, Loyda B. Méndez

CHAPTER 9: TRANSDISCIPLINARY COMMUNICATION IN RESEARCH TEAMS: INSTITUTIONAL CONSTRUCTS AND PRACTICES FROM A URUGUAYAN PERSPECTIVE
Bianca Vienni Baptista, Maria Goñi Mazzitelli, Florencia Ferrigno Came 253

CHAPTER 10: A MULTIFACETED DISCIPLINE-AGNOSTIC APPROACH TO TRAINING TRANSDISCIPLINARY TEAMS IN COMMUNICATION.. 293
Sawsan Khuri

Gaetano R. Lotrecchiano & Shalini Misra (Editors). 2020
Communication in Transdisciplinary Teams
Santa Rosa, CA: Informing Science Press

Preface

This edited volume serves two purposes. First, it highlights a range of conceptual and pragmatic dimensions of communication in transdisciplinary collaborative settings in diverse contexts and conditions. Advances in the "science of team science" and the study of inter- and trans-disciplinarity more broadly have been made mainly in Europe and North America. We believe that if scholars, professionals, policy makers, and community members – all participants in collaborative partnerships – are served only by facts and examples from Euro-American viewpoints, it would not only result in a culturally narrow body of work, but also have limited applicability to collaboration. With this concern in mind, several of the case studies, examples, and theories in this volume are international in origin. Presented in this manner, we hope that the research and findings reported in this volume will be more relevant to transdisciplinary collaboration.

Second, this volume addresses the critical importance of communication in collaboration at multiple levels of analysis – intrapersonal, interpersonal, organizational, and institutional, as well as the broader socio-political context. This volume is not one that contributes to communication theory in collaborative settings or relies heavily on the discipline of communication sciences. None of the authors, including ourselves, are staunch communication specialists. Rather, the research reported here scrutinizes the content and quality of interactions in a variety of cross-cultural settings and conditions; understands how the nature of dialogue influences interpersonal relationships and organizational learning; explores the epistemic and interpersonal demands communication in transdisciplinary teams places on leaders and members of such teams; identifies the institutional and organizational context for effective communication in TD settings; elucidates the socio-cognitive and behavioral skills, competencies, and knowledge repertoires for effective communication in transdisciplinary teams; and considers the potential contributions of advanced digital technologies in promoting knowledge integration.

The volume can be used as a first course in communication in transdisciplinary teams encouraging you to move on to reading further on topics and questions that interest you. We provide key definitions of concepts and brief overviews of theories where appropriate for readers who are new to the field. Each author also suggests pertinent readings relevant to the subject matter of their contributions.

For educators and trainers, two chapters in the volume focus exclusively on the development of communication competencies in collaborative settings. Almost all the other chapters can be used as cases in courses focusing on transdisciplinary problem-solving or team science training at the undergraduate and graduate levels and for professional participants in transdisciplinary teams because they highlight different aspects of communication in the collaborative process. You may use the chapters in the book as a starting point for discussion with students or collaborators to open the conversation on the nuances and complexities of communication in transdisciplinary teams. We are especially excited that the volume can be offered as an Open Education Resource (OER), meaning that the work can be shared for free for personal or classroom use. We are pleased to be able to contribute to a more affordable educational experience and promote greater access to educational resources to interested readers regardless of their financial or economic situation.

In working with our collaborators in this volume, we are reminded that not only do we rely on scholarly diversity to expand the discourse, but also that the conversation is emergent, some territory is uncharted, and some paths are overgrown and seemingly unnavigable. While this volume is not a survey of communication in transdisciplinary teams, it tries to serve as a compass directing the reader to what we know about this topic, identifying gaps, and suggesting new lines of research.

This work would not be possible without the committed engagement and diverse voices of our contributors. We thank them for their hard work and perserverence through all the stages of the publication process. This volume is an expression of our interdependency and trust. We greatly appreciate the meticulous and thorough support and contributions of our managing editor, Betty Boyd, for bringing this work into fruition. We thank Eli Cohen, managing editor of the Informing Science journals and founder and Executive Director of the Informing Science Institute, for inviting us to edit a volume on communication in transdisciplinary teams and supporting us tirelessly through this journey. And, nothing is possible without the love, encouragement, and support of our families, for which we are forever grateful.

Gaetano R. Lotrecchiano, EdD, PhD

Shalini Misra, PhD

Editors

Note: *We use the equal contributions approach for the sequence of the editors of this volume. The order of editorship is listed alphabetically.*

Gaetano R. Lotrecchiano & Shalini Misra (Editors). 2020
Communication in Transdisciplinary Teams
Santa Rosa, CA: Informing Science Press

Introduction: Communication in Inter- and Trans-disciplinary Teams

Julie Thompson Klein
Wayne State University, Detriot, MI, USA
julietklein@comcast.net

Shalini Misra
Virginia Tech, Arlington, VA, USA
shalini@vt.edu

Gaetano R. Lotrecchiano
George Washington University, Washington, DC, USA
glotrecc@gwu.edu

This volume on communication in transdisciplinary teams is timely for two reasons: the number and size of research teams has increased, and communication is a primary criterion for success in both inter- and trans-disciplinary collaborations. This introduction provides an overview of theory and practice aimed at orienting readers to pertinent literature then previews the chapters that follow. First, though, preliminary definition is in order. Relevant insights are dispersed across literatures on both inter- and trans-disciplinarity, raising the question of how they differ (Klein, 2017).

> **Interdisciplinarity (ID)** integrates information, data, methods, tools, concepts, or theories from two or more disciplines or bodies of knowledge in order to address a complex question, problem, topic, or theme. Solo interdisciplinarians work independently, but communication across boundaries is essential to collaboration.

> **Transdisciplinarity (TD)** transcends disciplinary worldviews by generating overarching synthetic frameworks and, in a connotation that arose in the late 20th century, problem-oriented research that crosses boundaries of academic, public, and private spheres by engaging stakeholders in co-production of knowledge. It also connotes teamwork aimed at generating new conceptual and methodological frameworks.

We combine insights from literatures on inter- and trans-disciplinarity in order to acknowledge parallels between the two concepts. Authors of chapters of this volume differ in their conceptualization and use of the terms, as well as the focus of their research. We

J. T. Klein's contribution to this introductory chapter draws on her chapter on "Learning in Transdisciplinary Collaborations: A Conceptual Vocabulary," in D. Fam, L. Neuhauser and P. Gibbs (Eds), (2018). *Transdisciplinary theory, practice, and education: The art of collaborative research and collective learning*, pp. 11-44. Springer: Cham, Switzerland: Springer; and on her forthcoming book "Beyond Interdisciplinarity: Boundary Work, Communication, and Collaboration in the 21st Century.

S. Misra's and G. R. Lotrecchiano's contributions to this introductory chapter draw from their series introduction to the Special Issue on transdisciplinary communication in the journal Informing Science (Misra, S., & Lotrecchiano, G. R. (2018). Transdisciplinary communication: Introduction to the special series. *Informing Science: the International Journal of an Emerging Transdiscipline, 21*, 14-50).

preserve their original uses of the two terms but synthesize lessons from both literatures in order to arrive at a more robust understanding of the dynamics of communication in teamwork that transcends knowledge boundaries. In the course of our discussion, we also employ nine related concepts defined in the text box: including *pidgin* and *creole, collaborative interdisciplinary reasoning, communicative action, collaborative communication competence, team climate, socio-cognitive platforms for interdisciplinary collaboration, a cooperation and communication culture, mutual* and *integrative learning,* and *knowledge convergence.*

Pidgin and *Creole:* A pidgin is an interim tongue that provides a medium for common ground between groups with different languages. A creole is a first language among members of a new cultural, social, or cognitive community.

Collaborative Interdisciplinary Reasoning: Integration of disciplinary contributions requires shared understanding and action through exchange, evaluation, and assertion of claims in a process of reasoning together.

Communicative Action: Cognitive rationality or scientific language cannot explain everything. Instrumental, ethical, and aesthetic forms of knowledge are all needed, and rational knowledge emerges from both "what we know" and "how we communicate" it.

Collaborative Communication Competence: Communication is essential to collective activities, factoring in participants' goals, ability to integrate knowledge, and expertise in interpersonal, relational, organizational, and pedagogical contexts.

Team Climate: A positive climate for transdisciplinary projects is based on shared imperatives that guide orientations and actions of teams or groups. Goals vary though, including innovation versus service or safety; so do types of interventions.

Socio-Cognitive Platforms for Interdisciplinary Collaboration: Group membership and collective norms require frameworks and spaces for communication and collaboration. They foster mutual understanding and shared goals, ideas, and measures.

Cooperation and Communication Culture: Cooperation helps facilitate collaboration through communication, interaction, mutual engagement, and co-elaboration of knowledge. It also attends to interfaces where the work of participants is co-dependent.

Mutual and Integrative Learning: Learning together evolves through social interaction. It is context-dependent and facilitates increased understanding and similarity of cognitive representations though collective exchange and engagement.

Knowledge Convergence: In inter- and trans-disciplinary work, convergence is a group-level phenomenon linked with collaborative learning resulting from increased common knowledge. Learners acquire shared knowledge and transactive memory.

Literature

The concept of communication is ambiguous because the term appears across popular, academic, and professional contexts. Academic studies also range from conversation analysis and dynamics of small-groups to complexities of dialogue in social networks, computer-mediated interactions, and training for communications industries. Moreover, Robert Craig

(1999) reported, specialties and schools of thought are informed by separate traditions of rhetorical, semiotic, phenomenological, cybernetic, socio-psychological, sociocultural, and critical analysis. Burtis and Turman (2006) contend all group communication involves boundary spanning, necessitating both internal and external boundary negotiations. However, boundary spanning, transferring information, sharing meaning, and negotiating take on greater importance in TD collaboration because it requires bridging knowledge domains with distinct logics, methods, and languages.

The formal study of teams, James Davis (1995) recalled, started in employment settings. Early studies of group behavior evolved into more specialized studies of human communication and the social psychology of groups. Lawrence Bass (1975) also reported "interdisciplinary task force management" has long been a feature of military operations, civilian affairs, engineering projects, feasibility studies, and industrial research and development. World War II was a watershed in the history of interdisciplinary research, highlighted by major initiatives such as the Manhattan Project and the emerging field of operations research. They tackled defense-related problems in team-based programs involving academic, governmental, and industrial experts at common sites such as institutes on campuses and national laboratories. Communication researchers also cite the World War II era as a heyday for small group communications, preceded by studies in the 1920s that adapted John Dewey's work on democratic group decision-making. Early management literature tended to focus on organizing teams and facilitating interactions, applying theories of the day to studies of interdisciplinary collaboration with emphasis on organizational structures, leadership strategies, and types of teams. Over time, though, the focus expanded to creating research cultures and behavioral dynamics of collaboration.

By the time the US-based National Research Council's (NRC) state-of-the-art report on team science appeared in 2015, the topic of communication was widespread. In addition to emergent literature on team science, the report's task force drew on related discussions in business and organizational management, sociology, economics, and science policy. It also acknowledged social science research on military, industrial research and development, production and sales, and sports teams. Accounts of communication in inter- and transdisciplinary contexts appear in other literatures as well, illustrating what library and information scientists call the problem of "scatter." Pertinent insights appear across philosophy, linguistics, communication studies, education, and discourses of inter- and transdisciplinarity. Other fields also informed the NRC task force's understanding of team research, including social studies of science, cognitive psychology, communication and information science, humanities, program evaluation research, small-group research, and case studies in the areas of transportation and healthcare (National Research Council, 2015).

Of added note, the NRC report repeatedly coupled communication and coordination. In a philosophical treatise on collaboration and interdisciplinarity, Hanne Andersen (2016) affirmed their increased role in science but cautioned they can come with epistemic costs. More people can produce and disseminate more results, but that advantage needs to be balanced against increased time demands involved in communication and coordination. Many science teams and large groups are also geographically dispersed, requiring electronic forms of communication with additional challenges stemming from differing work styles, time zones, and cultural ways of working. The difficulties are even greater when tasks are highly interdependent. Transparency is crucial, with explicit channels of communication and use of technologies for sharing knowledge and information. Challenges further complexify during translation of scientific findings into professional and community practices. Communication skills are thus an essential part of individuals' repertoires, and building communication strengths is a primary responsibility of team leaders.

The Role of Language

Language looms large across studies of communication in teamwork because it shapes the ways speakers think and act, thereby bridging cognition and behavior. The most commonly cited challenge arises from differences in specialized jargons. In an early study of interdisciplinary communication, Gerhard Frey (1973) reported discussions normally take place on a level similar to a popular scientific presentation accessible to a wide audience. Discussions become more precise as individuals combine every day and specialist languages. Teams might instead adopt formal languages such as metamathematics or general systems theory. Yet, Bergmann and colleagues (2010) cautioned in a primer on transdisciplinary methods that formal languages must be adapted to the "concrete occasions" and "constellations of disciplines and stakeholders' views within particular projects." Successful collaboration, they added, requires getting past non-specialist understandings of common colloquialisms and trying out terms that foster "interdisciplinary connectivity" through bridge words. Bilingualism is a popular metaphor of interdisciplinary communication. However, mastery of two disciplinary languages rarely occurs. Klein (1996) likened invention of an interlanguage to two concepts: *pidgin* and *creole*.

A pidgin is an interim tongue, providing a medium between groups with different languages. In contrast, a creole is a first language among members of a new social and cognitive community. These concepts are part of linguists' conceptual toolkit, and historian of science. Peter Galison (1997) borrowed them from anthropology to explain interactions in physics between scientific subcultures of theory and experiment. The core idea is that dissimilar subcultures can find common ground through exchange. Differing meaning of the same words is also a key challenge. In a case study of transdisciplinary research on urban development in the Swiss Lowlands, Baccini and Oswald (2008) identified two crucial communication tasks: learning each other's specialized languages and understanding perceptions hidden in words. Baccini, a scientist, and Oswald, an architect, realized they had a common interest in sustainable urban development. It expanded when other collaborators joined them. Yet, participants understood even basic words differently, such as "landscape," "urban," "project," and "process." Two years of mutual learning among team members resulted in a shared definition of the boundary concept of "urbanity." In yet another transdisciplinary project, the bridge concept "net city" (*Netzstadt*) functioned as a boundary object for communication across different approaches, connoting agglomeration of lowlands with connected knots or nodes rather than a fixed center. Likewise, the bridge word "mobility" enabled individuals in another project to cooperate and coordinate around the common objective of sustainable renovation of housing units (Bergmann & Jahn, 2008).

Discourse analysis also sheds light on dynamics of interdisciplinary conversations. Based on a study of academic seminars, Myra Strober (2011) stressed the importance of groups understanding that styles of communication derive from disciplinary cultures and habits of mind they instill. In a different study of eight team meetings, including five in systems biology, Choi and Richards (2017) focused on epistemics of communication. Their major insight is that collaborators occupy epistemic domains, individuated by what they know and how they situate themselves in order to contribute to interdisciplinary discourse. Individuals adopt a particular "epistemic stance" that reflects how they want to position themselves in light of their status. In analyzing excerpts from initial meetings, Choi and Richards identified four patterns by which they deploy expert knowledge: (1) marking their place to declare relevance; (2) telling territory through displaying, deploying, and directing their knowledge; (3) making connections; and (4) clarifying terminology. They subsequently move to more coordinated and integrated stages of mutual understanding and joint knowledge. Shifting from self-oriented communication to "supportive alignment" of contributions enables collaborative knowledge building and co-construction of responses, fostering "affiliative talk" rather than individual positioning.

Collaborative Reasoning, Action, and Competence

Three concepts deepen understanding of communication in inter- and trans-disciplinary teams: *collaborative interdisciplinary reasoning*, *communicative action*, and *collective competence*.

In a previous work and in her contribution to this book, **Bethany Laursen (2018, 2020)** calls communication the essential vehicle for *collaborative interdisciplinary reasoning*. She highlights two warrants. The first is Holbrook's (2013) consideration of whether interdisciplinary communication is possible. He identified three alternative answers in philosophy of science and social/political philosophy. The possibility of communication across boundaries is a matter of debate, though the first and dominant view asserts that integrating two or more disciplinary languages can generate a new common understanding. The keys to translation across disciplines are common vocabulary, shared knowledge, reciprocal comprehension, mutual trust, and social accord. Rival answers, though, hold that disciplinary languages are in principle and often in fact incommensurable: communication can only occur by a second view, learning the language of another discipline, or a third view, inventing a new language. Laursen adopts the first answer, but, in an investigation building on the work of Hanne Andersen, Vincenzo Politi (2017) suggested that "difference" rather than the restrictive notion of "incommensurability" can be the basis for coordinated efforts. Debate also continues on whether consensus and integration are mandatory. Laursen's second warrant is Jürgen Habermas' concept of "reasoning together." Through analysis of a conversational transcript of a multidisciplinary team, she scrutinized the process of synthesizing disciplinary perspectives at an individual level, enabling shared understanding and action at a team level. She defines this process of cognitive shifting at the individual and team level *collaborative interdisciplinary reasoning*.

In a different study of a transdisciplinary project aimed at revitalizing residential neighborhoods on the outskirts of Quebec City, Després and colleagues (2008) also invoked Habermas' (1987) theory of *communicative action*. It is based on the premise that cognitive rationality or scientific language cannot explain everything. Després and colleagues found that instrumental, ethical, and aesthetic forms of knowledge are all needed. In addition, rational knowledge comes out of not only "what we know" but "how we communicate" it, generating a form of "communicative rationality." When stakeholders enter into a process of negotiation they confront the four forms of knowledge in a series of encounters that allow representatives of each type to express their views and proposals. In the process, a fifth type of knowledge emerges. It is a hybrid product, the result of "making sense together." Fostering intersubjectivity, it requires ongoing efforts to achieve mutual understanding. As progressively shared meanings, diagnoses, and objectives emerge, individual interests and views are seen in different perspectives.

Jessica Leigh Thompson (2009) placed the third concept—*collective communication competence*—at the heart of interdisciplinary collaboration. Her ethnographic study of an academic team focused on human behaviors related to production of greenhouse gas emissions in urban areas examined processes that facilitate and hinder communication. Thompson's findings yielded four suggestions for team members and managers: (1) build in trust-building time, (2) host explicit discussions about language differences, (3) schedule social time, and (4) confront communication challenges early. She also recommended using a facilitator to navigate challenges. The common insights between Thompson's study and literature on transdisciplinary projects include openness, willingness to learn from others, and early negotiation of language differences. "Presence" in the form of engagement and "deep listening" are also crucial, and the process is ongoing. Reflexive communication helps members periodically reinforce mutual trust and gain confidence about sharing individual perspectives and insights.

Platforms, Cultures, and Conflict

The NRC report (2015) on team science also linked communication with the concept of a *team climate*, based on shared imperatives that guide orientations and actions. Hindenlang, Hoeb, and Roux (2008) highlighted the role of platforms for creating a team climate in transdisciplinary projects. They create a space for communication, fostering mutual understanding, shared goals, concrete ideas and measures, and common assessment. Comparably, based on a study of nine research programs and networks, Boix-Mansilla, Lamont, and Sato (2016) proposed a model of *socio-cognitive platforms for interdisciplinary collaboration*. Gains in communicative and collaborative capacity include greater clarity about disciplinary languages, increased comfort with unknown terrains, and recalibrated beliefs about other disciplines. Moreover, micro-social networks realign with growing "deliberative competency" at group and individual levels as well as socio-cognitive gains including the ability to provide honest and constructive feedback. Likewise, Wilhelm Vosskamp (1994) proposed that the quality of collaborative outcomes depends on development and richness of a shared language culture that Schmithals and Berhenhage (as cited in Bergmann, 2010, 2012) dubbed a project-specific *cooperation and communication culture*. It requires a conscious and targeted approach to communication, including interfaces where work of one participant is necessary for the work of another.

The second edition of the *Collaboration and Team Science: A Field Guide* (Bennett, Gadlin, & Marchand, 2018) also provided pragmatic strategies for building a team climate. Chapters focus on key topics of leadership, trust, vision, communication, and credit as well as sharing, managing difference and conflict, sustaining and strengthening a team, and navigating and leveraging networks and systems. They contain concrete checklists to determine whether the approach is working or not, and the authors recommended setting ground rules for how participants communicate in meetings and how disagreements and interpersonal conflicts will be handled. Moreover, they endorsed using Ledford's (2008) concept of "Collaborators Pre-Nup" to foster early attention to the overall communication process

(Bennett et al., 2018). Even with platforms and communication cultures in place, however, conflicts can arise. Conflict is associated with both technical issues (definition of a problem, methodologies, and scheduling) and interpersonal issues (leadership style and disciplinary ethnocentrism). Status conflicts are especially tenacious. They arise from disciplinary and professional pecking orders, quantitative versus qualitative approaches, academic rank, gender, race, and cultural backgrounds. The *Field Guide* further stipulated listening is a key skill to solving a problem collaboratively, as well as "principled negotiation" of interpersonal conflicts for mutual gain and objective criteria in evaluating options.

In this book **Chitvan Trivedi and Shalini Misra (2018, 2020**) also contribute a study of social enterprises that are working collaboratively across economic and societal sectors to solve problems such as child labor and poverty. In this process they further highlight the critical importance of cooperation and communication culture to promote "collective thinking" – a process by which tacit knowledge is transformed into explicit knowledge that leads in turn to organizational learning. Dialogic practices also lead to insights that could not be attained individually, including use of metaphorical language, activation of organizational values and norms, as well as design of organizational routines and physical settings that promote free flow of meaning and encourage open inter-personal exchanges. An organizational structure that promotes intra-organizational information exchange, a high level of decisional autonomy, and the ability for organizations to adapt quickly to environmental changes is a critical contextual condition for emergence of this type of communication culture. Their study found these two conditions in combination result in organizational learning, a collective capacity to make sense of and respond to internal and external changes.

In another chapter focused on the institutional level, **Nilda Medina, Loggina Báez, and Loyda Mèndez (2018, 2020)** emphasize the importance of continuous capacity building and collaborative readiness in order to promote collaborative communication and learning. In their study of a small, resource-scarce and minority-serving teaching-intensive institution in Puerto Rico, capacity building was critical to both success and sustainability of TD research initiatives. Capacity building includes systemic institutional efforts to promote shifts in a power structure, providing human, physical, and administrative infrastructure to promote communication and collaboration across individuals and departmental units and community participants, as well as settings and events designed to promote cross-disciplinary interaction and knowledge sharing. Capacity building efforts encouraged convergence across disciplines, the creation of common ground, and the development of new ideas for addressing complex problems.

Mutual and Integrative Learning

A variety of strategies and methods facilitate communication in TD teams, including mental mapping of stakeholder views, consensus conferences, and collaborative learning. McDonald, Bammer, and Deane's (2009) repertoire of dialogue methods covers hypothesis and model building, integrative assessment procedures, boundary objects and concepts, heuristics, research questions, artifacts and products, mutual learning, and stakeholder participation. In addition, teams engage in joint definition of a project, along with the core research problem, questions, and goals. Role clarification and negotiation also help members assess what they need and expect from each other while clarifying differences in disciplinary language and approaches. In addition, on-going interactions foster mutual learning and interdependence, expanding individual identities into group identity. Young teams, Stone (1969) found, exhibit secondary-group relations. Members are self-protective, thinking in terms of "I". Primary-group relations are characterized by dedication to a common task, thinking in terms of "we". Ideal models, Maurice DeWachter (1982) observed, start with the assumption that individuals will suspend their disciplinary/professional worldviews. Yet, his experience in bioethical decision-making indicated the best chance of success lies in starting by translating a global question into the specific language of each discipline then working back and forth in iterative fashion. By constantly checking the relevance of each answer to a core question, no single answer is privileged.

In the present volume, **Bianca Vienni Baptista, Maria Goñi Mazzitelli, and Florencia Ferrigno Came (2020)** analyze how different types of cross-disciplinary research (multi-, inter-, and trans-disciplinary) are being practiced in the Uruguayan context. One of the key insights is that the historical circumstances and cultural context shape how transdisciplinarity is conceptualized and practiced. In Uruguay, the Latin American Student Movement was a key driver of some of the features of transdisciplinary research, namely the creation of university outreach and extension activities and the commitment of universities to social conditions and problems. In fact, the concept of *integrality* in the Uruguayan context shares many features with transdisciplinarity. Integrality, according to these authors, concerns the university's orientation and practices toward the resolution of societal problems through interdisciplinary research and practice. They also analyze communicative processes in four transdisciplinary research centers in Uruguay. Five characteristics of communication stood out in these settings: (1) *one-way communication* (information moving in one direction), (2) *bidirectional communication* (dialogue occurring between two or more actors), (3) *integral spaces* (communication between actors contributing to teaching, extension and research while implies a learning process for all participants), (4) *co-construction* (hybridizing of knowledge, values, and interests by different actors, academic and non-academic), and (5) *diffusion platforms* (disseminating knowledge to different actors via articles, seminars, workshops, and other forums).

In a proposing a conceptual vocabulary for learning in transdisciplinary collaboration, Klein (2018) drew further insights on the nature of integrative learning in cross-disciplinary contexts framed by complexity and systems thinking. The relevant concepts were co-construction of knowledge, mutual learning, and a shift from adaptive and generative to transformational learning. The concepts of deep, collective, and double- and triple-loop learning are also associated with transdisciplinary collaboration, and they are paralleled, in turn, by concepts of collaborative knowledge, reflexivity, and transactivity. In the aggregate they underscore the crucial link between communication and learning. Because more attention has been paid to individual than group learning, their relationship remains an understudied area. Yet, Decuyper, Dochy, and Van den Bosschec (2010) contended, individual and collective learning are in a dialectical relationship that presupposes the other. Likewise, Volet, Vaurus, and Salonen (2009) cautioned against reducing analysis to either individual or social levels. In short, TD communication cannot be limited to either individual capacity or team dynamics. Yet, individuals still need to cultivate their personal capacity for collaboration.

Tanya Augsburg (2014) affirmed Bruce, Lyall, Tait, and Williams' (2004) list of ideal qualities in transdisciplinary individuals, including curiosity about and willingness to learn from other disciplines, flexibility and adaptability, openness in mind and creativity, good communication and listening skills, capacity to absorb information, teamwork, and, Augsburg added, reflection on processes of knowledge integration and willingness to take risks. Misra, Stokols, and Cheng (2015) further deemed competencies for collaboration a "transdisciplinary orientation." A synergistic combination of values, attitudes, beliefs, skills, knowledge, and behaviors predisposes individuals to collaboration. Values, in particular, are guiding principles that incline them to participate and work with others and to learn about unfamiliar theories and methods. Attitudes include willingness to invest time in learning and to adjust individual disciplinary conceptual schema to fit demands of teamwork, while behaviors include learning activities such as participating in a team project.

Two additional chapters in this volume scrutinize the role of leadership within TD science teams. **Maritza Salazar and Teresa Lant (2018, 2020)** examine intrapersonal qualities of leaders in fostering communication on TD medical research teams. In a study of leadership qualities in 52 multidisciplinary medical research teams, they found that leaders who possess multidisciplinary breadth of experience are best positioned to enable communication between team members who have never collaborated before and have little overlapping expertise. These leaders are moderately experienced but well versed in a variety of areas other than their own disciplines, so contribute insights deriving from breadth of research and practice. Their multidisciplinary breadth is key to stimulating interdependencies and information exchange among team members, in addition to summarizing and synthesizing different ideas during interactions. Salazar and Lant's study also showed that teams with leaders possessing multidisciplinary breadth of experience created more innovative outcomes than leaders who had too little or too much multidisciplinary breadth.

In contrast, **Elina Mäkinen (2018, 2020)** reports in this book, an ethnographic study of a newly formed medical research center revealed that leaders who became primary knowledge translators and brokers in nascent TD science teams became the focus of integrative knowledge creation, hindering creation of collective knowledge across all levels of the organization. She introduces the concept of entanglement to describe different types of leadership orientations, roles, and practices to foster interdependency among team members. Comparable to **Trivedi and Misra's (2018, 2020)** findings concerning the importance of fluidity in organizational structures for collective thinking and organizational learning, she also found that entanglement is critical for emergence of feedback loops of information and knowledge that flow through individuals and units across multiple levels of an organization and promote collective thinking as well as organizational learning.

Collaboration Knowledge

Achieving collective thinking in TD teamwork also requires developing a shared knowledge base that constitutes group intelligence (Krauss & Fussell, 1990). A pair of chapters by **Megan Potterbusch and Gaetano R. Lotrecchiano (2018, 2020)** and by **David Lebow (2018, 2020)** consider how digital technologies might promote creation of a shared knowledge base, including use of advanced digital technologies for sensemaking in TD teams. Challenging the traditional, linear, and mostly opaque information flow of the pre-digital era, Potterbusch and Lotrecchiano outline the potential of *Open Science* to serve as a new paradigm for facilitating communication, collaboration, and knowledge integration. For example, digital records of online interactions and artifacts created during the course of collaboration could open new avenues of communication, ease information flow across disciplinary lines, promote information exchange, and enhance trust among team members because of the increased transparency they afford. While the Open Science Framework and associated tools and technologies focus on macro-level team interactions and workflow, David Lebow focuses on the use of a social machine to facilitate knowledge integration in micro-level contexts, such as writing an integrative literature review.

In introducing the HyLighter tool designed for collaborative sensemaking, **Lebow (2018, 2020)** contends that social machines, as socio-cultural constructs, have the potential to reduce cognitive overload inherent in TD collaborative efforts. They can assist individuals and teams in their sensemaking efforts by facilitating identification of points of overlap or synthesis when dealing with large amounts of disparate pieces and types of digital information, a feature of our contemporary digital ecology. The HyLighter tool specifically focuses on addressing three commonly encountered problems inherent in conducting a transdisciplinary literature review within teams: disciplinary language barriers, information overload, and cognitive biases, such as cognitive inflexibility, active and passive information avoidance, confirmation bias, and group think. The features of this tool aim to assist team members in searching, organizing, and synthesizing important information from multiple sources, thereby facilitating collaborative sensemaking.

Other research on development of collaboration knowledge and learning has also focused on shared mental models. In a case study of an interdisciplinary team focused on education in STEM (science, technology, engineering, and mathematics), DuRussel and Derry (2011) integrated understandings of mental models with the concept of *situation awareness* in organizational literature. Prior knowledge helps shape individuals' mental models of a particular situation. As situational learning occurs, new models influence the content and the structure of permanent schemas. Alignment of mental models must be explicit, though, to achieve common understanding. In an overview of collaborative leadership, Barbara Gray (2008) further associated cognitive tasks with visioning and framing. Visioning stimulates creativity, modeled by divergent thinking, risk taking, and challenging established methods. Transdisciplinary leaders engaged in visioning are concerned with both content and collaborative process. Framing change entails grappling with the problem of language. Coupled with visioning it fosters reframing prior assumptions by constructing a new mental model that provides sense-making for team members.

Jeong and Chi (2011) also linked collaborative learning with the concept of *knowledge convergence*. It is evident in shared pieces of knowledge and mental models. Social interaction facilitates mutual understanding and increased similarity of cognitive representations. Weinberger, Stegmann, and Fischer (2007) likewise conceptualized knowledge convergence in terms of sharing and equivalence. Shared knowledge occurs when learners possess the same concepts, while equivalence connotes a similar degree of knowledge about a subject prior to collaboration. Reflexivity is also linked with collaborative learning. It is both transgressive, challenging dominant assumptions and power structures, and transcendent, engaging epistemological flexibility and synergies between contingent disciplinary and cultural knowledge (Bergmann et al., 2010, 2012). In addition, following Zittoun, Baucal, Cornish, and Gillespie (2007), reflexivity can generate collaboration knowledge, a concept that may be further likened to transactivity. And, Decuyper, Dochy, and Van den Bosschec (2010) associated transactivity with the degree to which learners acquire shared knowledge in the form of mental models or cognition and knowledge of who-knows-what.

To elaborate, Decuyper, Dochy, and Van den Bosschec (2010) explained that team learning processes foster a group level system for encoding, storing, and retrieving information. A transactive memory system develops in two phases: (1) specialization of each team member's expertise and (2) coordination and credibility through communication. Knowledge sharing can be unidirectional, but individuals can work together to create transactive and transformational forms of knowledge. Jack Mezirow (2003) defined transformational learning as "[l]earning that transforms problematic frames of reference—sets of fixed assumptions and expectations (habits of mind, meaning perspectives, mindsets)—to make them more inclusive, discriminating, open, reflective, and emotionally able to change." Transformational learning is emancipatory. Its purpose is enlightenment, transcending habitual thought patterns and behavior. Mutual and transformative learning have been associated with increased likelihood of lasting change. Rodrigo Lozano (2014) cautioned, however, that change in mental models and behavior associated requires constant learning in the life cycle of any project.

A final question lies at the heart of **Sawsan Khuri's (2020)** contribution to this volume. What core competencies foster transdisciplinary communication and collaboration skills among scientists and practitioners? Based on a review of the literature on inter- and transdisciplinary scholarship, non-profits, and businesses, Khuri identifies seven core competencies and associated behavioral patterns for TD communication and collaboration for practitioners. They include monitoring and presenting yourself, practicing communication ethics, adapting to others, practicing effective listening, expressing messages, identifying and explaining fundamental communication processes, and creating and analyzing message strategies. In this chapter, Khuri proposes a discipline-agnostic curricular framework for team training in communication based on these core competencies, which educators or facilitators can use in any type of TD team setting, regardless of the subject matter or problem focus.

For their part, the editors of this volume, **Gaetano R. Lotrecchiano and Shalini Misra (2018, 2020)**, adopt a complex adaptive systems approach to conceptual knowledge, skills, and competencies required for effective team functioning and knowledge integration in transdisciplinary teams. They use complexity theory to construct a typology of features of transdisciplinary knowledge producing teams and identify salient team processes that align with complex systems: namely complex problem-solving, stakeholder involvement, methodological pluralism, praxis, open systems capacity, shifting levels of reality, and collaborative construction and reconstruction. They elaborate on the foci of the conceptual knowledge, skills, and competencies for each feature of TD knowledge producing teams. They provide concrete examples of the socio-cognitive and behavioral indicators of these knowledge, skills, and competencies in TD teams with respect to each of these complexity features.

Taken together, the chapters that follow illuminate the range of conceptual and pragmatic dimensions of communication in transdisciplinary collaborative settings identified in the literature review. They illuminate the content and quality of what is conveyed in these interactions in a variety of cross-cultural settings and conditions; understand how they affect interpersonal relationships and organizational learning; explore the epistemic and interpersonal demands it places on leaders and members of TD collaborations; identify the institutional and organizational context for effective communication in TD settings; identify and elucidate the socio-cognitive and behavioral skills, competencies and knowledge repertoires for effective communication in TD teams, and consider the potential contributions of novel digital technologies in promoting knowledge integration. Specifically, we learn that:

1) Interpersonal communication holds a central and constitutive place in TD collaborative endeavors, and is not merely a component of it. Communication, therefore, needs to be studied as a part of the ecology of TD collaborative settings since it is linked inextricably to leadership, organizational structures and routines, institutional setups, mechanisms, and practices, and individuals' dispositions to cross-disciplinary collaboration.

2) Communication in TD settings entails transformational cognitive shifts at both the individual and organizational levels. One feature of this cognitive shift is collective thinking or sensemaking, where one becomes aware of one's own tacit knowledge, assumptions, and beliefs and makes them explicit through assertions and claims, questioning of these assertions and claims, and providing explanations for one's claims. Open, deep, and continuous interpersonal interaction and reflection are essential for cognitive shifting to occur at the individual and organizational level.

3) Integrative knowledge production is stifled if individual level cognitive shifts do not lead to shifts in organizational routines leading to the emergence of organizational learning or collective knowledge and wisdom. Organizational structure plays a decisive role in promoting collective thinking, sensemaking, and organizational learning. Organizational structures that facilitate shared adaptive dynamics or the free flow of knowledge and information through individuals and units across the organization promote communication in TD teams. Similarly, institutional capacity and readiness are macro-level features that can promote effective TD collaboration and communication.

4) Leaders play a critical role in promoting collective thinking and sensemaking. Leadership qualities, such as multidisciplinary breadth, and practices, such as the ability to foster interdependencies between team members, their use of metaphorical language to make tacit knowledge explicit, and their fostering of settings that encourage open interaction that activate organizational values, are key to collective sensemaking.

5) Conceptual knowledge, skills, and competencies that foster complex problem-solving, stakeholder involvement, epistemic and methodological pluralism, and collaborative construction and reconstruction are required for effective team functioning and knowledge integration in transdisciplinary teams.

6) Finally, intelligent and democratic digital technologies have the potential to facilitate knowledge integration in cross-disciplinary collaborative settings by reducing the cognitive burden on individuals and making information exchange between team members more transparent and equitable. The next generation of intelligent machines also offers promising methods for the study of TD communication and collaboration.

These chapters also raise a number of questions for the theory and empirical study of communication in transdisciplinary teams. For example, **are there clearly distinguishable stages of communication in TD settings?** What challenges are specific to each stage of collaboration and what are the leverage points for interventions to address these communication challenges? For example, cognitive shifts from tacit to explicit knowledge may be most evident in the integrating and generating stages of collaboration. However, what types of communication practices and routines support the stage in which synthesis of ideas occurs? Are there certain types of framing and launching communication practices that better enable the integrative communication in the later stages of the collaboration?

Another related question ripe for theoretical and empirical exploration is whether *different types of cognitive shifts* are entailed in communication in TD teams and what types of tools, technologies, routines, and practices can facilitate transformative cognitive shifts. A taxonomy of communication boundaries in TD settings and the associated cognitive shifts would be helpful in the understanding and supporting communication, including training the next generation of TD scholars and practitioners.

A final related set of questions concerns *the conditions and specific mechanisms that can support communication in TD teams.* For example, we learn from the chapters in this volume that skillful intellectual leadership can promote inclusive communication and synthesis. The types of *workflows, tools, and technologies that foster integrative communication is another potent area of research*.

In the epilogue of this volume, Professor Daniel Stokols **(Stokols, Misra, & Lotrecchiano, 2020)** responds to key findings and conclusions of the research reported in this volume and outlines some of the major gaps in the field and directions for further theoretical, methodological, and empirical inquiry. We hope that the research reported in this volume will lead to novel and creative research and practical innovations that further illuminate and improve communication in transdisciplinary contexts. Much remains to be learned about this very important topic.

References

Andersen, H. (2016). Collaboration, interdisciplinarity, and the epistemology of contemporary science. *History and Philosophy of Science, 56*, 1-10.

Augsburg, T. (2014). Becoming transdisciplinary: The emergence of the transdisciplinary individual. *World Futures: The Journal of New Paradigm Research, 70*, 233-247.

Baccini, P., & Oswald, F. (2008). Designing the urban: Linking physiology and morphology. In G. Hirsch Hadorn et al. (Eds.). *Handbook of transdisciplinary research* (pp. 79-88). Dordrecht: Springer.

Bass, L.W. (1975). *Management by task forces: A manual on the operations of interdisciplinary teams.* Mt. Airy, MD: Lomond.

Bennett, L., Gadlin, H. & Marchand, C. (2018). *Collaboration and team science: A field guide* (2nd ed.) Bethesda, MD: National Institutes of Health. Retrieved from http://teamscience.nih.gov

Bergmann, M., & Jahn, T. (2008). CITY: mobil: A model for integration in sustainability research. In G. Hirsch Hadorn et al. (Eds.), *Handbook of transdisciplinary research* (pp. 89-102). Dordrecht: Springer.

Bergmann, M., Jahn, T., Knobloch, T., Krohn, W., Pohl, C., & Schramm, E. (2010). *Methoden transdisziplinärer forschung: Ein uberblick mit anwendungsbeispielen.* Frankfurt/Main: Campus Verlag, Frankfurt/Main; English translation, *Transdisciplinary research methods* (2012). Frankfurt/Main and Chicago: Campus and University of Chicago Press.

Boix-Mansilla, V., Lamont, M., & Sato, K. (2016). Shared cognitive-emotional interactional platforms: Markers and conditions for successful interdisciplinary collaborations. *Science, Technology, & Human Values, 442,* 571-612.

Bruce, A., Lyall, C., Tait, J., & Williams, R. (2004). Interdisciplinary integration in Europe: The case of the Fifth Framework programme. *Futures, 36,* 457–470.

Burtis, J. O., & Turman, P. D. (2006). *Group communication pitfalls: Overcoming barriers to an effective group experience.* Thousand Oaks, SAGE.

Choi, S., & Richards, K. (2017). *Interdisciplinary discourse: Communicating across disciplines.* London: Palgrave, Macmillan.

Craig, R. (1999). Communication theory as a field. *Communication Theory, 9,* 119-161.

Davis, J. (1995). *Interdisciplinary courses and team teaching: New arrangements for learning.* Phoenix, AZ: American Council on Education, Oryx.

Decuyper, S., Dochy, F., & Van den Bosschec, P. (2010). Grasping the dynamic complexity of team learning: An integrative model for effective team learning in organizations. *Educational Research Review, 5,* 111–133.

Després, C., Fortin, A., Joerin, F., Vachon, G., Gatti, E., & Moretti, G. (2008). Retrofitting postwar suburbs: A collaborative design process. In G. Hirsch Hadorn et al. (Eds.), *Handbook of transdisciplinary research* (pp. 327-341). Dordrecht: Springer.

DeWachter, M. (1982). Interdisciplinary bioethics: But where do we start? A reflection on epochè as method. *Journal of Medicine and Philosophy, 7,* 275-287.

DuRussel, L. A., & Derry, S. J. (2011). Schema (mis)alignment in interdisciplinary teamwork. In S. Derry, C. D. Schunn, & M. A. Gernsbacher (Eds), *Interdisciplinary collaboration: An emerging cognitive science* (pp. 187-220). Mahwah, NJ: Earlbaum.

Frey, G. (1973). Methodological problems of interdisciplinary discussions. *RATIO, l5,* 161-182.

Galison, P. (1997). *Image and logic: A material culture of microphysics.* Chicago: University of Chicago Press.

Gray, B. (2008). Enhancing transdisciplinary research through collaborative leadership. *American Journal of Preventive Medicine, 35,* S124-S132.

Hindenlang, K. E., Heeb, J., & Roux, M. (2008). Sustainable coexistence of ungulates and trees: A stakeholder platform for resource use negotiations. In G. Hirsch Hadorn et al. (Eds.). *Handbook of transdisciplinary research* (pp. 315-326). Dordrecht: Springer.

Holbrook, J. B. (2013). What is interdisciplinary communication? Reflections on the very idea of disciplinary integration. *Synthese, 190,* 1865-1879.

Jeong H., & Chi, M. (2011). Knowledge convergence and collaborative learning. *Instructional Service, 35,* 287-315.

Khuri., S. (2020). A multifaceted discipline-agnostic approach to training transdisciplinary teams in communication. In G. R. Lotrecchiano & S. Misra (Eds), *Communication in transdisciplinary teams* (pp. 293-308)**.** Santa Rosa, CA: Informing Science Press.

Klein, J. T. (1996). *Crossing boundaries: Knowledge, disciplinarities, and interdisciplinarities.* Charlottesville, VA: University of Virginia Press.

Klein, J. T. (2017). Typologies of interdisciplinarity: The boundary work of definition. In R. Frodeman, J.T. Klein, & R. Pacheco (Eds), *The Oxford Handbook of Interdisciplinarity* (pp. 21-34). Oxford: Oxford University Press.

Klein, J. T. (2018). Learning in transdisciplinary collaborations: A conceptual vocabulary. In D. Fam, L. Neuhauser, & P. Gibbs (Eds), *Transdisciplinary theory, practice, and education: The art of collaborative research and collective learning* (pp. 11-44). Cham, Switzerland: Springer.

Krauss, R. M. & Fussell, S.R. (1990). Mutual knowledge and communicative reflectiveness. In J. Galegher, R. E. Kraut, & C. Egido (Eds.), *Intellectual teamwork: Social and technological foundations of cooperative work* (pp. 111-145). Hillsdale NJ: Erlbaum.

Laursen, B. (2018). What is collaborative, interdisciplinary reasoning? The heart of interdisciplinary team research. *Informing Science: the International Journal of an Emerging Transdiscipline, 21,* 75-106. https://doi.org/10.28945/4010

Laursen, B. (2020). What is collaborative, interdisciplinary reasoning? The heart of interdisciplinary team research. In G. R. Lotrecchiano & S. Misra (Eds), *Communication in transdisciplinary teams* (pp. 55-89)**.** Santa Rosa, CA: Informing Science Press.

Lebow, D. G. (2018). A social machine for transdisciplinary research. *Informing Science: the International Journal of an Emerging Transdiscipline, 21,* 201-217.

Lebow, D. G. (2020). A social machine for transdisciplinary research. In G. R. Lotrecchiano & S. Misra (Eds), *Communication in transdisciplinary teams* (pp. 203-226). Santa Rosa, CA: Informing Science Press.

Ledford, H. (2008). Collaborations: With all good intentions. *Nature, 452,* 682-684.

Lotrecchiano, G. R., & Misra, S. (2018). Transdisciplinary knowledge producing teams: Toward a complex systems perspective. *Informing Science: the International Journal of an Emerging Transdiscipline, 21,* 51-74. https://doi.org/10.28945/4086

Lotrecchiano, G. R., & Misra, S. (2020). Transdisciplinary knowledge producing teams: Team processes, knowledge, skills, and competencies. In G. R. Lotrecchiano & S. Misra (Eds), *Communication in transdisciplinary teams* (pp.19-54). Santa Rosa CA: Informing Science Press.

Lozano, R. (2014). Creativity and organizational learning as means to foster sustainability. *Sustainable Development, 22,* 205-216.

Mäkinen, E. I. (2018). Complexity leadership theory and the leaders of transdisciplinary science. *Informing Science: the International Journal of an Emerging Transdiscipline, 21*, 133-155.

Mäkinen, E. I. (2020). Complexity leadership theory and the leaders of transdisciplinary science. In G. R. Lotrecchiano & S. Misra (Eds), *Communication in transdisciplinary teams* (pp. 123-147). Santa Rosa, CA: Informing Science Press.

Medina, N. G., Báez, L. S., & Mendez, L. B. (2018). Collaborative transdisciplinary research in a small institution: Challenges and opportunities. *Informing Science: the International Journal of an Emerging Transdiscipline, 21*, 235-253.

Medina, N. G., Báez, L. S., & Mendez, L. B. (2020). Collaborative transdisciplinary research in a small institution: Challenges and opportunities. In G. R. Lotrecchiano & S. Misra (Eds), *Communication in transdisciplinary teams* (pp. 227-251). Santa Rosa, CA: Informing Science Press.

McDonald, D., Bammer, G., & Deane, P. (2009). *Research integration using dialogue methods.* Australian National University. Retrieved from http://epress.anu.edu.au/dialogue_methods_citation.html

Mezirow J. (2003). Transformative learning as discourse. *Journal of Transformation Education, 1*, 58-63.

Misra, S., Stokols, D., & Cheng, L. (2015). The transdisciplinary orientation scale: Factor structure and relation to the integrative quality and scope of scientific publications. *Journal of Translational Medicine and Epidemiology, 3*, 1042+.

National Research Council. (2015). *Enhancing the effectiveness of team science.* National Academies Press, Washington DC.

Politi, V. (2017). Specialization, interdisciplinarity, and incommensurability. *International Studies in the Philosophy of Science, 31*, 301-317.

Potterbusch, M., & Lotrecchiano, G. R. (2018). Shifting paradigms in information flow: An open science framework (OSF) for knowledge sharing teams. *Informing Science: the International Journal of an Emerging Transdiscipline,* 21,179-199.

Potterbusch, M., & Lotrecchiano, G. (2020). Shifting paradigms in information flow: An open science framework (OSF) for knowledge sharing teams. In G. R. Lotrecchiano & S. Misra (Eds), *Communication in transdisciplinary teams* (pp. 177-202). Santa Rosa, CA: Informing Science Press.

Salazar, M. R., & Lant, T. K. (2018). Facilitating innovation in interdisciplinary teams: The role of leaders and integrative communication. *Informing Science: the International Journal of an Emerging Transdiscipline, 21*, 157-178.

Salazar, M. R., & Lant, T. K. (2020). Facilitating innovation in interdisciplinary teams: The role of leaders and integrative communication. In G. R. Lotrecchiano & S. Misra (Eds), *Communication in transdisciplinary teams* (pp. 149-175). Santa Rosa, CA: Informing Science Press.

Stokols, D., Misra, S., & Lotrecchiano, G. R. (2020). Epilogue. In G. R. Lotrecchiano & S. Misra (Eds), *Communication in transdisciplinary teams* (pp. 309-327). Santa Rosa, CA: Informing Science Press.

Stone, A.R. (1969). The interdisciplinary research team. *Journal of Applied Behavioral Science, 5,* 351-365.

Strober, M. (2011). *Interdisciplinary conversations: Challenging habits of thought.* Palo Alto, CA: Stanford University Press.

Thompson, J. L. (2009). Building collective communication competence in interdisciplinary research teams. *Journal of Applied Communication Research, 37,* 278-297.

Trivedi, C., & Misra, S. (2018). Dialogue and the creation of transformative social change: The case of social enterprises. *Informing Science: the International Journal of an Emerging Transdiscipline, 21,* 107-132.

Trivedi, C., & Misra, S. (2020). Communicative processes in trans-sector transdisciplinary collaborations. In G. R. Lotrecchiano & S. Misra (Eds), *Communication in transdisciplinary teams* (pp. 91-121). Santa Rosa, CA: Informing Science Press.

Vienni Baptista, B., Goñi Mazzitelli, M., & Ferrigno Came, F. (2020). Transdisciplinary communication in research teams: Institutional constructs and practices from a Uruguayan perspective. In G. R. Lotrecchiano & S. Misra (Eds), *Communication in transdisciplinary teams* (pp. 253-291). Santa Rosa, CA: Informing Science Press.

Volet, S., Vaurus, M., & Salonen, P. (2009). Self- and social regulation in learning contexts: An integrative perspective. *Educational Psychologist, 44,* 215-226.

Vosskamp, W. (1994.) Crossing of boundaries: Interdisciplinarity as an opportunity for universities in the 1980s? *Issues in Integrative Studies, 12,* 43-54.

Weinberger, A., Stegmann, K., & Fischer, F. (2007). Knowledge convergence in collaborative learning: Concepts and assessment. *Learning and Instruction, 17,* 416-426.

Zittoun, T., Baucal, A., Cornish, F., & Gillespie, A. (2007). Collaborative research, knowledge, and emergence. *Integrative Psychological and Behavioral Science, 41,* 208-217.

Gaetano R. Lotrecchiano & Shalini Misra (Editors). 2020
Communication in Transdisciplinary Teams
Santa Rosa, CA: Informing Science Press

Chapter 1:
Transdisciplinary Knowledge Producing Teams:
Team Processes, Knowledge, Skills, and Competencies

Gaetano R. Lotrecchiano
George Washington University, Washington, DC, USA
glotrecc@gwu.edu

Shalini Misra
Virginia Tech, Arlington, VA, USA
shalini@vt.edu

Chapter Objectives

- To define Transdisciplinary Knowledge Producing Teams (TDKPTs) from a complex adaptive systems perspective and develop a typology of the features of TDKPTs.

- To distinguish between structural systemic complexities and interactive systemic complexities in TDKPTs.

- To identify the salient team processes in TDKPTs.

- To identify the foci of conceptual knowledge, skills, and competencies and align them with salient team processes.

- To provide concrete examples of socio-cognitive and behavioral indicators of knowledge, skills, and competence.

Introduction to the Chapter

This chapter offers a typology of the features of transdisciplinary knowledge producing teams (TDKPTs) using a complex adaptive systems (CAS) lens. TDKPTs are groups of stakeholder participants tasked with producing knowledge across disciplinary, sectoral, and ecological boundaries. TDKPTs reflect components of complex adaptive systems (CAS) and exemplify how CAS behave and function. Using literature from the Science-of-Team-Science (SciTS), complexity theory, and systems theory, we identify salient team processes for each feature of TDKPTs. Further, we elaborate on the conceptual knowledge, skills, and competencies needed for effective team functioning and integrative knowledge production. This chapter urges researchers of TD teams and TD team participants alike to reconsider the development and study of TDKPTs. Knowledge producing team members need

Significant portions of this chapter were published in Lotrecchiano, G. R., & Misra, S. (2018). Transdisciplinary knowledge producing teams: Toward a complex systems perspective. *Informing Science: the International Journal of an Emerging Transdiscipline, 21*, 51-74. https://doi.org/10.28945/4086

to engage in theoretical, epistemological, and methodological reflection to elucidate the dynamic nature of TD knowledge producing teams. Understanding how conflict, dissonance, and reciprocal interdependencies contribute to knowledge generation are key areas of future research and inquiry.

Background

Transdisciplinary (TD) teams are groups of researchers, scholars, practitioners, and community stakeholders who address problems at the intersection of scientific disciplines and/or societal sectors. They create knowledge that integrates the tools, techniques, and/or theories of disparate sectors that would not be achievable without collaboration (Somerville & Rapport, 2002). TD teams are, by nature, knowledge-producing teams (KPTs) that strive to increase methodological diversity, engage in cross-disciplinary knowledge building, and leverage pools of intellectual resources to understand and address real-world problems (Bear & Woolley, 2013; Jones, Wuchty, & Uzzi, 2008; Kyvik & Teigen, 1996; Lotrecchiano et al., 2016). "Transdisciplinary research project[s] rely on the transdisciplinary process of joint problem definition, problem-solving, and implementation that involves temporary cooperation between researchers and practitioners. Effects are intended and caused both in the scientific sphere and in practice—the societal sphere" (Walter, Helgenberger, Wiek, & Scholz, 2007, p. 326). In order to integrate and transcend the boundaries of any single discipline, members of transdisciplinary knowledge-producing teams (TDKPTs) must understand the connections between different knowledge communities (Gray, 2008) and focus on becoming adequately versed and skilled in disciplines and fields other than their own (Borner et al., 2010; Repko & Szostak, 2016). This type of social learning, one that allows cognitive shifts in understanding through observation of and participation with others, is a key component of successful and effective transdisciplinary teaming activity (Bandura, 1977). Collaborative learning is facilitated through the creation of shared conceptual frameworks (Park & Son, 2010) and mental models (Cannon-Bowers, Salas, & Converse, 1993) as teams engage in participatory approaches to generate new knowledge (Tress, Tress, & Fry, 2003). The co-evolving social learning that is a result in these collaborations allows teams to address and attempt to solve complex problems (Schwandt, 2008).

The study of the collaborative processes and outcomes of transdisciplinary knowledge producing teams (TDKPTs) poses some unique challenges. TDKPTs cope with *systemic complexities* while striving to maintain focus on their scientific and pragmatic goals (Hirsch Hadorn et al., 2007). One category of systemic complexity pertains to the barriers to TD integration arising from interpersonal interactions in TD team-based contexts, called *interactive systemic complexities*. Interactive systemic challenges to TD integration include perceived inequitable contributions to the project (Lotrecchiano, 2012), unbalanced problem ownership, discontinuous participation, fear of failure (Lang et al., 2012), variability in communication types and skills, overall lack of participant satisfaction with the project processes and outcomes (Crowston, Specht, Hoover, Chudoba, & Watson-Manheime, 2015), among others.

Structural systemic complexities, on the other hand, are barriers to TD integration that arise from characteristics inherent to the makeup of teams. These include differences in foundational training among team members, diverse and changing career paths, geographic dispersion, a lack of awareness of the breadth and complexity of the problem, perceived insufficient legitimacy of a team to solve the problem, conflicting methodological standards, conflicting epistemological and ontological orientations (Lang et al., 2012), and differing levels of transdisciplinary orientation among team members (Misra, Stokols, & Cheng, 2016).

Focusing on the tangible products of such teams, such as publication counts and bibliometric outcomes, is one approach to the study of the processes and outcomes of TDKPTs. The underlying assumption is that scientific outputs are indicators of successful team processes (Hall et al., 2012). Others studies have used cognitive, structural, and developmental approaches, focusing on teams' abilities to process information, their makeup, and/or interpersonal dynamics to understand the interactive dynamics of teams and support and develop them (Gray, 2008; Mickan & Rodger, 2005; Paletz & Schunn, 2010; Shuffler, DiazGranados, & Salas, 2011). Still other approaches have emphasized individual level analyses and competency-based approaches that highlight individual skills as they enable individual team members to be more effective team members and engage in complex problem-solving (Boon, Den Hartog, Boselie, & Paauwe, 2011; Salas, Shuffler, Thayer, Bedwell, & Lazzarra, 2015). Research approaches that emphasize any one level of analysis, or focus solely on products or processes, are likely to fall short of capturing the dynamism and emergent changes that occur within TDKPTs (Bedwell et al., 2012; Wheatley, 1999).

In this chapter, we conduct a descriptive analysis of characteristics of TDKPTs from a systems perspective (Cilliers, 2013) as an approach to the study of TDKPTs that address some of the limitations of prior approaches. We first describe how transdisciplinarity (TD), as a construct, could be used to frame an understanding of KPTs. Second, we go on to describe features of these teams using a complex systems lens and consider the types of knowledge, skills, and competencies members of TDKPTs might require for effective collaboration. Third, we provide examples of observable socio-cognitive and behavioral indicators of these knowledge, skills, and competencies.

Transdisciplinarity and Transdisciplinary Knowledge Producing Teams (TDKPTs)

In his treatise on the subject, Swiss psychologist Jean Piaget framed transdisciplinarity as a "higher stage of succeeding interdisciplinary relationships…which would not cover interactions or reciprocities between specialized research projects, but would place these relationships within a total system without any firm boundaries between disciplines" (Piaget, 1972, p. 138). Hence, from its inception transdisciplinary economies of knowledge production were grounded in systems thinking that aimed to understand entire multi-level networks of individuals, organizations, and knowledge. Numerous scholars have continued to refine and expand upon the theoretical and applied properties of transdisciplinarity in an attempt to bridge this definition to applied problem-solving (Gibbons et al., 1994; Jantsch, 1972a, 1972b; Klein, 1996; Kockelmans, 1979; Rosenfield, 1992). However, among others Basarab Nicolescu advanced the applicability of the term to contemporary problem-solving by emphasizing how transdisciplinary perspectives aided in understanding the world beyond the frameworks of any one discipline (Nicolescu, 2002). A number of lines of inquiry have focused on the conceptual work of defining transdisciplinarity and have contributed to our understanding of the nature of knowledge integration – complex and adaptive systems perspectives (Cilliers, 2013); humanities discourses (Klein, 2014); socially responsible science (Hirsch Hadorn et al., 2007; Maxwell, 2005); defining and dealing with "wicked problems"

(Brown, Harris, & Russell, 2010); re-imagining disciplinary silos and boundaries (Choi & Pak, 2007); and the multiplicity of realities in science (Nicolescu, 2002, 2012).

This conceptual research over the past two decades has permeated the research agendas of many sectors. Reference to the TD paradigm has appeared in documentation about learning, education, and science by organizations such as the United States National Science Foundation (NSF), National Institutes of Health (NIH), National Academy of Sciences (NAS), the United Nations Education, Scientific and Cultural Organization (UNESCO), and the International Center for Transdisciplinary Research (CIRET). Each has invited conversation about the tensions and complexities in interchange across knowledge systems (Cooke & Hilton, 2015; International Center for Transdisciplinary Research, 2018; National Science Foundation, 2018; UNESCO, 1998). This process of engaging in "boundary crossing" (Klein, 1996), "boundary blurring" (Becher, 1990), and identifying "zones of interdependence" (Thompson, 1967) between boundaries is fraught with barriers and challenges. Strategies and approaches to overcome some of these barriers and manage the challenges of cross-disciplinary collaboration are critical for solving global problems. As well, addressing the differences and fundamental limitations of certain types of knowledge economies and methodologies are essential to facilitate knowledge integration. Knowledge economies by nature are focused on "production and services based on knowledge-intensive activities that contribute to an accelerated pace of technical and scientific advancement, as well as rapid obsolescence…with a greater reliance on intellectual capabilities than on physical inputs or natural resources" (Powell & Snellman, 2004, p. 199). How integrative knowledge production occurs within knowledge economies is an important topic to address to facilitate complex problem-solving.

TDKPTs explicitly aim to integrate knowledge and address wicked problems. Transdisciplinary teams are distinct from unidisciplinary, interdisciplinary, and multidisciplinary teams. While each of these teams strives to produce knowledge and address a scientific problem, there are several distinctions between these economies of knowledge and the level of collaboration that occurs within each type of team. One set of differences concerns the representation of distinct disciplines, the diversity of knowledge systems, and attitudes towards other disciplinary worldviews and methodologies. Unidisciplinary teams work within the confines of the traditions or expectations of a single disciplinary history and scope. Sometimes these teams have negative biases toward other disciplines and deny the validity, rigor and usefulness of certain disciplines, approaches, ontological assumptions, epistemics, and methods (Allan, 2007). For the purpose of comparison to other more cross-disciplinary interactive modalities, unidisciplinary teams typically adopt the oneness of a disciplinary approach with little consideration of parallel or adjacent disciplines.

Multidisciplinary teams involve individuals from two or more disciplines working together on a common problem (Graybill, Dooling, Vivek, & John, 2006). This economy is employed in many cross-disciplinary teams throughout many sectors that require professional expertise to interface with scientific and scholarly expertise. Each participant brings to the discourse their own theories, methods, and techniques and provides insights within the confines of a discipline. Multidisciplinary teams, though extremely effective in incorporating multiple perspectives to understand or address a problem, often lack the inventiveness to put forth new techniques or models, modify mainstream approaches, or construct new frameworks that integrate or transcend the confines of any one discipline. They are effective in solving problems that are less complex than those attempted by other more interactive cross-disciplinary teams. These teams often attempt to achieve greater understanding and knowledge through the multiplication of methods and not through hybridization of approaches (Klein, 1990).

Moving further along the continuum of cross-disciplinary collaboration, when teams made up of individuals from distinct disciplines modify (or synthesize) existing methods or theories stemming from the cross pollination of two or more disciplines they are interdisciplinary in nature (Klein, 1990). However, interdisciplinary teams, though more intent on integrating knowledge are less focused on generating new knowledge that might result in new methods or frameworks that are the result of collaborative efforts. In both cases (multi- and interdisciplinary teams), a new level of discourse does emerge which ultimately leads to a further integration of knowledge (Graybill et al., 2006; Klein, 1990). Klein suggests that interdisciplinarity is a paradox, generating productive tensions that supplement, complement, and critique existing structures (Klein, 1998). This is in line with contemporary complexity thinking on adaptation in groups and organizations where tension and conflict can breed change and innovation (Burnes, 2005; Plsek & Wilson, 2001; Wheatley, 1999). The tensions promote the expansion of individual worldviews and the creation of new frameworks to manage knowledge. Without development of new frameworks to manage such new knowledge, exchanges cannot have a lasting impact on problems requiring new theoretical or constitutive lenses (Klein, 1996).

Even with limits, interdisciplinarity offers new ways of working in teams. New styles of thought begin to emerge and upend traditional methodologies and analytical enterprises to generate new frames of knowledge (Pirrie, Wilson, & Elsewood, 1998). This viewpoint echoes that of earlier theorists, who also focused on the shifts that occur between disciplinary boundaries resulting in novel perspectives and paradigm shifts, but highlighted different mechanisms like scientific paradigm shifts, differentiation and integration of scientific knowledge, and interdependences (Kuhn, 1970; Lawrence & Lorsch, 1967; Thompson, 1967).

Even with their merits, multi- and interdisciplinary team approaches all fall short of knowledge integration and collaboration in a manner unique to TDKPTs. Transdisciplinarity is a departure from mere considerations of hybridization and synthesis of disciplinary perspectives, methods, or frameworks. While multidisciplinary and interdisciplinary teams focus on exchange between disciplines, TDKPTs teams operate from a fundamentally different paradigm that endeavors to work across disciplines and non-disciplinary knowledge systems with the goal of engaging in participatory knowledge-creation across epistemic and methodological boundaries (Dillon, 2008; Huutoniemi, Klein, Bruun, & Hukkinen, 2010). Maasen and Lieven (2006) describe transdisciplinarity as a new mode of governing science where "…practices are directed toward solving complex policy issues and address scientific knowledge production proper. It promises to circumvent the schism between scientific expertise and policy-making by… the involvement of stakeholders [that] make sure the 'right problem' gets addressed 'in the right way'"(Maasen & Lieven, 2006, p. 400). Transdisciplinarity, therefore, moves us from a consideration of science as bound by disciplines and gravitates to a more holistic and systemic schema that considers the dynamics of entire systems of actors and concepts (Hammond & Dubé, 2012; Klein, 1990; Lotrecchiano, 2010; Tress et al., 2003). Maasen and Lieven (2006) characterize TDKPTs as "extending expertise", and "legitimation through participation" rather than "legitimation through knowledge".

In TDKPTs participants are challenged to relate to and reconcile with different levels of reality (Wickson, Carew, & Russell, 2006) thus challenging the very core of their beliefs and assumptions about knowledge. Furthermore, the transfer of power, reinterpretations of service delivery, training and education requirements, and questions of legitimacy all contribute to a general resistance to transdisciplinarity (Fine, 2007). These tensions become real as traditional roles and disciplines are challenged to change and evolve in TD collaborations. TD team interactions are subject to unfavorable conditions that make it difficult to transition from an interdisciplinary mode to this more novel and integrative one. TDKPTs therefore require a reappraisal and a reconsideration of the systemic features and properties if integration and synthesis are to truly occur. Figure 1 provides a graphical representation of the distinctions between uni-, multi-, inter-, and transdisciplinarity. We now turn our focus to a systems analysis of the features of TDKPTs.

Figure 1 depicts the differing levels of interdependency for the various types of cross-disciplinary collaboration. There is no interdependency between different disciplines in unidisciplinary knowledge producing teams. In multidisciplinary teams, multiple closed systems (O) participate in problem-solving through overlapping interests, but with little or no integration. Multidisciplinarity, therefore, is driven by standardization and a general investment into the entire system through unidisciplinary representation of one's own profession or disciplinary perspective. In interdisciplinary economies of knowledge, integration occurs as different disciplines interact and integrate perspectives, theories, or methods (□). Transdisciplinary knowledge producing teams are driven by goals that include integrated input/output (□), but also transform and transcend disciplines by different types of reorientation (e.g., creation of new conceptual frameworks that go beyond the knowledge of any single discipline) (□, Δ, etc.)

UNIDISCIPLINARITY

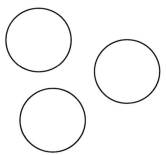

- Singularized histories, traditions, and expectations
- Linear perspective
- Closed systems
- Common knowledge within disciplines
- Non-interactive, no interdependence
- Codified reality
- Adaptation not required

MULTIDISCIPLINARITY

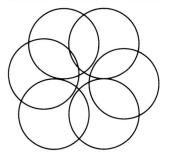

- Shared histories, traditions, and expectations
- Poly-linear perspectives
- Permeable system
- Shared knowledge across disciplines, stakeholders, or sectors
- Dialogic interaction, pooled interdependence
- Similar reality
- No adaptation

INTERDISCIPLINARITY

- Intersecting histories, traditions, and expectations
- Intersecting perspectives
- Interactive system
- Adjusted knowledge across disciplines, stakeholders, or sectors
- Blended interaction, Sequential interdependence
- Common reality
- Adaptive

TRANSDISCIPLINARITY

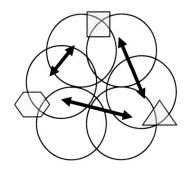

- Holistic histories, traditions, and expectations
- Amalgamated perspective
- Open system
- Generating knowledge across disciplines, stakeholders, or sectors
- Reciprocal interdependence
- Multiple realities
- Transformative

Figure. 1 Complexity Perspectives of Cross-Disciplinary Knowledge Economies (adapted from Lotrecchiano, 2011).

Features of Transdisciplinary Knowledge Producing Teams (TDKPTs)

To describe the overlapping themes in transdisciplinary knowledge economies and TDKPTs we look to complexity science to understand how one might strive toward defining and developing the skills necessary to work within these teams. In the sections below, we introduce a typology of TD features under two categories—*structural systemic complexities* and *interactive systemic complexities*, and elucidate the complexity factors they parallel and the distinctive team processes in TD environments. Underlying these features are several key assumptions about TDKPTs that are important to consider as we articulate the shared elements of TDKPTs with complex adaptive systems. We additionally offer definitions associated with Complex Adaptive Systems (CAS) as they are key to the descriptions that follow.

Assumptions about TDKPTs

TDKPTs operate within evolving environmental conditions as they strive to create new frameworks for managing novel knowledge outputs (N. Morgan, 2002). This evolving environment is recognizable through the dynamic interactions of teams (Stokols et al., 2003).

TDKPTs by nature express adaptive qualities (those required for change) that are often manifested during moments of conflict and tension that are byproducts of evolution and change (Hagemeier-Klose, Beichler, Davidse, & Deppisch, 2004). These conflicts are moments of knowledge awareness and exchange and not necessarily barriers to teaming (Blau, 1964; Buckley, 1998).

TDKPT mechanisms are not bound to any one feature. There is an enormous amount of overlap between different TDPKT features. To consider otherwise would be contrary to the systems approach being adopted here.

TDKPT features are found on the individual, group and organizational levels of any system affecting individuals and teams as they interface with their environment (Borner et al., 2010). Any description of features needs to be cognizant of the individual, team, and environmental factors that contribute to any knowledge economy.

TDKPTs are complex and adaptive environments (complex adaptive systems) that utilize techniques for communication and exchange that ascribe to principles found in systems theory like adaptation, nonlinearity, openness, and self-organization (Cilliers, 2013).

Having delineated the basic assumptions for a systems understanding of the features of TDKPTs, we present key features of TDKPTs, the systems principles invoked in the feature, the salient team processes for each TDKPT feature along with the key conceptual knowledge, skills, and competencies needed for effective team functioning and integrative knowledge production. Table 1 summarizes this information.

A Complex Adaptive Systems (CAS) Primer

- Information exchange occurs through the interactions of multiple elements.
- Non-linearity in CAS is the result of a lack of any one dominant framework bounding the flow of information.
- CAS are open systems with feedback loops, both positive and negative. Both kinds are necessary.
- CAS are open systems where feedback loops serve as entropy in the system stimulating and inhibiting flow at any given time.
- Change is a continual steady state in CAS where equilibrium is equated with death of the system.
- The depth and history of a complex adaptive system is common knowledge but not depicted through any one entity, event or actor in the system. All activities contribute to the growing knowledge about the system.
- Interactions between systems components is a foundational feature of CAS.

(Adapted from Cilliers, 2013)

Table 1. Features of TDKPTs, salient team processes, and foci conceptual knowledge, skills, and competencies using a complexity lens

Structural System Complexities

Examples of Teamwork Challenges:
- Perceived inequitable contributions to the project (Lotrecchiano, 2012).
- Unbalanced problem ownership, discontinuous participation, fear of failure (Lang et al., 2012).
- Variability in communication types and skills, overall lack of participant satisfaction with the project processes and outcomes (Crowston et al., 2015)

Feature of TDKPTs	Systems Principle	Salient Team Processes	Foci of Conceptual Knowledge, Skills, and Competencies	Examples of Observable Socio-Cognitive & Behavioral Indicators of Knowledge, Skills, and Competence
Complex problem-solving	Information exchange occurs through the interactions of multiple elements.	A heightened focus on anticipated future states (Hirsch Hadorn et al., 2007; Weisbord, 2004)	Understanding of scientific holism, explanatory theories and generation of system-wide knowledge over reductionism and predictive theories (Rigler & Peters, 1995)	Developing a cohesive picture of the system and determining what aspects belong with each other.

Shifting the focus of goals or reprioritizing goals in response to changing environment |
| | | Goal alignment with conditions of a changing world (Entin & Serfaty, 1999)

Focus on dealing with interpersonal team challenges | Understanding of non-linearity of cause and effect, time-lag between cause and effect, intangible and unfamiliar factors, and closed loop structures and inter-causal relationships (Dorner, 1997; Senge, 2006; Sternman, 1989) | Demonstrating self-awareness during discourse (e.g., acknowledgement of limitations of one's own discipline, methodology, or expertise)

Demonstrating team behaviors that promote team processes (e.g., willingness to share ideas and information, willingness to listen to and understand perspectives and |

	CAS are open systems with feedback loops, both enhancing, stimulating (positive) or detracting, inhibiting (negative).	Co-development of shared mental models within KPTs (Cannon-Bowers et al., 1993) Social learning as part of team engagement (Schwandt, 2008)	Understanding of and sensitivity to team dynamics and their effect on team processes and outcomes. Identifying points of conflict and complementarity and working toward integration of perspectives (Jehn & Chatman, 2000). Receptiveness to learning as a normative byproduct of social interactions (Schwandt, 2009).	worldviews different from one's own, awareness of conflict and willingness to address it, willingness to change one's perspective). **Demonstrating increase in transdisciplinary orientation** (values, attitudes, beliefs, conceptual skills, and behaviors) (Misra, Stokols, & Cheng, 2015) **through learning through team engagement**
Stakeholder involvement		Translation of knowledge across disciplines (Colditz, Wolin, & Gehlert, 2012) Development and sustainability of scientific and non-scientific partnerships (Maasen & Lieven, 2006) Establishing interdependence between knowledge partners (Lawrence & Lorsch, 1967).	Focusing on problems and questions that are society driven with the goal of transforming disciplinary knowledge (Klein, 2010). Advocating for the inclusion of diverse societal sectors relevant to the problem / question including marginalized cultures (Roloff, 2008). Focusing on both addressing a problem and integrating disciplinary and non-disciplinary insights to	**Demonstrating understanding of disciplinary inadequacy to address a complex problem** (e.g., lack of breadth of disciplines, disciplines are not able to offer broad-based comprehensive solutions to problems, lack of tools to grasp complex reality) (Newell & Meek, 2003). **Demonstrating preference for a more open understanding of knowledge** (e.g., openness to inclusion of lived experiences, oral traditions) (Vickers, 1997). **Achieving disciplinary adequacy for the disciplines relevant to understanding and addressing the problem** (Repko & Szostak, 2016)

				construct a more comprehensive understanding (Klein, 1996a; Repko & Szostak, 2016)	**Critically evaluating disciplinary insights to the problem** (Repko & Szostak, 2016) **Engaging in the process of creating common ground among conflicting and complementary insights to generate a more comprehensive understanding of the problem** (e.g., contextualizing, mapping problems, connecting disciplines, modifying disciplinary and cultural insights, generating bridging constructs).
			Focusing on accommodating (but not completely resolving) epistemological differences. Developing appreciation of the contributions of diverse disciplinary and stakeholder perspectives to understanding and addressing the problem. Evaluating the capacity of diverse disciplinary and stakeholder perspectives to addressing the problem.		**Demonstrating inclusive and integrative thinking, as opposed to exclusive thinking** **Demonstrating responsiveness to divergent disciplinary and non-scientific perspectives** (e.g., not showing bias toward employing perspectives and methods with which one is familiar) **Demonstrating intellectual flexibility** (e.g., willingness to learn more about unfamiliar theories and methods, reading outside one's primary field) **Working with knowledge of the disciplinary, non-disciplinary, cultural, and experiential parts of the problem while simultaneously focusing on the whole** **Developing skill in multilevel analysis of data.** **Demonstrating inductive and deductive thinking** (e.g., employing existing theories to
		Boundary spanning over boundary forming (Klein, 2004) **Shifting awareness of problems** (Nicolescu, 2005b) **Pluralism as a normative reality** (Lamont & Swidler, 2014) **Translation of knowledge** (Larson, Landers, & Begg, 2011).			
	Change is a continual steady state in CAS where equilibrium is equated with death of the system.				
Methodological pluralism					

| Praxis | Interactions between systems components is a foundational feature of CAS. | Experience-based learning is necessary for impact-based solutions (Kolb, 1984)

Combining formal and informal knowledge (Horlick-Jones & Sime, 2004)

Reintegrating co-created knowledge (Lang et al., 2012) | Developing frameworks that inclusive of, but not dominated by any one perspective.

Engaging explicitly in reflective, reflexive, integrative process

Focusing on synthesis and combination of diverse types of knowledge, as opposed to mere juxtaposition

Focusing on progressing toward holistic understanding of the problem and using that understanding to address a real-world problem. | pose questions while building constructs and theories from observations and data)

Ability to develop constellations of methods to understand the complexity of a problem.

Uncovering one's own assumptions, biases, and beliefs through a process of introspection and dialogue with team members

Engaging in questioning and communicating one's own assumptions, biases, and beliefs during team discussions

Modifying concepts and/or theories in light of discursive team processes (e.g., expanding the range of theories, refining concepts, identifying implicit assumptions)

Engaging in "conceptual blending" (Henry, 2011). That is, figuring out ways to utilize similarities between different types of knowledge to build a new and more comprehensive concept. |

Interactive System Complexity

Examples of Teamwork Challenges

- Differences in foundational training among team members, diverse and changing career paths, geographic dispersion, a lack of awareness of the breadth and complexity of the problem, perceived insufficient legitimacy of a team to solve the problem, conflicting methodological standards, conflicting epistemological and ontological orientations (Lang et al., 2012),
- Differing levels of transdisciplinary orientation among team members (Misra et al., 2016)

Feature of TDKPT	Systems Principle	Salient Team Processes	Foci of Conceptual Knowledge, Skills, and Competencies	Examples of Observable Socio-Cognitive & Behavioral Indicators of Knowledge, Skills, and Competence
Open systems capacity	Non-linearity in CAS is the result of a lack of any one dominant framework bounding the flow of information.	Reception to knowledge from outside of one's system of knowledge (Tress et al., 2003)	Focusing on cultivating openness to divergent perspectives, worldviews, and experiences	Engaging in active listening, probing team members' and one's own ideas and viewpoints.
				Willingness to learn new vocabulary and orient oneself to the broad contours of disciplines, fields, and topics that are unfamiliar.
		Conflict and power struggles can breed innovative thought (Eldridge & Crombie, 1975)	Understanding and appreciation of power dynamics and different types of conflict within teams.	Explicitly learning about different institutional arrangements of team members (e.g., experience, seniority, expectations, incentives for participation, motives, and goals)
		Interdependent relationships between actors need to contribute to shared goals (Katz & Kahn, 1966)	Ability to distinguish between sources of conflict (interpersonal versus intellectual conflicts).	Demonstrating knowledge of conflict resolution strategies (e.g, recognition of biases – one's own and others', acknowledging other interests and goals, identification of causes of conflict)

Different (shifting) levels of reality	CAS are open systems where feedback loops serve as entropy in the system stimulating and inhibiting flow at any given time.	Navigation of multiple realities related to a single problem (McGregor, 2011; Nicolescu, 2006) Mastering the consideration of diversity over different timescales, landscapes, and experiential episodes (Cilliers, 2013)	Paying explicit and purposeful attention to the full range of aspects and relationships involved in addressing the question / problem (including temporal, spatial, cultural, political, and economic dimensions) Adequately contextualizing the problem to aid understanding drawing from a variety perspectives (includ-	Navigation of multiple realities related to a single problem

Focusing on building transactive knowledge (who knows what) of team members

Focusing on the development of team routines and task designs that create interdependencies between team members

Engaging in repeated interactions with team members to understand team members' expertise, breadth of knowledge, and experience

Facilitating the flow of information between individuals and / or units through creation online and offline infrastructures, communication and organizational routines and norms

Including perspectives that are different or divergent from the team's worldview

Receptivity to new inputs

Focus on outputs that are the result of team processes

Demonstrating reflection (through discourse, writing, or other forms of communication) on learning from the collaboration, one's own biases, and one's limited understanding of the disciplines, theories, and methods relevant to the problem (e.g., asking questions such as what draws one to the problem, why were certain members or views selected to be part of the team)

Developing and applying perspective taking techniques

	Adaptation through self-organization (Heylighen, 2008)	ing the historical and experiential perspectives) **Continuous comparison of team-level understanding generated over the course of the collaboration compared to prior narrower / incomplete discipline-based individual understanding of the problem**		Evaluating discipline-based and cultural insights by questioning team members' biases Evaluating the quality and strength of arguments, evidence, and propositions to reach reasoned conclusions as team Recognizing of how differences in discourse are the result of different interpretations of reality due to diversity of worldviews found in a team. Viewing approaches, products, and processes of relevant disciplines that are part of the collaboration from a comparative viewpoint (Toynton, 2005).
Collaborative construction and reconstruction	The depth and history of a complex adaptive system is common.	**Openness to rearranging collaborative and knowledge arrangements** (Balsiger, 2004) **Direct contact with those affected by the problem attempting to be solved** (Klein, 2004)	Focus on actively leveraging understanding gained from transdisciplinary collaboration to integrate disciplinary views so that inform one another (VB Mansilla, 2005) Acknowledging the partial nature of all insights, dependence of all knowledge	Developing structural knowledge of the problem through concept maps, systems maps, and social ecological analysis (Trivedi & Misra, 2015). Questioning one's learning from the collaborative experience Engaging in a process of considered judgement and critique as a team (e.g., weighing different options, adjusting goals and

	on contextual conditions and focusing on relationships between elements of systems (Welch, Szostak, & Repko, 2011).	strategies to achieve proposed aims, reflecting on and evaluating successful and ineffective team processes, recognizing the limitations of one's approach and product) (VB Mansilla, Duraisingh, Wolfe, & Haynes, 2009)
	Knowing and describing reality through first person perspectives and knowledge.	**Producing and communicating cognitive advancement or transdisciplinary knowledge** (e.g., new insight, solution, policy, explanation, product)
		Reconfiguring team membership in light of new information (e.g., including new stakeholders, other types of expertise)

Structural Systemic Complexities

Complex Problem-Solving

The complex problem-solving feature is the basis for all other features of TDKPTs. This characteristic is rooted in TDKPTs' dedication to bridging scientific inquiry and pragmatic real world outcomes (Brown et al., 2010). Hirsch Hadorn et al. (2007) assert that different types of knowledge are needed to address wicked problems. *System knowledge* relates to how things can be observed in the present state and depends on the unidisciplinary expertise of those working in a specific area of impact, the existing literature, local communities of stakeholders, etc. This form of knowledge is routine in multi- and interdisciplinarity economies and often serves as the bases for exchange among team members and stakeholders. *Target knowledge* emphasizes the future state of a problem. Values and priorities, policies and trends, planning documents and stakeholders all have specific roles in providing solutions to wicked problems that will contribute to a future state of the environment. As target knowledge these artifacts directly impact solutions and become the focus of inquiry. This level of knowledge widens the investments and participation of team members and stakeholders to include information that will inform a solution. *Transformational knowledge* is knowledge that will aid in the transition from the present state to a future state that considers the problem in a new light or through alternative lenses. This process is specific to TD knowledge economies and emphasizes the emerging dimension of TDKPTs that yields unique methods and processes in addition to novel solutions (Hirsch Hadorn et al., 2007).

The transition between different types of knowledge and the way these contribute to the impact on real life problems occurs through a number of interactions on multiple levels contributing to the complexity of the problem being impacted by an inquiry (Cilliers, 2013). Complex problem-solving can conjure new problems for teams as they attempt to anticipate future states, meet the conditions of the changing environment, while simultaneously dealing with interpersonal team challenges. Effective teams can counteract certain challenges by co-developing shared mental models and common goals that serve as a blueprint for bringing teams together toward a common purpose and hence targeted outcomes (Bennet, Gadlin, & Levine-Finley, 2010; Cannon-Bowers et al., 1993; Tuckman, 1965; Tuckman & Jensen, 1977). Lang et al. (2012) emphasize that the co-evolution of individuals and teams engaged in these sorts of endeavors is parallel to the complexity of the problems that teams are trying to solve and therefore requires similar skills to manage its complexity. This co-evolution and social learning becomes part of the process in which complex problems may become more solvable as team interactions develop, change, and grow through intimacy with the complexity of the problem which they seek to solve through a process of social learning (Bandura, 1977; Schwandt, 2009). Framing of the problem and how a team might approach it may require team building techniques that respond to the wicked nature of problems being considered. This process will include a management of the different types of knowledge (system, target, and transformational) that are required for addressing the problem.

The explicit problem focus in TDKPTs bridges human and natural systems related to a problem with little emphasis on the confines and boundaries found related to differing sectors, disciplines, and traditions of thought (Klein, 1996). This feature of TDKPTs views problems as multidimensional, void of the disconnections that can occur between theoretical and practical solutions (Wickson et al., 2006). As such, team members co-evolve in their understanding of abilities and skills along with the uncharted territory of the problem landscape as they become more facile in dealing with the shifting environment that it represents (Schwandt, 2009).

Transformative knowledge creation requires individual team members to operate in an environment that tests and challenges their ways of knowing, compels them to recognize and reconcile with conflicts, and creatively synthesize diverse knowledge bases. Such challenges can be overcome through individual and teaming behaviors that emphasize boundary crossing and build skills that are likely to forecast the future state of a problem (Weisbord, 2004), adaptability to emerging and changing perspectives that come from often challenging interpersonal interactions in teams (Entin & Serfaty, 1999), and the ability to learn from the process of developing shared mental models (Cannon-Bowers et al., 1993; Schwandt, 2009).

A Case of Transdisciplinary Knowledge Producing Teams

A report by Walsh and Wicks (2014), describes how students from multiple courses of study were introduced to a transdisciplinary approach geared toward understanding the complexity of wetland and coastal land loss in Louisiana, USA through a field site experience at the Chenier Caminada near Port Fourchon. The problem was addressed from perspectives of three disciplines -- environmental management, geology, and landscape architecture. The integrative process required a multifold approach that incorporated different types of *system knowledge* about the river delta that informed and clarified the complexity of the overall problem. The course instructors challenged students to apply disciplinary knowledge *(system knowledge)* to a host of target particularities relating to land owner priorities, community needs, and geographical changes that could affect the overall long-term solutions to the complex problem of land erosion and loss *(target knowledge)*. Ultimately, these areas of focal interest were to be applied to 5, 10, and 25-year plans for the sustainability of the environment being studied leading to *transformational knowledge* that would integrate discipline-based knowledge of the environment in its present state with the diverse needs and concerns of those directly affected by the problem.

Instructors reported "…change in attitude [about the extent of the geological problem] of the non-geology students when they developed a real understanding of the delta cycle. The final plans were truly transformative and integrative. The students understood how to link across disciplinary boundaries" (p. 51). However, this was not a unilateral experience across all disciplines involved, highlighting how team members co-evolve at different rates. Geology graduate students, presumably the most equipped with the target knowledge to address the problem, were found to be less confident in their teaming abilities after the teaming experience. The authors surmised that through the introduction of new perspectives, they in fact felt less equipped to tackle the problem. In other cases, where expertise was considered less developed, as in landscape architecture students, confidence in was even more diminished as a result of the project. As the instructors of the class reported, the abilities of students to share knowledge across boundaries within the project was heightened even though their confidence in their own teaming skills may have diminished as a result of the project (Walsh & Wicks, 2014).

Stakeholder Involvement

While it can be easily surmised that multiple stakeholders representing different interests are needed to attempt complex problem-solving, it is in the details of this sort of engagement where unique challenges emerge within TDKPTs. Interacting in ways that challenge unidisciplinary viewpoints requires an expansion of perspectives about the breadth of knowledge required in a process of inquiry and problem-solving. Conflicts arise usually as a result of the lack of facility in translating knowledge to ensure accessibility across a team of stakeholders (Bennett & Gadlin, 2012). Maasen and Lieven (2006) find that these stifling dynamics can be observed when stakeholders representing both scientific and applied concerns interact and highlight "the separation between scientific expertise and policy making" (p. 401).

The emphasis here is not on conflict, but rather the barriers that are the result of singularizing perspectives around a problem. It reminds us to consider the reasons for multi-stakeholder interaction. Multi-stakeholder engagement is key to complex problems solving (Roloff, 2008). In TDKPTs multi-stakeholder involvement arises from the need for task interdependence between actors to achieve a transdisciplinary end goal. If there is no interdependence between stakeholders within the system, there is no need for coordination across the system (Lawrence & Lorsch, 1967; Thompson, 1967). Cohesion and interdependency amongst stakeholders stemming from their unique investments and agendas can be an opportunity for psychosocial investment in addressing a problem.

Differences in stakeholder understanding of problems in TDKPTs are not just a matter of the degree of involvement but also the ability to embrace the totality of the problem. The ability to integrate stakeholders with highly diverse perspectives including those who personally experience the problem is markedly different than that of other knowledge economies where knowledge production is left to those identified as knowledge specialists (Maasen & Lieven, 2006). While the integration and synthesis of knowledge is of primary concern in these instances, such teaming engagements might lack the breadth of experiential knowledge to adequately engage all stakeholder perspectives. Translation between these factions requires an openness to seeking solutions across disciplines (Colditz et al., 2012) establishing interdependent relationships as the core basis teaming (Lawrence & Lorsch, 1967). It is through the engagement of those who typically solve problems with those who typically are burdened with real-world problems where a unique stakeholder engagement specific to TDKPTs can be identified.

Methodological Pluralism

Complex problem-solving depends on the freedom to employ multiple approaches toward understanding and resolving the problem, with no single methodological approach dominating problem-solving providing only a narrowly constructed solution (Wickson et al., 2006). If complex problem-solving relies on a series of systematically and contextually related real-world factors, then solutions to these problems are just as complex. For this reason, no one method can adequately supply potential solutions. Constellations of methods are often employed in TDKPTs and they coexist as do the multiple realities that emerge as part of the problems seeking to be solved (Nicolescu, 2005a). The logic behind this construction of problem-solving processes is antithetical to many traditional unidisciplinary means to problem-solving that rely on 'risk reduction' over 'risk production', or the ability to gain insight through non-linear and often more conflict-laden perspectives. Similarly, conflict becomes an opportunity for knowledge production and boundary spanning. Increasing risk in problem-solving can be a means to expanding the scope of the problem and seeking greater input from different actors toward the resolution of the problem (Maasen and Lieven, 2006). This multi-method approach to problem-solving shows that more than one legitimate description of a problem exists and more than one potential solution is possible within a complex and adaptive system (Cilliers, 2013). Different descriptions will decompose the system in different ways and are not reducible to one another. Different descriptions may also have different degrees of complexity (Cilliers, 2013).

Environments that adopt multiple methods toward problem-solving are inherently complex. The adaptive nature of these environments will require the consideration of converging and diverging methodological practices and conflict may lead to both tension and creativity within the same teaming environment. When team members interface with different stakeholders and consider the ways in which they might utilize standardized methodologies from a host discipline in their quest to contribute to the solution of a problem, others will provide for complementary and possibly even contradictory ways of knowing and solving problems. As stated, this is a normative dynamic in a teaming environment where trust in methodological pluralism (Lamont & Swidler, 2014), shifts in reality perceptions (Nicolescu, 2005a), and boundary spanning (Klein, 2004) is a constant state. Translation therefore becomes the dominant behavior in TDKPTs, where individuals and the team are continually challenged to show the relational characteristics between different methods and how through selection and hybridization they can provide novel approaches to complex problems (Larson et al., 2011).

Praxis

The term praxis is an often-used word with many contextual underpinnings. Here we draw on the Aristotelian definition that emphasizes the relationship between thinking, making, and doing or transdisciplinary practice, knowledge, process, and application. The term was a key cornerstone in Marxist philosophy that challenged philosophical criticism to focus on the goals of philosophy to interpret the world for the sake of change and not just for the sake of critical analysis (Engels, 1886).

For the purposes of the consideration of praxis as a feature of TDKPTs one should think about praxis as a process unique to TD teams that takes action, considers impact, analyzes through reflection, alters and revises plans, and then implements plans for future actions. The praxical orientation of TDKPTs is not unlike what Kolb (1984) refers to as the experiential learning cycle, one grounded in experiential learning as a cyclical process of concrete learning, reflective observation, abstract conceptualization and active experimentation. Here new experiences give way to personal reflection on how the experience affects the individual, and ultimately, abstraction and the application of new ideas into practice. This is an interplay between what some would refer to as the intersection of formal and informal knowledge, or that which is practiced and that which is experienced (Horlick-Jones & Sime, 2004). This process is one where different forms of knowledge from divergent sources are related and reintegrated so as to represent a co-created knowledge form that is the result of the interactions between different components within a complex system (Cilliers, 2013). This reintegration results in evidence-based practical applications incorporated into scientific discourse. All the while this process also provides a means by which new ways of knowing and decision-making can be observed as the byproduct of a praxical approach (Lang et al., 2012). This process can contradict implementation science that is based on linear planning processes like those often found in scientific management (Taylor, 1911) that emphasize the product orientation of scientific inquiry for a more knowledge-based purpose for inquiry. Praxis provides the vehicle for moving beyond system knowledge (Hirsch Hadorn et al., 2007). It is the summation of the relationships and dimensionality of systems, target, and transformational knowledge states.

In many ways praxis underpins how individuals and teams might embrace the transition from unidisciplinary knowledge to action oriented transformational and applied knowledge that results in structural change. In light of the coexistent multiple perspectives that make up the transdisciplinary environment, praxis becomes the normative model for integrating multiplicity. Praxis assumes that theory and practice are related and each should inform each other in reciprocal relationship. In itself the achievement of a praxical orientation to knowledge building is a type of transdisciplinary endeavor. Wickson et al. (2006) state that transdisciplinary praxis "should co-evolve to a point where they are integrated and/or resonant. How this process proceeds in practice is one of the integrative challenges" (p. 1053) yet to be fully understood. However, it suggests that application and conceptualization are unified entities in the transdisciplinary process (Lotrecchiano, 2013).

Interactive Systemic Complexities

Open Systems Capacity

The wicked problem-solving ability of teams rests on their capacity to operate as part of an open system (von Bertalanffy, 1956) allowing for knowledge from sources outside system to permeate within the system and be considered alongside other types of knowledge. An open system presumes interactions with entities from outside of a group of bounded actors, ideas and/or entities with the intended result of recirculating knowledge through outputs back into the greater environment. Open systems are receptive to the input of tangible elements like resources and materials as well as the actors and ideas that are part of the input-output relationship between bounded systems (disciplines, teams, organizations, knowledge sets, etc.) and its interactions with other entities outside of it (Tress et al., 2003). The capacity to learn from this permeable environment and adapt behavior for better fit can enhance knowledge integration. Under these conditions, TDKPTs can integrate and synthesize disciplines by providing "synthetic reconfiguration of available knowledge regarding the social, economic, and ecological conditions" (Pregernig, 2006, p. 446).

In an open system team members must expand the range of considerations beyond traditional outlets one is accustomed to. As input into a system occurs, conflict, and power struggles between discipline-defined team members can emerge as traditional ways of knowing are challenged by the integration of approaches from outside system. Ideas and information are key environmental inputs in this kind of open system. When ideas and information are exchanged in a TD team, individuals' internal knowledge frameworks are challenged. This destabilizes the system and can lead to conflict. Engaging with the information, questioning one's own assumptions, reconciling with the limitations of the discipline, and finding ways to synthesize ideas toward the common problem, results in TD integration. These moments of tension and conflict are exchanges of information which represent 'triggers' of new awareness (Blau, 1964; Buckley, 1998) that have the potential to bring about novel awareness related to knowledge development (Eldridge & Crombie, 1975). These energetic input-output boundary-spanning events highlight that TDKPTs "consist of patterned activities of a number of individuals and the activities are complementary or interdependent with respect to some common output or outcome" (Katz & Kahn, 1966, p. 20) even though they may seem to be unrelated to a common goal as they are being played out. This exchanging of energy between individuals (interdependencies) within the system leads us to be able to identify the exchanges occurring within and without a system (Thompson, 1967).

A TDKPT working under these conditions deals with the challenge of including all necessary inputs. Such inclusion may foster and breed conflict, as the multiple inputs might require a team to behave in transparent and freely uninhibited ways. This feature draws our attention to the input-output mechanisms associated with all groups and organizations that must include knowledge from alternative sources and provide outputs that are targeted to multiple audiences. Here input-output interactions strive to develop a new integrated perspective (Katz & Khan, 1996). This is a highly nonlinear pattern as outputs of these interactions are a function of future inputs. The state of the system is determined by the values of the inputs and outputs over time and in relation to the evolution of new problems within the same wicked problem (Cillers, 2013).

Different (Shifting) Levels of Reality

One of the trademarks of scientific inquiry is the ability to frame and identify problems in light of their context within an agreed upon conceptual lens and analytic strategy (Burrell & Morgan, 1979). TDKPTs engage in inquiry that challenges this trademark based on the possibility that in doing so a series of divergent realities can be considered alongside one another. Nicolescu (2006) describes the intersection of these sometimes oppositional or conflicting realities as a zone of non-resistance where human-based considerations like political, social, and individual realities intersect with natural realities like the environment, the cosmos, and physical law. This intersection is where exchanges in knowledge can flow freely (McGregor, 2011; Nicolescu, 2006). A systems perspective to complex problems includes experiences of multiple actors and approaches from a range of lenses that may suggest that multiple realities exist in problem-solving depending on one's proximity to it. In addition, reality itself can be skewed based on one's disciplinary lens or even the level of comfort one has with the complexity of a problem. Complex systems display reality over a diverse range of timescales, environmental landscapes, and experiential episodes (Cilliers, 2013).

As adaptive complex systems themselves, the network of actors involved in TDKPTs will display change as different stakeholders interface with one another, adjust their own disciplinary perspective, and contribute to new and emergent realities as part of their problem-solving efforts. Simultaneously, shifts occur within these complex systems as they adapt to a changing environment and self-organize themselves (Heylighen, 2008). This is necessary in order for the system to cope with its environment, and in TDKPTs this adaptation brings teams closer to considering problems with a more holistic viewpoint. Change is at the heart of such systemic emergence and it is a constant state that requires adaptation as a constant function (Barnes, Matka, & Sullivan, 2003; Cilliers, 2013; Nicolescu, 2010).

Complex systems like those represented in TDKPTs display behaviors that are a direct result of interactions between actors and the knowledge being generated. In other words, the goal of generating new knowledge is more dependent on processes of creating knowledge, even if measured using different or divergent realities, than solely the synthesis of existing knowledge. Emergence is key to this feature as one of the goals of TDKPTs is to develop holistic approaches that are not subject to the parts of disciplines that make them up, but rather are the culmination of including multiple states of reality related to a problem. As such, the environment of these teams can be one of disorientation where the environment is a constantly changing reality requiring individuals to develop skills that are multidimensional and access multiple states of reality as perceived through different stakeholders.

Collaborative Deconstruction and Reconstruction

As teams work toward affecting new arrangements of knowledge in their problem-solving activities, new arrangements of collaborators and stakeholders emerge (Wickson, 2006). This is partly due to inclusiveness and partly due to the creation of novel approaches and insights that may not lie within the perceived boundaries of a given problem. This process of boundary spanning in the interpretation of the complexity of problems invites new relationships between stakeholders that may be unusual or novel either because of their novel disciplinary arrangement or because of the viewpoint they may bring to solving the problem (Balsiger, 2004). Often these unexpected relational arrangements are the result of involving those who are directly affected by problems to work along those who merely work to solve problems (Klein, 2004). Such construction of relationships can often deconstruct others and create strong ties out of loosely constructed ones (Simmel, 1955).

Active exchanges between professionals of different disciplines or even from the same traditions can develop into novel interdependencies (Thompson, 1967). As coordination and collaboration develop into new interdependencies between actors of the system, increasing complexity of these relationships can support a reordering of the collaborative functions between those who work together in the same team (Maasen & Lieven, 2006). These relationships may become more asymmetric than equal as team construction becomes a reflection of the complex environment in which the team works, adapting to complex arrangements of relationships through an internal dynamic process. Overall team structure is maintained even through the components themselves are exchanged or renewed (Cilliers, 2013).

Groups, where changes in relationships and the strengthening and weakening of ties are a normative activity, can make for a challenging team environment. The consequences of these dynamics in parallel with the shifting landscape of problems and their solution seeking processes can cause emotional strain to existing relationships as disciplinary communal ties are tested and reshaped. There may even be emotional stresses requiring stakeholders to reevaluate their dedication to a strain of thought and the relationships with stakeholders that constitute one's loyalty. Such shifts can result in dissension from one's previously espoused epistemological commitments and require mediation and reflective skills as team members adapt through recombination. Recombination is the process of taking existing compositions and breaking them down into constituent elements and recombining them to form new ones (Kerne, 2005). Such reorganization of one's placement in the system of knowledge, often results in reevaluating team values and can result in modifying behaviors to better navigate these relational changes.

Conclusion: Viewing Transdisciplinary Learning and Engagement through a Complexity Lens

Unique to transdisciplinarity is the evolution of integrated and synthesized knowledge beyond the boundaries that often separate it. The challenge is to involve participants in the theoretical, epistemological, and methodological evolutions that are the source and summit of transdisciplinary communication and collective learning. Baiyin Yang's (2003) description of learning environments that accept the social dynamism embedded in knowledge integration is in concert with TDKPTs and is useful for a discussion on bridging the gap between structural and interactive systemic complexities. It supports the expectation that knowledge production is an enterprise of change, learning, and influence by multiple agents, not all of which are human actors. TD learning, with its social, conceptual, behavioral and psychological facets, hints at describing settings where "knowledge is defined as human beings' understanding about reality through mental correspondence, personal experience, and emotional affectation with outside objects and situations" (p. 108) not solely focusing on behavior or traits.

The mechanisms of how TD learning can be observed and operationalized on the individual level may inform collective efficacy and communities of practice once uncovered in more detail. Some work has been conducted already in this area. The structural relationship between personal self-efficacy and collective efficacy have been studied in light of change, socio-economic status and communal activity resulting in conversations about the role of individuals in collective work groups (Fernandez-Ballestros, Diez-Nicolas, Caprara, Barbaranelli, & Bandura, 2002). "Micro social order" has been proposed as a link to collective-oriented behavior, positive affect, and group perceptions into a network that generates recurrent patterns of exchange (Lawler, Thye, & Yoon, 2008). Research on collective efficacy, and its measurement has been taken up by Roger Goddard who, while focusing on collective belief, has also begun to consider the individual in light of collective efficacy (Goddard, 2002; Goddard, Hoy, & Hoy, 2004). Some studies have been conducted that attempt to show the impact of individual interactions on collective efficacy with teachers and principals (Wahlstrom & Seashore Louis, 2008) in leader verbal behavior (Sims & Manz, 1984) and in multi-agency work settings (Daniels, Leadbetter, & Warmington, 2007; Stokols et al., 2003; Stokols, Hall, Taylor, & Moser, 2008; Stokols, Misra, Moser, Hall, & Taylor, 2008)

Another theoretical area in need of attention is that of the role of cognitive dissonance within reciprocal interactions. The role of dissonance and, more importantly, the consequences of gravitation toward psychological consonance have a direct effect on the achievement of TD learning with its requirement for maintaining multiple realities and conversations. As Leon Festinger (1957) has claimed, "the reality which impinges on a person will exert pressures in the direction of bringing the appropriate cognitive elements into correspondence with that reality" (p. 11). Scholars in the area of cognitive dissonance have been more active in their attempt at focusing on how dissonance affects the individual learner and empirical studies range from intragroup studies on agreement/disagreement dynamics (Glasford, Pratto, & Dovidio, 2008; Matz & Wood, 2005), to workplace learning behavior (Dechawatanapaisal & Siengthai, 2006), and to behavior regulation through deval-uation of positive stimuli (Veling, Holland, & van Knippenberg, 2008). Even in these rig-orous studies, a match between research on individual learning mechanisms and TD set-tings is lacking.

For a context specific research paradigm that focuses on individual learning mechanisms in the context of TD settings, scholars will need to construct their endeavors in ways similar to the tenets of TD settings themselves: interpenetration of epistemologies, methodological pluralism, shifting realities, etc. In fact, most of the work in dissecting TD has been con-ducted in the realm of research paradigms and the TD characteristics suggested in this chapter stem from those inquiries. Scholars need to ask questions of the problem with phenomenological and cybernetic lenses (Brier, 2003; Nicolescu, 1995) that, by their very nature, are more well equipped to harvest the multilayered data in intersecting phenomena that are in constant dynamic flux. Social mechanisms may serve well as dynamic variables in these sorts of studies where changing interactive indicators are used to establish codes and themes more suited than static variables for research (Hëdstrom, 2005; Hedström & Swed-berg, 1998). Worth noting are the successful attempts of scholars like Grandon Gill of the University of South Florida and Eli Cohen who have recently proposed research techniques on individual coping with complexity and its effect on information processing that are highly adaptable to TD settings (Gill & Cohen, 2008).

If individual learning in complex TD settings is to be understood for the purpose of en-lightening practical leadership, a variety of contributions will need to be synthesized focus-ing on real-life TD situations. At the moment, these are limited or at least underdeveloped. However, many sectors like cancer research (Croyle, 2008; Hiatt & Breen, 2008; Sellers, Caporaso, Lapidus, Peterson, & Trent, 2006), tobacco and substance abuse research (Abrams, Leslie, Mermelstein, Kobus, & Clayton, 2003; G. Morgan, Kobus, & Gerlach, 2003; Provan, Clark, & Huerta, 2008; Unger et al., 2003), aerospace technology develop-ment (Jeffrey, Allen, & Seaton, 2000), and translational team science (Morrison, 2008; Na-tional Center for Advancing Translational Sciences, 2010) are paving the way. The conclu-sion to any conversation about TD learning must ultimately return to the question of the models, structure, and characteristics of TD environments but also must include the indi-vidual psychosocial functioning that provide individual access to these sorts of social and conceptual interactions.

Wickson et al. (2006) suggest that reflection is a necessary skill for transdisciplinary en-gagement for it encourages participants to assess frames of reference, values, beliefs, and assumptions in light of emerging problems and solutions rather than simply being observa-tional in the process of problem-solving. This leads to a full-participation in the develop-ment of methods of investigation and learning.

By defining the features of TDKPTs we are able to consider the role of complexity theory in researching such teams, while simultaneously considering the skills needed to work with-in TD teams. Ultimately, these features draw our attention to the role of communication in knowledge generation. Such research takes seriously the need to understand team dynam-ics, explores research methodologies that can uncover the social nature of knowledge pro-ducing teams, and deciphers the indicators of their productivity from the standpoint of transdisciplinary knowledge generation. While research on communication in TD teams continues to be illusive and partially lacking rigor, scholars can inform the major challenges that transdisciplinary teams face on a regular basis: integration, praxis, and engagement by examining the functional and cognitive elements of teaming behavior both at onset and during teaming engagement. This is particularly important for multiple stakeholder projects with scientific, practice and community implications as problems and priorities are sure to emerge over time with the changing state of a system and as team members change and co-evolve with their wicked problems. Evaluation methodologies used with scientific and practice participants may be challenged to clearly capture both practitioner and researcher scientist perspectives which at times may represent opposing viewpoints because of their own temporal biases.

Questions to Further the Discourse

1. How can we employ the examples of socio-cognitive and behavioral indicators of knowledge, skills, and competencies to operationalize and observe communication and learning at the team level in TDKPTs?

2. How might theory and research on cognitive dissonance be applied to the study of cognitive shifting and transdisciplinary learning in TDKPTs?

3. How might learning theories and mechanisms focused on individual learners be extended to TDKPTs using a complex systems lens?

Must Reads

Cilliers, P. (2013). Complexity and postmodernism. Understanding complex systems. In C. Martin & J. Strumberg (Eds.), *Handbook of systems and complexity in health*. New York: Springer.

Hirsch Hadorn, G., Hoffmann-Riem, H., Biber-Klemm, S., Grossenbacher-Mansuy, W., Joye, D., Pohl, C., & Zemp, E. (2007). *Handbook of transdisciplinary research*. Springer.

Lotrecchiano, G. R. (2010). Complexity leadership in transdisciplinary (TD) learning environments: A knowledge feedback loop. *International Journal of Transdisciplinary Research, 5*(1), 29-63.

Stokols, D., Misra, S., Moser, R., Hall, K., & Taylor, B. (2008). The ecology of team science. *American Journal of Preventative Medicine, 35*(2S), S96-S115.

References

Abrams, D., Leslie, F., Mermelstein, R., Kobus, K., & Clayton, R. (2003). Transdisciplinary tobacco use research. *Nicotine and Tabacco Research, 5*(S1), S5-S10.

Allan, K. (2007). *The social lens: An invitation to the social and sociological theory*. Thousand Oaks, CA: Pine Forge Press.

Balsiger, P. (2004). Supradisciplinary research practices: History, objectives and rationale. *Futures, 36*(4), 407-421.

Bandura, A. (1977). *Social learning theory*. Upper Saddle River, NJ: Prentice Hall.

Barnes, M., Matka, E., & Sullivan, H. (2003). Evience, understanding and complexity. *Evaluation, 9*(3), 265-284.

Bear, J., & Woolley, A. (2013). The role of gender in team collaboration and performance. *Interdisciplinary Science Reviews, 36*(2), 146-153. https://doi.org/10.1179/030801811x13013181961473

Becher, T. (1990). The counter culture of specialization. *European Journal of Education, 25*(2), 333-346.

Bedwell, W., Wildman, J., DiazGranados, D., Salazar, M., Kramer, W., & Salas, E. (2012). Collaboration at work: An integrative multilevel conceptualization. *Human Resource Management, 22*(2), 128-145. https://doi.org/10.1016/j.hrmr.2011.11.007

Bennett, L. M., & Gadlin, H. (2012). Collaboration and team science. *Journal of Investigative Medicine, 60*(5), 768.

Bennet, L. M., Gadlin, H., & Levine-Finley, S. (2010). *Collaboration and team science: A field guide*. Retrieved from Bethesda, MD:

Blau, P. (1964). *Exchange and power in social life*. New York: J. Wiley.

Boon, C., Den Hartog, D., Boselie, P., & Paauwe, J. (2011). The relationship between perceptions of HR practices and employee outcomes: Examining the role of person-organisation and person-job fit. *International Journal of Human Resource Management, 22*(1), 138-162.

Borner, K., Contractor, N., Falk-Krzesinski, H. J., Fiore, S., Hall, K., Keyton, J., & Uzzi, B. (2010). A multi-level stystems perspective for the science or team science. *Science Translational Medicine, 2*(49), 1-5.

Brier, S. (2003). Cybersemiotics and the question of semiotic and informational thresholds. *World Futures, 59*, 361-380.

Brown, V., Harris, J., & Russell, J. (2010). *Tackling wicked problems: Through the transdisciplinary imagination*. London: Earthscan.

Buckley, W. (1998). *Society: A complex adaptive system. Essays in social theory*. Gordon and Breach.

Burnes, B. (2005). Complexity theories and organizational change. *International Journal of Management Reviews, 7*(2), 72-90.

Burrell, G., & Morgan, G. (1979). *Sociological paradigms and organisational analysis: Elements of the sociology of corporate life*. London: Heinemann.

Cannon-Bowers, J., Salas, E., & Converse, S. (1993). Shared mental models in expert team decision making. In N. Castellan (Ed.), *Current issues in individual and group decision making* (pp. 221-246). Mahwah, NJ: Erlbaum.

Choi, B. C. K., & Pak, A. W. P. (2007). Multidisciplinarity, interdisciplinarity, and transdisciplinarity in health research, services, education and policy: 2. Promotors, barriers, and strategies of enhancement. *Clinical & Investigative Medicine, 30*(6), E224-E232. Retrieved from http://search.ebscohost.com/login.aspx?direct=true&db=aph&AN=28105676&site=ehost-live

Cilliers, P. (2013). Complexity and postmodernism. Understanding complex systems. In C. Martin & J. Strumberg (Eds.), *Handbook of systems and complexity in health*. New York: Springer.

Colditz, G., Wolin, K., & Gehlert, S. (2012). Applying what we know to accelerate cancer prevention. *Science Translational Medicine, 4*(127), 127rv124. https://doi.org/10.1126/scitranslmed.3003218

Cooke, N., & Hilton, M. (2015). *Enhancing the effectiveness of team science*. Washington, DC: National Academies Press.

Crowston, K., Specht, A., Hoover, C., Chudoba, K., & Watson-Manheime, M. (2015). Perceived discontinuities and continuities in transdisciplinary scientific working groups. *Science of the Total Environnmennt, 534*, 159-172. https://doi.org/10.1016/j.scitotenv.2015.04.121

Croyle, R. (2008). The National Cancer Institute's transdisciplinary centers initiaives and their need for building a science of team science. *American Journal of Preventative Medicine, 35*(2S), S90-249.

Daniels, H., Leadbetter, J., & Warmington, P. (2007). Learning in and for multi-agency working. *Oxford Review of Education, 33*(4), 521-538.

Dechawatanapaisal, D., & Siengthai, S. (2006). The impact of cognitive dissonance on learning work behavior. *Journal of Workplace Learning, 18*(1/2), 42-54.

Dillon, P. (2008). A pedagogy of connection and boundary crossings: Methodological and epistemological transactions in working across and between disciplines. *Innovations in Education, 45*(3).

Dorner, D. (1997). *The logic of failure*. Reading, MA: Addison Wesley.

Eldridge, J., & Crombie, A. (1975). *A sociology of organisations*. New York: International Publications Service.

Engels, F. (1886). *Marx/Engels selected works* (Vol. 1). Moscow, USSR: Progress Publishers.

Entin, E., & Serfaty, D. (1999). Adaptive team coordination. *Human Factors The Journal of the Human Factors and Ergonomics Society, 41*(2), 312-325. https://doi.org/10.1518/001872099779591196

Fernandez-Ballestros, R., Diez-Nicolas, J., Caprara, G. V., Barbaranelli, C., & Bandura, A. (2002). Determinants and structural relations of personal efficacy and collective efficacy. *Applied Psychology: An International Review, 51*(1), 107-125.

Festinger, L. (1957). *A theory of cognitive dissonance*. Stanford, CA: Stanford University Press.

Fine, H. (2007). Transdisciplinarity: Trying to cross boundaries. *Tamara Journal of Critical Organisation Inquiry, 6*(3/4), 16. Retrieved from http://proxygw.wrlc.org/login?url=http://proquest.umi.com/pqdweb?did=1482120841&Fmt=7&clientId=31812&RQT=309&VName=PQD

Gibbons, M., Limoges, C., Nowotney, H., Schwartzman, S., Scott, P., & Trow, M. (1994). *The new production of knoweldge: The dynamics of science and research in contemporary societies*. London: SAGE.

Gill, T., & Cohen, E. (2008). Research themes in complex forming. *Informing Science: the International Journal of an Imerging Transdiscipline, 11*, 147-164. https://doi.org/10.28945/444

Glasford, D., Pratto, F., & Dovidio, J. (2008). Intragroup dissonance: Responses to ingroup violation and personal values. *Journal of Experimental Social Psychology, 44*, 1057-1064.

Goddard, R. (2002). A theoretical and empirical analysis of the measurement of collective efficacy: A development of a short form. *Educational and Psychological Measurement, 62*(1), 97-110.

Goddard, R., Hoy, W., & Hoy, A. (2004). Collective efficacy beliefs: Theoretical developments, empirical evidence, and future direction. *Educational Researcher, 33*(3), 3-13.

Gray, B. (2008). Enhancing transdisciplinary research through collaborative leadership. *American Journal of Preventative Medicine, 35*(2S), S124-132.

Graybill, J., Dooling, S., Vivek, S., & John, W. (2006). A rough guide to interdisciplinarity: graduate student perspectives. *Bioscience, 56*(9), 757. https://doi.org/10.1641/0006-3568(2006)56[757:argtig]2.0.co;2

Hagemeier-Klose, M., Beichler, S., Davidse, B., & Deppisch, S. (2004). The dynamic knowledge loop: Inter- and transdisciplinary cooperation and adaptation of climate change knowledge. *International Journal of Disaster Risk Science, 5*(1), 21-32.

Hall, K., Stokols, D., Stipelman, B., Vogel, A., Feng, A., Masimore, B., . . . Berrigan, D. (2012). Assessing the value of team science: A study comparing center- and investigator-initiated grants. *American Journal of Preventative Medicine, 42*(2), 157-163.

Hammond, R., & Dubé, L. (2012). A systems science perspective and transdisciplinary models for food and nutrition security. *PNAS, 109*(31), 12356-12363.

Hëdstrom, P. (2005). *Dissecting the social.* Cambridge, MA: Cambridge University Press.

Hedström, P., & Swedberg, R. (1998). *Social mechanisms: An analytic approach to social theory.* Cambridge: Cambridge University Press.

Henry, S., & Bracy, N. L. (2011). Integrative theory in criminology applied to the complex social problem of school violence. In A.F. Repko, W.H. Newell, & R. Szostak (Eds), *Case studies in interdisciplinary research* (pp. 259-282). Thousand Oaks, CA: Sage.

Heylighen, F. (2008). Complexity and self-organization. In M. Bates & M. Maack (Eds.), *Encyclopedia of library and information sciences*: Taylor and Francis.

Hiatt, R., & Breen, N. (2008). The social determinants of cancer. *American Journal of Preventative Medicine, 35*(2S), S141-S150.

Hirsch Hadorn, G., Hoffmann-Riem, H., Biber-Klemm, S., Grossenbacher-Mansuy, W., Joye, D., Pohl, C., & Zemp, E. (2007). *Handbook of transdisciplinary research.* Springer.

Horlick-Jones, T., & Sime, J. (2004). Living on the border: Knowledge, risk and transdisciplinarity. *Futures, 36*(4), 441-456.

Huutoniemi, K., Klein, J. T., Bruun, H., & Hukkinen, J. (2010). Analyzing interdisciplinarity: Typology and indicators. *Research Policy, 39*(1), 79-88.

International Center for Transdisciplinary Research. (2018). *CIRET*. Retrieved from http://ciret-transdisciplinarity.org/index_en.php

Jantsch, E. (1972a). Inter- and transdisciplinary university: A system approach to education and innovation. *Higher Education, 1*(1), 7-37.

Jantsch, E. (1972b). *Toward interdisciplinarity and transdisciplinarity in education and innovation.* Paper presented at the Center for Education Research and Innovation (CERI), Paris, France.

Jeffrey, P., Allen, P., & Seaton, R. (2000). *Cross-disciplinary knoweldge as a guide to the study and management of complexity: The case of product definition in the aerospace industry.* Paper presented at the International Transdisciplinarity Conference, Zurich, Switzerland.

Jehn, K., & Chatman, J. (2000). The influence of proportional and perceptual conflict composition on team performance. *The International Journal of Conflict Management, 11*(1), 56-73.

Jones, B. F., Wuchty, S., & Uzzi, B. (2008). Multi-university research teams: Shifting impact, geography, and stratification in science. *Science, 322*, 1259-1262.

Katz, D., & Kahn, R. (1966). *The social psychology of organizations.* New York: Wiley.

Klein, J. T. (1990). *Interdisciplinarity: History, theory, and practice.* Detroit: Wayne State University Press.

Klein, J. T. (1996). *Crossing boundaries: Knowledge, disciplinarities, and interdisciplinarities.* Charlottesville, VA.: University Press of Virginia.

Klein, J. T. (1998). The discourse of interdisciplinarity. *Liberal Education, 84*(3), 4. Retrieved from http://proxygw.wrlc.org/login?url=http://proquest.umi.com/pqdweb?did=35960675 &Fmt=7&clientId=31812&RQT=309&VName=PQD

Klein, J. T. (2004). *A platform for a shared discourse of interdisciplinary education.* Paper presented at the Fenner Conference on the Environment, Guadalajara, Mexico.

Klein, J. T. (2010). A taxonomy of interdisciplinarity. In R. Frodeman, J. T. Klein, & C. Mitcham (Eds.), *The Oxford handbook of interdisciplinarity* (pp. 15-30). Oxford: Oxford University Press.

Klein, J. T. (2014). Inter- and trans-disciplinary boundary work in collaboration science and translational medicine. *Journal of Translational Medicine and Epidemiology, 2*(Special Issue: Collaboration Science and Translational Medicine), 1024-1030.

Kerne, A. (2005, August). Doing interface ecology: The practice of metadisciplinary. In *ACM SIGGRAPH 2005 Electronic Art and Animation Catalog* (pp. 181-185). ACM.

Kockelmans, J. (1979). Why interdisciplinarity? In J. Kockelmans (Ed.), *Interdisciplinarity in higher education* (pp. 123-160). Pennsylvania State University Press.

Kolb, D. (1984). *Experiential learning: Experience as the source of learning and development.* Prentice Hall.

Kuhn, T. (1970). *The structure of scientific revolutions* (2d ed.). Chicago: University of Chicago Press.

Kyvik, S., & Teigen, M. (1996). Child care, research collaboration, and gender differences in scientific productivity. *Science, Technology, and Human Values, 21*(1), 54-71. https://doi.org/10.1177/016224399602100103

Lamont, M., & Swidler, A. (2014). Methodological pluralism and the possibilities and limits of interviewing. *Qualitative Sociology, 37*(2). https://doi.org/10.1007/s11133-014-9274-z

Lang, D., Wiek, A., Bergmann, M., Stauffacher, M., Martens, P., Moll, P., . . . Thomas, C. (2012). Transdisciplinary research in sustainability science: Practice, principles, and challenges. *Sustainability Science, 7*(1), 25-43. https://doi.org/10.1007/s11625-011-0149-x

Larson, E., Landers, T., & Begg, M. (2011). Building interdisciplinary research models: A didactic course to prepare interdisciplinary scholars and faculty. *Clinical Translational Science, 4*(1), 38-41.

Lawler, E., Thye, S., & Yoon, J. (2008). Social exchange and micro social order. *American Sociological Review, 73*(August), 519-542.

Lawrence, P., & Lorsch, J. (1967). *Organization and environment: Managing differentiation and integration.* Boston: Division of Research, Graduate School of Business Administration, Harvard University.

Lotrecchiano, G. R. (2010). Complexity leadership in transdisciplinary (TD) learning environments: A knowledge feedback loop. *International Journal of Transdisciplinary Research, 5*(1), 29-63.

Lotrecchiano, G. R. (2011). Leadership is as simple as a game of marbles: Transdisciplinary, learning and complexity in fairies, keepsies and mibs. *Integral Leadership Review, 11*(1). http://integralleadershipreview.com/2011/2008/leadership-is-as-simple-as-a-child%e2012%2080%2099s-game-of-marbles/

Lotrecchiano, G. R. (2012). *Social mechanisms of team science: A descriptive case study using a multilevel systems perspective employing reciprocating struturation theory.* George Washington University, Washington DC.

Lotrecchiano, G. R. (2013). A dynamical approach toward understanding mechanisms of team science: Change, kinship, tension, and heritage in a transdisciplinary team. *Clinical and Translational Science, 6*(4), 267-278.

Lotrecchiano, G. R., Mallinson, T., Leblanc-Beaudoin, T., Schwartz, L., Lazar, D., & Falk-Krzesinski, H. (2016). Motivation and threat indicators for collaboration readiness in knowledge generating teams (KPTs): A scoping review and domain analysis. *Heliyon, 2*(5).

Maasen, S., & Lieven, O. (2006). Transdisciplinarity: A new mode of governing science? *Science & Public Policy (SPP), 33*(6), 399-410. https://doi.org/10.3152/147154306781778803

Mansilla, V. B. (2005). Assessing student work at disciplinary crossroads. *Change: The Magazine of Higher Learning, 37*(1), 14-21.

Mansilla, V. B., Duraisingh, E., Wolfe, C., & Haynes, C. (2009). Targeted assessment rubric: An empirically grounded rubric for interdisciplinary writing. *The Journal of Higher Education, 80*(3), 334-353.

Matz, D., & Wood, W. (2005). Cognitive dissonance in groups: The consequences of disagreement. *Journal of Personality and Social Psychology, 88*(1), 22-37.

Maxwell, J. A. (2005). *Qualitative research design.* Thousand Oaks, CA: SAGE Publications.

McGregor, S. (2011). Demystifying transdisciplinary ontology: Multiple levels of reality and the hidden third. *Integral Leadership Review, 11*(2). Retrieved from http://integralleadershipreview.com/1746-demystifying-transdisciplinary-ontology-multiple-levels-of-reality-and-the-hiddenthird

Mickan, M., & Rodger, S. (2005). Effective health care teams: A model of six characteristics developed from shared perceptions. *Journal of Interprofessional Care, 19*(4), 358-370.

Misra, S., Stokols, D., & Cheng, L. (2015). The transdisciplinary orientation scale: Factor structure and relation to the integrative quality and scope of scientific publications. *Journal of Translational Medicine and Epidemiology, 3*(2), 1042.

Morgan, G., Kobus, K., & Gerlach, K. (2003). Facilitating transdiciplinary research: The experience of the transdisciplinary tobacco use research centers. *Nicotine and Tobacco Research, 5*(1S), S11-S19.

Morgan, N. (2002). Notions of transdisciplinarity. In M. Somerville & D. Rapport (Eds.), *Transdisciplinarity: reCreating Integrated Knowledge* (p. 38-41). Oxford, UK: EOLSS Publishers Co. Ltd.

Morrison, L. (2008). The CTSAs, the Congress, and the scientific method. *Journal of Investigative Medicine, 56,* 7-10.

National Center for Advancing Translational Sciences (2010). *Clinical and Translational Science Awards.* Retrieved from https://ncats.nih.gov/ctsa

National Science Foundation. (2018). *Convergence Research at NSF.* Retrieved from https://www.nsf.gov/od/oia/convergence/index.jsp

Newell, W., & Meek, J. (2003). Complexity and interdisciplinarity. Knowledge management, organizational intelligence and learning, and complexity. In *Encyclopedia of life support systems.* Oxford, UK: EOLSS Publishers.

Nicolescu, B. (1995). Cybernetics: The bridge between divided knowledge and transdisciplinarity. *Kybernetes: The International Journal of Systems and Cybernetics, 24*(7), 21-24.

Nicolescu, B. (2002). *Manifesto of transdisciplinarity* (K.-C. Voss, Trans.). Albany, NY: State University of New York Press.

Nicolescu, B. (2005a). Towards a transdisciplinary education. *The Journal for Transdisciplinary Research in Southern Africa, 1*(1), 5-16.

Nicolescu, B. (2005b). *Towards transdisciplinary education and learning.* Paper presented at the Science and Religion: Global Perspectives, Philadelphia, PA.

Nicolescu, B. (2006). Hidden third theory. In B. Haverkott & C. Reijntjes (Eds.), *Moving Worldviews Conference Proceedings* (pp. 142-165). Leusden, the Netherlands: ETC/Compas.

Nicolescu, B. (2010). Methods of transdisciplinarity-Levels of reality, logic of the included middle and complexity. *Transdisciplinary Journal of Engineering & Science, 1*(1), 19-38.

Nicolescu, B. (2012). Transdisciplinarity: The hidden third, between the subject and the object. *Human and Social Studies, 1*(2), 13-28.

Paletz, S. B., & Schunn, C. (2010). A social-cognitive framework of multidisciplinary team innovation. *Topics in Cognitive Science, 2*, 73-95.

Park, J.-Y., & Son, J.-B. (2010). Transitioning toward transdisciplinary learning in a multidisciplinary environment. *International Journal of Pedagogies and Learning, 6*(1), 82-93.

Piaget, J. (1972). *The epistemology of interdisciplinary relationships.* Paper presented at the Center for Educational Research and Innovation (CERI), Paris, France.

Pirrie, A., Wilson, V., & Elsewood, J. (1998). *Evaluating multidisciplinary education in health care.* Edinburgh: The Scottish Council for Research in Education.

Plsek, P., & Wilson, T. (2001). Complexity science: Complexity, leadership, and management in healthcare organizations. *British Medical Journal, 323*(7315), 746-749.

Powell, W., & Snellman, K. (2004). The knowledge economy. *Annual Review of Sociology, 30*, 199-220.

Pregernig, M. (2006). Transdisciplinarity viewed from afar: Science-policy assessments as forums for the creation of transdisciplinary knowledge. *Science & Public Policy (SPP), 33*(6), 445-455. https://doi.org/10.3152/147154306781778867

Provan, K., Clark, P., & Huerta, T. (2008). Transdisciplinarity among tobacco harm-reduction researchers. *American Journal of Preventative Medicine, 35*(2S), S173-181.

Repko, A., & Szostak, R. (2016). *Interdisciplinary research: Process and theory.* SAGE.

Rigler, F., & Peters, R. (1995). *Science and limnology* (Vol. 6). Luhe, Germany: Ecology Institute.

Roloff, J. (2008). A life cycle model of multi-stakeholder networks. *Business Ethics: A European Review, 17*(3), 311-325.

Rosenfield, P. (1992). The potential of transdisciplinary research for sustaining and extending linkages between the health and social sciences. *Social Science and Medicine, 25*(11), 1343-1357.

Salas, E., Shuffler, M., Thayer, A., Bedwell, W., & Lazzarra, E. (2015). Understanding and improving teamwork in organizations: A scientifically based practical guide. *Human Resource Management, 54*(4), 599-622.

Schwandt, D. (2008). Individual and collective coevolution. In M. Uhl-Bein & R. Marion (Eds.), *Complexity leadership, Part 1: conceptual foundations.* Charlotte: IAP Publications.

Schwandt, D. (2009). Collective learning as social change: Integrating complex adaptive systems and structuration with Parsons's theory of action. In C. Hart (Ed.), *Essays in honor of Talcott Parsons* (pp. 125-150). Poynton: Midrash Publications.

Sellers, T., Caporaso, N., Lapidus, S., Peterson, G., & Trent, J. (2006). Opportunities and barriers in the age of team science. *Cancer Causes & Controls, 17*(3), 229-237.

Senge, P. (2006). *The fifth discipline: The art and practice of the learning organization.* Broadway Business.

Shuffler, M., DiazGranados, D., & Salas, E. (2011). There's a science for that: Team development interventions in organizations. *Current Directions in Psychological Science, 20*(6), 365-372.

Simmel, G. (1955). *Conflict.* New York: Free Press.

Sims, H., & Manz, C. (1984). Observing leader verbal behavior: Toward reciprocal determinism in leadership theory. *Journal of Applied Psychology, 69*(2), 222-232.

Somerville, M., & Rapport, D. (2002). *Transdisciplinarity: reCreating Integrated Knowledge.* Oxford, UK: EOLSS Publishers Co. Ltd.

Sternman, J. (1989). Modelling managerial behaviour: Misperceptions of feedback in a dynamic decision making environment. *Management Science, 35*, 23-43.

Stokols, D., Fuqua, J., Gress, J., Harvey, R., Phillips, K., Baezconde-Garbanati, L., . . . Trochim, W. (2003). Evaluating transdisciplinary science. *Nicotine and Tabacco Research, 5*(S1), S21-S39.

Stokols, D., Hall, K., Taylor, B., & Moser, R. (2008). The science of team science. *American Journal of Preventative Medicine, 35*(2S), S77-S88.

Stokols, D., Misra, S., Moser, R., Hall, K., & Taylor, B. (2008). The ecology of team science. *American Journal of Preventative Medicine, 35*(2S), S96-S115.

Taylor, F. W. (1911). *The principles of scientific management.* New York, London: Harper & Brothers

Thompson, J. (1967). *Organizations in action: Social science bases of administrative theory.* New York: McGraw Hill.

Toynton, R. (2005). Degrees of disciplinarity in equipping mature students in higher education for engagement and success in lifelong learning. *Active Learning in Higher Education, 6*(2), 106-117.

Tress, M., Tress, G., & Fry, G. (2003). *Potential and limitations of interdisciplinary and transdisciplinary landscape studies.* Wageningen: Delta Program.

Trivedi, C., & Misra, S. (2015). Relevance of systems thinking and scientific holism to social entrepreneurship. *The Journal of Entrepreneurship, 24*(1), 37-62.

Tuckman, B. (1965). Developmental sequence in small groups. *Psychological Bulletin, 63.*

Tuckman, B., & Jensen, M. (1977). Stages of small group development revisited. *Group and Organization Studies, 2*(4), 419-427.

UNESCO. (1998). *Transdisciplinarity: Stimulating synergies, integrating knowledge.* Paper presented at the Division of Philosophy and Ethics, Royaumont Abbey, Val-d'Oise, France.

Unger, J., Cruz, T., Shakib, S., Mock, J., Shields, A., Baezconde-Garbanati, L., . . . Johnson, C. (2003). Exploring the cultural context of tobacco use: A transdisicplinary framework. *Nicotine and Tobacco Research, 5*(Supplement 1), S101-S117.

Veling, H., Holland, R., & van Knippenberg. (2008). When approach motivation and behavioral inhibition collide: Behavior regulation through stimulus devaluation. *Journal of Experimental Social Psychology, 44*, 1013-1019.

Vickers, J. (1997). [U]nframed in open, unmapped fields: Teaching the practice of interdisciplinarity. *ARACHNE, 4*(2), 11-42.

von Bertalanffy, L. (1956). General systems theory. *General Systems, 1*, 1-10.

Wahlstrom, K., & Seashore Louis, K. (2008). How teachers experience principal leadership: The roles of professional community, trust, efficacy, and shared responsibility. *Educational Administration Quarterly, 44*(4), 458-495.

Walsh, M., & Wicks, C. (2014). Introducing transdisciplinary problem-solving to environmental management systems and geology students through a case study of disturbed coastal systems. *Journal of College Science Teaching, 43*(3), 48-53.

Walter, A., Helgenberger, S., Wiek, A., & Scholz, R. (2007). Measuring societal effects of transdisciplinary research projects: Design and application of an evaluation method. *Evaluation and Program Planning, 30*, 325-338.

Weisbord, M. (2004). *Productive workplaces revisited: Dignity, meaning, and community in the 21st Century*. San Francisco: Jossey-Bass.

Welch, I., Szostak, R., & Repko, A. (2011). The emergence of interdisciplinarity from epistemological thought. *Issues in Integrative Studies, 29*, 1-39.

Wheatley, M. (1999). *Leadership and the new science*. San Francisco: Berrett-Koehler.

Wickson, F., Carew, A., & Russell, A. (2006). Transdisciplinary research: Characteristics, quandaries and quality. *Futures, 38*, 1046-1059.

Yang, B. (2003). Toward a holistic theory of knowledge and adult learning. *Human Resource Development Review, 2*(2), 106-129.

Gaetano R. Lotrecchiano & Shalini Misra (Editors). 2020
Communication in Transdisciplinary Teams
Santa Rosa, CA: Informing Science Press

Chapter 2:
What Is Collaborative, Interdisciplinary Reasoning? The Heart of Interdisciplinary Team Research

Bethany K. Laursen
Departments of Philosophy and Community Sustainability Michigan State University, Laursen Evaluation & Design, LLC
laursen3@msu.edu

Chapter Objectives

- To persuade the reader that an argument is a basic unit of analysis for interdisciplinary integration.

- To define collaborative, interdisciplinary reasoning (CIR) as "the attempted integration of disciplinary contributions to exchange, evaluate, and assert claims that enable shared understanding and eventually action in a local context."

- To explain that exchanging and evaluating claims requires agreeing with teammates about what is assertible (and why) according to shared standards for what counts as good reasons and inferences.

- To explain that asserting a claim together legitimately requires using those shared standards of reasonableness to make a cogent, integrated argument.

- To demonstrate that to assess the argument's cogency, it can be helpful to reconstruct it using pragma-dialectic principles as a form of discourse analysis.

Introduction to the Chapter

Collaborative, interdisciplinary research is growing rapidly, but we still have limited and fragmented understanding of what is arguably the heart of such research—collaborative, interdisciplinary reasoning (CIR). This article integrates neo-Pragmatist theories of reasoning with insights from literature on interdisciplinary research to develop a working definition of collaborative, interdisciplinary reasoning: namely, it is the attempted integration of disciplinary contributions to exchange, evaluate, and assert claims that enable shared understanding and eventually action in a local context. In other words, to assert something together legitimately requires making a cogent, integrated argument, and this requires agreeing with teammates about what is assertible and why according to shared standards of reasoning. The article then applies this definition to an empirical example to demonstrate its utility. The empirical example is an excerpt from a Toolbox workshop transcript. The arti-

An earlier version of this chapter was published as Laursen, B. K. (2018). What is collaborative, interdisciplinary reasoning? The heart of interdisciplinary team research. *Informing Science: the International Journal of an Emerging Transdiscipline, 21,* https://doi.org/10.28945/4010

cle reconstructs a cogent, inductive, interdisciplinary argument from the excerpt to show how CIR can proceed in an actual team, one of the first uses of discourse analysis on interdisciplinary talk. The study contributes operational definitions of 'reasoning together' and 'collaborative, interdisciplinary reasoning' to existing literature. It also demonstrates empirical methods for operationalizing these definitions, with the argument reconstruction also providing a brief case study in how teams reason together.

Background

Collaborative, interdisciplinary research has grown dramatically in recent decades—both in prevalence as well as promise (Van Noorden, 2015). The National Academies recently reported that 90% of scientific and engineering articles are now written by two or more authors (National Research Council, 2015, pp. 19-20), and many of these teams are interdisciplinary. In six domains, articles from 2005 referenced an average of 50% more disciplines than articles from 1975 (Porter & Rafols, 2009). The trend towards interdisciplinary referencing practices—and by implication, interdisciplinary reasoning among author teams—has been especially marked since the mid-1980s (Lariviere & Gingras, 2014).

Rapid expansion in collaborative, interdisciplinary research has been justified by both the epistemic and instrumental promises of this mode of research (National Research Council, 2005). Epistemically, the claim is that many problems—especially so-called "grand challenges" (De Grandis & Efstathiou, 2016) or "wicked problems" (Brown, Harris, & Russell, 2010; Rittel & Webber, 1973)—cannot be understood by a single discipline. Rather, insights are claimed to be more relevant and more incisive when knowledge is integrated across disciplinary boundaries and interstices (National Research Council, 2005, pp. 16-17). Instrumentally, it often "takes a village" to access the material, human, temporal, and technical resources needed to research such wicked problems (Hagstrom 1964; Lewis, Ross, & Holden 2012).

However advantageous, this form of research poses its own challenges, which have in turn sparked meta-research on collaborative, interdisciplinary processes—a literature to which this study contributes (e.g., Frodeman, Klein, & Mitcham, 2010; Frodeman, Klein, & Pacheco, 2017). Meta-research and lessons learned in practice have together produced a plethora of tools, frameworks, and constructs aimed to help us understand and address challenges inherent in cross-disciplinary teamwork (e.g., i2insights.org, n.d.; National Institutes of Health National Cancer Institute, n.d.).

What has been underrated in this meta-research and practice, however, is a clear understanding of what could be considered the most basic task of these research teams: collaborative, interdisciplinary reasoning. By reasoning, here, I mean making inferences from what we understand to what we don't understand (Scriven, 1976). Making inferences entails exploring implications of a claim, using some claims to justify or cast doubt on other claims. That is, reasoning assesses the "warranted assertibility" (Dewey, 1938, p. 9) of a claim by evaluating the implications of other, more well-established claims.

Broadly speaking, we engage in reasoning when someone wants to assert an idea and others want to assess the right to assert it. These desires create different kinds of discourse settings in which assertions are made and defended. Sometimes, what is asserted is an answer to a question. These discourse settings constitute inquiries. Research is a type of inquiry, and, therefore, reasoning is essential to it. Failing to understand this most essential activity results in limited progress in improving theory and practice of collaborative, interdisciplinary research.

This investigation contributes to filling the related conceptual gap by first proposing a definition of collaborative, interdisciplinary reasoning (CIR) based on the neo-Pragmatist reasoning and argumentation literature. Next follows an in-depth example of CIR so understood to illustrate that this form of reasoning in interdisciplinary teams is plausible. The example also demonstrates perhaps the first application of argument reconstruction as a form of discourse analysis of interdisciplinary talk. The article concludes by reflecting on areas for future research.

The tasks for future research include investigating situations in which reasoning goes poorly. This article presents the ideal for CIR as a goal for which to aim. However, an ideal—by definition—is never fully realized. A full, ethical, and useful treatment of CIR must, therefore, consider non-ideal situations, providing conceptual frameworks and practical suggestions for engaging the real world. This article provides an orienting direction for such future work.

Future directions also include extension into collaborative, transdisciplinary reasoning. This article focuses on interdisciplinary research as the integration rather than transcendence of disciplines, or as the incorporation of academic and non-academic stakeholders. This is because there is more literature on interdisciplinarity than transdisciplinarity and because interdisciplinarity remains a common goal in the research world. This article aims, therefore, to contribute to interdisciplinary work directly and to transdisciplinary work by extension or transfer.

Collaborative, Interdisciplinary Reasoning

Reasoning Together Defined

To reiterate, this article focuses upon reasoning that should occur among members of an interdisciplinary research project. *Research* here distinguishes inquiries that are planned and conducted systematically from those conducted more haphazardly. More specifically, Leedy and Ormrod (2005, p. 2), state, "Research is a systematic process of collecting, analyzing, and interpreting information (data) in order to increase our understanding of the phenomenon about which we are interested or concerned." Research, in other words, is a type of formal inquiry that seeks to increase understanding. In this conception, research occurs not only in academic settings but also in industrial and national laboratories, law enforcement offices, and non-profit organizations, to name a few places. Research projects might involve only one person, but the focus here is projects involving two or more collaborators.

CIR is a specific kind of the more general activity of reasoning together, requiring first an understanding of that more general concept. Communication is the vehicle for collaborative reasoning. J. Britt Holbrook (2013) helpfully identified three ways to understand communication, particularly as it applies to interdisciplinary research. One view is the Kuhn-MacIntyre thesis that reasoning across perspectives is not possible, because perspectives amount to incommensurable paradigms. Any collaborative reasoning that does occur requires one of the participants to acquire "native fluency" in the relevant disciplinary languages, an accomplishment that is extremely difficult, rare, and in the end, not the integration of two paradigms. A second view, the Bataille-Lyotard thesis, holds that collaborative reasoning can proceed only by inventing a new language, built expressly for that discourse. Like the Kuhn-MacIntyre thesis, the Bataille-Lyotard thesis contends that different perspectives amount to incommensurable paradigms. However, unlike its Kuhn-MacIntyre counterpart, this thesis argues that commensurability is possible—but only through the invention of a custom-built language. A third major understanding of reasoning together is the Habermas-Klein thesis, which holds that collaborative reasoning is possible through *integration* of perspectives. While Holbrook's article does not acknowledge this, other work from the Habermas-Klein perspective discusses many possible paths to integration (Klein, 1996, 2014, pp. 20-22; O'Rourke, Crowley, & Gonnerman, 2016; Repko, Szostak, & Buchberger, 2016). Some paths may involve the creation of a new language but others may integrate existing languages. Moreover, although the Habermas-Klein thesis emphasizes integration as the ideal, the thesis acknowledges that in reality some perspectives are incommensurable (whether for inherent or contextual reasons is up for debate in each case). Thus, while Holbrook may disagree with me, I believe the Habermas-Klein thesis accommodates both the Bataille-Lyotard and Kuhn-MacIntyre theses while also affirming what most of us tend to believe: that reasoning together does happen across different perspectives.

Therefore, for the purposes of this project the Habermas-Klein thesis is most appropriate. I emphasize one strand of this thesis with a conception of "reasoning together" found in neo-Pragmatist works by Jürgen Habermas (1985), Larry Wright (1995, 2001), and Christian Campolo (Campolo, 2005; Campolo & Turner, 2002). This approach differs from perspectives of reasoning that have been more common in interdisciplinary literature, such as interdisciplinary learning (Augsburg & Chitewere, 2013), thinking (Dreyfuss, 2011), and cognition (Derry, Schunn, & Gernsbacher, 2013; Nikitina, 2005). The difference is that this neo-Pragmatist approach centers the social practice of giving reasons through discourse for the sake of coordinated action. It elevates the role of communication as a learning-for-doing tool while minimizing communication, learning, or doing treated separately: to neo-Pragmatists, collaborative reasoning is cognitive and communicative and contextually practical all at once. With such a focus, new facets of interdisciplinary communication come into the spotlight. As discussed and exemplified below, these new facets include types of discourse, standards for assertion, argument structures (including premises and conclusions), and conversational moves. The article attempts to show these are valuable insights.

Habermas's theory of "reasoning together" unfolds several types of argumentation that differ based on differing goals of discourse (Habermas, 1985). Possible goals include finding truth ("theoretical discourse"), determining what is right action ("practical discourse"), establishing standards for value ("aesthetic criticism"), assessing authenticity of expression ("artistic critique"), and—as a meta-purpose—clarifying the appropriate forms of the above discourses ("explicative discourse") (Habermas, 1985, p. 23). Regarding the last goal, we need such meta-discourse because we always risk reasoning about different types of things in inappropriate ways, e.g., confusing the way things are (finding truth) with the way things should be (determining what is right action, or establishing standards of value). Explicative discourse is especially important in interdisciplinary contexts as disciplines disagree about the appropriate way(s) to discuss many topics (Eigenbrode et al., 2007); indeed the interdisciplinary example analyzed below illustrates explicative discourse.

Habermas (1985) emphasizes that rational discourse toward the above goals always involves argumentation because rational discourse depends upon one's ability to evaluate reasons and inferences against shared ("transsubjective") standards of adequacy (p. 9). Such discourse can be understood as reasoning together, both because the claims and reasons are given in *social contexts* and because the standards by which those reasons are evaluated are *socially constructed*.

Intersubjective Standards of Reasoning

Intersubjective (a.k.a. shared) standards of reasoning are statements whose meaning is shared between interlocutors and used to judge the acceptability of claims.

Alternatively

Intersubjective (a.k.a. shared) standards of reasoning are thresholds of criteria of reasonable-ness understood and endorsed by all participants, where criteria of reasonable-ness indicate what is assertible and why in this local context.

Intersubjective standards, as Wright and Campolo call them, are statements whose meaning is shared between interlocutors and is used to judge the acceptability of claims. A standard indicates a threshold of acceptability on a certain criterion. For example, a common intersubjective standard in quantitative research is that statistical inferences must have a p value below 0.05 to be considered credible (Wasserstein & Lazar, 2016). Qualitative researchers, on the other hand, often require credible findings to be member checked (i.e., given approval by the respondents themselves) (Lincoln & Guba, 1985). Both of these standards are socially constructed by epistemic communities. These standards can therefore change.

Moreover, these standards can have different meanings, even to members within the same epistemic community or the same person in two different contexts. For example, 0.05 is the threshold for which statistical test? With what kind of data? Similarly, member checking must include which members? And how should the check be performed? These questions identify key features of the *meaning* of each standard. Intersubjectivity of these standards requires participants agree upon the answers to such key questions. The best test we have of agreement is the ability to coordinate actions that depend upon the meaning. For example, if I ask for the data so I can test for significance, and if you give me the data in the form I expect, then I can be fairly confident you and I have the same test in mind and therefore a shared meaning of "statistical significance." Intersubjectivity, therefore, is best evidenced in localized social exchanges where actions serve as evidence of agreement across subjects (see Example 1).

Example 1: Climate Change Discourses

For examples of the kinds of discourse Habermas discusses, consider the following pair of climate change discourses. To set context, imagine a city has adopted a climate change adaptation plan that involves spending $12 million to raise the elevation of causeways in and out of town. The action of causeway renovation is a non-linguistic claim approximately translated linguistically as, "We believe climate change is real and that this is a right way to deal with it." This statement prompts two different kinds of discourse in local meetings, coffee shops, and newspapers. First is the "theoretical" or truth-finding question, "Is climate change really real?" Second is the practical question, "If it is real, what is the right way to deal with it?" These two questions have different assertion goals and therefore require distinct forms of reasoning. What shapes those distinct forms ought to take would be decided in an "explicative" discourse about each question that clarifies their appropriate form. In all cases, for these discourses to count as discourses, multiple parties must participate, and participation requires their ability to evaluate each other's claims. As Habermas observes, "[My] reflections point in the direction of basing the rationality of an expression on its being susceptible of criticism and grounding" (Habermas, 1985, p. 9).

It is important to note that Habermas's conception of rational discourse includes both "linguistic and non-linguistic actions," where non-linguistic expressions might include "delays, surgical interventions, declarations [waging] of war, [and] repairs" (1985, p. 8). Both linguistic and non-linguistic expressions communicate, but only linguistic expressions use words to do so. What matters is that the expression effectively makes a claim addressing one of the purposes listed above, and that this claim can be evaluated against shared standards of reasoning.

Expanding on Habermas's insights, Wright (1995) and Campolo (2005) theorize that "reasoning together" is the activity of establishing or repairing intersubjectivity about the implications of a claim for the sake of continuing a shared effort. Or, as Campolo puts it, "It is a way of restoring or initiating purposeful coordination to our several actions or behaviors" (2005, p. 38). Purposeful coordination is exactly what is at stake in collaborative projects; without it, a group is unlikely to accomplish its goals. Examples of coordinated action include meeting together, defining a research question, collecting and analyzing data, and submitting an article.

Here's how reasoning together supports such coordinated action. The initial result of a session of reasoning together is an assertion, which is a type of action ("communicative action," according to Habermas (1985)). This initial action then enables a chain of other actions: assertions enable understanding, understanding enables belief, and belief enables actions (see bottom half of Figure 1). This chain must occur for each of the innumerable decisions an interdisciplinary team must make. Moreover, the project itself is the first link in this chain as the understanding it generates should go onto influence beliefs and actions beyond the project.

Collaborative reasoning in research can be triggered by a disruption in any one of these links in the chain of action—originating either within or beyond the project. John Dewey (1910) called such a break "the feeling of a discrepancy, or difficulty" (p. 73), and it is the first step in an inquiry. An example of disruption within the team might come when team-mates do not agree on how to complete the data analysis, or when someone doesn't understand what someone else wrote in the manuscript so they can't approve its submission. Disruptions beyond the team might arise even before the team assembles; these might be disruptions that start the team's entire project as an inquiry into an external disruption. For instance, when colleagues in a field no longer understand a phenomenon (perhaps the claims are controversial, incoherent, or absent), the coordinated action of understanding has been disrupted, and this event can manifest as a research question. In another instance, resource users might be at a loss about what to do because they are questioning some long-held beliefs (e.g., they question if climate is stable), and if researchers are listening to their needs, this disruption in daily life might prompt a research question. Research projects are attempts to restore disrupted chains of action in the world (including disrupted understanding, such as curiosity) by answering research questions, and this requires answering many other kinds of questions within the team's work. Answering questions *as a team* requires reasoning *together*.

Integrating the insights of Habermas, Wright, and Campolo, in the present project I understand *reasoning together* as follows:

> Reasoning together is (linguistic or non-linguistic) discourse in which the participants exchange, evaluate, and assert claims that enable coordinated action in a local context.

This proposition is worth unpacking. Recall that reasoning involves assessing one claim's dependence on other, more well-established claims. To evaluate these claims, participants must agree upon the standards by which they will evaluate them. The following questions arise: What counts as a "supportive" claim? How do we judge when one claim legitimately "depends on" another? What do we accept as "well-established"? If members of a team are not yet on the same page about these standards, they need to resolve their misunderstandings using a meta-, "explicative" discourse. Otherwise, they might go ahead and apply a shared or dominant standard in any of Habermas's four other forms of discourse.

Therefore, in order to exchange, evaluate, and assert claims together, participants need shared standards of what counts as good reasons and inferences. Well-supported, shared inferences then enable coordinated action. An expanded definition of reasoning together, therefore, follows:

> Reasoning together is the co-application and, perhaps, co-revision or even co-creation of intersubjective standards for what counts as a good reasons and inferences in a localized social exchange so that people can continue working together.

The prefix "co-" specifies that these activities occur collaboratively, through conversation and other forms of communication. Co-application consists of applying existing standards of reasoning. For instance, a team may have already decided that "good" claims in their project must be based at least partly on inferential statistics. They could then apply that standard to a questionable claim to see how good it is. Co-revision modifies an existing standard to restore shared understanding of it. Co-creation, however, is the synthesis of a new standard from existing, shared understanding. Note that reasoning together cannot create shared understanding *ex nihilo*; much must already be shared (Campolo, 2005).

Reasoning Together

Reasoning together is (linguistic or non-linguistic) discourse in which the participants exchange, evaluate, and assert claims that enable coordinated action in a local context.

Alternatively

Reasoning together is the co-application and, perhaps, co-revision or even co-creation of intersubjective standards for what counts as a good reasons and inferences in a localized social exchange so that people can continue working together.

This conception of "reasoning together" emphasizes that (1) team members must have shared standards for evaluating a claim and (2) the goal of reasoning depends on the local context of a targeted action. Participants in collaborative *research* are trying to take an action of assertion that leads to the subsequent action of shared *understanding*, whether understanding of truth, action, value, authentic expression, or discourse itself. This shared understanding, ideally, enables further coordinated actions beyond the research project, e.g., spending $12 million to upgrade causeways (Example 1).

To clarify relationships among key concepts thus far: We reason to go from understanding less to understanding more by making inferences. We make inferences by evaluating whether some relatively well-established claims support other claims. Evaluating support involves applying standards for what counts as support, where applying such standards may first require creating or revising them. When reasoning as a team, all participants must agree upon and understand those standards. Reasoning then results in warranted, assertible conclusions that enable a series of coordinated actions. Assertion itself is a kind of coordinated communicative action, but it typically serves a more distal action. In a surgery team, that action is a successful surgery. In a research team, that action is shared understanding of a phenomenon. Eventually, shared understanding from research may influence actions beyond the research project, such as a more successful surgery. The top half of Figure 1 charts this definition of "reasoning together."

Collaborative, Interdisciplinary Reasoning Defined

From here, to define CIR we need only specify what it means to reason together in an interdisciplinary way. Given the prevalence and promise of interdisciplinary research described above, a relatively clear consensus has emerged about what it means to be "interdisciplinary." The authoritative definition from the National Academies in their 2005 report *Facilitating Interdisciplinary Research* is widely recognized: interdisciplinarity entails "integrat[ing] information, data, techniques, tools, perspectives, concepts, and/or theories from two or more disciplines or bodies of specialized knowledge" (National Research Council, 2005, p. 2). Combining this definition with the above definition of "reasoning together" suggests the definition of CIR given in the box. The bottom half of Figure 1 shows how this definition of CIR specifies and mirrors the more general definition of "reasoning together."

Collaborative, Interdisciplinary Reasoning

Collaborative, interdisciplinary reasoning is the attempted integration of disciplinary contributions to co-apply, co-revise, or co-create intersubjective standards for what counts as good reasons and inferences in a local social exchange so that people can gain understanding and then continue working together.

Alternatively

CIR is the attempted integration of disciplinary contributions to exchange, evaluate, and assert claims that enable shared understanding and eventually action in a local context.

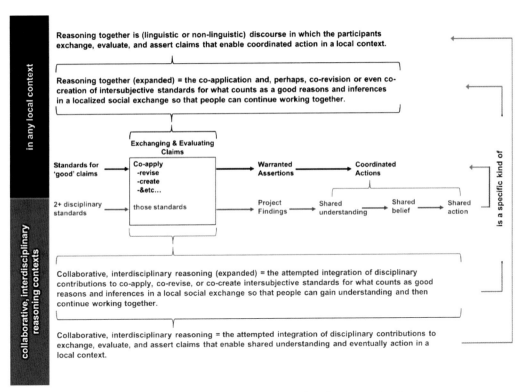

Figure 1. Reasoning together in any local context (top) vs. collaborative, interdisciplinary contexts (bottom).

Standards for reasoning already exist in most disciplinary discourses, but they must often be revised or created in interdisciplinary discourses because all disciplinarians bring their own standards to the team (Eigenbrode et al., 2007; Knorr Cetina, 2009). Disciplinary standards may not only have different thresholds (e.g., $p < 0.1$ versus 0.05), they may also have different content and meanings altogether (e.g., "significant" = relevant, credible, actionable; versus $p < 0.05$). Co-revision consists in sorting out mismatched understandings of standards, while co-creation consists in establishing new standards. Some teams may be able to co-apply an intersubjective standard right away—perhaps having worked together before. Usually, however, teams will first need to co-revise or co-create such a standard through the process of explicative discourse.

As Habermas (1985) observed, a discourse that makes claims can be understood as an argument, where the more established claims are premises and the inferred claim is the conclusion. A reasoning team is trying to craft a cogent argument all of its members endorse. The argument contains premises each interlocutor can evaluate for "allegations of support" of the conclusion (Wright, 1995, p. 570), and the conclusion captures the result of co-applying the standard to those premises. In some cases, the conclusion will itself be a standard to co-apply in another argument. In such cases, as an instance of explicative discourse, the argument is co-repairing or co-creating a shared standard for later reasoning. For example, the city council that approved the causeway renovation probably had an earlier meeting or series of meetings in which they decided that conclusions about climate change and what to do about it require certain kinds of evidence (e.g., regional climate models, climate risk assessment). Therefore, when they got this evidence, they were able to make an argument asserting climate change is real and causeway renovation is an appropriate next step. In an interdisciplinary group (perhaps the city council qualifies), the argument premises will often be crafted from various disciplinary contributions. The example in the next section illustrates how collaborative, interdisciplinary conversations can be understood as instances of CIR. It focuses specifically on explicative discourse—the co-creation of standards for group reasoning about another topic.

First, though, it is crucial to emphasize that interlocutors need not succeed in achieving intersubjectivity to engage in CIR. All three philosophers above emphasize, as Wright observes, "The practice of giving reasons is of value in our deliberations *when and because we are equipped* to evaluate the allegation of support [of a reason]" emphasis added (1995, p. 570). When we are not so equipped, reasons don't help much. In other words, it is quite possible to give reasons in a way that is *not* valuable and nevertheless be engaged in reasoning together. We often reason together quite poorly. Defining exactly what it means to reason together well or poorly in CIR remains a future project, but some warnings about the general process of reasoning together apply.

Wright (1995) and Campolo (2005; Campolo & Turner, 2002) stress that we are equipped to evaluate allegations of support when the standards by which we evaluate them are (in my paraphrasing) (a) shared, (b) relevant, and (c) informed. If any one of these three criteria is absent, then we ought not to reason together. Here's why.

There are two options when participants realize they do not share enough foundational, relevant, informed commitments to make reliable inferences that solve the problem. One option is to stop reasoning and try another coordination approach, such as following orders. The other option is to continue reasoning, but this option is dangerous. To continue reasoning using claims they do not hold or understand, participants must create an appearance of informed consensus. This illusion can be constructed in at least two ways: either stronger participants force weaker participants to adopt their views and/or participants feign understanding. In the first case, great harm might be done through epistemic oppression *and* valuable understanding might be suppressed that could have helped solve the problem (Dotson, 2012; 2014). In the second case, which might also be a form of testimonial injustice (Dotson, 2011), it is unlikely the group will solve the problem and this could be harmful in itself. In addition, any success participants might have will be due to luck—good inferences will have nothing to do with it. This can also be harmful as it may reinforce bad reasoning habits (Campolo, 2005).

Collaborators must therefore have quite a bit in common before reasoning together becomes possible or useful. While it is possible to have *an* explicative discourse, i.e., to reason together to co-create a shared standard for another discourse, it is not possible to have explicative discourses about explicative discourses *ad infinitum*. We must, eventually, agree on some standard for reasoning to get off the ground. These basic shared standards arise from our shared experiences; for instance, our experience as academics. As Campolo (2005) puts it,

> Reasoning together in a fruitful way depends upon our existing shared practice, shared knowledge, and shared competence. Under the right conditions, reasoning together can restore that intersubjectivity. Under almost no circumstances can reasoning together create that intersubjectivity where it does not already exist (p. 45).

Thus, to judge whether a group is reasoning well or poorly, we must know the nature of their shared background. Therefore, the example below goes so far as to affirm reasoning did succeed to some extent, but a full evaluation is beyond the scope of this study.

Collaborative, Interdisciplinary Reasoning Exemplified

CIR can be found in many places. Excerpts from a transcript of a Toolbox workshop as well as the analysis I performed on the transcript, are described in this section. Toolbox workshops host lightly facilitated, cross-disciplinary team discussions about project-related work.

The facilitator rarely speaks, but the written instrument each participant completes provides some structure in the form of a menu of project-related assumptions participants can discuss at will. (For more information about the Toolbox Dialogue Initiative, formerly known as the "Toolbox Project", see O'Rourke and Crowley, 2013). Table 1 (at the end of this chapter) is a conversation thread about 40 speaking turns long, including minor interruptions and affirmations such as "Mmmhmm," and "Right" excluded from this analysis. In this thread, interlocutors discuss what counts as modeling in their interdisciplinary project. They evaluate and integrate each other's claims into a coherent argument supporting a conclusion about modeling that allows them to go on together. Of the twelve team members present, only three participate in this thread: a sociologist, a hydrologist, and an engineer. They integrate contributions from their three disciplines into five argument premises (P1-5) that together support a single conclusion about what counts as modeling in their project.

This section begins by overviewing the argument. Next, it describes the methods used in reconstructing the argument and then the reconstruction itself, i.e., how each premise is developed in the dialogue. To my knowledge, it is the first use of argument reconstruction to analyze interdisciplinary discourse at the conversation level (cf. Choi & Richards 2017). Lastly, the section concludes by showing how this example of explicative discourse enables future coordinated action for the participants. This section is an example that other analysts can follow with interdisciplinary conversations wherever they occur.

Argument overview

The numbers in parentheses below after a given premise refer to speaking turns that contribute to that premise. The first premise is mostly implicit in the dialogue, which is indicated by brackets. (Noteworthy: the sociologist does utter a few words gesturing in this direction). Similarly, the conclusion does not appear in any speaking turns because no one spoke the entire conclusion out loud; it also appears in brackets. However, implicit conclusions are not necessarily unreasonable or problematic. Explicit articulation is not logically required since the conclusion follows from the premises, which were already well-established, and it summarizes the general position that participants in the excerpt constructed.

P1. [The practices of the people here decide what modeling is in our project.] (64, 66)

P2. Everyone here uses statistics with empirical observations to build their models. (66, 68, 69, 79, 89, 91)

P3. Hydrologists and engineers use statistics to correlate inputs and outputs according to processes they already know. (70, 75-79, 83, 85, 87)

P4. Sociologists use statistics to discover processes. (70, 77, 81, 85, 92, 94, 96, 98, 100)

P5. These two practices both use the input-process-output framework although their operationalizations of the framework differ. (72, 74, 88, 91, 103, 104)

C. [Therefore, modeling in our project involves using statistics with empirical observations to operationalize the input-process-output concept.]

With this conclusion, conversational participants are now on the same page about what modeling is in their project, enabling them to continue modeling together. Because their modeling practice was at stake, interrupted by misunderstanding, they co-revised their standard for what counts as a reasonable claim about modeling. Now, they could co-apply this standard to their shared modeling practices in future interdisciplinary dialogues—until another disruption requires them to co-revise. Their conclusion is an inference that allowed them to go from understanding less about modeling to understanding more. It is an assertion that enables future chains of coordinated action.

Argument reconstruction methods

Reconstructing arguments from ordinary language—especially un-rehearsed dialogues—is difficult and controversial. Pragma-dialectical argumentation scholars recognize the tension between getting the reconstruction right while also assuming the speakers are making the strongest argument possible, consistent with their argumentative intentions (van Eemeren et al., 2014). This assumption requires an analyst to fit the speakers' words into a cogent argument form—even if it is not the form in which the speaker presented claims. Indeed, everyday conversations rarely proceed as linear arguments. In most cases, one must give the speaker the benefit of the doubt when it comes to re-constructing a cogent argument but also capture the conversational moves actually used to argue. That is, the analyst must be charitable but also descriptively accurate. There is no easy to way to resolve the tension between accuracy and charity, although pragma-dialectical (schematic) reconstructions combined with conversation analysis can help, and that is what I have tried to do here (Sandvik, 1997). Nevertheless, we can think of argument reconstruction as more of an art than a science. Others may see a different argument in the excerpt than the one I present in Table 1.

However, any such disagreement merely illustrates the proposition that reasoning together is about exchanging and evaluating reasons for one's assertions. Specifically, some might give reasons to disagree with the reconstruction, underscoring that we rely upon reason-giving in research discourse and this difficult task requires balancing accurate and charitable interpretations of what others have said. Thus, the main purpose of this example is not to get the reconstruction "objectively right" (if there is such a thing). The purpose, rather, is to illustrate collaborative, interdisciplinary reasoning, whether through the example itself and/or how we talk about it.

1. The definition of CIR identifies four nodes or knots in the reasoning tapestry: dis-cussants, disciplines, premises, and a conclusion that increases understanding and eventually leads to action.

2. Brief verbal affirmations such as "Mmmhmm," and "Right" are not content con-tributions but rather indicate acceptance, and so they are excluded from the analy-sis.

3. The remaining, substantive speaking turns may contain more than one distinct idea.

4. Each distinct idea is coded as a separate "contribution."

5. The speaker's own disciplinary identity indicates which disciplinary perspective is driving the contribution, *unless* the speaker explicitly notes they are taking on the perspective of another discipline or disciplinarian.

6. These disciplinary contributions contribute to argument premises, and the premis-es a conclusion.

7. The premises and conclusion are assumed to be grammatically complete, contextu-ally meaningful, and logically coherent (i.e., "well-formed") claims.

8. A well-formed claim may or may not be spoken aloud. In cases where it is not, the analyst supplies the missing pieces by surmising what the speakers intended to say or believe they did say. Listening to the audio recording can help in resolving am-biguity.

The full application of these principles to the excerpt is documented in Table 1.

Argument reconstruction

P1. [The practices of the people here decide what modeling is in our project.] Un-derstanding the origin of Premise 1 requires first looking at the dialogue's context. Partici-pants requested a Toolbox workshop *because* they wanted to get on the same page about key concepts in their project. Thus, this excerpt about modeling takes place in a conversational context designed to help them increase mutual understanding, which includes mutual un-derstanding about what modeling is in their project. The assumption behind the dialogue is that the people present have a significant role to play in determining how things are understood within their project. In fact, the sociologist implies as much when he opens the ex-cerpted dialogue:

> Sociologist (64, 66): "Well one of the things I found working with many of the people in the room is a term I'm still trying to wrap my mind around, that I don't think we all use the same way is the word 'modeling'…We actually confronted this one when we tried to write our grant."

The sociologist references use of the term "modeling" in their proposal writing process, indicating that the following discussion is about use of the term in this project by people participating in the project. The others take up this conversation in future turns, implying they agree with this first premise.

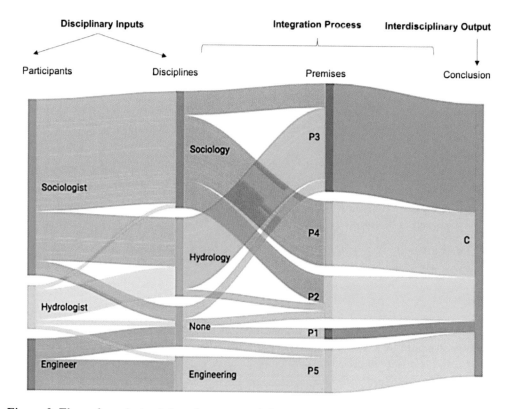

Figure 2. Flow of words (and therefore reasons) from speakers to disciplines, premises, and conclusion in the dialogue excerpt (26 speaking turns, 34 contributions, 1294 words). The width of the link represents the number of words.

What has happened is that the participants immediately applied a shared, unspoken stand-ard about what is assertible by the sociologist. What is assertible seems to be whatever has been experienced by anyone in the group—individually or collectively. It is not clear how they came to share this assertibility standard. They may have affirmed the validity of each other's experiences in previous discussions, or they may simply share that assumption based on their shared lifeworld as academics, where (usually) one's expertise is not ques-tioned by those from other disciplines. When applying this standard to his claim, the sociologist here is not speaking as a sociologist but more generally as a member of the project. Indeed, Figure 2 shows P1 comes from no particular disciplinary perspective.

P2. Everyone here uses statistics with empirical observations to build their models. Premise 2 takes quite a while to become a full thought in the dialogue. Not until speaking turn 89 do participants discover what exactly they all have in common when modeling. They spend much of the dialogue trying to find the commonality by showing how they use terms related to modeling, such as "calibration" and "significance." For example, the Sociologist explains that when he models,

> Sociologist (66): … we [Sociologists] go and do a fairly standardized set of mathematical type things that say, ok that is, that explains this much of what we were trying to explain, this well or with this much degree of confidence….

> Sociologist (68): [cont.] Um, but you're actually inferring sort of this significance of relationships and so.

> Hydrologist (69): [overlap] Well you just described what <u>we</u> do.

In this brief exchange, the hydrologist and sociologist agree that for them, significance means mathematically significant, a definition that likely refers to statistics given the use of the terms "degree of confidence" and "significant." The engineer never disagrees with this conclusion, suggesting that it also describes his practice. A longer exchange (75-89) centers on the term "calibration," but in fact the process of calibration is so technical they cannot fully compare the various meanings-in-practice during this brief dialogue. They are satisfied to know calibration eventually ends by determining the statistical significance of their empirical observations.

By comparing and contrasting related terms such as "calibration" and "significance," the interlocutors (the sociologist, hydrologist, and engineer) can triangulate on where the focus term, "modeling," fits in their respective meaning structures (Mohr, 1998). In locating the target term in relation to other terms, they can discern its core meaning: they examine which terms it is related to in the same way in the meaning structures of all participants. They decide that the core feature of modeling for them is use of statistics with empirical observations.

> Sociologist (66): "[The way] we model in the social sciences – some of us do – is basically an exercise of developing some theoretical models and testing them against the world and seeing how well that model fits."

> Hydrologist (89): "But what you described is what you do for a model <u>anyway</u>, you're approach to modeling? I'm just sitting here going, hmmm yep."

Again, we see the participants applying their shared standard for what is assertible, namely, whatever has been experienced by the participants. When they apply this standard to the anecdotes given by the sociologist and hydrologist, they establish a new claim about the necessary role of statistics. Now that they know what they have in common, they must articulate their differences to develop an integrative definition of modeling. Figure 2 shows P2 is an interdisciplinary premise, established by sociology, hydrology, and a general perspective integrated into a coherent claim.

P3. Hydrologists and engineers use statistics to correlate inputs and outputs according to processes they already know. Premises 3 and 4 take even longer than Premise 2 to formulate. In fact, not until the engineer introduces the boundary-crossing metaphor of a "box" do the sociologist and hydrologist/engineering camps articulate their practices in a shared language or terminology so they can compare them.

> Engineer (72): "I think one aspect of it is, there's like, think about it as a box. There's inputs, and there's outputs. One type of model is trying to correlate those and show how inputs match with the outputs just however mathematically or statistical description. The other type is processes."

Most modelers are aware of the box metaphor. It provides a common framework within which are different components—inputs, processes, and outputs (the IPO framework)—with different roles for different modelers. Still, interlocutors in this example struggle for a while to locate each other within this framework. Applying their "whatever we've experienced" standard is not as easy as it was in the first two premises. The difficulty seems to stem from the fact that, in contrast to their common use of statistics, they either don't use the IPO framework to understand their own modeling practices or, if they do, they use it differently from each other. Reconciling those different uses takes some conversational work.

Taking up the engineer's "box" proposal, the hydrologist leans into the IPO framework to describe her modeling practice in detail in speaking turns 75 and 77. She ends with a provocative summary, "We [hydrologists] have some fundamental processes we <u>know</u> occur." The sociologist immediately understands and critiques this sort of modeling, signaling that this approach is somehow essential to the differences between sociological and hydrological IPO modeling; premises 3 and 4 co-evolve. The engineer identified two ways to use the IPO framework: (1) correlating inputs and outputs, and (2) specifying the processes. Once it becomes clear the sociologist does the latter, it is simultaneously clear the hydrologist and engineer do the former. Hence the fullness of Premise 3 depends conversationally but not logically upon Premise 4. Figure 2 shows P3 is also an interdisciplinary premise, established by the same contributing perspectives as P2, but from different utterances. The figure also shows that P3 takes the most words and therefore the longest to establish; it proved to be the trickiest premise for everyone to understand. This makes sense since P3 initiated P4 yet also depends conversationally upon it.

P4. Sociologists use statistics to discover processes. Because Premises 3 and 4 unfold simultaneously, it is worth requoting the hydrologist's summary from speaking turn 77 more completely:

> Hydrologist (77): "[You sociologists are] trying to – your conceptual knowledge is trying to get put together somehow. We [hydrologists] have some fundamental processes we <u>know</u> occur [in the world], so we have to figure out whether or not we're missing some [in this model]."

This comment distinguishing the two modeling practices makes more sense later in the dialogue, after discussing the particular practice of calibration:

> Sociologist (92): "We [sociologists] just don't start with any process relationships, those are all to be discovered."

That is, if hydrologists and engineers are correlating inputs and outputs because they already know (a potential list of) the processes involved, then what is different is that sociologists do not yet know their processes. One can see how this integrated understanding of modeling would serve their project very well because the disciplinary practices complement each other. Figure 2 shows P4 is actually a disciplinary claim from sociology; the sociologist is, after all, speaking for himself. However, we know he is responding to hydrological and engineering perspectives, so again we see that P4 depends conversationally but not logically upon P3. P4 therefore takes almost as many words as P3 to establish. Applying the "whatever we've experienced" standard to this claim takes as much effort as that for the previous claim.

P5. These two practices both use the input-process-output framework although their operationalizations of the framework differ. Finally, now that participants have identified their common use of empirical statistics and their different roles in the IPO framework, they need to show how the commonality and the difference are both part of the same practice, namely modeling. This is a bit of a conversational formality as they have been assuming all along that these practices are part of modeling. But they are not satisfied until they explicate exactly how those practices relate. Near the end, the hydrologist has an epiphany that brings it all together:

> Hydrologist (103): "Hey! So maybe it's just that we all come up with conceptual models similarly, but it's [the difference is] the actual implementation of it?"

> Sociologist (104): "Seems to be. It's yeah the practice of what we actually do when say we go out and model."

The epiphany rests on the realization that the IPO framework is a conceptual model shared by both camps; everyone is assuming there are inputs, processes, and outputs in their models. However, when it comes time to build a model—to operationalize it—participants make different assumptions about what inputs, processes, and outputs to include. This is another application of the "whatever we've experienced" standard. In their experience, hydrologists and engineers (in this dialogue) assume they know what processes could be involved, so what is to be discovered through the model is to what extent the inputs and outputs correlate based on which processes are actually involved and what values their parameters have. Sociologists, on the other hand, do not assume they know which processes could be involved; "those are all to be discovered." In this way, both camps model using the IPO concept although they operationalize it in two different ways—but always with statistics! Figure 2 shows P5 is also integrative, established by the engineering and general perspectives present.

C. [Therefore, modeling in our project involves using statistics with empirical observations to operationalize the input-process-output concept.] The argument's conclusion follows logically and immediately from its five premises; essentially, participants have already reached this conclusion after expositing premise 5. The conclusion is a generalization from two kinds of modeling to all modeling that occurs or will occur in the project. Specifically, this takes the form of an inductive argument, also known as an inductive generalization. Such an argument establishes that certain features shared by a sample of members of a set are likely shared by all members of that set. Just how likely is this prospect depends upon how representative the sample is of the set. In this case, our discussants believe they are remembering past instances of their modeling practices that accurately represent the types of modeling they will do in the future. This is what justifies their application of the "whatever we've experienced is assertible" standard. Time will tell how accurate this belief is, but for now they have good reasons to believe their memories accurately reflect the past and predict the future. Therefore, this inductive argument yields a strong, cogent, interdisciplinary conclusion that allows them to move forward with modeling. Figure 2 shows that all five premises, and therefore the total volume of words spoken in the exchange, contribute to the conclusion. Because these premises were established by several disciplines, and because we know the premises and conclusion are cogent, Figure 2 shows us that interdisciplinary integration resulted in the conclusion discussed above.

This conclusion (of an explicative discourse) functions as a standard they can apply in future forms of discourse. It is a standard that was co-created from the application of another standard that was already shared. If participants did not already share that standard, they would not have been able to have this conversation. In other words, instances of CIR depend upon shared, intersubjective standards that must pre-exist the focal question. Such pre-existing standards can be established through other rounds of CIR or shared lifeworld experiences that create shared assumptions.

Argument visualization

Visual analysis complements argument reconstruction. Argument reconstruction highlights the logical structure and rhetorical presentation of the discourse. In doing so, it de-emphasizes the amount of conversation that occurs, the overall sources and locations of integration, and who plays particular roles across the entire argument. A parallel sets chart, on the other hand, emphasizes those very things (Figure 2). A parallel sets chart illustrates flows between sets, e.g., visualizing the flow of money through accounts or energy through trophic levels (See https://datavizcatalogue.com/methods/parallel_sets.html for the basics of parallel sets charts. Sometimes these are also called Sankey diagrams, e.g., https://developers.google.com/chart/interactive/docs/gallery/sankey)

In our case, we are tracking the reasoning process from individual participants to a shared conclusion. The "sets" are sources and sites of inference along the way, viz., (1) participants, (2) disciplines, (3) premises, and (4) argument conclusion. (Participants are separate from disciplines since participants can infer the perspective of several disciplines.) The "flow" is the reasons asserted, viz., words uttered. By tracking the words through the reasoning process, we can visualize sources and sites of integration and participant reasoning roles in the entire conversation at a glance. These quantitative insights complement the qualitative argument reconstruction, helping analysts and practitioners identify which disciplines tend to make certain kinds of contributions to the integrative work, and who tends to represent those disciplines in what ways.

While not the only way to visualize reasoning, this set-and-flow chart falls directly out of the definition of CIR given above. In that definition, CIR is the transformation of disciplinary contributions into an interdisciplinary conclusion through the exchange of reasons. In this example, words flow from participants, pictured on the left side of the chart (Figure 2), through various disciplines and premises to the conclusion, on the right side. The word flows represent the exchange, evaluation, and assertion of claims between participant-disciplines (inputs), coherent premises (process), and a conclusion or warranted assertion (output), per the IPO model of integration offered by O'Rourke and colleagues (O'Rourke et al., 2016).

Note that the chart alone *does not* visualize integration or intersubjectivity; those must be assessed through the argument reconstruction. To wit, just because two disciplinary contributions are relevant to the same premise does *not necessarily* mean they are integrated beyond a mere, multidisciplinary "stapling together." We must examine the construction of the premise to assess its integration. Likewise, just because two people contribute to two disciplines which contribute to a single premise does *not necessarily* mean the people each understand that premise in the same way. We must carefully read the transcript. Integration and intersubjectivity are *qualities* of the exchange, not *quantities* that can be charted. We can only locate integration and intersubjectivity in the chart if we use our qualitative knowledge of what the chart represents.

While we cannot use the chart without the argument reconstruction, the argument reconstruction can stand alone as evidence of CIR. However, because it pictures the entire exchange at once, the chart does make some dynamics of CIR more visible than in the reconstruction alone.

Figure 2 helps us identify disciplinary sources of integration and participant reasoning roles. We see the conversation takes 1294 words, which is not very many, so we must keep that in mind when interpreting the chart. The colors in Figure 2 identify the originating nodes; therefore each node has a unique color. (Remember that participants are distinct from disciplines, so the sociologist has a different color from sociology). This helps us track who or what is contributing to a given node. Through the chart we can quantify both the number of disciplines contributing to integration points and also the volume or amount of their contribution. This approach may help evaluate the breadth and/or depth of the interdisciplinarity, depending on how those constructs are measured (Kelly, 1996).

Figure 2 also showcases clues about conversational roles other studies have shown are important for interdisciplinary communication: dominators (Bondy, 2010; Reed, 2008), boundary spanners (Klein, 2014), and integration specialists (Bammer, 2013). Figure 2 shows the sociologist speaks most; he may be a controller or dominator in this exchange. The reconstruction can help us interpret the nature of his control. Figure 2 also shows the hydrologist is the most flexible thinker as she contributes to all perspectives in the exchange; she acts as the boundary spanner with interactional expertise (Collins & Evans, 2002). The engineer may be the integration specialist as nearly one-third of his words fall into a general perspective that applies to all parts of the argument, except P3. Indeed, most of the engineer's words contribute to P5, which is the final premise needed to tie all the others together in a coherent, cogent conclusion. Thus, we see Figure 2 not only identifies sources and sites integration, it also aids the quick, visual identification of key conversational roles that can spark further analysis or team interventions. Together, the parallel sets chart and argument reconstruction provide a quantitative and qualitative understanding of the nature of interdisciplinary integration in this discourse. The new definition of CIR proposed above makes these analyses possible.

From Disruption to Conclusion to Action

The above dialogue excerpt is an example of what Habermas (1985) calls "explicative discourse," which is discourse about the standards for discourse, as noted above. Habermas explains,

> *Explicative discourse* is a form of argumentation in which the comprehensibility, well-formedness, or rule-correctness of symbolic expressions is no longer naively supposed or contested but is thematized as a controversial claim. (emphasis original, p. 23)

"Thematized" means abstracted from specifics into a principle that can be interrogated. In this case, specific instances of purportedly "well-formed" definitions of modeling are abstracted into a general definition of modeling for their project. Another way of describing this form of discourse is a shift to a meta-level—from the current topic to *how we ought to talk about the topic*. The team is not trying to model right now; they are talking about *how* to model within their project. This shift to explicative discourse is triggered because they keep using the term in different ways, disrupting their shared understanding of modeling in their project. The sociologist opens this discussion by noticing this disruption and bringing it to the group, shifting discourse from a naïve supposition to a controversial claim. As a result, they want to know what counts as a good reason to trust each other's modeling approaches. Explicative discourse, like any other discourse, becomes interdisciplinary when these standards for "good reasons" are created or revised through the integration of disciplinary contributions. As the example illustrates, choosing a team modeling approach is a common example of interdisciplinary explicative discourse, and therefore is also an instance of CIR.

Now that they have an intersubjective standard for what counts as modeling, they can go on with modeling; their practice will require co-applying this standard in other kinds of discourse. For example, they might try to get at the truth of something, and therefore apply this standard of modeling in a future theoretical discourse. They might ask, "What could be the impact of residential water use on this aquifer?" Collaborative consideration of this question will be another instance of CIR, but it is also the action-outcome of the first instance. Their first instance of CIR established what modeling is. This step will enable them to take the action of modeling the aquifer, which will be the second instance of CIR. In short, since actions count as non-linguistic expressions, the outcome of one discourse is another discourse, and so on. Humans are in ongoing conversation with each other, and interdisciplinary research is no exception.

Collaborative, Interdisciplinary Reasoning Qualified

Of course, to introduce the concept of CIR I chose an example that successfully reached an integrated, logical conclusion (in only 6 minutes of conversation!). Its brevity might lead one to believe CIR is easy. It is not. Toolbox transcripts also contain muddled, confused arguments that never resolve. Dialogical impasses can be caused by many factors, including: the illusion of agreement; the illusion of disagreement; fuzzy concepts; information overload; implicit (or explicit) bias; competing values; moral dilemmas; incommensurable epistemologies and ontologies; and, almost inevitably, the jerk in the room.

Freeing these impasses requires first diagnosing which factor—among others—is the root cause. Thinking in terms of CIR can help with this diagnosis. By tracking which disciplinary standards are being integrated into an argument and how, a theorist or practitioner will find the point of impasse. Several tracking questions aid this process: Does everyone agree on the type of discourse we're having right now (e.g., explicative, practical)? If so, which reasons nevertheless fell flat? Who disagreed or got confused? Gently digging into the sticking point like a surgeon examining a wound will reveal the root causes. At bottom may be a difference in meanings, values, goals, or personalities that can be resolved. One must continue querying reasons for the impasse and considering answers from many perspectives. The solution to problems with CIR is often more CIR, increasingly targeted where there is lack of intersubjectivity.

However, sometimes more reasoning is not the solution. For instance, it is not clear that reasoning alone would be enough to involve the other nine participants in the exchange analyzed above. Perhaps some did not speak due to testimonial quieting or smothering by more powerful members (Dotson, 2011). If so, more CIR would simply perpetuate this harm, making things worse. Perhaps some did not agree with the assumed standard of assertibility ("whatever we've experienced is assertible.") This may be a deep disagreement that is unresolvable; no matter what is said the disagreement would remain and participation would be divided. Although it was successful, the excerpt above is not perfectly ideal; intersubjectivity only extended to one-fourth of the group members.

While a lot of CIR is not as quickly resolved as the example I analyzed above, unresolved attempts at CIR are not complete failures. In the process of genuinely engaging one another's disciplinary standards, we learn a lot that will help us down the road—so long as we keep an open mind. We learn intellectual humility, charity, and patience (Ferkany & Whyte, 2011). We learn new vocabulary words (Jeffrey 2003). We learn who is motivated by what (Boix Mansilla, Lamont, & Sato, 2015). We learn how to midwife half-formed ideas (Burnyeat 1977; Plato 369 BCE/1997, 148e-151d). By building these and other capacities (Salazar, Lant, Fiore, & Salas, 2012), we may eventually be able to integrate our reasons into a shared assertion. But perhaps, more importantly, we become better people along the way.

Conclusion

This article has argued that CIR entails integration of disciplinary contributions to co-apply, co-revise, or co-create intersubjective standards for what counts as "good" reasons and inferences in a team research project. The extended example illustrates this definition. Disciplinary integration is the intended consequence of people from different disciplines trying to reason together. As Habermas, Wright, and Campolo conceive of it, reasoning together requires intersubjective standards for evaluating claims. These intersubjective standards constitute standards for reasonableness in the dialogue, whether talking about reasonable standards of modeling, evidence, methodological adequacy, advocacy, or figure design—to name a few areas of possible conflict in research teams. Achieving such intersubjectivity requires teammates to integrate their respective standards for epistemic (e.g., truth, justification) and non-epistemic success (e.g., justice, feasibility) as well as the meaning of shared concepts, because these standards and meanings often vary in different disciplines. That is, CIR changes not only with the purpose of the dialogue but also with the epistemic cultures of the interlocutors. Engineers, for example, employ different standards of reasonableness and meaning than sociologists.

To conclude, CIR is a unique instance of reasoning together that has heretofore been under-theorized by both argumentation theorists and scholars of interdisciplinarity. While all instances of reasoning together depend upon intersubjectivity, as shown above CIR co-applies, co-revises, or co-creates that intersubjectivity *by integrating disciplinary contributions*. Identifying the reasoning moves within communicative actions facilitates intersubjectivity, enabling both theorists and practitioners to more effectively diagnose dialogical impasses and analyze the structure of interdisciplinary inferences. CIR is the engine of knowledge integration in interdisciplinary teams, but it doesn't always work well. Nonetheless, if we can better understand the mechanism, we can better understand and improve the transformation of disciplinary contributions into interdisciplinary insights.

Questions to Further the Discourse

1. How is interdisciplinary reasoning similar to and different from transdisciplinary reasoning?

2. How does collaborative, interdisciplinary reasoning relate to more familiar constructs such as interdisciplinary "learning" (Boix Mansilla, 2010; Boix Mansilla et al., 2015) and "cognition" (Derry et al., 2013; Nikitina, 2005)?

3. What standards mark CIR done well or poorly?

Must Reads

Campolo, C. (2005). Treacherous ascents: On seeking common ground for conflict resolution. *Informal Logic, 25*(1), 37–50.

Eigenbrode, S. D., O'Rourke, M., Wulfhorst, J. D., Althoff, D. M., Goldberg, C. S., Merrill, K., et al. (2007). Employing philosophical dialogue in collaborative science. *BioScience, 57*(1), 55–64. http://doi.org/10.1641/B570109

Klein, J. T. (2014). Communication and collaboration in interdisciplinary research. In M. O'Rourke, S. Crowley, S. D. Eigenbrode, & J. D. Wulfhorst (Eds.), *Enhancing communication & collaboration in interdisciplinary research.* Thousand Oaks: SAGE Publications.

Habermas, J. (1985). *The theory of communicative action: Volume I.* (T. McCarthy, Trans.). Boston, MA: Beacon Press.

National Research Council. (2005). *Facilitating interdisciplinary research.* Washington, DC: National Academies Press.

References

Augsburg, T., & Chitewere, T. (2013). Starting with worldviews: A five-step preparatory approach to integrative interdisciplinary learning. *Issues in Integrative Studies, 31*, 174–191.

Bammer, G. (2013). *Disciplining interdisciplinarity.* Canberra: Australian National University E Press. http://doi.org/10.2307/j.ctt2jbkj5

Boix Mansilla, V. (2010). Learning to synthesize: The development of interdisciplinary understanding. In R. Frodeman, J. T. Klein, & C. Mitcham (Eds.), *The Oxford handbook of interdisciplinarity* (pp. 288–306). New York City: Oxford University Press.

Boix Mansilla, V., Lamont, M., & Sato, K. (2015). Shared cognitive-emotional-interactional platforms: Markers and conditions for successful interdisciplinary collaborations. *Science, Technology & Human Values*, 1–42. http://doi.org/10.1177/0162243915614103

Bondy, P. (2010). Argumentative injustice. *Informal Logic*, *30*(3). http://doi.org/10.22329/il.v30i3.3034

Brown, V. A., Harris, J. A., & Russell, J. Y. (2010). *Tackling wicked problems through the transdisciplinary imagination*. Washington, DC: Earthscan.

Burnyeat, M. F. (1977). Socratic midwifery, Platonic inspiration. *Bulletin of the Institute of Classical Studies*, *24*(1), 7–16. https://doi.org/10.1111/j.2041-5370.1977.tb00363.x

Campolo, C. (2005). Treacherous ascents: On seeking common ground for conflict resolution. *Informal Logic*, *25*(1), 37–50.

Campolo, C., & Turner, D. (2002). Reasoning together: Temptations, dangers, and cautions. *Argumentation*, *16*(1), 3–19. http://doi.org/10.1023/A:1014958422056

Choi, S., & Richards, K. (2017). *Interdisciplinary discourse*. London: Palgrave MacMillan.

Collins, H. M., & Evans, R. (2002). The third wave of science studies: Studies of expertise and experience. *Social Studies of Science*, *32*(2), 235–296. http://doi.org/10.1177/0306312702032002003

De Grandis, G., & Efstathiou, S. (2016). Introduction—Grand challenges and small steps. *Studies in History and Philosophy of Science Part C: Studies in History and Philosophy of Biological and Biomedical Sciences*, *56*, 39–47. http://doi.org/10.1016/j.shpsc.2015.11.009

Derry, S. J., Schunn, C. D., & Gernsbacher, M. A. (2013). *Interdisciplinary collaboration: An emerging cognitive science*. New York, NY: Psychology Press.

Dewey, J. (1910). *How we think*. Boston: DC Heath & Co.

Dewey, J. (1938). *Logic: The theory of inquiry*. New York: Henry Holt and Company.

Dotson, K. (2011). Tracking epistemic violence, tracking practices of silencing. *Hypatia*, *26*(2), 236–257. http://doi.org/10.1111/j.1527-2001.2011.01177.x

Dotson, K. (2012). A cautionary tale: On limiting epistemic oppression. *Frontiers: A Journal of Women Studies*, *33*(1), 24. http://doi.org/10.5250/fronjwomestud.33.1.0024

Dotson, K. (2014). Conceptualizing epistemic oppression. *Social Epistemology*, *28*(2), 115–138. http://doi.org/10.1080/02691728.2013.782585

Dreyfuss, S. (2011). Something essential about interdisciplinary thinking. *Issues in Integrative Studies*, *29*, 67–83.

Eigenbrode, S. D., O'Rourke, M., Wulfhorst, J. D., Althoff, D. M., Goldberg, C. S., Merrill, K., et al. (2007). Employing philosophical dialogue in collaborative science. *BioScience*, *57*(1), 55–64. http://doi.org/10.1641/B570109

Ferkany, M., & Whyte, K. P. (2011). The importance of participatory virtues in the future of environmental education. *Journal of Agricultural and Environmental Ethics*, *25*(3), 419–434. http://doi.org/10.1007/s10806-011-9312-8

Frodeman, R., Klein, J. T., & Mitcham, C. (Eds.). (2010). *The Oxford handbook of interdisciplinarity*. New York, NY: Oxford University Press.

Frodeman, R., Klein, J. T., & Pacheco, R. C. S. (Eds.). (2017). *The Oxford handbook of interdisciplinarity* (2nd ed). Oxford: Oxford University Press.

Habermas, J. (1985). *The theory of communicative action*. (T. McCarthy, Trans.). Boston, MA: Beacon Press.

Hagstrom, W. O. (1964). Traditional and modern forms of scientific teamwork. *Administrative Science Quarterly*, *9*(3), 241. https://doi.org/10.2307/2391440

Holbrook, J. B. (2013). What is interdisciplinary communication? Reflections on the very idea of disciplinary integration. *Synthese*, *190*(11), 1865–1879. http://doi.org/10.1007/s11229-012-0179-7

i2insights.org. (n.d.). i2insights.org. Retrieved February 26, 2018, from http://i2insights.org

Jeffrey, P. (2003). Smoothing the waters. *Social Studies of Science*, *33*(4), 539–562. https://doi.org/10.1177/0306312703334003

Kelly, J. S. (1996). Wide and narrow interdisciplinarity. *The Journal of General Education*, *45*(2), 95–113. http://doi.org/10.2307/27797294

Klein, J. T. (1996). *Crossing boundaries: Knowledge, disciplinarities, and interdisciplinarities*. Charlottesville, VA: University of Virginia Press.

Klein, J. T. (2014). Communication and collaboration in interdisciplinary research. In M. O'Rourke, S. Crowley, S. D. Eigenbrode, & J. D. Wulfhorst (Eds.), *Enhancing communication & collaboration in interdisciplinary research*. Thousand Oaks: SAGE Publications.

Knorr Cetina, K. (2009). *Epistemic cultures*. Cambridge, MA: Harvard University Press.

Lariviere, V., & Gingras, Y. (2014). Measuring interdisciplinarity. In B. Cronin & C. R. Sugimoto (Eds.), *Beyond bibliometrics: Harnessing multidimensional indicators of scholarly impact* (pp. 187–200). Cambridge, MA.

Leedy, P. D., & Ormrod, J. E. (2005). *Practical research: Planning and design*. Upper Saddle River, NJ: Pearson.

Lewis, J. M., Ross, S., & Holden, T. (2012). The how and why of academic collaboration: Disciplinary differences and policy implications. *Higher Education*, *64*(5), 693-708. https://doi.org/10.1007/s10734-012-9521-8

Lincoln, Y. S., & Guba, E. G. (1985). *Naturalistic inquiry*. SAGE.

Mohr, J. W. (1998). Measuring meaning structures. *Annual Review of Sociology*, *24*, 345–370.

National Institutes of Health National Cancer Institute. (n.d.). *Team Science Toolkit*. Retrieved May 23, 2015, from https://www.teamsciencetoolkit.cancer.gov/Public/Home.aspx

National Research Council. (2005). *Facilitating interdisciplinary research*. Washington, DC: National Academies Press.

National Research Council. (2015). *Enhancing the effectiveness of team science*. (N. J. Cooke & M. L. Hilton, Eds.) Washington, DC: National Academies Press. http://doi.org/10.17226/19007

Nikitina, S. (2005). Pathways of interdisciplinary cognition. *Cognition and Instruction, 23*(3), 389–425. http://doi.org/10.1207/s1532690xci2303_3

O'Rourke, M., & Crowley, S. J. (2013). Philosophical intervention and cross-disciplinary science: The story of the Toolbox Project. *Synthese, 190*(11), 1937–1954. http://doi.org/10.1007/s11229-012-0175-y

O'Rourke, M., Crowley, S., & Gonnerman, C. (2016). On the nature of cross-disciplinary integration: A philosophical framework. *Studies in History and Philosophy of Science Part C: Studies in History and Philosophy of Biological and Biomedical Sciences, 56*, 62–70. http://doi.org/10.1016/j.shpsc.2015.10.003

Plato. (1997). Theaetatus. In J. M. Cooper & D. S. Hutchinson (Eds.), M. J. Levitt & M. Burnyeat (Trans.), *Plato Complete Works* (pp. 157–234). Hackett Publishing Company: Indianapolis, IN. (Original work published about 369 BCE.)

Porter, A. L., & Rafols, I. (2009). Is science becoming more interdisciplinary? Measuring and mapping six research fields over time. *Scientometrics, 81*(3), 719–745. http://doi.org/10.1007/s11192-008-2197-2

Reed, M. S. (2008). Stakeholder participation for environmental management: A literature review. *Biological Conservation, 141*(10), 2417–2431. http://doi.org/10.1016/j.biocon.2008.07.014

Repko, A. F., Szostak, R., & Buchberger, M. P. (2016). *Introduction to interdisciplinary studies* (2nd ed.). Thousand Oaks, CA: SAGE Publications.

Rittel, H., & Webber, M. M. (1973). Dilemmas in a general theory of planning. *Policy Sciences, 4*, 155–169.

Salazar, M. R., Lant, T. K., Fiore, S. M., & Salas, E. (2012). Facilitating innovation in diverse science teams through integrative capacity. *Small Group Research, 43*(5), 527–558. http://doi.org/10.1177/1046496412453622

Sandvik, M. (1997). Reconstructing interactive argumentative discourse. *Argumentation, 11*(4), 419–434.

Scriven, M. (1976). *Reasoning*. New York, NY: McGraw-Hill Book Company.

van Eemeren, F. H., Garssen, B., Krabbe, E. C. W., Henkemans, A. F. S., Verheij, B., & Wagemans, J. H. M. (2014). The pragma-dialectical theory of argumentation. In F. H. van Eemeren, B. Garssen, E. C. W Krabbe, A. F. Snoeck Henkemans, B. Verheij, & J. H. M. Wagemans, *Handbook of argumentation theory* (2nd ed., pp. 517–613). Dordrecht: Springer, Dordrecht. http://doi.org/10.1007/978-90-481-9473-5_6

Van Noorden, R. (2015). Interdisciplinary research by the numbers. *Nature, 525*(7569), 306–307. http://doi.org/10.1038/525306a

Wasserstein, R. L., & Lazar, N. A. (2016). The ASA's statement on p-values: Context, process, and purpose. *The American Statistician, 70*(2), 129–133. http://doi.org/10.1080/00031305.2016.1154108

Wright, L. (1995). Argument and deliberation: A plea for understanding. *The Journal of Philosophy, 92*(11), 565–585. http://doi.org/10.2307/2941088

Wright, L. (2001). Justification, discovery, reason and argument. *Argumentation, 15*(1), 97–104. http://doi.org/10.1023/A:1007800732356

Table 1. This excerpt from a Toolbox Dialogue Initiative workshop exemplifies collaborative, interdisciplinary reasoning (CIR).

Full Speaking Turn	Contribution	Speaker	Disciplinary Perspective Used	Word Count	Premise Contributed To
10:56 64 SOCIOLOGIST: Well one of the things I found working with many of the people in the room is a term I'm still trying to wrap my mind around, that I don't think we all use the same way is the word modeling.	Well one of the things I found working with many of the people in the room is a term I'm still trying to wrap my mind around that I don't think we all use the same way is the word modeling.	Sociologist	Sociology	41	P1
65 P2: Yeah, that's one that...				0	
66 SOCIOLOGIST: [cont'] We actually confronted this one when we tried to write our grant, we came to a heavy place that allowed us to write the grant. [laughter] And it was actually trying to engage the fact that modeling can mean such different things to different fields. And in engineering particularly I've come to appreciate as a view... And until I got going on our little bear project five years ago, to me modeling – we model in the social sciences – some of us do --is basically an exercise of developing some theoretical models and testing them against the world and seeing how well that model fits. And so we specify the model that fits, as certain relationships among things we can measure, and then we go and do a fairly standardized set of mathematical type things that say, ok that is, that explains this much of what we were trying to explain, this well or with this much degree of confidence. And then you might go back to the drawing board and re-specify and tweak and try to figure out how to make your	We actually confronted this one when we tried to write our grant	Sociologist	Sociology	12	P1

Full Speaking Turn	Contribution	Speaker	Disciplinary Perspective Used	Word Count	Premise Contributed To
model fit those data better.	to me modeling – we model in the social sciences – some of us do –is basically an exercise of developing some theoretical models and testing them against the world and seeing how well that model fits. And so we specify the model that fits, as certain relationships among things we can measure, and then we go and do a fairly standardized set of mathematical type things that say, ok that is, that explains this much of what we were trying to explain, this well or with this much degree of confidence. And then you might go back to the drawing board and re-specify and tweak and try to figure out how to make your model fit those data better.	Sociologist	Sociology	120	P2
67 P2: [overlap] mm hmm				0	
68 SOCIOLOGIST: [cont'] Um, but you're actually inferring sort of this significance of relationships and so.	but you're actually inferring sort of this significance of relationships and so.	Sociologist	Sociology	12	P2
69 HYDROLOGIST: [overlap] Well you just described what we do.	Well you just described what we do.	Hydrologist	Hydrology	7	P2
70 SOCIOLOGIST: [cont'] So I thought it would be part of our project to explain, you know variability in water quality, that we would get all this raw data in water quality variability and we would try to explain it using behavioral variability and so forth at these various scales. And what I found	So I thought it would be part of our project to explain, you know variability in water quality, that we would get all this raw data in water quality variability and we would try to explain it using behavioral variability and so forth at these various scales. And what I found was we weren't actually	Sociologist	Sociology	120	P4

Full Speaking Turn	Contribution	Speaker	Disciplinary Perspective Used	Word Count	Premise Contributed To
was we weren't actually doing that. What we were doing was we were simulating rigid models and calibrating to measured outcomes and there was, it kind of works or it doesn't work. There wasn't the same kind of process as I was, it's different in some fundamental way. I'm still trying to understand what that difference is because I feel like we're going to have to figure this out.	doing that. What we were doing was we were simulating rigid models and calibrating to measured outcomes and there was, it kind of works or it doesn't work. There wasn't the same kind of process as I was, it's different in some fundamental way. I'm still trying to understand what that difference is because I feel like we're going to have to figure this out.				
	So I thought it would be part of our project to explain, you know variability in water quality, that we would get all this raw data in water quality variability and we would try to explain it using behavioral variability and so forth at these various scales. And what I found was we weren't actually doing that. What we were doing was we were simulating rigid models and calibrating to measured outcomes and there was, it kind of works or it doesn't work. There wasn't the same kind of process as I was, it's different in some fundamental way. I'm still trying to understand what that difference is because I feel like we're going to have to figure this out.	Sociologist	Hydrology	120	P3
71 PP: yeah				0	
72 ENGINEER: [overlap] We were talking about this is morning, [name], and I think one aspect of it is, there's like, think about it as a box. There's inputs, and there's outputs. One type of model is trying to correlate those and show how inputs match with the outputs just however mathemati-	We were talking about this this morning, [name], and I think one aspect of it is, there's like, think about it as a box. There's inputs, and there's outputs. One type of model is trying to correlate those and show how inputs match with the outputs just however mathematically or statistical	Engineer	Engineering	100	P5

Full Speaking Turn	Contribution	Speaker	Disciplinary Perspective Used	Word Count	Premise Contributed To
cally or statistical description. Then other type is processes. Trying to explain how you start here and where you go next, and where you go next, and where you go next, and where you go next. And then ultimately what comes out that you can measure or see.	description. Then other type is processes. Trying to explain how you start here and where you go next, and where you go next, and where you go next, and where you go next. And then ultimately what comes out that you can measure or see.				
73 P?: [overlap] mm hmm				0	
74 ENGINEER: [cont'] And there's I think probably other aspects of the problem that do that too, but that seemed to, that definitely resonates with me.	And there's I think probably other aspects of the problem that do that too, but that seemed to, that definitely resonates with me.	Engineer	Engineering	25	P5
75 HYDROLOGIST: [overlap] So I think maybe one of the key differences of that whole, you know you get all these data and then you calibrate you know the model to match what happens with the data or what you see and it seems like you're kind of like you're just tuning things to just to make it all work.	So I think maybe one of the key differences of that whole, you know you get all these data and then you calibrate you know the model to match what happens with the data or what you see and it feels like you're kind of like you're just tuning things to just to make it all work.	Hydrologist	Hydrology	57	P3
76 SOCIOLOGIST: [overlap] Just like turning knobs.	Just like turning knobs.	Sociologist	Hydrology	4	P3
77 HYDROLOGIST: Yeah, but in reality there's very fundamental concepts or processes that are represented through physics, whatever, that we have representations in there and then those pa-rameters are the question marks.[BL1] So you guys maybe are more empirically based and you're trying to, your conceptual knowledge is trying to get put together somehow. We have some funda-	Yeah, but in reality there's very fundamental concepts or processes that are represented through physics, whatever, that we have representations in there and then those parameters are the question marks	Hydrologist	Hydrology	30	P3

Full Speaking Turn	Contribution	Speaker	Disciplinary Perspective Used	Word Count	Premise Contributed To
mental processes we know occur, so we have to figure out whether or not we're missing some.					
	So you guys maybe are more empirically based and you're trying to, you conceptual knowledge is trying to get put together somehow.	Hydrologist	Sociology	22	P4
	We have some fundamental processes we know occur, so we have to figure out whether or not we're missing some.	Hydrologist	Hydrology	20	P3
14:23 78 SOCIOLOGIST [interrupting]: this becomes a really big issue in building human dimensions in, because we're not usually able -- and we're always asked, I was asked just today -- to serve up a sort of direct process relationship. So "if you do this, this is what happens," or "this is how people will behave," because it's like we need to know that to be able to use this in this framework. We understand sort of how water moves in the soil in this really complicated way with all these equations, and now we need to understand if the humans are going to be a part of that process model, how do we write the code to represent [cut off by laughter]	this becomes a really big issue in building human dimensions in, because we're not usually able -- and we're always asked, I was asked just today -- to serve up a sort of direct process relationship. So "if you do this, this is what happens," or "this is how people will behave," because it's like we need to know that to be able to use this in this framework. We understand sort of how water moves in the soil in this really complicated way with all these equations, and now we need to understand if the humans are going to be a part of that process model, how do we write the code to represent	Sociologist	Sociology	115	P3
15:00 79 ENGINEER: [overlap] Well you can do it two ways though right? Because you could just, say the hydro-economic stuff that I presented last time was just embedding that, that economic understanding, the empirics of that into that process without really understanding in detail what's driv-	Well you can do it two ways though right? Because you could just, say the hydro-economic stuff that I presented last time was just embedding that, that economic understanding, the empirics of that into that process without really understanding in detail what's driving that behavior	Engineer	Engineering	45	P3

Full Speaking Turn	Contribution	Speaker	Disciplinary Perspective Used	Word Count	Premise Contributed To
ing that behavior, or you can try and, you can try and go with that some more too. [long pause] It seems like though, that as I'm thinking about it, and I'm curious to hear what everyone else's thoughts are on this, is that if you have an empirically based model, that's a method of calibration in a sense.					
	or you can try and, you can try and go with that some more too.	Engineer	Engineering	15	P3
	It seems like though, that as I'm thinking about it, and I'm curious to hear what everyone else's thoughts are on this, is that if you have an empirically based model, that's a method of calibration in a sense.	Engineer	Engineering	39	P2
80 HYDROLOGIST: Right.				0	
81 SOCIOLOGIST: I actually calibrated a model just the other day so I could tell you if that's true or not.	I actually calibrated a model just the other day so I could tell you if that's true or not.	Sociologist	Sociology	19	P4
82 HYDROLOGIST: Right.		Hydrologist		0	
[laughter]				0	
83 SOCIOLOGIST: I'd like to sit down when you're calibrating some models, or I'd be willing to take name's class	I'd like to sit down when you're calibrating some models, or I'd be willing to take name's class	Sociologist	Hydrology	18	P3
84 P?: [overlap] mm hmm				0	
16:00 85 SOCIOLOGIST: [cont'] so I can tweak	so I can tweak some knobs and find out, ok, "now	Sociologist	Hydrology	41	P3

Full Speaking Turn	Contribution	Speaker	Disciplinary Perspective Used	Word Count	Premise Contributed To
some knobs and find out, ok, "now I actually understand what you mean when you say that," um and whether it's really the same or different from what I'm used to doing, training my students to do. When I do just my sociology it's over here, and that's what I do. And when I work on these teams I've not always been able to bring that into the conversation, especially in modeling part.	I actually understand what you mean when you say that," um and whether it's really the same or different from what I'm used to doing, training my students to do.	Sociologist	Sociology	36	P4
	When I do just my sociology it's over here, and that's what I do. And when I work on these teams I've not always been able to bring that into the conversation, especially in modeling part.				
86 P?: [overlap] mm hmm				0	
87 SOCIOLOGIST: [cont'] The modeling part is always sort of what you guys are used to doing and I'm trying to figure out, how to insert important things that I understand into that, but it doesn't strike me as the same exercise. Or maybe it's more so the same and I don't understand.	The modeling part is always sort of what you guys are used to doing and I'm trying to figure out, how to insert important things that I understand into that, but it doesn't strike me as the same exercise. Or maybe it's more so the same and I don't understand.	Sociologist	Hydrology	50	P3
88 ENGINEER: I think it could be both. Meaning there's similarities, and there's obviously different contexts, [unclear] so there's the opportunity for difference as well.	I think it could be both. Meaning there's similarities, and there's obviously different contexts, [unclear] so there's the opportunity for difference as well.	Engineer	Engineering	23	P5
89 HYDROLOGIST: But what you described is what you do for a model, you're approach to modeling? I'm just sitting here going, hmmm yep.	But what you described is what you do for a model, you're approach to modeling? I'm just sitting here going, hmmm yep.	Hydrologist	Hydrology	23	P2
90 P?: [overlap] mm hmm				0	

Full Speaking Turn	Contribution	Speaker	Disciplinary Perspective Used	Word Count	Premise Contributed To
91 HYDROLOGIST: [overlap] cont Sounds like what we do. So it's kind of interesting that we can do this and sometimes diverge at the end, at least in terms of understanding each other.	Sounds like what we do.	Hydrologist	Hydrology	5	P2
	So it's kind of interesting that we can do this and sometimes diverge at the end, at least in terms of understanding each other.	Hydrologist	Engineering	24	P5
92 SOCIOLOGIST: We just don't start with any process relationships, those are all to be discovered.	We just don't start with any process relationships, those are all to be discovered.	Sociologist	Sociology	14	P4
93 HYDROLOGIST: [overlap] Right.		Hydrologist		0	
94 SOCIOLOGIST: [cont'] And tested, so we don't understand anything at the outset that we can put into that model that says this will always do that or these will be the fixed relationships.	And tested, so we don't understand anything at the outset that we can put into that model that says this will always do that or these will be the fixed relationships.	Sociologist	Sociology	31	P4
95 ENGINEER: [overlap] mm hm.		Engineer		0	
HYDROLOGIST: Right		Hydrologist		0	
96 SOCIOLOGIST: [cont'] We do in fact do that in the sense that we specify a model with a certain structure and it defines how it could work,	We do in fact do that in the sense that we specify a model with a certain structure and it defines how it could work,	Sociologist	Sociology	25	P4
97 P?: [overlap] Right.		P?		0	
98 SOCIOLOGIST: [cont'] but people – some people like me -- obsess about getting specification right,	but people – some people like me -- obsess about getting specification right,	Sociologist	Sociology	13	P4

Full Speaking Turn	Contribution	Speaker	Disciplinary Perspective Used	Word Count	Premise Contributed To
99 P?: [overlap] Right.				0	
100 SOCIOLOGIST: [cont'] and others don't worry about it – throw a model out there. Move on to the next paper. You know. Who cares if your operationalization was stupid.	and others don't worry about it – throw a model out there. Move on to the next paper. You know. Who cares if you're not operationalization was stupid.	Sociologist	Sociology	28	P4
101 P?: [overlap] yeah				0	
17:43 102 SOCIOLOGIST: [cont'] you know whatever, but [unclear]				0	
103 HYDROLOGIST: Hey! So maybe it's just that we all come up with conceptual models similarly, but it's the actual implementation of it?	Hey! So maybe it's just that we all come up with conceptual models similarly, but it's the actual implementation of it?	Hydrologist	Engineering	21	P5
104 SOCIOLOGIST: Seems to be. It's yeah the practice of what we actually do when say we go out and model.	Seems to be. It's yeah the practice of what we actually do when say we go out and model.	Sociologist	Sociology	19	P5

Note: See text for explanation of column headers.

Gaetano R. Lotrecchiano & Shalini Misra (Editors). 2020
Communication in Transdisciplinary Teams
Santa Rosa, CA: Informing Science Press

Chapter 3:
Communicative Processes in Trans-Sector Transdisciplinary Collaborations

Chitvan Trivedi
Gettysburg College, Gettysburg, PA, USA
ctrivedi@gettysburg.edu

Shalini Misra
Virginia Tech, Arlington, VA, USA
shalini@vt.edu

Chapter Objectives

- To understand the process of social change creation in social entrepreneurial ventures (SEVs), specifically emphasizing the role and nature of the communicative process in social change creation.

- To discover the individual, interpersonal, and organizational conditions that facilitate the process of social change that are central to the design of effective trans-sector transdisciplinary problem-solving ventures.

- To explore the role of collective wisdom and knowledge networks for long-term collaborative community capacity building.

- To discover the role of deep and continuous social interaction, or dialogue in fostering organizational learning.

- To understand the role of deliberative democratic practices among stakeholders to address complex social problems.

Introduction to the Chapter

There is little scholarship about the process of social change creation and the necessary conditions to promote social change over time. The aim of this chapter is to understand the process of social change creation in social entrepreneurial ventures (SEVs), specifically emphasizing the role and nature of the communicative process. Understanding the individual, interpersonal, and organizational conditions that facilitate the process is central to design of effective trans-sector transdisciplinary problem-solving ventures. Drawing on data from seven SEVs from India and the US and employing a grounded theory methodology, this research scrutinizes the social change process and uncovers the role and characteristics of dialogue in this process. The reflections and experiences of members of SEVs revealed that social entrepreneurship is a collective endeavor and this collective character is critical

An earlier version of this chapter was published as Trivedi, C., & Misra, S. (2018). Dialogue and the creation of transformative social change: The case of social enterprises. *Informing Science: the International Journal of an Emerging Transdiscipline, 21,* 107-132. https://doi.org/10.28945/4012

to its success. Collective organization and synergy, deep intra-organizational communication, and a conducive organizational context are essential conditions for the creation of collective wisdom and knowledge networks for long-term collaborative community capacity building. Dialogue emerged as a central category linking the other categories to explain the process of social change creation. Organic organizational structure enables knowledge creation and integration through the process of organizational learning through deep and continuous social interaction, or dialogue.

Background

Transformative and sustained social change remains elusive despite unprecedented efforts by trans-national development institutions like the United Nations, federal and local governments, and the social sector to tackle global problems like extreme poverty, hunger, and disease. At the UN Millennium Development Summit in the year 2000, world leaders took stock of global challenges and proposed eight goals as a blueprint for the world's countries and leading development institutions to drastically mitigate the most pressing societal challenges of our time by the year 2015 and create transformative social change (e.g., reducing extreme poverty by 50%, providing universal primary education). These Millennium Development Goals (MDG) spurred unprecedented efforts by governments and the social sector to tackle these problems. By 2015, while there was progress on all of the indicators based on the MDG targets, most goals were not achieved (Galatsidas & Sheehy, 2015; United Nations, 2015). In its progress report on the Millennium Development Goals (MDGs), the UN identified four critical limitations in governmental and institutional approaches to addressing societal problems and creating social change. These were (1) inadequate emphasis on the role of local government participation in the problem-solving process; (2) lack of diversity of stakeholders in the problem-solving process and insufficient understanding of the relationships among them; (3) weak institutional capacity because of lack of diversity of participants from diverse sectors (government, civil society, business); and (4) a deficit of culturally sensitive and contextually compatible approaches to societal problems (United Nations Development Group, 2014).

A large body of research has similarly identified the critical importance of participatory and culturally sensitive approaches, the need for building institutional capacity through intersectoral partnerships, including partnerships with the private sector, and participatory monitoring and accountability in solving complex societal problems (Austin, 2000; Barringer & Harrison, 2000; Bovaird, 2004; Child & Faulkner, 1998; Peredo & Chrisman, 2006). Other research has uncovered implicit prerequisite conditions entrenched in these approaches, such as the reliance on long term external funding and political commitment to institute structural and policy changes (Trivedi, 2010). For example, scores of NGOs work with communities to improve personal and public health through personal and home hygiene education. Nevertheless, their success rates are low as personal health is closely tied to sanitary conditions of the community. Structural conditions such as the lack of proper sewage disposal systems seriously undermine their efforts in health promotion and disease prevention (UN News Center, 2013).

Despite the broad scope of this literature, there is little scholarship about the process of social change creation and the necessary conditions to promote social change over time. This chapter focuses on the process of social change creation in a specific type of complex problem-solving organization, namely social entrepreneurial ventures (SEVs), with an emphasis on the role and nature of the communicative process in social change creation. We address two primary questions: What is the process of social change creation in trans-sector TD problem-solving organizations? What contextual conditions support the process of social change creation? In the following sections, we define trans-sector transdisciplinary problem-solving and social entrepreneurship, and summarize the literature on social change creation in the context of social entrepreneurial ventures to provide background and context for the present research.

Social Entrepreneurship and Trans-Sector Transdisciplinary Problem-Solving

In recent decades, the potential of social entrepreneurship for addressing intractable societal problems has gained tremendous momentum throughout the world evidenced by large investments in social entrepreneurial ventures by foundations such as Ashoka, Schwab, and Skoll (Ashoka, n.d.; Schwab Foundation, n.d.; Skoll Foundation, n.d.). Because of their unique combination of private structure and public purpose, their generally smaller scale, connections to citizens, flexibility and capacity to tap private initiative in support of public purposes, social entrepreneurial ventures (SEVs) have surfaced as strategically important potential partners in the effort to forge new solutions to existing social problems (Trivedi & Stokols, 2011).

SEVs are collaborative and participatory organizational forms whose goal is to address *long standing social problems* and *facilitate sustained positive social change* (Trivedi & Stokols, 2011). Included among the objectives of such organizations are providing goods and services that the market or public sector is either unwilling or unable to provide, developing skills, creating employment, and fostering pathways for the integration of socially excluded people (Martin & Osberg, 2015; Trivedi, 2010; Trivedi & Stokols, 2011). In fact, recognized social needs, market failure, and repeated unsuccessful attempts by the government to address socio-environmental problems are the primary reasons for the existence of SEVs. While SEVs can provide private means to pursue public good, their core aim is to address deeprooted social problems and social injustice, reverse societal imbalance, and transform the structural and political system through processes of social change creation and sustenance.

SEVs are characterized by a particular type of trans-sector transdisciplinary (TD) problem-solving (Klein, 2010) in which a diversity of members, organizations, and stakeholders contribute knowledge, skills, expertise, and other resources and cooperate for democratic and holistic solutions to societal problems (TD Net, 2009). While one strand of trans-sector TD problem-solving centers on academic collaborations between universities and industrial/private sectors to address scientific or translational problems, SEVs are characterized by a different type of TD problem-solving. Here members from different sectors of society (including academia, non-profits, governmental organizations, for-profits, and individual community members) collaborate using deliberative democratic practices (Fischer, 2012) to address complex social problems like environmental sustainability and poverty (TD Net, 2009). In this sense, trans-sector TD problem-solving transcends the relatively narrow scope of individual societal sectors through the creation of hybrid knowledge systems, synthesizing technical or scientific, political, economic and local knowledge systems, toward the resolution of social problems.

In order to contextualize problems, understand the linkages among problems, and identify leverage points for interventions SEVs are characterized by democratic and participatory modes of collaboration (Nowotny, Scott, & Gibbons, 2001) to draw on the experience of community members, employees and partners to create "socially robust knowledge" (Klein, 2010) that creates collaborative capacity. Toward that goal, SEVs develop group objectives and shared aims, and decision-making power is distributed and not based on capital ownership (Bull, 2008; Dart, 2004). SEVs rely on high quality leaders (Orloff, 2002), who embrace end values such as liberty, social justice, and equality (J. M. Burns, 1978) to foster feelings of community, value-added collaboration, and collective purpose among employees and partners, and mobilize interpersonal and professional networks to create economic and social capital by encouraging citizen engagement and empowering individuals and communities (Bornstein, 2007; Dees, 2001; Martin & Osberg, 2007; Thompson, 2002; Trivedi & Stokols, 2011; Waddock & Post, 1991). From this perspective, SEVs can be conceptualized as exemplar TD systems that are social, collaborative, and collective in their orientation toward addressing complex social problems.

While there is some clarity about the goals and purposes of SEVs and their defining features, very little is understood about the process by which they address societal problems and create sustained positive social change. Many researchers have emphasized the innovativeness of the solution as a key contributing factor (Alvord, Brown, & Letts, 2004; Ashoka.org; Bornstein, 2007; Dees, 2001; Mair & Martí, 2006; Schwab Foundation, n.d.; Wei-Skillern, Austin, Leonard, & Stevenson, 2007). However, in examining how these organizations have overcome struggles and challenges they have faced over time, it becomes obvious that it takes more than just a brilliant idea to create and sustain social change (Bhatt, 2005; Bornstein & Davis, 2010; Martin & Osberg, 2015; Trivedi, 2010; Trivedi & Stokols, 2011). For example, it took the Grameen bank in Bangladesh and Self-Employed Women's Association (SEWA) in India (both organizations dedicated to uplifting the social status of women) years before they saw the impacts of their work on women's empowerment (Bhatt, 2005; Hulme, 2008). For example, the Grameen bank provided micro-credit loans to impoverished people who did not have access to the banking system, which enabled them to start small businesses and become part of the financial system. For the first time in the history of the banking industry, banks went door to door to the customers to collect money, demonstrating their flexibility and willingness to change their collection system. They also developed educational programs to promote saving among their customers. Later, they realized the advantages and transformative potential of granting loans to women (over men) and its impact on women's status in their families and society (Rahman, 1999; Yunus & Jolis, 2007). Their innovative idea was successful because it was supported by the organizational structure. Understanding the process of social change creation and the individual, interpersonal, and organizational conditions that facilitate the process is central to design of effective trans-sector TD problem-solving ventures.

Prior grounded theory development efforts have focused on the how SEVs conceptualize social problems. This research has revealed that systems thinking and scientific holism in the conceptualization of social problems are critical factors in the creation of social change (Trivedi & Misra, 2015). These findings are briefly summarized in the following section before moving on to describe the current research, which scrutinizes the role and nature of dialogue and the contextual conditions that support dialogue in the social change process.

SEV - Childline India Foundation (CIF), a 24-hour toll free child helpline for street children in distress, which started in Mumbai and now operates in 81 of India's largest cities. It also supports child helplines in 145 countries worldwide, through Child Helpline International (CHI), to provide care and protection to children who live and work on the streets from abuse and violence, trafficking, child labor, armed conflicts and drug abuse. The CIF has established Childline centers across India and functions as a national center for awareness, advocacy and training on issues related to child protection. The CHI facilitates the establishment of child helplines around the world. It offers assistance to newly developing child helplines in other countries in choosing the helpline model that best fits the situation of the children in that country, planning the start-up, training, awareness campaigns, child participation, networking and partnership building with other organizations including the telecom sector and fundraising activities.

Toward Social Change: Understanding the Ecology of the Social Problem

Since social change is produced by the same factors that produce continuity, one needs to understand the process of social continuity to understand social change creation (Calhoun, 2000). Social continuity is closely linked to prevailing social norms, specifically collective social norms. Social norms are evaluative beliefs that synthesize affective and cognitive elements to orient people to the world in which they live. Social norms are beliefs about the acceptability of behavior. Norms are linked to and reinforced by existential beliefs about human nature, the human condition, and interpersonal relations. Thus, a major cause of resistance to social change is individuals' beliefs in the value of existing social norms (Lewin, 1951). To bring about social change, we need to understand the value individuals place on the norms of the 'collective'. Collective social norms are rooted in the relationship between social action and social structure and can only be understood and influenced by understanding the interconnections between the components of a social system in which social problems are embedded. However, this view has yet to be empirically explored in the context of complex problem-solving in social enterprises. Prior research has found that SEVs recognize, expose, and address the underlying structure that leads to patterns of behavior in the system (Trivedi, 2013; Trivedi & Misra, 2015). Identifying these interconnections requires identifying focal points in the social context where these interconnections occur—an important first step for influencing social norms (Ensminger & Knight, 1997).

SEVs, as collaborative entities, are unique in the way they frame and approach complex social problems. Social entrepreneurs are especially skilled systems thinkers and understand what we term the *ecology of the social problem*. The ecology of social problems means the relationship and interaction between a social problem and its context, which includes other social problems (Trivedi & Misra, 2015). Systems thinking enables them to understand the forces at play in the social system and reveals the underlying structure of the system allowing SEVs to identify leverage points. Social problems are invariably entrenched in the particular social, physical, political, economic, and cultural contexts and are interlinked with other social problems forming an ecosystem. The way in which a society defines their social problems determines the life cycle of the problem, how they are approached, and what is done about them. This is a highly contested process as it deals with divergent and conflicting interests, intentions, and objectives. This interplay of interests influences a society's approach to defining and addressing the social problem (Blumer, 1971).

Key Definitions

- *Social Problem* is defined as a generic term that applies to the range of conditions that are a direct or indirect outcome of aberrant behaviors held to be manifestations of social disorganization. Examples of social problems include poverty, illiteracy, crime, prostitution, mental illness, drug addiction, environmental denudation, pollution, climate change, etc.

- *Social Norms* are evaluative beliefs that synthesize affective and cognitive elements to orient people to the world in which they live.

- *Collective Social Norms* are culturally established rules prescribing appropriate behavior that are shared by the group, community, or culture.

- *Ecology of a Social Problem* refers to the relationship and interaction between a social problem and its context, which includes other social problems.

- *Complex Social System* is a complex system whose behavior is primarily the result of the behavior of social agents. Examples are families and nations.

- *High Functioning System* is a system capable of making necessary adjustments to achieve its goals more effectively.

- *Social Entrepreneur* is an individual with innovative solutions to society's most pressing social problems.

- *Structural Knowledge* is the knowledge of how the social variables are related and how they influence one another. It helps form a cohesive picture, and helps determine what belongs together. Structural knowledge is one's assumptions about these variables, which can be partly implicit and partly explicit but it is the crucial factor for finding order in apparent chaos.

Effective SEVs conceptualize society as a complex social system in order to develop a holistic understanding of the social problem. According to general systems theory (von Bertalanffy, 1950, 1952), society can be understood as a complex configuration of many systems engaged in overlapping and interlocking patterns of relationships with one another. These subsystems are generally arranged in a hierarchy and work in an integrated fashion to accomplish the goal of the system (Dörner, 1997; Sawyer, 2005). Complex social systems generally have more than one subsystem connected to each other. Each such subsystem has its own boundaries, goals, and input and output processes and continually exchanges feedback with other subsystems. Since each system/subsystem interacts with its environment, they are considered open or dynamic systems. A high functioning system continually exchanges feedback among various subsystems to ensure that they are closely aligned to achieve the overall goals of the system. When this is achieved, the system can move from its original state to a more desired state (Dörner, 1997). Conceptualizing social problems in this way allows SEVs to comprehend which entities and stakeholders should be involved while developing a solution to the problem (Trivedi & Misra, 2015).

Social entrepreneurs often reflect on their own behavior, comment critically on it, and make efforts to modify it (Trivedi, 2013) in an effort to identify imporant stakeholders and gain structural knowledge about the social system. They conceptualize the ecology of the social problem incrementally through a cyclical thought process of conception, planning, and action. Social entrepreneurs structure their thoughts by asking more 'why' questions than 'what' questions to help them understand the dynamic structure of the social problem (Trivedi, 2013). Jayeshbhai Patel of Manav Sadhna, a social entrepreneurial organization in Ahmedabad, India committed to uplifting underserved children, explains:

> *I wanted to know why urban slum kids are not interested in education and going to school. So I visited the schools and found that they suffer from an inferiority complex. Whenever they are not able to answer the question asked by the teacher, the teacher would insult them. Eventually they would stop going to school and start working on the street. Working as a child laborer, they have their freedom, have enough money to buy and eat food, and can freely go anywhere they want. They like such freedom. And they also start gaining respect from their parents as they start earning. This simple quest to find the reason made the whole structure of interconnections visible.*

Social problems are not isolated entities, but one or more highly organized systems that interact with and depend on each other. These inter-relations are highly abstract and opaque in nature and are controlled by their internal dynamic, making them even harder to identify (Dörner, 1997). SEVs that are successful in creating social change are capable of understanding the non-linearity of cause and effect that are or may be distant in time and space (Trivedi & Misra, 2015). Moreover, there are other intangible and unfamiliar factors such as the social, political, environmental, and cultural context that may alter these systems creating closed loop structures. In such cases, effects feedback to change one or more of the causes and therefore causes affect other causes. In the example of the slum children served by Manav Sadhna, gaining economic freedom and respect from their parents are examples closed-loop structures (effects feedback to one or more causes). Understanding this non-unidirectional relationship between cause and effect, along with how dominance among causes may change over time is vital to understanding the ecology of the social problem and facilitating social change.

Understanding these interactions and interrelations between the subsystems is what Dörner (1997) terms *structural knowledge* – the knowledge of how the variables in a system are related and how they influence one another. Structural knowledge is essential for complex problem-solving (Jonassen, Beissner, & Yacci, 1993). Comprehending the social system's structure involves (1) organizational knowledge creation and learning that stems from understanding the ecology of social problems and (2) the ability to sense changes in signals from the environment, both internal and external, and adapt accordingly and in a timely manner. Understanding a complex social problem is an iterative process, understood progressively at various levels of analysis (individual, organizational, societal) requiring the coordinated effort of many different actors and integration of activities across functions and knowledge domains. Such ecological knowledge enhances SEVs' ability to recognize and identify the structure of the social problem and structural patterns or archetypes that help them discover constraints and bottlenecks in the system, and devise ways to transform these bottlenecks into leverage points to facilitate social change (Trivedi & Misra, 2015). The case of SEWA Bank, India, described later in the chapter, explicates the process of social change creation.

The research reported here focuses on the role and nature of the communicative process in social change creation in the context of SEVs. Drawing on data from seven SEVs from India and the US and employing a grounded theory methodology, this research scrutinizes the social change process and uncovers the role and characteristics of dialogue in this process. We find that under the appropriate organizational conditions, *dialogue is the glue that links together three conditions necessary for social change*– conceptualizing the *ecology of social problems* (structural knowledge creation) (Trivedi & Misra, 2015), *community empowerment*, and *collaborative capacity* (Trivedi, 2013). In understanding the dialogic process and qualities of dialogue, we propose a grounded theoretical conceptual framework linking dialogue to the creation of knowledge networks and collective wisdom, which collectively lead to the creation of positive social change. This framework also elaborates on the organizational conditions that support dialogue in social entrepreneurial organizations as revealed by our research.

Research Methodology

This research draws on a larger research project on how SEVs create sustained social change (Trivedi, 2013). A grounded theory approach was used with theoretical sampling (Glaser & Strauss, 1967) to understand the local interaction and meanings as related to the social context in which they occur. In grounded theory development, the process of data collection is controlled by the emerging theory. This approach is particularly well suited to studying local interaction and meanings as related to the social context in which they occur. It places more emphasis on participants' own accounts of social and psychological events and their associated local phenomenal and social worlds. Hence, this approach helps in understanding a phenomenon within the socio-political, cultural, economic, spatial, and temporal context in which it occurs (Richardson, 1996). Grounded theory is generated by an iterative process involving *continual sampling* and *analysis of unstructured data* collected from interviews, participant observation, and archival research. There are two main components of grounded theory development: (1) *constant comparison* of the data to the emerging theory and (2) the use of *theoretical sampling* to build conceptual and theoretical depth of analysis.

"Theoretical sampling" (Glaser & Strauss, 1967), in which the researcher selects individuals or groups based on the *relevance* and *expected level of novel insights* for developing and elaborating the theory, offers an appropriate sampling strategy for this research. In theoretical sampling, groups must be chosen according to well-defined theoretical criteria and decisions about what data to collect next are based on the knowledge drawn from prior material collected. Sampling and integration of material ceases when "theoretical saturation" of a category or group of cases is reached, that is, new insights no longer emerge. Thus, in this method of data collection, coding, and analyses are conducted simultaneously. For example, the objective of this research was to study different types of SEVs that vary in their social missions, developmental trajectories, and socio-political, geographical, and cultural contexts to reveal the full range and variation of SEVs. We, therefore, strove for maximum variation in the sample (Flick, 2002) and included cases that were as different as possible from each other (in terms of their features, processes, and experiences). We selected seven SEVs in India and USA based on their willingness to participate, availability, and potentially novel insights they were able provide to the research.

Method

Qualitative data was collected from seven social entrepreneurial organizations over a period of eight months from July 2011 to February 2012 (see Table 1). This research involved site visits to all seven organizations. Site visits included visits to the headquarters or main office, satellite or field offices, and the actual locations in which the SEVs work such as urban slums, schools, and workshops. Semi-structured interviews were conducted with a wide range of members within these social entrepreneurial organizations (n=27), taking care to ensure that they have the necessary knowledge and experience to provide information relevant to the research. Approximately four to five members from each organization participated in this research. These included the social entrepreneurs/founders, executive directors, associate directors, coordinators, research coordinators, administrative staff, health administrators, teachers, volunteers, interns, employees, site coordinators, and collaborators/partners. Additional informal interviews were conducted with twenty field workers and volunteers in all of these organizations. All participants in this research have consented to being identified in publications by their real names. Each interview was approximately about 90 minutes long. Data also included informal observations during group meetings and field trips in some of the organizations in a participant-observer role.

Table 1: List of organizations and description of their activities

ORGANIZATION	DESCRIPTION OF ACTIVITIES
Delancey Street Foundation, USA	Delancey Street is residential self-help organization for former substance abusers, ex-convicts, homeless and others who have hit bottom. Delancey Street residents receive a high school equivalency degree (GED) and are trained in three different marketable skills. Beyond academic and vocational training, residents learn important values, and the social and interpersonal skills that enable them to live successfully in the mainstream of society.
SAATH, India	SAATH is a non-governmental organization in Gujarat, India that utilizes market-based strategies and facilitates participatory processes to create inclusive cities by empowering India's urban and rural poor. SAATH's one-stop, integrated services reach over 100,000 slum dwellers in Ahmedabad, and many more in Gujarat and Rajasthan states of India.
MAM Movies, India	MAM Movies is an open source network of voluntary independent filmmakers who use media, the arts, and technology to inform, inspire, and empower others to create positive action in the world. They believe that inner transformation leads to outer change. The aim is to bring these stories of inner transformation to the general public through film making and other media (such as blogs).

ORGANIZATION	DESCRIPTION OF ACTIVITIES
Gramshree, India	The Gramshree Trust was established in 1995 by Anarben Patel to encourage the empowerment of underprivileged women through self-reliant activities. Gramshree provides women artisans in Gujarat a place where they can leverage their handicraft skills to save and earn for their families. In 2002, Gramshree established a handicraft training program and a production center. Today Gramshree works with 750 women in Gujarat, providing them with skill training, employment opportunities, and a chance to live with dignity, financial security and self-reliance. In 2005, Gramshree opened a retail outlet to establish a larger platform from which to market goods produced by women and artisans.
Manav Sadhna, India	Manav Sadhna, an NGO based at Gandhi Ashram-Ahmedabad works to assist and uplift poor and needy children. Inspired by Gandhian philosophy, Manav Sadhna works in the area of education, nutrition, alternatives to child labor and medical aid to women and children living in the slums.
THINK Together, USA	THINK Together is one of USA's largest and leading non-profit providers of extended learning time programs (after-school, small group tutoring, summer learning, early literacy, etc.) in California serving tens of thousands of students at several hundred sites across the four-county region of Southern California (Los Angeles, Orange, Riverside, and San Bernardino Counties). THINK is an acronym that stands for Teaching, Helping, and Inspiring & Nurturing Kids. THINK Together's mission is to provide high-quality, academically oriented out-of-school programs for students regardless of race, creed, or socioeconomic status.
The Self-Employed Women's Association (SEWA), India	SEWA is an organization of poor, self-employed women workers with 700,000 members who have full employment (mainly through small businesses) and are ensured income, food, work, social security, health and child care, old age benefits, as well as banking and legal services. By providing these employment opportunities, the SEWA movement has raised the status of women individually and collectively. The SEWA model has been successfully replicated not only in urban and rural India but also in other socio-political and cultural contexts such as in South Africa, Turkey, and Yemen.

Data Analytic Strategies

Data from the semi-structured interviews and notes from observations were integrated with analyses of archival resources. The archival analysis examined popular media and academic articles about the organization, the organization's website, financial strategy and portfolios, and annual reports pertaining to the organizational structure and goals, financial strategies, as well as the organization's achievements. The documented textual interview data and the archival material were coded, analyzed, and categorized through the "theoretical coding" procedure described by Glaser and Strauss (1967). In the process of interpreting the data and comparing the different cases and processes, coding procedures including "open coding", "axial coding", and "selective coding" were used (Flick, 2002).

"Open coding" aimed to identify themes/categories and associated subcategories emerging from the data (Flick, 2002). The goal, therefore, was to create multi-dimensional categories from which a preliminary framework for analysis can be generated. Open coding was achieved by analyzing the interview text line by line, by each sentence or by each paragraph. In this research, *organic organizational structure and context, ecological understanding of the social problem*, and *dialogue* emerged as the primary categories through which SEVs create and sustain social change. Further sub-categories emerged from the process of "axial coding", in which the goal was to refine and differentiate the categories that emerged from open coding and detect and uncover relationships between the categories and sub-categories. For example, within the primary category of dialogue, *tacit to explicit knowledge creation, skilled facilitation using metaphorical language,* and *preserving organizational values through dialogue* emerged as secondary categories. Figure 1 (later in this chapter) shows the relationships between the various categories and sub-categories that emerged in this research.

"Selective coding" is the last step of coding that aimed to identify and elaborate the core rubrics or constructs that were used to group the categories developed earlier through open and axial coding (Flick, 2002). Since the process of gathering and incorporating additional data ended as theoretical saturation was reached, this phase facilitated development of a theory and identified and explained patterns in the data and the conditions under which these applied. For example, one way in which selective coding was used in the present research was to explain the organizational conditions under which large-scale positive social change is created and sustained and the contextual conditions that facilitate and/or constrain the social change creation process, based on the categories, subcategories, and relationships between them found through open and axial coding.

Cross-validation measures such as data triangulation were used to gain a deeper understanding of the organizations and groups participating in this study. For example, in addition to the interviews of the leaders or social entrepreneurs, this research analyzed (1) archival data -- including objective data such as financial portfolios and annual reports of the organization; (2) the mission or vision statement of the organization; (3) past organizational and strategic decisions; and (4) interviews of multiple stakeholders, collaborators, and employees. In this way, theoretical coding and interpretation of the interview and archival data were enriched and corroborated.

We applied Flick's (2014) *principle of sequentiality* to navigate through the variety of data sources in this research. This means that we followed the data from beginning to end following its temporal development so that the categories emerge, rather than looking for excerpts for substantiating pre-conceived categories. Our data analysis, therefore, aimed to classify and interpret the data to make statements about implicit and explicit dimensions, structures, routines, and practices of meaning-making in the interview, archival, and observational material. Our final aim was to arrive at generalizable statements by comparing various materials or various texts or several cases. Therefore, the quotes and examples provided below serve as exemplars and are not meant to represent the sole data source that substantiates the emergent categories.

Findings and Emerging Theory

The reflections and experiences of the members of social entrepreneurial ventures revealed that social entrepreneurship is a collective endeavor and this collective character is essential to its success. Collective organization and synergy, deep intra-organizational communication, and a conducive organizational context are critical for the creation of *collective wisdom* and *knowledge networks* for long-term collaborative community capacity building. The theory emerged as the relationships between the concepts combined into an integrated framework that explained the process of social change creation (Strauss & Corbin, 1990). *Dialogue* emerged as a central category linking the other themes to explain the process of social change creation. *Organic organizational structure* enables knowledge creation and integration through the process of *organizational learning* through *deep and continuous social interaction*, or *dialogue*. Illustrative quotations from the participants are included in the each of the categories to tell the story of the theory.

Organic Organizational Structure

An appropriate organizational structure is vital to an organization's success as it provides coordination for organizational processes and facilitates the achievement of collective goals. According to Van de Ven (1986), organizational structural features play an important role in enhancing the morale, efficiency, and effectiveness of the organization. Clemmer (1995) found that organizational structures, if inappropriate, can hinder the performance of motivated employees. Organic organizational structures work well under dynamic conditions and usually have a high level of adaptation. They are most appropriate for an unstable, turbulent, unpredictable environment and for non-routine tasks. SEVs in this research typically employed an organic structure that provided employees with decisional autonomy and control over activities, shifting the primary focus from individual performance to group performance. An organic organizational structure places greater emphasis on social interaction characterized by discussion, elaboration and continuous refinement of tasks and are, therefore, better suited for SEVs (T. A. Burns & Stalker, 1961; Courtright, Fairhurst, & Rogers, 1989; Weick, 1987). Organic structures usually exhibit a low degree of formalization defined as the extent to which policies, procedures, job descriptions, and rules and regulations are codified in writing (Carpenter, Bauer, & Erdogan, 2010) thus making them amenable to respond quickly and effectively to environmental challenges by enabling employees to exercise a great deal of discretion.

Since the effectiveness of SEVs depends on their ability to acquire accurate structural knowledge, a key requirement for their success would be to foster greater flexibility in acquiring, relating, and interpreting information. Such flexibility requires a low degree of formalization of policies and procedures to allow employees to exercise greater autonomy.

Hence, SEVs in this research engaged in what Nonaka (1994) calls "communities of inter-action" to facilitate the creation and refinement of structural knowledge. Communities of interaction are formed through social interaction in self-designed and self-managed groups that collectively develop ideas, knowledge, and practices as they learn together through shared repertoires of routines and vocabularies. Dyer and Nobeoka (2000) assert that such communities of interactions are effective in generating, amplifying, transferring, and re-combining knowledge. The SEVs that participated in this research exhibited a decentralized structure that supported *collective learning*. For example, Randy Barth of THINK Together reported:

> *The culture at THINK Together promotes a collaborative approach that encourages employees to combine their diverse knowledge, talents and expertise in flexible, manageable group-work efforts. This approach aims to foster a supportive structure that facilitates innovation, efficiency and agility to embrace change and keep up with rapid growth. We strive to develop, maintain and reward a culture of trust and teamwork. To support this we have a matrix organization structure which seems a natural step to building collaborative organization.*

Thus, SEVs put into practice a structure in which authority could be delegated based on structural knowledge to those who are best able to understand and respond to the issue and not based on the employee's position or role in the organization. Jobs are not clearly or precisely defined in such organizations. Positions, roles, job descriptions, and standard op-erating procedures are broad and generalized rather than specific and specialized (T. A. Burns & Stalker, 1961). Such an organizational process nurtures the culture of commitment to knowledge creation and sharing among employees. Keren Nazareth at SAATH ex-plained:

> *We believe in providing lot of autonomy. There is lot of sense of psychological ownership among people working at SAATH. The structure is very organic; that allows us to be flexible and the decision power is distributed. We provide that autonomy to our employees as they are many a times more in tune with the community. We want to understand that and support that. We do question it, but at the end of the day, we give that person a space to make that decision. In our [organizational] history, no person has stepped on anyone's toes when it comes to decision making.*

Organic structures foster a *consultative communication approach* (Courtright et al., 1989) where all knowledgeable contributors participate in decision-making processes irrespective of their position within the organization. An organic structure facilitates open communication, em-powerment, and delegation of authority creating a path for innovation (Pierce & Delbecq, 1977; Sine, Mitsuhashi, & Kirsch, 2006). These types of structures also are well suited to organizations dealing with complex tasks (Hull & Hage, 1982). It facilitates effectiveness, problem-solving, responsiveness, flexibility, adaptability, creativity, and innovation – all critical aspects for complex problem-solving (Jonassen et al., 1993; Maani & Maharaj, 2004; Schein, 1993). Adaptability comes from empowering employees to be creative, to experi-ment, and to suggest new ideas. Information sharing coupled with decentralized decision-making at all levels of the organization facilitates the generation of fast and suitable re-sponses.

Empowerment of and value-added participation by employees is very motivating because it meets the human need for autonomy, responsibility, challenge, esteem, social interaction, and personal development. This helps SEVs in the development and capitalization of collective intellectual capital generated by employees at various levels of an organization (Helms, 2006). Sunil Vaghela, Health Administrator, at Manav Sadhna explained:

> *I have complete autonomy to do my work. I am given an annual budget and I have to manage things on my own. If I feel I need to engage in one activity or other at a particular point of time, I have that autonomy and support from the organization and that helps in faster resolutions of problems. And I provide the same kind of autonomy to community leaders that I work with. This also facilitates information flow and helps in identifying emerging issues.*

Furthermore, enabling and empowering employees to communicate across traditional organizational boundaries regardless of position, level, or unit through an organic organizational structure improved SEVs' ability to sense and respond to environmental changes. As indicated before, in order to understand and influence structural patterns, SEVs must sense changes in signals from the environment, both internal and external, and continually assess and modify their roles, structures, and processes to adapt to environmental needs and respond innovatively to challenges. This requires the coordinated effort of many different actors and integration of activities across functions, knowledge domains, and contexts. It was found that organic organizational structures facilitated this type of knowledge creation, integration, and action.

Organizational Learning

Organizational learning is a useful lens to understand cooperative and communicative processes in knowledge creation and integration (Dodgson, 1993). Organizational learning enhances organizations' ability to sense and respond to environmental changes (Flood, 1999). Organizational learning encompasses both processes and outcomes, occurs in all activities of the organization, and is defined as *"an organization wide continuous process that enhances its collective ability to accept, make sense of, and respond to internal and external changes"* ("Organizational learning", para 1).

Putting the right organizational structure in place is the first step in creating learning organizations. The data in this research uncovered that for SEVs organizational structures that facilitated social interaction and dialogue were critical for organizational learning and knowledge creation. Solving complex problems requires tapping into the collective intelligence of groups of knowledgeable people. Learning takes place in a social context and it is the nature and boundaries of the context that facilitate the identification of the system constraints or bottlenecks (Easterby-Smith & Lyles, 2011; Nonaka, 1994; Weick, 1995; Weick, Sutcliffe, & Obstfeld, 2005). The data revealed that to translate learning into knowledge the informally shared understanding among various actors needed to be crystallized as a part of a *knowledge network* (formal and informal knowledge held by the members of organization, within written rules, and in the oral transmission of knowledge through routines and practices). Organizational learning, therefore, is the process of encoding inferences from individual experiences into routines that guide behavior. Thus, organizational learning led to *collective knowledge* -- the accumulated knowledge of the organization stored in its rules, procedures, routines, and shared norms (Levitt & March, 1988). This systematic integration and collective interpretation of new knowledge led to collective action.

This iterative nature of knowledge creation and integration also indicates a tacit and subjective form of knowledge creation that is deeply rooted in action, commitment, and involvement in the specific context and requires constant, open, and deep interpersonal communication (Weick, 1995). Dialogue, therefore, was found to play a critical role in knowledge creation and facilitate the conversion of tacit knowledge to explicit knowledge. Open communication, delegation of authority, empowerment of employees and stakeholders, and autonomy led to greater flexibility in acquiring, relating, interpreting, and integrating information and locating bottlenecks. Locating bottlenecks enabled SEVs to influence how these bottlenecks work and how they could be maneuvered to meet the organizations' mission. SEVs could, therefore, capitalize on collective intellectual capital and convert the bottlenecks to leverage points to create social change. For example, the biggest problem that SEWA Bank encountered in its early days was developing a reliable and fair method of accessing the credit worthiness of its clients. These clients were extremely poor, lacked any kind of documentation, and were most likely illiterate. After many encounters with their clients, field employees suggested considering tangible and intangible assets such as ownership of cattle, availability of trade equipment, cash savings, jewelry, basic literacy, or having a husband without a drinking problem as markers of credit worthiness. This is arguably one of the most innovative features of the SEWA Bank model. This organizational learning could not have emerged without continuous, long-term, and deep interpersonal communication across all levels of the organization, and employee autonomy and empowerment.

Continuous and Deep Social Interaction through Dialogue

Dialogue is the most fundamental of human skills for complex problem-solving (Schein, 1993). Rapidly changing external environments create increased need for learning. Learning organizations accept change as an ongoing and dynamic process. Engaging in dialogue, disclosing and testing assumptions, building trust, and generating shared mental models that cut across organizational boundaries are key characteristics that distinguish learning organizations from other types of organizations (Patterson, 2009). Such organizations collect data from their external environment, translate events through deep and open communication, and develop shared understanding and conceptual schema (Daft & Weick, 1984). This is done through what Weick et al. (2005) call *sensemaking*. In the process of sensemaking, events are open to interpretation and many possible meanings can be synthesized. Here strong and supportive leaders clarify values, preferences, and priorities (Patterson, 2009). Thus, leaders are central to the process of creating, sharing, and exploring knowledge at an organizational level (Bryant, 2003). Knowledge creation and organizational learning can be fostered through the appropriate organizational context, as found here, but it also requires strong organizational support and leadership.

Continuous "Samvaad": From tacit to explicit knowledge.

Weick et al. (2005) assert that sensemaking is a social and collective process involving dialogue and communication, a process of collective thinking that relies on mastering the practice of dialogue and discussion that work in a complementary fashion (Senge, Kleiner, Roberts, Ross, & Smith, 2010). Dialogue is central to organizational learning because it holds promise as a means for promoting collective thinking and communication (Bohm, 2014; Isaacs, 2001; Senge et al., 2010). Thus, organizational learning starts with dialogue where employees suspend their assumptions and start thinking together (Isaacs, 1993). Jayeshbhai Patel, founder of Manav Sadhna, terms this practice "continuous *samvaad*" (a Gujarati word that translates to "dialogue" in English). Dialogue, in this context, means a free-flow of meaning through the group, allowing the discovery insights not attainable individually (Senge, 1993).

Among other distinct uses and purposes of a dialogue, Gustavsen (1992) has proposed two that are particularly relevant to SEVs, namely, to defuse conflict and to encourage the pooling of ideas or meaning to enable individuals to master complex system realities and become more effective at limiting self-defeating and unintended consequences. Our tacit ways of thinking govern how we formulate our views, deal with differences, pay attention, make causal connections which in turn govern the ways we perceive the world, and take action in it (Cowan, David, & Foray, 2000; Nonaka, 1994; Nonaka & Von Krogh, 2009). Thus, dialogue is a process in which the group learns to watch or experience its own tacit process in action whereby an attempt is made to bring this tacit infrastructure to the surface, perceive its impact, and alter it (Bohm & Factor, 1985; Isaacs, 2001). In other words, dialogue provides the platform for the transformation of tacit knowledge into explicit knowledge, which can in turn be converted into organizational routines.

The SEVs in this research provided an environment for individuals to think better collectively and to create and share knowledge. Organizational knowledge creation by SEVs is a process that amplifies the knowledge created by individuals and crystallizes it as a part of the knowledge network of an organization (Dodgson, 1993; Nonaka, 1994). For example, Manav Sadhna promoted organizational learning through the process of dialogue (or samvaad). Every morning, employees came together, sat on the floor in a circle, and started their day with a payer from each major world religion. Such an organization of physical space and organizational routine provided a sense of equality among employees and facilitates the sharing of experiences and perspectives (Schein, 1993). Then one person from the group read a passage from Gandhi's autobiography, *My Experiments with Truth*, which was followed by a discussion and elaboration of values underlying the text. This is what Isaacs (2001) refers to as "side by side" interaction, which encourages free exchange between members to enable them to learn to talk together. Jayeshbhai encouraged everyone to share his or her experiences with specific examples. This way, members spoke to the group as a whole rather than speaking directly to one another. Such a process created an environment in which people can express their differences without any effort to reconcile them (Isaacs, 2001). This process invited members to reflect on the quality of language and inquiry they bring to the conversation, and to become self-reflective about how their filters governed their thinking and acting.

It is important not to misunderstand dialogue as any type of verbal communication. Communication can be one-way, but dialogue engages all members in a productive exchange of thoughts and ideas. Isaacs (1993) defines dialogue as, "a sustained collective inquiry into the processes, assumptions, and certainties that compose everyday experience" (p. 25). Hence dialogue, as understood in this context, focuses on thinking processes so that an individual becomes more conscious of his/her thought processes enabling him/her to think better collectively. Dialogue, in the SEVs in this research, was found to center on the transformation of the quality of tacit thinking that underlay all interactions (Isaacs, 2001). In these SEVs, engaging in the process of dialogue implied developing a capacity to interact in a way that suspended the habitual processes of thought and meaning that typically controlled members. Reflection coupled with inquiry skills provided the foundation for fruitful dialogue in these organizations as the usage of such skills freed the process of dialogue from particulars of circumstance (Senge et al., 2010), such as the chemistry among team members. Stefano, Gino, Pisano, and Staats (2014) have similarly found that reflection is a powerful mechanism by which experiences are translated into learning. They also found that reflection increases ones' ability to achieve a goal, which in turn translates to higher rate of learning.

Skilled facilitation using metaphorical language

The data showed that dialogue required a challenging stance of being both an observer and a participant simultaneously requiring the cultivation of reflective awareness and proprioceptive awareness (awareness of what one is doing as one is doing it). With skilled facilitation, this type of stance triggered meaningful dialogue surrounding the organization's work and employees' experiences in the field. Skilled facilitation was found to be critical for the emergence of insights as the facilitator/leader modeled how to suspend habitual thought processes, uncover assumptions, and allow insights to emerge.

Jayeshbhai Patel, founder of Manav Sadhna, enabled members to articulate their perspectives by the use of *metaphorical language* to express the meaning and feelings involved in the learning process, thereby revealing hidden and tacit knowledge that is otherwise difficult to communicate. For instance, on the topic of mentorship he explained:

> *Leaders have to balance between molding the employee's values toward right direction as well as supporting them at each step to realize those values. It is like the work of a potter, who uses his upper hand to shape the clay to turn in to a beautiful earthen pot, while always supporting that action by other, invisible, hand from inside so that the created form retains its shape and does not break.*

On the idea of leadership, Jayeshbhai said:

> *One should not strive to be a "yogi" (preacher), but instead try to be "upyogi" (helpful). There is no place for assumption or judgement. There is only equality or viewing each other with equanimity (Samdhristi). When you change your perspective, we change the world around us. I am not here to preach or teach anyone. I am here to share my thoughts. A leader is the one who centralizes, while a ladder is the one who decentralizes. In centralization your "I" [ego] becomes capital, in decentralization it becomes small "i". In decentralization, you have sharing, you have caring. This can become a movement, a mission. While centralization often evolves ambition. One should try to be a ladder for other to achieve their success, rather than becoming a leader.*

Further, on the idea of success Madhusudan of MAM Movies explained in one of the group sessions:

> *Success is form of external validation. Once you start following your swagyan (self-understanding), you do not require external validation and it does not matter whether you help one person or ten or one hundred in a day. This enlightenment makes you very fearless of success and failure. And second, it helps you to understand that you are just an instrument and that helps you with the understanding that MAM (organization) is just a vehicle and you can do work with or without it.*

And Mimi Silbert of Delancey Street Foundation, wrote on the idea of continuing in the face of difficulties,

I'm like a mother figure. I love them. They love me and we're climbing a mountain together. I tell them, "I might be closer to the top of the mountain, and you might feel closer to the bottom but the truth is; the people at the bottom hold the power. If you pull in a negative direction, we'll all fall down the mountain – and Delancey Street will be over. If you pull each other up, we'll all make it up. And the pie is big enough for all of us, so here we go." (McCoy, 2014)

Social interaction is the key and is accomplished through communal living and with open interactions with various elements of community. The stress is on fun, humor, and interpersonal communication skills (Silbert, 1984).

The usage of metaphors is an effective method of converting tacit knowledge to explicit knowledge (Nonaka, 1994). "The essence of metaphor is understanding and experiencing one kind of thing in terms of another" (Lakoff & Johnson, 1980, p. 5). Metaphors enable individuals to experience new behaviors by making inferences from models of other behaviors. While perception through prototype is in many cases limited to concrete, mundane concepts, metaphor plays an important role in associating abstract, imaginary concepts. When two concepts are presented in a metaphor, it is possible not only to think of their similarity, but also to make comparisons that discern the degree of imbalance, contradiction or inconsistency involved in their association.

Metaphors enable the finding of fresh ways of seeing, understanding, and shaping the situation we want to organize and manage (Morgan, 2006). The latter process becomes the basis for creating new meaning. Some metaphors provide familiar ways of thinking while others develop new insights and perspectives. Overall, metaphors can generate a range of complementary and competing insights and help to build on the strengths of different perspectives. Additionally, metaphors serve as a way of *creating a network of concepts* that can help generate future knowledge using existing information. Hence, the process of dialogue is a creative, cognitive process that relates seemingly disparate concepts within an individual's cognitive schema. Dialogue thus becomes a vehicle for thinking generatively, creatively, and importantly thinking together. It facilitates the natural flow of conversations and allows members to be self-reflective.

This continuous interplay of enhancing the creation of tacit knowledge through self-reflection with relevant aspects of explicit knowledge improves the total quality of the individual's structural knowledge (Nonaka, 1994). At MAM Movies, for example, the regular sharing of experiences enabled this. Sharing experiences through dialogue facilitated the creation of common perspectives and helped establish a common basis for understanding each other and the organization's goals and objectives. Thus, social interaction through dialogue created shared understanding and common interpretive schemas that could then facilitate organizational learning.

Activating organizational values using dialogue

This research found that dialogue served the purpose of preserving the organizational values and keeping them cognitively active as exemplified by Jayeshbhai Patel's role in tying organizational learning to organizational values at the end of each such session of "samvaad" or dialogue. For example, Manav Sadhna displayed its values all across the organization -- "Happiness depends on what you can give and not what you can get"; "Service to mankind"; "Home for the underprivileged", "Be the change you want to see in this world."

Verplanken and Holland (2002) have found that individuals make choices consistent with their values when those values are cognitively activated. Thus, the knowledge generated along with cognitively active organizational values facilitates behavior and processes that crystallize the new knowledge into behavior and routines. Such a learning process creates strong organizational culture that encourages normative behavior (Schein, 1993). Organizational culture is defined here as (a) a pattern of basic assumptions, (b) invented, discovered, or developed by a given group, (c) as it learns to cope with its problems of external adaptation and internal integration, (d) that has worked well enough to be considered valid and, therefore (e) is to be taught to new members as the (f) correct way to perceive, think, and feel in relation to those problems (Schein, 1990). Values have been found to influence habitual behavior through affective mechanisms (Bardi & Schwartz, 2003). Social interaction, therefore, has the capacity to generate synergy. That is, the added value results not from the cumulative effects of elements present in the milieu but from the interaction. Thus, the practice of dialogue helps SEVs strengthen organizational learning and better realize their organizational values.

The core of the grounded theory of dialogue in the context of trans-sector TD problem-solving organizations presented here is built on the premise that the effect of people's shared attention can alter the quality and level of inquiry possible at any particular time. People can gradually learn to refine their modes of collective awareness to promote increasingly more subtle and intelligent modes of interaction. The process is very demanding, and at times frustrating; it is also deeply rewarding. Figure 1 depicts graphically the relationships between the constructs that emerged from the data and centrality of dialogue in the process of knowledge creation, organizational learning, and collective action.

In the next section, we use the case of Self-Employed Women's Association (SEWA) Bank to clarify the linkages between these concepts and explain how they are critical to the creation and sustenance of positive social change.

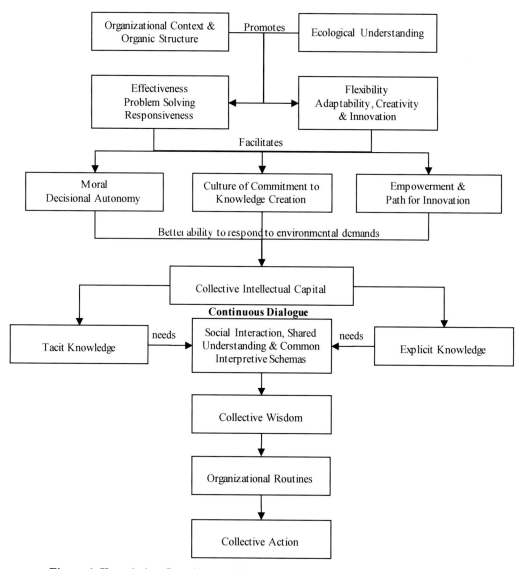

Figure 1: Knowledge Creation and Organizational Learning through Dialogue

The Process of Social Change: The Case of SEWA Bank

SEWA Bank was started against all odds – the clients were illiterate, there was no system to evaluate the credit worthiness of clients, and the savings deposited were marginal. And yet, SEWA bank shattered the myth that the poor are not bankable and turned their bank into a viable, profitable, financial venture without any aid or subsidy year after year since its inception in early 1970s by devising new and innovative solutions to all these problems (Bhatt, 2005).

Complexity of the Social Problem

The informal or unorganized sector constitutes about 50% of the GDP of India and provides livelihood to almost 90% of the work force (Government of India, 2012; Kabra, 2003; Sakthivel & Joddar, 2006). The unorganized sector in India consists of people who earn their living through their own small business or by selling their own labor. Despite their hard work and significant contribution to the national economy, they do not have access to financial services (Bhatt, 2005). Hence, they face two major challenges – lack of working capital and non-ownership of assets. As a result, a big portion of their little income goes toward interest on working capital and renting trade equipment. Paying high interest leads to the lack of business infrastructure, which in turn leads to the lack of capital, savings, and assets. The Government of India has attempted, in the form of various financial schemes implemented by nationalized banks, to help the unorganized sector gain access to financial services (Bhatt, 2005). However, these have not been effective in uplifting the self-employed poor in the informal sector, largely owing to the structure of banking in India. For example, most workers in the unorganized sector live hand to mouth, which is very labor intensive. They have no time bring their earnings to the bank during regular bank hours. Also, they need to make frequent deposits in order to be able to save or else they spend everything they earn. Furthermore, it is uneconomical for them to spend money on transportation to the bank for small amounts of money that have to be deposited frequently. Even for those who are a little better off economically, in order to get a loan they need collateral deposits and a strong credit history. They need to be literate to be able to open a bank account, to be able to fill out the forms, and they need some type of asset to qualify for a loan. Thus, these structural conditions limit the benefits of government initiated financial schemes for participants in the informal sector. The system boundaries are so rigidly defined that the entities involved are not able to understand each other's needs. Banks implementing such financial schemes to help the poor do not understand their clients and do not have adequate means to measure the credit worthiness of self-employed people. The poor feel intimidated by the formal office and banking environments, where they would have to deposit a crumbled pile of currency in small denomination. At the same time, bankers have a distrust of the poor and are condescending toward them and their economic activities.

Innovativeness of SEVs: Organizational Context, Organic Structure, Ecology of the Social Problem

SEWA established their own bank (SEWA Bank) in 1974. It was based on the cooperative model where members were also the shareholders of the bank. To remain true to their cooperative model, not only are the banking services for poor women, the management is also comprised of poor women (Bhatt, 2005). Thus, there was a strong alignment of interests and objectives between the board, the management, and the customers. The women who constituted the bank were the women for whom the bank was constituted. Therefore, the bank was able to comprehend their customers' needs as it was the same critical mass of women who demanded and provided the services. SEWA bank employed unconventional systems thinking principles to build a banking system for their clientele. Perseverance, egalitarianism, inclusion, and participation are actively incorporated into meetings and organizational practices (Blaxall, 2004). The organizational structure encouraged experimentation and learning and willingness to take advantage of the partnership.

To tackle the challenge of illiteracy, SEWA Bank started providing photo identity cards for account holders and supplemented it with a dedicated person in the bank to help anyone with the forms and other paperwork. SEWA Bank devised a door-to-door service and a daily collection schedule to facilitate and cultivate the habit of saving. Such a flexible system, coupled with decentralized decision-making power, promoted motivation and commitment in employees. This made the system boundaries porous and gave them the ability to understand their customers' needs. Empowered employees developed their own system of assessing credit worthiness of their customers. For example, availability of trade equipment, cash, savings, jewelry, a roof over their head, real estate, owning a cow or other animals, food ration card, or having any certificate or license are considered valuable assets by SEWA Bank. SEWA bank also takes into account intangible assets, such as education, basic literacy, number of children, a husband without a drinking problem, in-laws who are liberal and allow a woman to work outside the house, when assessing the credit worthiness of a client. It took a combination of unconventional thinking and a constant reevaluation of clients' needs through continuous dialogue to identify assets that clients can turn into capital and build and sustain successful banking model for the poor (Bhatt, 2005).

Further, bank frontline workers, known as 'bank-saathis', who typically belong to the same community and live in the same neighborhood as customers, help identify these assets and help with the daily collection of savings. They also assist with loan application assessments. They have considerable autonomy in assessing the customers' credit worthiness. SEWA bank, like other SEVs in this study, has an organic organizational structure whereby decision-making power is based on knowledge rather than position. Such practices allow the creation of new knowledge, which is then crystallized into predictable organizational routines. The leadership at SEWA bank facilitated the establishment of participatory management and behavioral practices to reduce the social distance between the management and the community members. This included regular rotation of office holders, highly compressed pay scales, a stable core management cadre, and a conscious policy of developing new leaders (Blaxall, 2004). SEWA bank understood that in order to serve their customers effectively, they need to understand their work and their requirements. Through bank-saathis, SEWA bank refined its structural knowledge and understanding of interconnections among different social variables, which was then codified into organizational routines.

At the same time, SEWA Bank understands the ecology of the social problem and provides other supportive services such as, advice on how to cook and feed a family with limited resources and where and how to spend money. It also provides assistance in finding the best and most affordable deals for purchasing trade equipment, so that customers can start exercising financial discipline. The bank also identifies potential areas where it can provide supplementary help such as legal services, medical services, insurance, capacity building, and marketing knowhow to its clients. For the extreme poor, whose credit worthiness is impossible to assess, or where the identity of a person cannot be verified, the Bank helps them in procuring a ration card, a voting card, or an electricity connection. In addition, to equip women in making sound financial choices, the bank conducts training programs, where women can learn about financial planning. The Bank also places great importance on the redemption of old debts with moneylenders, pawnshops, or property owners as it frees women from life-long indebtedness and helps to increase their bargaining power with wholesalers and suppliers.

Crystallization of Social Change

Once a saving pattern is established, things start turning around. Women feel more self-confident once they realize they have money accumulating in their account. Bhatt (2005) notes that when financial tensions ease for women, their husband's attitude softens and they start considering women as partners rather than a burden. Gradually, women begin to have a voice in the family, and family-by-family and neighborhood-by-neighborhood; social change starts to gain momentum. Wilson (1996) argues that individual change is a prerequisite for community and social change. Page and Czuba (1999) refer to this phenomenon as empowerment, which is a "multi-dimensional social process that helps people gain control over their own lives" (para 11).

Over years, the bond between SEWA Bank and the women they serve became stronger and most women developed a strong support structure to help them realize their dreams. This process of raising the status of women individually and collectively is a long-term process that involves hard work by many. Continuous social support leads to greater awareness of new opportunities. This is a subconscious process whereby society gradually progresses as knowledge of new forms of social institutions spreads over time (Jacobs & Asokan, 1999). Social entrepreneurs play a key role in making this knowledge broadly available. Though social entrepreneurs or leaders appear to act individually, they are conscious and enlightened representatives of the society and hence their role should be viewed in that light (Cleveland & Jacobs, 1999). The success of SEVs encourages subsequent imitation and propagation in their immediate communities and beyond. Growing success leads to the assimilation of the new practices in the society and over the course of time these practices become regularized and institutionalized.

Conclusion

This research employs a social ecological perspective (Stokols, 2018) to develop a grounded theory of knowledge creation and organizational learning in trans-sector TD problem-solving contexts, such as social entrepreneurial ventures. Three salient conclusions emerge from this study of the social change process in seven SEVs in India and the US.

1. Dialogue and its ability to generate knowledge networks and collective wisdom play a vital role in the complex problem-solving and social change process. We developed a grounded theoretical framework elucidating the role of dialogue in the process of social change creation and sustenance with particular attention to the organizational conditions and context.

2. This research highlighted how the appropriate organizational context can support dialogue, promote the generation of individual and organizational learning, amplify the knowledge created by individuals, and allow the crystallization of knowledge as a part of the knowledge network of the organization, which in turn leads to collective wisdom and action. Key elements of such an organizational context include (a) understanding the *ecology of the social problem*; (b) *organic organizational structure*; (c) *continuous and deep social interaction among all levels of the organization through dialogue*; (d) *employee and community autonomy and empowerment*; and (e) *attention to subtle environmental changes in the system*. These elements in combination lead to the creation of collective wisdom. Collective wisdom then feeds back into the conception, planning, and ac-

tion stages of the iterative cycle of organizational knowledge creation to create positive social change. Figure 1 maps the relationship between the various categories and sub-categories that emerged from the data.

3. At the same time, this research identified the nature and characteristics of the dialogic process that lead to the generation of organizational learning and collective wisdom – *continuous samvaad* (open and deep communication), *skilled facilitation using metaphorical language*, and *cognitive activation of organizational values* to promote organizational norms.

In summary, we found that in order to create and sustain positive social change, SEVs first understand the interconnections between the components of the social structure that produce and maintain social continuity and collective social norms. This ecological understanding of the dynamic nature of the structure of the social problem is gained through a process of questioning and probing, experimentation, evaluation, and learning. Gaining knowledge of the ecology of the social problem is an iterative process, understood progressively at various levels of analysis (individual, organizational, societal) and requires the coordinated effort of many different actors and the integration of activities across functions and knowledge domains. It was found that multiple actors at different levels of the organization are engaged in a continuous and iterative cycle of conception, planning, and action.

Each action, in turn, produces both intended and unintended consequences. Through consolidation and accumulation, these consequences result in the creation and refinement of *structural knowledge*. Structural knowledge can be *tacit or explicit*. Tacit and subjective forms of knowledge creation need constant, open, and deep interpersonal communication to convert them into explicit knowledge. This transformation was found to be facilitated by dialogue. Dialogue aided the creation of shared understanding and common interpretive schemas, while empowering the community and building collaborative community capacity, and led to the creation of collective wisdom. This wisdom fuels the next round of conception, planning, and action as structural knowledge is further refined through this iterative process of gaining ecological understanding.

In addition to ecological understanding, the ability to sense internal and external environmental changes is required for the organization to adapt to these changes. This in turn depends on actors' (employees, community, and other stakeholders) ability to acquire, relate, and interpret information. Organizational structures that promote empowerment and autonomy are better suited to promote ecological understanding of the social problem, sense external changes, and create structural knowledge. Such an organizational context fosters effective problem-solving, flexibility, adaptability, creativity, and innovation.

The research methodology employed in this study is progressive and discovery based. It is interpretative, emphasizes thick description of multiple cases, and is contextually sensitive. It emphasizes the meaning of experiences and behavior in context and its full complexity. The method provides a richer and deeper understanding of trans-sector TD problem-solving using the case of social entrepreneurship and social entrepreneurial ventures compared to a quantitative approach that can provide greater generalizability. However, this approach also has number of limitations. For instance, the range and number of SEVs that can be studied is limited. It was not possible to study a broader range of SEVs that likely would have yielded additional insights, due to geographical, language, economic, time, and other constraints. Further, there are some limitations inherent to qualitative methodology. For example, since only a small group of cases or organizations are studied, the results might not be generalizable to all contexts and populations. Additionally, it may be difficult to disentangle interviewee biases in interview data. However, the research presented here did not rely solely on interview data. Cross-validation strategies such as data triangulation were used to gain a deeper understanding of the organizations and groups involved and avoid interviewee biases.

Questions to Further the Discourse

1. What personality attributes and contextual factors promote effective ways of creating sustained positive social change?

2. How do we replicate such efforts in different socio-environmental, political, economic, and spatial contexts?

3. How do we promote specific insights from successful ventures and create inclusive and participatory frameworks for different TD problem-solving contexts?

4. How can organizational culture foster critical components of knowledge creation, systems thinking, and cultural intelligence, in the way they construct, disseminate and share collective wisdom?

5. How do we foster commitment to collective action among leaders in different sectors?

Must Reads

Dörner, D. (1997). *The logic of failure: Recognizing and avoiding error in complex situations*. Basic Books.

Isaacs, W. N. (1993). Taking flight: Dialogue, collective thinking, and organizational learning. *Organizational Dynamics, 22*(2), 24-39.

Trivedi, C., & Misra, S. (2015). Relevance of systems thinking and scientific holism to social entrepreneurship. *Journal of Entrepreneurship, 24*(1), 37-62.

References

Alvord, S. H., Brown, L. D., & Letts, C. W. (2004). Social entrepreneurship & societal transformation: An exploratory study. *Journal of Applied Behavioral Science, 40*(3), 260-282. https://doi.org/10.1177/0021886304266847

Ashoka. (n.d.) *Ashoka: Innovators for the public*. Retrieved from http://www.ashoka.org/support/criteria

Austin, J. E. (2000). *The collaboration challenge: How nonprofits and businesses succeed through strategic alliances* (1st ed.). San Francisco, Calif.: Jossey-Bass Publishers.

Bardi, A., & Schwartz, S. H. (2003). Values and behavior: Strength and structure of relations. *Personality and Social Psychology Bulletin, 29*(10), 1207-1220. https://doi.org/10.1177/0146167203254602

Barringer, B. R., & Harrison, J. S. (2000). Walking a tightrope: Creating value through interorganizational relationships. *Journal of Management, 26*(3), 367-403. https://doi.org/10.1177/014920630002600302

Bhatt, E. R. (2005). *We are poor but so many: The story of self-employed women in India*. New Delhi: Oxford University Press.

Blaxall, J. (2004, May 25-27). *India's Self-Employed Women's Association (SEWA): Empowerment through mobilization of poor women on a large scale*. Paper presented at the Scaling Up Poverty Reduction: A Global Learning Process and Conference, Shanghai.

Blumer, H. (1971). Social problems as collective behavior. *Social Problems, 18*(3), 298-306. https://doi.org/10.2307/799797

Bohm, D. (2014). *On dialogue*. London: Routledge.

Bohm, D., & Factor, D. (1985). *Unfolding meaning: A weekend of dialogue with David Bohm*. New York, NY: Routledge.

Bornstein, D. (2007). *How to change the world: Social entrepreneurs and the power of new ideas* (updated ed.). NY: Oxford University Press Inc.

Bornstein, D., & Davis, S. (2010). *Social entrepreneurship: What everyone needs to know*. New York, NY: Oxford University Press, USA.

Bovaird, T. (2004). Public–private partnerships: From contested concepts to prevalent practice. *International Review of Administrative Sciences, 70*(2), 199-215. https://doi.org/10.1177/0020852304044250

Bryant, S. E. (2003). The role of transformational and transactional leadership in creating, sharing and exploiting organizational knowledge. *Journal of Leadership & Organizational Studies, 9*(4), 32-44. https://doi.org/10.1177/107179190300900403

Bull, M. (2008). Challenging tensions: Critical, theoretical and empirical perspectives on social enterprise. *International Journal of Entrepreneurial Behaviour & Research, 14*(5), 268-275. https://doi.org/10.1108/13552550810897641

Burns, J. M. (1978). *Leadership*. New York, NY: Harper & Row.

Burns, T. A., & Stalker, G. M. (1961). *The management of innovation*. London: Tavistock Publications.

Calhoun, C. (2000). Social change. In E. F. Borgatta & R. J. V. Montgomery (Eds.), *Encyclopedia of sociology* (2nd ed., Vol. 4, pp. 2641-2648). New York: Macmillan Reference.

Carpenter, M., Bauer, T., & Erdogan, B. (2010). *Principles of management*. Irvington, NY: Flatworld Knowledge.

Child, J., & Faulkner, D. (1998). *Strategies of cooperation: Managing alliances, networks and joint ventures*. London: Oxford University Press.

Clemmer, J. (1995). *Pathways to performance: A guide to transforming yourself, your team, and your organization*. Toronto, Canada: Clemmer Group.

Cleveland, H., & Jacobs, G. (1999). The genetic code for social development. In H. Cleveland, G. Jacobs, R. Macfarlane, R. v. Harten, & N. Asokan (Eds.), *Human choice: The genetic code for social development* (p. 7). Minneapolis, MN: World Academy of Art and Science.

Courtright, J. A., Fairhurst, G. T., & Rogers, L. E. (1989). Interaction patterns in organic and mechanistic systems. *The Academy of Management Journal, 32*(4), 773-802. https://doi.org/10.2307/256568

Cowan, R., David, P. A., & Foray, D. (2000). The explicit economics of knowledge codification and tacitness. *Industrial and Corporate Change, 9*(2), 211-253. https://doi.org/10.1093/icc/9.2.211

Daft, R. L., & Weick, K. E. (1984). Toward a model of organizations as interpretation systems. *The Academy of Management Review, 9*(2), 284-295. https://doi.org/10.2307/258441

Dart, R. (2004). The legitimacy of social enterprise. *Nonprofit Management and Leadership, 14*(4), 411-424. https://doi.org/10.1002/nml.43

Dees, J. G. (2001). *The meaning of "Social Entrepreneurship"*. Retrieved from https://entrepreneurship.duke.edu/news-item/the-meaning-of-social-entrepreneurship/

Dodgson, M. (1993). Organizational learning: A review of some literatures. *Organization Studies, 14*(3), 375-394. https://doi.org/10.1177/017084069301400303

Dörner, D. (1997). *The logic of failure: Recognizing and avoiding error in complex situations*. Basic Books.

Dyer, J. H., & Nobeoka, K. (2000). Creating and managing a high-performance knowledge-sharing network: The Toyota case. *Strategic Management Journal, 21*(3), 345-367.

Easterby-Smith, M., & Lyles, M. A. (2011). *Handbook of organizational learning and knowledge management* (2nd ed.). Chichester, West Sussex: Wiley.

Ensminger, J., & Knight, J. (1997). Changing social norms: Common property, bridewealth, and clan exogamy. *Current Anthropology, 38*(1), 1-24. https://doi.org/10.1086/204579

Fischer, F. (2012). Participatory governance: From theory to practice. In D. Levi-Faur (Ed.), *The Oxford handbook of governance* (pp. 457-471). Oxford, New York: Oxford University Press. https://doi.org/10.1093/oxfordhb/9780199560530.013.0032

Flick, U. (2002). *An introduction to qualitative research* (2nd ed.). Thousand Oaks, CA: Sage Publications.

Flick, U. (Ed.). (2014). *The Sage handbook of qualitative data analysis*. London, UK: Sage. https://doi.org/10.4135/9781446282243

Flood, R. L. (1999). *Rethinking the fifth discipline: Learning within the unknowable*. London: Routledge.

Galatsidas, A., & Sheehy, F. (2015, July 6). What have the millennium development goals achieved? *The Guardian*. Retrieved from https://www.theguardian.com/global-development/datablog/2015/jul/06/what-millennium-development-goals-achieved-mdgs

Glaser, B. G., & Strauss, A. L. (1967). *The discovery of grounded theory: Strategies for qualitative research*. Chicago: Aldine Publishing Company.

Government of India. (2012). *Report of the committee on unorganised sector statistics*. Retrieved from http://www.lmis.gov.in/sites/default/files/NSC-report-unorg-sector-statistics.pdf

Gustavsen, B. (1992). *Dialogue and development: Theory of communication, action research and the restructuring of working life*. Assen, Netherlands: Van Gorcum.

Helms, M. M. (2006). Organic organizations. In M. M. Helms (Ed.), *Encyclopedia of management* (5th ed., Vol. 1): Gale Cengage.

Hull, F., & Hage, J. (1982). Organizing for innovation: Beyond Burns and Stalker's organic type. *Sociology, 16*(4), 564-577. https://doi.org/10.1177/0038038582016004006

Hulme, D. (2008). The story of the Grameen Bank: From subsidised microcredit to market-based microfinance. *Brooks World Poverty Institute Working Paper* (60). https://doi.org/10.2139/ssrn.1300930

Isaacs, W. N. (1993). Taking flight: Dialogue, collective thinking, and organizational learning. *Organizational Dynamics, 22*(2), 24-39. https://doi.org/10.1016/0090-2616(93)90051-2

Isaacs, W. N. (2001). Toward an action theory of dialogue. *International Journal of Public Administration, 24*(7-8), 709-748. https://doi.org/10.1081/PAD-100104771

Jacobs, G., & Asokan, N. (1999). Towards a comprehensive theory of social development. In H. Cleveland, G. Jacobs, R. Macfarlane, R. v. Harten, & N. Asokan (Eds.), *Human choice: The genetic code for social development* (pp. 152). Minneapolis, MN: World Academy of Art and Science.

Jonassen, D. H., Beissner, K., & Yacci, M. (1993). *Structural knowledge: Techniques for representing, conveying, and acquiring structural knowledge*. Hillsdale, New Jersey: Lawrence Erlbaum.

Kabra, K. N. (2003). The unorganised sector in India: Some issues bearing on the search for alternatives. *Social Scientist, 31*(11/12), 23-46. https://doi.org/10.2307/3517948

Klein, J. T. (2010). A taxonomy of interdisciplinarity. In R. Frodeman, J. T. Kelin, & C. Mitcham (Eds.), *The Oxford handbook of interdisciplinarity*. Oxford, UK: Oxford University Press.

Lakoff, G., & Johnson, M. (1980). *Metaphors we live by*. Chicago, IL: University of Chicago Press.

Levitt, B., & March, J. G. (1988). Organizational learning. *Annual Review of Sociology, 14*, 319-340. https://doi.org/10.1146/annurev.so.14.080188.001535

Lewin, K. (1951). *Field theory in social science*. New York: Harper.

Maani, K. E., & Maharaj, V. (2004). Links between systems thinking and complex decision making. *System Dynamics Review, 20*(1), 21-48. https://doi.org/10.1002/sdr.281

Mair, J., & Martí, I. (2006). Social entrepreneurship research: A source of explanation, prediction, and delight. *Journal of World Business, 41*(1), 36-44. https://doi.org/10.1016/j.jwb.2005.09.002

Martin, R. L., & Osberg, S. R. (2007). Social entrepreneurship: The case for definition. *Stanford Social Innovation Review, Spring*, 29-39.

Martin, R. L., & Osberg, S. R. (2015). *Getting beyond better: How social entrepreneurship works.* Boston, MA: Harvard Business Review Press.

McCoy, D. L. (2014). *Remarkable leaders: Risk takers who dare us!* American Spirit Foundation.

Morgan, G. (2006). *Images of organization* (Updated ed.). Thousand Oaks: Sage Publications.

Nonaka, I. (1994). A dynamic theory of organizational knowledge creation. *Organization Science, 5*(1), 14-37. https://doi.org/10.1287/orsc.5.1.14

Nonaka, I., & Von Krogh, G. (2009). Perspective — Tacit knowledge and knowledge conversion: Controversy and advancement in organizational knowledge creation theory. *Organization Science, 20*(3), 635-652. https://doi.org/10.1287/orsc.1080.0412

Nowotny, H., Scott, P. B., & Gibbons, M. T. (2001). *Re-thinking science: Knowledge and the public in an age of uncertainty.* Cambridge: U: Polity Press.

Organizational learning. (n.d.), In *BusinessDictionary.com.* Retrieved from http://www.businessdictionary.com/definition/organizational-learning.html

Orloff, A. (2002). *Social Venture Partners Calgary: Emergence and early stages: A case study.* Canadian Centre for Social Entrepreneurship. Retrieved from https://www.ualberta.ca/business/-/media/business/centres/cccsr/ccse/documents/programs/research/svpcalgarycasestudy.pdf

Page, N., & Czuba, C. E. (1999). Empowerment: What is it? *Journal of Extension, 37*(5), 1-5.

Patterson, J. A. (2009). Organisational learning and leadership: On metaphor, meaning making, liminality and intercultural communication. *International Journal of Learning and Change, 3*(4), 382-393. https://doi.org/10.1504/IJLC.2009.026220

Peredo, A. M., & Chrisman, J. J. (2006). Toward a theory of community based enterprise. *Academy of Management Review, 31* 309-328.

Pierce, J. L., & Delbecq, A. L. (1977). Organization structure, individual attitudes and innovation. *Academy of Management Review, 2*(1), 27-37. https://doi.org/10.5465/AMR.2006.20208683

Rahman, A. (1999). *Women and microcredit in rural Bangladesh: Anthropological study of the rhetoric and realities of Grameen bank lending.* Boulder, Colo.: Westview Press.

Richardson, J. T. E. (Ed.) (1996). *Handbook of qualitative research methods for psychology and the social sciences.* Malden, MA: Blackwell Publishers.

Sakthivel, S., & Joddar, P. (2006). Unorganised sector workforce in India: Trends, patterns and social security coverage. *Economic and Political Weekly*, 2107-2114.

Sawyer, R. K. (2005). *Social emergence: Societies as complex systems*. Cambridge University Press. https://doi.org/10.1017/CBO9780511734892

Schein, E. H. (1990). Organizational culture. *American Psychologist, 45*(2), 109-119. http://doi.org/10.1037/0003-066X.45.2.109

Schein, E. H. (1993). On dialogue, culture, and organizational learning. *Organizational Dynamics, 22*(2), 40-51. https://doi.org/10.1016/0090-2616(93)90052-3

Schwab Foundation. (n.d.). *Schwab Foundation for Social Entrepreneurship*. Retrieved from http://www.schwabfound.org/sf/index.htm

Senge, P. M. (1993). *The fifth discipline: The art & practice of the learning organization*. New York, NY: Currency Doubleday.

Senge, P. M., Kleiner, A., Roberts, C., Ross, R. B., & Smith, B. J. (2010). *The fifth discipline fieldbook: Strategies and tools for building a learning organization*. New York: Nicholas Brealey Publishing.

Silbert, M. (1984). Delancey Street Foundation: A process of mutual restitution. In F. Reissman & A. Garrtner (Eds.), *Self-help revolution*. New York: Human Sciences Press Inc.

Sine, W. D., Mitsuhashi, H., & Kirsch, D. A. (2006). Revisiting Burns and Stalker: Formal structure and new venture performance in emerging economic sectors. *The Academy of Management Journal, 49*(1), 121-132. https://doi.org/10.5465/AMJ.2006.20785590

Skoll Foundation. (n.d.). *Connecting and celebrating social entrepreneurs*. Retrieved from http://www.skollfoundation.org/

Stefano, G. D., Gino, F., Pisano, G., & Staats, B. (2014). *Learning by thinking: How reflection aids performance*. Working Paper No. 14-093. Boston: Harvard Business School.

Stokols, D. (2018). *Social ecology in the digital age: Solving complex problems in a globalized world*. London: Elsevier Academic Press.

Strauss, A., & Corbin, J. (1990). *Basics of qualitative research: Grounded theory procedures and techniques*. Newbury Park: Sage.

TD Net. (2009). *Transdisciplinary research*. Retrieved from http://www.transdisciplinarity.ch/en/td-net/Transdisziplinarit-t.html

Thompson, J. L. (2002). The world of the social entrepreneur. *The International Journal of Public Sector Management, 15*(5), 412-431. https://doi.org/10.1108/09513550210435746

Trivedi, C. (2010). Towards a social ecological framework for social entrepreneurship. *Journal of Entrepreneurship, 19*(1), 63-80. https://doi.org/10.1177/097135570901900104

Trivedi, C. (2013). Social entrepreneurship: Ecological consciousness and collective processes. (Order No. 3563422, University of California, Irvine). *ProQuest Dissertations and Theses*, 232.

Trivedi, C., & Misra, S. (2015). Relevance of systems thinking and scientific holism to social entrepreneurship. *Journal of Entrepreneurship, 24*(1), 37-62. https://doi.org/10.1177/0971355714560658

Trivedi, C., & Stokols, D. (2011). Social enterprises and corporate enterprises: Fundamental differences and defining features *Journal of Entrepreneurship, 20*(1), 1-32. https://doi.org/10.1177/0971355714560658

UN News Center. (2013). *World toilet day: UN urges breaking taboos, making sanitation for all a global reality.* Retrieved from http://www.un.org/apps/news/story.asp?NewsID=46529

United Nations. (2015). *The Millennium Development Goals Report.* New York Retrieved from http://www.un.org/millenniumgoals/2015_MDG_Report/pdf/MDG%202015%20rev%20(July%201).pdf

United Nations Development Group. (2014). *Delivering the post-2015 development agenda: Opportunities at the national and local levels.* New York Retrieved from https://sustainabledevelopment.un.org/content/documents/1909UNDP-MDG-Delivering-Post-2015-Report-2014.pdf

Van de Ven, A. H. (1986). Central problems in the management of innovation. *Management Science, 32*(5), 590-607. https://doi.org/10.1287/mnsc.32.5.590

Verplanken, B., & Holland, R. W. (2002). Motivated decision making: Effects of activation and self-centrality of values on choices and behavior. *Journal of Personality and Social Psychology, 82*(3), 434-447. https://doi.org/10.1037/0022-3514.82.3.434

von Bertalanffy, L. (1950). The theory of open systems in physics and biology. *Science, 111*(2872), 23-29. https://doi.org/10.1126/science.111.2872.23

von Bertalanffy, L. (1952). *Problems of life.* London: Watts.

Waddock, S. A., & Post, J. E. (1991). Social entrepreneurs and catalytic change. *Public Administration Review, 51*(5), 393-401. https://doi.org/10.2307/976408

Wei-Skillern, J. C., Austin, J. E., Leonard, H. B., & Stevenson, H. H. (2007). *Entrepreneurship in the social sector.* Thousand Oaks, CA: Sage Publication.

Weick, K. E. (1987). Theorizing about organizational communication. In F. M. Jablin, L. L. Putnam, K. H. Roberts, & L. W. Porter (Eds.), *Handbook of organizational communication: An interdisciplinary perspective* (pp. 97-122). Newbury Park, CA: Sage Publications.

Weick, K. E. (1995). *Sensemaking in organizations.* Thousand Oaks: Sage Publications.

Weick, K. E., Sutcliffe, K. M., & Obstfeld, D. (2005). Organizing and the process of sensemaking. *Organization Science, 16*(4), 409-421. https://doi.org/10.1287/orsc.1050.0133

Wilson, P. A. (1996). Empowerment: Community economic development from the inside out. *Urban Studies, 33*(4-5), 617-630. https://doi.org/10.1080/00420989650011753

Yunus, M., & Jolis, A. (2007). *Banker to the poor: Micro-lending and the battle against world poverty.* New York: Public Affairs.

Gaetano R. Lotrecchiano & Shalini Misra (Editors). 2020
Communication in Transdisciplinary Teams
Santa Rosa, CA: Informing Science Press

Chapter 4:
A New Paradigm for Research Organization: Academic Leadership in Transdisciplinary Science Teams

Elina I. Mäkinen
Faculty of Management and Business, Tampere University, Finland
elina.makinen@tuni.fi

Chapter Objectives

- To create an understanding of the role of academic leaders in transdisciplinary science.
- To shed light on the challenges for transdisciplinary science in the context of new research collaborations.
- To assess leadership actions and activities from the perspective of complexity leadership theory.
- To demonstrate how leadership practices can lead to top-down rather than bottom-up knowledge creation processes.
- To emphasize the importance of placing knowledge brokers and hybrid researchers in strategic leadership positions at different organizational levels.

Introduction to the Chapter

Prior research has shown that leadership plays a key role in knowledge-producing organizations and their efforts to create innovative discoveries. Yet, we know very little of leadership in the context of transdisciplinary science. This chapter reports on a longitudinal qualitative case study where the author examined the kind of leadership roles and practices academic leaders draw on when seeking to promote emerging transdisciplinary collaboration in a complex adaptive system (Mäkinen, 2018a). Complex adaptive systems are places for actors to engage in knowledge-intensive cooperation in a collaborative network that has a common goal (e.g., Hazy, 2007; Marion & Uhl-Bien, 2001; Uhl-Bien, Marion & McKelvey, 2007). Transdisciplinary research organizations are like complex adaptive systems, because they bring together actors from varied backgrounds, promote interdependence among them, and form dynamic collectives with common goals (Cilliers, 1998; Lotrecchiano, 2010; Marion, 1999).

The empirical analysis presented in this chapter shows how academic leaders addressed these kinds of challenges and supported transdisciplinary collaboration in a newly formed transdisciplinary research organization. The research center was formed through a partnership between a School of Medicine and a non-profit foundation. It brought together physicians, medical researchers, and scientists from different fields to study a specific problem,

An earlier version of this chapter was published as Mäkinen, E. I. (2018). Complexity leadership theory and the leaders of transdisciplinary science. *Informing Science: the International Journal of an Emerging Transdiscipline, 21,* 133-155. https://doi.org/10.28945/4009

premature birth. Despite decades of research on premature birth, the problem remains unsolved. Premature birth is an adaptive challenge: solving it requires new learning, innovation, and new patterns of behavior (Heifetz, 1994; Heifetz & Linsky, 2002).

This chapter focuses on analyzing the role of the leaders of transdisciplinary science. The findings demonstrate that when it comes to attracting researchers from different disciplinary backgrounds to advance knowledge on a single research problem collaboratively, the leaders of transdisciplinary science must rely on different leadership roles and practices. The leaders first drew on practices related to enabling leadership: they modelled transdisciplinary behavior and took on roles as knowledge translators and brokers (Hazy & Uhl-Bien, 2013, Uhl-Bien et al., 2007; Mäkinen, Evans, & McFarland, 2019). While brokering and bridging practices often support innovation (Lomas, 2007; Ward, House, & Hamer, 2009; Waring, Currie, Crompton, & Bishop, 2013), these activities began to reinforce administrative leadership and made the leaders the focal point of transdisciplinary knowledge integration. This hindered the creation of shared adaptive dynamics.

Background

Transdisciplinary research collaborations have developed at such an increasing rate that researchers interested in how they should be managed have had a difficult time keeping up. Transdisciplinary science aims at solving complex problems, crossing disciplinary boundaries, including different stakeholders in the research process, and enhancing the practical value of findings (Klein, 2014; Maasen & Lieven, 2006). The multidisciplinary, collaborative, and multi-organizational nature of transdisciplinary research calls for academic leadership that is able to nurture collaboration across different kinds of knowledge boundaries (Shrum, Genuth, & Chompalov, 2007; Sonnenwald, 2007).

In the context of non-academic organizations, leadership researchers have declared that the relationships between leaders and organizational members matter for how organizations perform (Barge & Musambira, 1992). Moreover, both theoretical and empirical contributions in leadership research have demonstrated that leadership plays a key role in knowledge creation processes in non-academic organizations (Bryant, 2003; Lakshman, 2007; Politis, 2002; Srivastava, Bartol, & Locke, 2006). Yet, the role of leaders in institutions of higher education has attracted little empirical attention (Bryman, 2007).

Those leading transdisciplinary research in academic contexts face particular challenges. First, cross-disciplinary research units are different from discipline-based departments. Biancani, McFarland, and Dahlander (2014) defined interdisciplinary research centers as semiformal organizations that are temporary and fluid, and where participation is voluntary. The authors argued that university departments, in comparison, are formal units where organizational memberships are assigned as a term of employment. These disciplinary and departmental communities offer their members safety, familiarity, and a clear understanding of academic norms (Abbott, 2001). Instead, transdisciplinary collaboration requires that scholars view knowledge creation beyond their disciplinary units and consider the goals of a broader knowledge system (Klein, 1990). Therefore, leaders of transdisciplinary science have to attract scholars from departmental to transdisciplinary units and support their voluntary participation in the shared, transdisciplinary research endeavor.

Challenge 1: Promoting participation	**Example:** Schmidt and Pröpper (2017) studied an international multi-institutional collaboration dealing with sustainable land management in Angola, Botswana, and Namibia. Participation in the transdisciplinary effort, team-building, and generation of shared goals were challenged by varied incentive structures, roles, and responsibilities in the participants' home institutions.

Once leaders of transdisciplinary science have succeeded in attracting talented scholars across departments, they face another leadership challenge: how to motivate scholars to interact across disciplinary boundaries. Some have conceptualized this challenge as one of cognitive incommensurability (Cummings & Kiesler, 2005; Dougherty, 1992; Lamont, 2009; Murray, 2010). Collaborators' different disciplinary orientations, motivations, and professional interests can come in the way of collaboration. These challenges are highlighted in transdisciplinary science, because it brings together not only academics from different disciplines, but also non-academic actors, such as practitioners, policymakers, and industry representatives, who all have their own reasons to participate (Klein, 2014; Maasen & Lieven, 2006).

Challenge 2: Communication across fields and interests	**Example:** A study by Suldovsky, McGreavy, and Lindenfeld (2018) analyzed communication in the context of a transdisciplinary project focusing on strengthening decision making for beach and shellfish flat management in Maine and New Hampshire. Collaborative communication was challenging, if not impossible, due to the collaborators' internalized epistemic authority of particular forms of knowledge production.

As a third challenge, after researchers are in place and collaborating in the transdisciplinary research organization, leaders of transdisciplinary science have to manage the tension between the need to innovate and the need to produce (Uhl-Bien & Arena, 2018). In order to survive, complex adaptive systems, such as transdisciplinary research organizations, have to produce innovative knowledge rapidly (Uhl-Bien et al., 2007). The creation of innovative outcomes requires risk taking, experimentation, and play (March, 1991). This can create a tension in a transdisciplinary research organization, because the familiar disciplinary research approach may appear as a faster path to productivity (Mäkinen et al., 2019). In relation to their work on leadership and organizational adaptability, Uhl-Bien and Arena (2018) have noted that it is important not to let "the pressure to produce overwhelm the need to innovate" (p. 11). Leaders of transdisciplinary science, then, need to make sure that scholars do not fall back on their disciplinary ways of creating knowledge when there is pressure to produce outcomes.

Challenge 3: Producing transdisciplinary outcomes	**Example:** Pohl (2005) studied two transdisciplinary environmental research programs that sought to promote collaboration between social and natural scientists. The pressure to produce results led to a division of labor among the social and natural scientists, where they remained in and took responsibility for their own disciplinary areas, instead of engaging in transdisciplinary collaboration.

The next section gives an overview of the complexity leadership theory. It is followed by a description of the empirical setting, data collection, and data analysis. When reporting on findings from the longitudinal qualitative case study, I explain the different roles and practices the leaders relied on when mobilizing transdisciplinary collaboration and seeking to overcome the previously discussed challenges (Mäkinen, 2018a). Finally, the chapter concludes with a discussion on what complexity leadership theory can add to our understanding of transdisciplinary science and the role of academic leaders.

Conceptualizing Leadership in Transdisciplinary Science

Organizations focusing on knowledge-intensive work and outcomes operate in an increasingly fast-paced environment, where traditional leadership models, often bureaucratic and centralized in nature, are insufficient (Marion & Uhl-Bien, 2001; Schneider & Somers, 2006). Scholars have questioned the extent to which traditional leadership models can support modern organizations, where the main purpose is to create innovative products by combining the expertise of different individuals. As a result, leadership researchers have begun to consider leadership as practices distributed throughout the organization rather than as actions of a few leaders at the top-level of the organization (Hargadon, 2003; Pearce & Sims, 2000; Yukl, 2005). Figure 1 demonstrates the changes in leadership models over the course of the last century (Lotrecchiano, 2019). Instead of leader-centrism, leadership models have become aligned with systems thinking. The new theories also emphasize a relational kind of leadership that focuses on dynamic and interactive social processes occurring throughout the organization (Drath, 2001; Uhl-Bien, 2006).

Building on this work, scholars have developed new conceptualizations of leadership that are grounded in complexity theory (Hazy, 2007; Lichtenstein et al., 2006; Marion & Uhl-Bien, 2001; Uhl-Bien et al., 2007). Complexity leadership theory emerged from the idea that a nuanced understanding of leadership in the Knowledge Era is needed (Marion & Uhl-Bien, 2001). In such a context, leadership is dynamically evolving, emergent, and distributed (Bolden, 2011; Dervitsiotis, 2005). Uhl-Bien et al. (2007) defined the complexity leadership theory model as "connective, distributed, dynamic, and contextual" (p. 302). The purpose of this research has been to understand what leadership means in knowledge-intensive complex adaptive systems, where individuals collaborate and share a common goal.

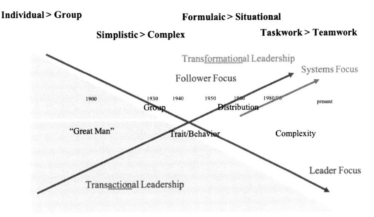

Figure 1. Typology of Leadership Models in the Twentieth Century: From Leader-Centrism to Systems-Centrism (Lotrecchiano, 2019)

Complexity Leadership Theory: Roles and Practices

Complexity leadership theory perceives leadership as an interplay between many forces: administrative, enabling, and adaptive leadership (Marion & Uhl-Bien, 2001; Uhl-Bien et al., 2007). In order to create effective adaptive dynamics—*that is, the generation of creative knowledge, that exhibits significance and impact*—finding a balance between different leadership roles is important.

Administrative leadership resembles the traditional, bureaucratic, and hierarchical type of leadership (Uhl-Bien et al., 2007). It includes practices such as building vision, implementing strategy, and assigning work responsibilities (Hazy & Uhl-Bien, 2013). While these are often seen as strategies for building stable organizations, complexity leadership theory recognizes their importance for creating managed chaos (Nag, Corley, & Gioia, 2007; Uhl-Bien & Marion, 2009). After all, the goal is not to spin out of control, but to stimulate innovation and creativity in a way that is in line with the mission of the organization (Dess & Picken, 2000). More recently, Uhl-Bien and Arena (2018) have argued that administrative leadership should be relabeled as operational leadership, which focuses on how formal leaders enable the production of results through selection, execution, and efficiency.

Enabling leadership operates between administrative and adaptive leadership and it draws attention to the ways in which leaders can structure conditions that are optimal for problem-solving, adaptability, and new learning (Uhl-Bien and Marion, 2009; Uhl-Bien et al., 2007). It involves building an environment where diversity is appreciated and work groups are structured to enable interaction and collaboration. Enabling leaders are individuals who adopt behaviors for enhancing interactive and adaptive dynamics (Uhl-Bien & Arena, 2018). They can act as brokers who bring individuals, ideas, and resources together and support exchange of information (Arena, Cross, Sims, & Uhl-Bien, 2017; Uhl-Bien & Arena, 2018). They also monitor the organization to better understand the different forces influencing the emerging adaptive dynamics.

Adaptive leadership is a complex dynamic rather than a role assigned to a person. It is an interactive type of leadership and it underlies emergent change activities. Ultimately, all heterogeneous knowledge-producing organizations should strive for adaptive dynamics and adaptive leadership. As the authors noted (Uhl-Bien et al., 2007), "adaptive change is produced by the clash of existing but (seemingly) incompatible ideas, knowledge, and technologies; it takes the form of new knowledge and creative ideas, learning, or adaptation" (p. 307). Later Uhl-Bien and Arena (2018) suggested that perhaps a better label for adaptive leadership was entrepreneurial leadership, which emphasizes the creation of new knowledge, skills, products, and processes in order to sustain the organization's success.

Table 1. Leadership Skills and Competencies

Administrative Leadership	Enabling Leadership	Adaptive Leadership
Vision, strategy, and distribution of work tasks.	Brokering people, knowledge, and resources.	Promotion of a complex dynamic for creativity.
Skills and Competencies		
Goal setting in a changing context (Entin & Serfaty, 1999) Understanding differences in knowledge production across disciplines (Cilliers, 2013) Openness to rearranging collaborative arrangements (Balsiger, 2004).	Communication, dialogue, and learning (Eigenbrode et al., 2007; Suldovsky et al., 2018) Translation of knowledge across disciplines (Colditz, Wolin, & Gehlert, 2012).	Interpersonal conflict and change management (Lotrecchiano & Misra, 2018).

Table 1 summarizes the three different leadership roles and provides a list of skills and competencies needed in each role. Complexity leadership theory suggests that by mobilizing enabling leadership, it is possible to find an optimal balance between administrative and adaptive forces. While administrative, enabling, and adaptive leadership roles are distinct, they are all simultaneously present, entangled, and interdependent when leaders seek to facilitate innovation (Kontopoulos, 1993; Uhl-Bien et al., 2007).

Connecting Activities

Complexity leadership theory highlights the importance of connecting activities that can link ideas, information, people, resources, and technology in ways that scale novelty and innovation (Uhl-Bien & Arena, 2018). Connecting activities are typically associated with enabling leadership. These activities may include knowledge brokering, joint training opportunities, and shared decision-making. Connecting activities are critical in the facilitation of adaptability and change in knowledge-intensive organizations (Arena et al., 2017; Taylor & Helfat, 2009; Uhl-Bien & Arena, 2018).

Indeed, knowledge brokering and bridging have been shown to foster learning and innovation in different professional contexts, for instance in healthcare (Lomas, 2007; Ward et al., 2009; Waring et al., 2013). While boundary spanning in collaborative knowledge work is known to be important, it has also been shown to be difficult to accomplish (Bechky, 2003; Haas, 2006; Huising, 2014; Kellogg, 2014; Majchrzak, More, & Faraj, 2012). In transdisciplinary contexts, a significant challenge is that the number of different boundaries is relatively high as collaborators come from, for example, academia, industry, and policy sectors. Furthermore, no matter which sector they come from, individuals have varying capabilities to facilitate boundary-crossing (Lotrecchiano, 2010; Lotrecchiano, 2014; Uhl-Bien et al., 2007).

In relation to these challenges, Uhl-Bien and Arena (2018) have noted that in complex adaptive systems connections will co-occur with conflicts. Conflicts are inevitable, but they can be productive if leaders simultaneously help individuals connect across differences and link up around adaptive responses (Arena et al., 2017). Both adaptive and enabling leadership play a role in how conflicts are managed. According to Lotrecchiano (2010), adaptive leadership strives to develop collaborators' conflicting perspectives into resolute outcomes. Enabling leadership, in turn, fosters interactions and interdependency and in this way supports the interactive and adaptive dynamics of complex systems.

Methodology

The findings presented in this chapter are based on a longitudinal qualitative research project on a new transdisciplinary research center in the field of medicine. The center was located in a research university in the United States. It was formed through a partnership between the university's School of Medicine and a non-profit foundation that wanted to fund research directed at solving and reducing premature birth. Senior scholars from the School of Medicine—who later became the center's leadership team—wrote a research proposal to form a transdisciplinary research center focusing on premature birth.

The center's mission was to create new knowledge about premature birth through a transdisciplinary team science approach. The goal was to study and understand what leads to premature birth and ultimately translate this research into clinical interventions and policy changes. The organizational setup included four transdisciplinary research teams and a leadership team, which all contributed to the center's research activities. Each of the research teams had a methodological focus based on the team leader's previous research, but the participants of the transdisciplinary teams came from different disciplines. The four research teams focused on 1) understanding the role of the placenta in premature birth, 2) identifying temporal and geographical premature birth patterns, 3) finding biomarkers associated with premature birth related diseases, and 4) uncovering the role of microbial communities in cases of premature birth (see Mäkinen, 2018b; Mäkinen, 2019).

In addition to the meeting data, the five leaders and the administrator were interviewed at two different time points: when the center was formed and two years after. On both rounds, interviews were conducted based on a semi-structured interview protocol. While each interviewee was asked the same general questions, there was flexibility in how the varied issues they brought up were discussed in more detail. In practice, the interviewer asked different kinds of follow-up questions depending on how the informants responded to the planned questions (Corbin & Strauss, 2015).

The interview protocol for the first round of interviews focused on how the transdisciplinary research center was planned and formed. For example, the protocol included the following questions:

- What is your role in the premature birth center? How do you envision enacting this role in the center?
- What led you to current research on premature birth?
- What the teams' and their members' roles are? What are they expected to do?
- Are there things researchers seem to agree on? What do they disagree on?
- Can you describe some concrete ways in which the research will get translated into medical practice?

The interview protocol for the second round of interviews was concerned with how the center had evolved during the first two years, what kind of scientific progress had been made, what transdisciplinary science looked like in practice, and what challenges the leaders had experienced since the formation of the center. The interview protocol included questions such as:

- How have you experienced the past couple of years that you have been part of the center?
- How would you describe your current tasks and responsibilities in the center?
- How have your responsibilities changed during the past two years?
- How has the center changed during the past couple of years?
- How and where do you interact with members of the center?
- How have you experienced the regularly organized meetings?

A team of social scientists, which the author was part of, collected data on the center for almost three years since its formation. The team observed and recorded all of the meetings the center organized during this time. These meetings related to the center's varied research activities (e.g., work of the four research teams, center leadership team, and data collection efforts). A detailed description of the longitudinal data collection effort on the new transdisciplinary research center can be found in the author's article "Complexity Leadership Theory and the Leaders of Transdisciplinary Science" (Mäkinen, 2018a). In what follows, I briefly describe the four transdisciplinary teams and then explain how data on the center's leadership team was collected and analyzed.

Data collection on the leadership meetings started in August 2011 and continued until November 2014. During this time, 128 leadership meetings, each lasting an hour, were observed. In the meetings, the leaders were gathered around an oval-shaped table in a seminar room at the School of Medicine. When observing the meetings, the author sat around the same table taking notes, but without participating in the conversations. The author used her laptop to jot down and write up observations from the leaders' meeting interactions and conversations (Emerson, Fretz, & Shaw, 1995). In addition to note taking, there was permission to record the meeting discussions. These recordings were extremely helpful during the analytical stage as they allowed for double-checking that the content of discussions was understood correctly.

Transdisciplinary Research Teams

The center had four transdisciplinary research teams: placenta team, premature birth pattern team, bioinformatics team, and microbiome team. The placenta team studied the role of placental cells in premature birth and focused on cases of placental failure. The team leader was a geneticist and his main collaborators came from the fields of genetics, OB-GYN, and pathology. Funding for the project was cut after the first year and the reasons for this outcome are analyzed elsewhere (Mäkinen, 2019). The premature birth pattern team identified geographical and temporal premature birth trends in the United States birth record dataset by using cluster analysis approaches. The team was led by a computer scientist and the team members included statisticians, epidemiologists, and clinicians and medical researchers from OB-GYN, neonatology, and pediatrics. The bioinformatics team studied which biological markers were associated with pregnancy related diseases. The team was led by a bioinformatician and most of the project's analytical work was done by bioinformaticians. However, there were also clinicians and medical researchers from OB-GYN and pediatrics who regularly attended meetings and contributed to the project. Finally, the microbiome team explored how changes in the mothers' microbial communities over the course of pregnancy contributed to premature birth (see Mäkinen, 2018b). The team was led by a microbiologist and its members included scientists from microbiology, immunology, and epidemiology. The center's leadership team consisted of five senior academics (all male) and one administrator (female). The academics represented different medical and scientific fields. They were tenured and established scholars in neonatology, pediatrics, OB-GYN, and epidemiology.

Because the transdisciplinary research center did not have its own building, meetings organized regularly for each of the previously described transdisciplinary research teams became an important strategy for supporting collaboration across disciplines (see Mäkinen et al., 2019). The meetings were opportunities for interaction as well as contexts for influencing how researchers should behave as members of the new transdisciplinary research organization.

The leaders had certain objectives for jumpstarting transdisciplinary collaboration in the center. First, it was essential to create a context for transdisciplinary conversations that went beyond the established lines of research that had dominated premature birth investigation for decades. Second, the shared team meetings were seen as the most likely context in which transdisciplinary interactions would take place. As the leaders participated in the team meetings, they allowed the leaders to monitor how transdisciplinary collaboration was progressing and use different leadership roles and practices to promote the creation of adaptive dynamics.

In an effort to exchange ideas and plan the center's activities, the leaders organized weekly meetings also for their own group. In these meetings, the leaders discussed issues relating to the management of the center. In their leader roles, they were responsible for a number of things, such as, making sure scientific progress was made, identifying and attracting new talents into the teams, fundraising, preparing annual progress reports, and determining annual research budgets.

Analytical Approach to Meeting and Interview Data

The analysis of the previously described meeting and interview data was motivated by the theoretical and empirical observation that leadership plays an important role in knowledge creation processes (Bryant, 2003; Lakshman, 2007; Politis, 2002; Srivastava et al., 2006). The author developed analytical codes that aligned with complexity leadership framework for uncovering how the leaders of transdisciplinary science mobilized and managed adaptive dynamics.

The analysis of ethnographic field notes from leadership meetings and interviews with the leaders consisted of two stages that can be characterized as initial and focused coding (Lofland & Lofland, 1995). During the initial coding stage, the author went through the 128 leadership meetings in chronological order and searched for evidence for different kind of leadership practices aimed at promoting transdisciplinary collaboration. These initial codes were defined, for example, as leadership practices aimed at developing a shared understanding of the problem of premature birth, engaging members in transdisciplinary conversations, and encouraging passive researchers to participate in research collaborations.

Before moving to the stage of focused coding, the author reviewed literature on leadership in knowledge-intensive organizations and used this prior research to make sense of the initial codes. This analytical stage required a modified grounded theory approach of comparison and contrast, where the initial codes were compared against the complexity leadership theory framework (Strauss & Corbin, 1990). Through an iterative process of reading literature and going through the initial codes, the author became convinced that the complexity leadership theory provided a useful framework for structuring the analytical coding of meeting observations even further. The leadership roles—administrative, enabling, and adaptive—and their related practices thus provided a set of focused codes for winnowing out less useful initial codes and focusing in on a selected number of themes (Lofland & Lofland, 1995; Uhl-Bien et al., 2007). This analytical process involved the identification of the three leadership roles and then connecting them with leadership practices present in the data (e.g., modelling transdisciplinary behavior, translation, brokering) (Uhl-Bien et al., 2007; Uhl-Bien & Arena, 2018).

Next, I present the empirical findings. I draw on meeting observations and quotes from interviews with members of the leadership team. When we began data collection, leaders were assigned identity numbers, which can be seen after each quote (e.g., ID-29).

Creating Adaptive Dynamics

When creating a context for transdisciplinary collaboration, the leaders emphasized the need to generate innovative ideas about premature birth that were different from existing lines of research. While the leaders thought it was important to have premature birth experts in the center, they also wanted to make sure that new research paths were emerging. Researchers who had no experience with premature birth, but were included based on their analytical skills, were particularly important for achieving this goal. They could develop unexplored hypotheses about the health problem. They would help in making sure that the transdisciplinary center created new and innovative discoveries rather than produced traditional research outcomes due to the pressure to produce (Uhl-Bien & Arena, 2018).

Adaptive dynamics emerge from a given interactive context characterized by complex social dynamics and patterns of behavior that have the power to generate innovative outcomes (Uhl-Bien et al., 2007). In the new transdisciplinary research center, the interactive context can be understood as the previously described shared weekly meetings, where members of the center came together to discuss research projects. In these meetings, researchers interacted, exchanged knowledge, and sought to produce transformative outcomes relating to premature birth.

Shared Meetings as a Context for Adaptive Dynamics

Immediately after the center was launched, premature birth experts, who had spent their careers researching and taking care of pregnant women and premature babies, dominated the project meeting conversations. The threat of falling back on creating knowledge through disciplinary approaches was real. One leader said, "It's easier to fall back into a traditional mold and do studies that look a lot like all the studies we've done before in our careers, and so it gives us the semblance of the perception of progress, of success because we're publishing" [ID-29]. Connected to this, the leaders felt the meeting conversations were focused on what was already known about the health problem:

> They understand the problem according to the current paradigms. We don't know whether—well, the current paradigms have not been yielding with respect to solving the problem, right? We are missing something. That's why having a disposition that's focused on transdisciplinary discovery is so important. We want people to be open to new paradigms that would actually completely change the way you think about pre-term birth…It's changing the paradigm that's really important in research to solving these kinds of problems. Until you change the paradigm and know the new rules and new operations, you can't solve the problem; you just spin within the existing paradigm. [ID-27]

For transdisciplinary discovery to be successful, the leader thought it was important to separate the center's work from the current paradigms. To resist the influence of established lines of research, the leader emphasized that the center needed researchers who were "open to new paradigms." In fact, the leaders hoped that researchers would be able to internalize foreign research approaches to the extent that they would become unrecognizable to their home disciplines:

> We want people to think beyond where they are routinely thinking. If [name of an epidemiologist] has never dealt with a biological question in the signaling pathway, we would want him to do that more often, ultimately. Same for [name of a pediatrician]. If I'm not used to dealing with the way they think, then I want to do that—I do enough of that, actually. I'm learning about their fields. Pretty soon, if you met me for the first time, you would think I might be an epidemiologist or something, but I'm not. That's sort of where we are headed is that I would be able to have multiple cloaks, and so would they, have multiple cloaks. What we are hoping is that the students who are in these environments will naturally wear multiple cloaks. [ID-27]

This leader used himself as an example. He said he was not initially familiar with epidemiology, but increasingly, due to his interactions and collaborations with an epidemiologist, an outsider would have a difficult time identifying his disciplinary background. The leaders wanted everyone in the center to experience this transformation and to become hybrid researchers able to "wear multiple cloaks."

However, in order to initiate the process where existing expertise was broken down, rearranged, and recombined to generate something different, the meeting participants had to begin to interact. One leader said that the challenge they were facing was how to connect different researchers' mental frameworks:

> It is how you look at a problem. I think that what we are dealing with are different mental frameworks. The difficulty is how to appreciate what another person's mental framework would look like and how to get it to relate to your mental framework. [ID-8]

This cognitive incommensurability can prevent collaboration across knowledge boundaries (Cummings & Kiesler, 2005; Dougherty, 1992; Lamont, 2009; Murray, 2010). While in the context of the transdisciplinary research center there were multiple knowledge boundaries that needed to be crossed, the most challenging boundary was the one between premature birth experts and researchers with no prior experience with the health condition:

> The science gets deep for them [practitioners] pretty fast. They probably understand some of it but not all of it, and maybe not enough to really react to what people are saying, and the reverse is certainly true. We have basic scientists in the room who really know very little about pregnancy and premature birth. [ID-23]

When planning the transdisciplinary research effort, the leaders emphasized the importance of creating a new paradigm for premature birth research, which required learning from others and valuing their research approaches. These kinds of adaptive goals called for enabling leadership practices, which could promote interactions, interdependency, and adaptive tension (Uhl-Bien et al., 2007).

Enabling Leadership Practices

Complexity leadership theorists argue that enabling leadership practices are necessary for creating, protecting, and maintaining a space for adaptive dynamics (Uhl-Bien & Arena, 2018). In order to create an environment where physicians, medical researchers, and scientists from different backgrounds could engage in learning and collaboration, the leaders of transdisciplinary science wanted to develop strategies for easing the crossing of knowledge boundaries. The leaders used modelling of transdisciplinary behavior and knowledge translation and brokering as their main enabling leadership practices.

Modelling Transdisciplinary Behavior

The leaders promoted transdisciplinary learning and collaboration by modelling transdisciplinary behavior. They hoped that this enabling leadership practice would build researchers' confidence towards independently taking part in transdisciplinary interactions. The shared meetings were the best opportunity to influence the behavior of everyone involved with the center. The leaders believed that demonstrating how to interact in a transdisciplinary environment was important for those who came from a science background.

> Traditionally, in medical science and sciences…the expression is that the more you can be expert at some tiny little field, the more likely you are to be very successful. Also, I think that the more you can present stuff that people can't understand, the more points you seem to get. If you can do a terrific presentation so that people know that you know what you're talking about, but they don't understand half of what you're saying, then that really builds your thing. [ID-8]

In a transdisciplinary environment, scientists had to demonstrate their expertise differently from the previous interviewee's description of typical seminar or conference behavior. The leaders were in a good position to demonstrate openness to new areas of knowledge to the other members of the organization. They were all established and respected scholars in their fields, so crossing disciplinary boundaries was not as risky for them as it was for junior researchers. For example, one leader was particularly effective in demonstrating to researchers how to interact across disciplinary boundaries. He acted as a sort of rebellious academic and thought out loud ideas that many perceived as nontraditional.

> I'm trying to push the envelope, so by example saying look, I'm willing to say stuff that maybe is outrageous and maybe it can stimulate something. Other people may be more timid about saying things that they feel might make them look non-expert or look foolish or something like that. Part of it, maybe they are not trained to do that, to make those jumps. [ID-8]

By being active in the meeting settings and expressing untraditional ideas, the leader hoped he could support intellectual risk taking in others. Risk taking, experimentation, flexibility, and play are crucial activities in complex adaptive systems and they can be promoted through enabling leadership (March, 1991; Uhl-Bien & Arena, 2018).

Leaders noted that even after their efforts to model transdisciplinary behavior, the senior researchers engaged in transdisciplinary discussion more often than the junior researchers did. Senior researchers seemed to be more at ease in transdisciplinary meetings. Of course, from the perspective of academic careers, the tenured senior scholars had less to lose.

> I think it is the more senior people who talk comfortably to each other, but it is sort of like demonstrating. It is sort of like showing—it is like kids watching their parents. The kids are modeling. If the scientists are modeling their interactions, in a way, then I think the students learn that that's the way it should be done. That's where you are going to get productivity. It's okay, actually, to ask these questions. 'Look at my mentor getting quizzed by [name of a senior scholar] and [name of a senior scholar]', you know? Or, 'Look at my mentor asking a question back to them which is getting them to say something that we don't really think about.' Once they get used to that, then it will be easier for the next generation to do these things, I think. It is modeling. [ID-27]

Although this modelling did not engage everyone in transdisciplinary conversation, this leader was not concerned. He perceived it as seniors modelling transdisciplinary interactions to juniors, like "kids watching their parents." Over time, the junior scholars would learn to participate in transdisciplinary thinking, ask questions, and share their expertise.

Knowledge Translation and Brokering

Over the course of several months, the leaders came to realize that modelling transdisciplinary behavior was not enough for initiating learning and collaboration within the center. One leader said they had to continue to guide and manipulate collaborative interactions: "Transdisciplinary discussion has not evolved spontaneously. A little bit, but I think it really still requires a lot of manipulation or guidance" [ID-8]. Therefore, the leaders began to rely on another enabling leadership practice: knowledge translation and brokering. Arena and Uhl-Bien (2016) have pointed out that enabling leaders can establish adaptive space by brokering and bringing individuals together. In the transdisciplinary research organization, the shared meetings brought members of the center together physically, but knowledge translation and brokering were needed to connect actors intellectually. The leaders practiced these connecting activities both in and outside of meetings.

One-on-one interactions between a leader and a member of the transdisciplinary research community were important when the center was formed and nobody knew each other, or when new researchers joined the effort. These interactions allowed the leaders to get to know the specific researchers and get a sense of what their expertise was like. Consequently, they could make plans for how to integrate a researcher with particular expertise to on-going research projects. Once the leader understood what the researcher was able to do, he could translate this expertise to the other members of the center. One leader explained how he approached a researcher who had recently joined the center:

> Like, I asked [name of a scientist], I said, 'Tell me what you are doing in more detail, like a paragraph,' so he sent it to me. I have that; no one else has that yet. I had a sense of what he was doing from what he told me, and I said, 'Well, do you have papers that you have published?' 'No.' I said, 'Well, then, tell me yourself, in your own words, in about a paragraph what you do.' I will take that and I will then massage that in a way that begins to make sense to other people. I will translate what he is doing in-to their worlds. [ID-27]

This example demonstrates the work the leaders did as translators. First, the leader familiarized himself with the work of the researcher, and then introduced his work to others whose projects might benefit from the new researcher's input. The leader invited the researcher to attend project meetings, supported his presence in the meeting, and suggested ways in which he could contribute.

The translation work continued in every interaction the leader had with members of the center. He wanted to understand how the researchers approached research problems and then tried to guide them to think in new ways. This practice relates to "injecting tension into the system," which is one strategy for opening up the adaptive space (Uhl-Bien & Arena, 2018, p. 11). The leader had to do this delicately so as not to create too much tension and conflict between differing perspectives.

> When I interact with people, I want to know what they are thinking about. I will ask them questions like, 'How do you think that relates to such-and-such?' and then let them think out loud about it. If they are comfortable, they

will think about it. They may not necessarily say, 'Well, I have got a bit of an idea.' Instead, I will say, 'Well, did you ever think about this?' and then they will say, 'Hmm, interesting' and it goes from there. [ID-27]

While in the shared meetings, researchers' different ways of doing research and thinking about premature birth sometimes clashed, the one-on-one conversations between a leader and a researcher had a different tone. The leader did not challenge the researcher's work, but instead expressed interest in it and suggested new ways of approaching it. In a similar manner to how the leaders modelled transdisciplinary behavior in shared meetings, this leader demonstrated how researchers from different backgrounds could interact without too much confrontation.

In addition to this behind the scenes translation work, the leaders acted as knowledge brokers. Uhl-Bien and Arena (2018, p. 12) have noted that "connecting involves linking up agents (i.e., ideas, information, people, resources, technology) in ways that scale novelty and innovation into beneficial new order in the operational system." In line with this, the leaders developed brokering tactics to connect the different individuals and their perspectives.

The challenge was that, while in private conversations the leaders could motivate researchers to talk about their work, in the shared meetings many researchers became silent. This was because in the heterogeneous project meetings the conversation could go in multiple directions and include topics a researcher was not familiar with. As this leader described: "You just talk to people about the things that they are good at doing, then they will talk about them easily. If you talk about things they don't do on a regular basis, they don't talk" [ID-27]. As such, the leaders sought to first activate individuals who were more silent in order to make sure that different perspectives were heard. This was easier when the leaders were leading the meeting. This leader described his own role:

> I saw my role as to try to at least foster transdisciplinary discussion around whatever we were doing. I tried, and this has evolved over time, to provoke transdisciplinary discussion either by calling on people or asking questions or to try to get people involved to get the transdisciplinary perspective. [ID-8]

When heading the meeting, the leader relied on tactics such as calling on people and asking them questions. In this way, the meeting conversations included more perspectives. The next step was to connect different individuals or groups at a concrete level.

> I see that as an important role, trying to promote transdisciplinary thought and trying to get people linked up. Often I will try to suggest that maybe two projects that are doing things that are different, but could combine them, would actually work together or at least to think something out. That's just starting to emerge. I have been trying to do that for a long time, but I think it's finally starting to come together…I think that building a transdisciplinary team takes a long time. [ID-8]

The leader paid attention to everyone present in the project meetings he led. He made sure participants were active and made connections with others in the room.

The statement that transdisciplinary thought was "just starting to emerge"—made two years after the formation of the center—highlights how much time and effort the leaders had to put into mobilizing new transdisciplinary research collaborations. While the discussed enabling leadership practices were critical for promoting transdisciplinary collaboration, their benefits did not materialize right away.

Administrative Leadership and the Management of Transdisciplinary Science

The described enabling leadership practices were crucial for jumpstarting learning and collaboration, but demanded that the leaders take a central role in the management of transdisciplinary science. When the leaders brokered researchers and projects, they identified promising projects, decided on how research resources were used, and provided roles for collaborators. In complexity leadership theory, these practices are associated with administrative leadership (Uhl-Bien et al., 2007; Uhl-Bien & Arena, 2018). This section discusses the delicate relationship between different leadership roles and suggests that an imbalance in this relationship can prevent some actors from contributing to research collaborations and can jeopardize the creation of adaptive dynamics.

Enabling leadership practices began to shift towards administrative leadership, when more and more researchers became interested in the transdisciplinary research organization. As research funds from the NIH were increasingly difficult to get, medical researchers and scientists, beyond those initially included in the effort, began to show interest in the transdisciplinary study of premature birth. The center had a biweekly research seminar, where researchers outside the center could come pitch their research ideas to the leadership team. One leader explained that the increased interest in the center's premature birth grant forced them to deal with an overabundance of promising research ideas:

> Having funding from a foundation and having restricted funds on the NIH side actually makes it a little bit more likely that investigators that were otherwise perfectly fine and happy, because they had plenty of money, are now headed in this direction to see if they can find money to do work. That's an irony of the circumstance, which actually provides incentive to people to congregate and begin to work on this [transdisciplinary study of premature birth]… The trouble is, we don't have enough money to incent everybody. They can come and present a great idea, and then the next thing they want is money, and we don't have enough. [ID-27]

The leader was pleased that researchers from different fields were interested in the effort and proposed ideas for how to study the syndrome. However, there was not enough money to support every project, no matter how promising the research ideas were. Ultimately, the leaders had to decide what was worth funding, which was a great responsibility in a situation where nobody knew what was causing premature birth.

Furthermore, while premature birth seemed like a narrow research problem, there were multiple different research paths that could have been taken to create new knowledge on the topic. The leaders had to make sure there was a sense of direction for the research effort; otherwise it would be challenging to make progress. Here is how one leader explained it:

> The biggest problem is that every [research] avenue looks exciting. It looks 'oh my God, it's so interesting.' The leadership group, our job is to try and be sure that we keep the train going forward because otherwise we are going to

be going like this [gestures a circle]. That's difficult because everything's exciting. Everything looks great, but you have to be able to keep focus and try to bring it all together. [ID-7]

One strategy for keeping "the train going forward," as the leader said, was the initial decision to focus on four transdisciplinary research projects. The leaders selected these projects already before the center was formed. As these projects led to discoveries, new research avenues began to emerge. In many ways, this development was something positive. Multiple interesting research avenues could be signs of intellectual chaos that could lead to more creativity and development (Nonaka & Yamanouchi, 1989). Again, the leaders had to decide which research ideas were worth the limited resources. One leader confessed that they had made some mistakes along the way:

> We have to think about, practically speaking, what are the synergies that we might fund? What are the people that are likely to actually work well together and make choices that reflect that? So far we are doing okay, but we have made some mistakes, too…. It's self-serving their goals in trying to understand [referring to a project on infection and premature birth], which is what [a scientist] is interested in. It's just not engaging enough for a lot of the people, so that's money that we spent that probably is going to go nowhere. Now, it might ultimately get her a grant and it might get her a few papers, but I am not sure it's going to contribute much to premature birth, to be blunt. [ID-27]

The leaders did not want to pick projects only on the basis of what was a promising idea. They wanted to identify researchers who were able to work with others and create collaborative synergies across the center and its projects. They wanted researchers who were "open to new paradigms." While the leader said they were "doing okay" in their attempt to support the best possible projects, they had also made some mistakes. One project they had decided to fund was helping the individual scholar and her career, but not necessarily the transdisciplinary study of premature birth.

When a complex adaptive system relies on administrative leadership too heavily, the relationship between different leadership functions becomes unbalanced, which can threaten the creation of adaptive dynamics. The leadership team was in a position to guide knowledge creation toward directions that they selected based on their knowledge of premature birth research, new discoveries from ongoing projects, and synergies among members of the center. While this behavior may have guaranteed the production of research outcomes, the adaptive dynamics suffered from a lack bottom-up processes, such as experimentation (Uhl-Bien & Arena, 2018).

Discussion: Establishing Entanglement and Interdependency in a New Transdisciplinary Environment

Complexity leadership theory provides a framework for analyzing how leaders of transdisciplinary science mobilize and manage collaboration across disciplinary boundaries. The purpose of this chapter was to shed light on the role of leaders in a newly formed transdisciplinary research organization. Next, I reflect on the challenges for establishing entanglement of leadership functions and interdependency among organizational members in a new research center. I discuss how the lack of entanglement and interdependency can explain why the leaders became the focal points of knowledge creation and how such a development can be prevented.

Complexity leadership theory emphasizes that while administrative, enabling, and adaptive leadership roles are distinct forms of leadership, in effectively functioning organizations they need to work together (Hazy & Uhl-Bien, 2013; Uhl-Bien & Marion, 2009; Uhl-Bien et al., 2007). Ideally, these different forms of leadership exist in a dynamic relationship, entangled with one another. In this way, they support the creation of adaptive dynamics in complex systems. However, in this new transdisciplinary research organization, it seemed that the different leadership functions were not sufficiently entangled. Instead, they formed a kind of leadership toolbox from where the leaders selected a function and related leadership practices that suited a given situation.

In addition to weak entanglement of the different leadership functions, the leaders had a difficult time with fostering interdependency among the members of the transdisciplinary research center. Uhl-Bien et al. (2007, p. 310) noted, "While interaction permits the movement and dynamic interplay of information, interdependency creates pressure to act on information." This means that simply increasing information flow in a complex adaptive system is not enough. Experts need to develop interdependency among themselves so that there is a real incentive to collaborate. The leaders of transdisciplinary science relied on practices that fostered the movement and interplay of different types of expertise, but in the new research organization, the researchers were not immediately dependent on each other. When collaborative relationships between people were not yet established, it was not clear where interdependencies could develop or where they were even necessary.

Weak entanglement of leadership functions and lack of interdependency among members of the organization challenges the creation of adaptive dynamics. The leaders were eager to support the creation of adaptive dynamics by relying on enabling leadership practices. They saw value in connecting activities, which are important for the facilitation of adaptability and change in complex adaptive systems (Arena et al., 2017; Taylor & Helfat, 2009; Uhl-Bien & Arena, 2018). Knowledge brokering and translation were particularly important, because most of the collaborators were not familiar with each other or the problem of premature birth.

Yet, quite quickly, the leaders faced a situation where there was a pressure to produce results. Transdisciplinary research organizations—especially when they are new and have not yet developed stable knowledge creation processes—can struggle with jumpstarting collaborations that can lead to innovative research outcomes. The risk tends to be that the pressure to produce products comes in the way of the need to innovate (Uhl-Bien & Arena, 2018). In order to ensure transdisciplinary research outcomes, the leaders began to rely on an administrative leadership role. These challenges—connecting members in the new center and ensuring that progress was made—and the leaders' responses to them made the leaders the focal point of transdisciplinary knowledge integration. When the leaders translated and brokered knowledge in line with enabling leadership, they became knowledgeable of all the expertise present in the center. They then used the gained knowledge to broker expertise and people on transdisciplinary research projects. Finally, they had the opportunity to assess research ideas and decide which projects to support.

Leaders becoming the focal point of knowledge integration has consequences for a system's adaptive dynamics. According to Lotrecchiano (2010), successful transdisciplinary environments require knowledge feedback loops that run throughout the organization on multiple levels. If formal leaders act as the focal points of knowledge integration, the knowledge feedback loop is not likely to draw on the expertise of all organizational members in an optimal way. Similarly, in relation to facilitating adaptive processes, Uhl-Bien and Arena (2018) emphasize the importance of both top-down and bottom-up processes. Both are important, but they need to be integrated in a dynamic way.

It is important to remember, though, that the empirical context of the present study sheds light on the challenges of building adaptive dynamics in a new transdisciplinary center. Despite the tendency of the leaders to take charge of transdisciplinary knowledge creation in these early stages does not determine what the organization's future will be. While these findings increase our understanding of what goes on in recently established transdisciplinary environments, they do not presume a long-term outcome for the center. When organizational members gain collaboration experience, familiarity, and trust, transdisciplinary collaboration at all organizational levels is likely to become easier.

How to, then, mobilize transdisciplinary collaboration in a new center and avoid the described challenges? This chapter suggests that knowledge brokers capable of interacting at knowledge boundaries should be placed throughout the organization in strategic positions. These strategic positions might include individuals who lead teams, recruit researchers, and head meetings. A study on brokering activities in the area of patient safety by Waring et al. (2013) showed that those in more informal roles can be more effective at knowledge brokering, because they rely less on bureaucratic authority and more on professional and relational qualities. Recruiting individuals who are open to new knowledge and skillful at knowledge brokering is important in transdisciplinary research organizations. When the role of knowledge brokers is not based on bureaucratic authority, they are in a position to form connections across projects and to generate interdependency more easily than formal leaders.

Conclusion

Transdisciplinary research organizations are complex adaptive systems in the sense that they bring together experts from varied backgrounds, promote interdependence among them, and form dynamic collectives with common goals (Cilliers, 1998; Lotrecchiano, 2010; Marion, 1999). This chapter examined what kind of leadership roles and practices leaders of transdisciplinary science rely on when seeking to promote adaptive dynamics. The analysis of empirical findings utilized complexity leadership theory, because it provided analytical tools for understanding the role of leaders in emergent collaborative contexts (Hazy & Uhl-Bien, 2013; Uhl-Bien & Marion, 2009; Uhl-Bien et al., 2007).

The chapter demonstrated that although academic leaders relied on different types of leadership practices, finding an optimal balance between administrative, enabling, and adaptive leadership was challenging. The leaders first drew on practices related to enabling leadership. Later on, they took on an administrative role, as there was an increasing pressure to show progress. In this role, the leaders decided on promising research ideas, the use of resources, and project composition. As these practices relate to top-down leadership and decision-making, the leaders became the focal point of transdisciplinary knowledge integration. This, in turn, created an obstacle for the creation of shared adaptive dynamics throughout the research organization.

Questions to Further the Discourse

1. What is the role of leaders at different developmental stages in the transdisciplinary research process?

2. How can shared leadership be promoted throughout organizations?

3. How do different organizational members take part in the creation of adaptive dynamics?

Must Reads

Hargadon, A. (2003). *How breakthroughs happen: The surprising truth about how companies innovate.* Cambridge, MA: Harvard Business School Press.

Majchrzak, A., More, P. H. B., & Faraj, S. (2012). Transcending knowledge differences in cross-functional teams. *Organization Science, 23*(4), 951-970. https://doi.org/10.1287/orsc.1110.0677

Hazy, J. K., & Uhl-Bien, M. (2013). Towards operationalizing complexity leadership: How generative, administrative and community-building leadership practices enact organizational outcomes. *Leadership, 11*(1), 79-104. https://doi.org/10.1177/1742715013511483

References

Abbott, A. (2001). *Chaos of disciplines.* Chicago, IL: University of Chicago Press.

Arena, M., Cross, R., Sims, J., & Uhl-Bien, M. (2017). Groundswell: Tapping the power of employee networks to fuel emergent innovation. *MIT Sloan Management Review, 58*(4), 39-47.

Balsiger, P. (2004). Supradisciplinary research practices: History, objectives and rationale. *Futures, 36*(4), 407-421. https://doi.org/10.1016/j.futures.2003.10.002

Barge, J. K., & Musambira, G. W. (1992). Turning points in chair-faculty relationships. *Journal of Applied Communication, 20,* 54-77. https://doi.org/10.1080/00909889209365319

Bechky, B. A. (2003). Sharing meaning across occupational communities: The transformation of understanding on a production floor. *Organization Science, 14*(3), 312-330. https://doi.org/10.1287/orsc.14.3.312.15162

Biancani, S., McFarland, D. A., & Dahlander, L. (2014). The semiformal organization. *Organization Science, 25*(5), 1306-1324. https://doi.org/10.1287/orsc.2013.0882

Bolden, R. (2011). Distributed leadership in organizations: A review of theory and research. *International Journal of Management Reviews, 13,* 251-269. https://doi.org/10.1111/j.1468-2370.2011.00306.x|

Bryant, S. E. (2003). The role of transformational and transactional leadership in creating, sharing and exploiting organizational knowledge. *Journal of Leadership and Organizational Studies, 9*, 32-44. https://doi.org/10.1177/107179190300900403

Bryman, A. (2007). Effective leadership in higher education: A literature review. *Studies in Higher Education, 32*(6), 693-710. https://doi.org/10.1080/03075070701685114

Cilliers, P. (1998). *Complexity and postmodernism. Understanding complex systems*. London, UK: Routledge.

Cilliers, P. (2013). Understanding complex systems. In J. Sturmberg & C. Martin (Eds.), *Handbook of systems and complexity in health* (pp. 27-38). New York, NY: Springer.

Colditz, G., Wolin, K., & Gehlert, S. (2012). Applying what we know to accelerate cancer prevention. *Science Translational Medicine, 4*(127), 127rv4. https://doi.org/10.1126/scitranslmed.3003218

Corbin, J., & Strauss, A. (2015). *Basics of qualitative research: Techniques and procedures for developing grounded theory*. Thousand Oaks, CA: Sage.

Cummings, J. N., & Kiesler, S. (2005). Collaborative research across disciplinary and organizational boundaries. *Social Studies of Science, 35*(5), 703-722. https://doi.org/10.1177/0306312705055535

Dervitsiotis, K. N. (2005). Creating conditions to nourish sustainable organizational excellence. *Total Quality Management & Business Excellence, 16*(8, 9), 925-943. https://doi.org/10.1080/14783360500163078

Dess, G., & Picken, J. C. (2000). Changing roles: Leadership in the 21st century. *Organizational Dynamics, 28*(3), 18-34. https://doi.org/10.1016/S0090-2616(00)88447-8

Dougherty, D. (1992). Interpretive barriers to successful product innovation in large firms. *Organization Science, 3*(2), 179-202. https://doi.org/10.1287/orsc.3.2.179

Drath, W. (2001). *The deep blue sea: Rethinking the source of leadership*. San Francisco, CA: Jossey-Bass and Center for Creative Leadership.

Eigenbrode, S. D., O'Rourke, M., Wulfhorst, J. D., Althoff, D. M., Goldberg, C. S., Merrill, K., Morse, W., Nielsen-Pincus, M., Stephens, J., Winowiecki, L., & Bosque-Pérez, N. A. (2007). Employing philosophical dialogue in collaborative science. *BioScience, 57*(1), 55-64. https://doi.org/10.1641/B570109

Emerson, R., Fretz, R., & Shaw, L. (1995). *Writing ethnographic fieldnotes*. Chicago, IL: University of Chicago Press.

Entin, E., & Serfaty, D. (1999). Adaptive team coordination. *Human Factors: The Journal of the Human Factors and the Ergonomics Society, 41*(2), 312-325. https://doi.org/10.1518/001872099779591196

Haas, M. R. (2006). Acquiring and applying knowledge in transnational teams: The roles of cosmopolitans and locals. *Organization Science, 17*(3), 367-384. https://doi.org/10.1287/orsc.1060.0187

Hargadon, A. (2003). *How breakthroughs happen: The surprising truth about how companies innovate.* Cambridge, MA: Harvard Business School Press.

Hazy, J. K. (2007). Computer models of leadership: Foundation for a new discipline or meaningless diversion? *Leadership Quarterly, 18*(4), 391-410. https://doi.org/10.1016/j.leaqua.2007.04.007

Hazy, J. K., & Uhl-Bien, M. (2013). Towards operationalizing complexity leadership: How generative, administrative and community-building leadership practices enact organizational outcomes. *Leadership, 11*(1), 79-104. https://doi.org/10.1177/1742715013511483

Heifetz, R. A. (1994). *Leadership without easy answers.* Cambridge, MA: Harvard University Press.

Heifetz, R. A., & Linsky, M. (2002). *Leadership on the line: Staying alive through the dangers of leading.* Boston, MA: Harvard University Press.

Huising, R. (2014). The erosion of expert control through censure episodes. *Organization Science, 25*(6), 1633-1661. https://doi.org/10.1287/orsc.2014.0902

Kellogg, K. C. (2014). Brokerage professions and implementing reform in age of experts. *American Sociological Review, 79*(5), 912-941. https://doi.org/10.1177/0003122414544734

Klein, J. T. (1990). *Interdisciplinarity: History, theory, and practice.* Detroit, MI: Wayne State University Press.

Klein, J. T. (2014). Interdisciplinarity and transdisciplinarity: Keyword meanings for collaboration science and translational medicine. *Journal of Translational Medicine & Epidemiology, 2*(2), 1024.

Kontopoulos, K. M. (1993). *The logics of social structure.* Cambridge, MA: Cambridge University Press.

Lakshman, C. (2007). Organizational knowledge leadership: A grounded theory approach. *Leadership & Organization Development Journal, 28*, 51-75. https://doi.org/10.1108/01437730710718245

Lamont, M. (2009). *How professors think: Inside the curious world of academic judgment.* Cambridge, MA: Harvard University Press.

Lichtenstein, B., Uhl-Bien, M., Marion, R., Seers, A., Orton, D., & Schreiber, C. (2006). Leadership in emergent events: Exploring the interactive process of leading complex situations. *Emergence: Complexity and Organization, 8*(4), 2-12.

Lofland, J., & Lofland, L. H. (1995). *Analyzing social settings. A guide to qualitative observation and analysis.* Belmont, CA: Wadsworth Publishing Company.

Lomas, J. (2007). The in-between world of knowledge brokering. *British Medical Journal, 334*(7585), 129-132. https://doi.org/10.1136/bmj.39038.593380.AE

Lotrecchiano, G. R. (2010). Complexity leadership in transdisciplinary (TD) learning environments: A knowledge feedback loop. *International Journal of Transdisciplinary Research, 5*(1), 29-63.

Lotrecchiano, G. R. (2014). Defining collaboration science in an age of translational medicine. *Journal of Translational Medicine and Epidemiology, 2*(2), 1023.

Lotrecchiano, G.R. (2019). *Motivation and threat research to measure readiness in team collaborations.* Presentation delivered at the Milken Institute School of Health Policy. George Washington University, Washington, DC. April 17, 2019

Lotrecchiano, G. R., & Misra, S. (2018). Transdisciplinary knowledge producing teams: Toward a complex systems perspective. *Informing Science: The International Journal of an Emerging Transdiscipline, 21,* 51-74. https://doi.org/10.28945/4086

Maasen, S., & Lieven, O. (2006). Transdisciplinarity: A new mode of governing science? *Science & Public Policy, 33*(6), 399-410. https://doi.org/10.3152/147154306781778803

Majchrzak, A., More, P. H. B., & Faraj, S. (2012). Transcending knowledge differences in cross-functional teams. *Organization Science, 23*(4), 951-970. https://doi.org/10.1287/orsc.1110.0677

March, J. G. (1991). Exploration and exploitation in organizational learning. *Organization Science, 2*(1), 71-87.

Marion, R. (1999). *The edge of organization: Chaos and complexity theories of formal social organizations.* Newbury Park, CA: Sage.

Marion, R., & Uhl-Bien, M. (2001). Leadership in complex organizations. *Leadership Quarterly, 12,* 389-418. https://doi.org/10.1016/S1048-9843(01)00092-3

Murray, F. (2010). The oncomouse that roared: Hybrid exchange strategies as a source of distinction at the boundary of overlapping institutions. *American Journal of Sociology, 116*(2), 341-388. https://doi.org/10.1086/653599

Mäkinen, E. I. (2018a). Complexity leadership theory and the leaders of transdisciplinary science. *Informing Science: The International Journal of an Emerging Transdiscipline, 21,* 133-155. https://doi.org/10.28945/4009

Mäkinen, E. I. (2018b). Tuning clinical recruitment around cultural taboos in a human microbiome study. *Science as Culture, 27*(4), 464-487. https://doi.org/10.1080/09505431.2018.1508429

Mäkinen, E. I. (2019). The power of peer review on transdisciplinary discovery. *Science, Technology, & Human Values,* available online and forthcoming in print. https://doi.org/10.1177/0162243918822741

Mäkinen, E. I., Evans, E. D., & McFarland, D. A. (2019). The patterning of collaborative behavior and knowledge culminations in interdisciplinary research centers. *Minerva,* available online and forthcoming in print. https://doi.org/10.1007/s11024-019-09381-6

Nag, R., Corley, K. G., & Gioia, D. A. (2007). The intersection of organizational identity, knowledge, and practice: Attempting strategic change via knowledge grafting. *Academy of Management Journal, 50*(4), 821-847. https://doi.org/10.5465/amj.2007.26279173

Nonaka, I., & Yamanouchi, T. (1989). Managing innovation as a self-renewing process. *Journal of Business Venturing, 4,* 299-315. https://doi.org/10.1016/0883-9026(89)90003-7

Pearce, C., & Sims, H. (2000). Shared leadership: Toward a multi-level theory of leadership. In M. Beyerlein, D. Johnson, & S. Beyerlein (Eds.), *Advances in the interdisciplinary studies of work teams,* volume 7, (pp. 115-139). New York, NY: JAI.

Pohl, C. (2005). Transdisciplinary collaboration in environmental research. *Futures, 37,* 1159-1178. https://doi.org/10.1016/j.futures.2005.02.009

Politis, J. D. (2002). Transformational and transactional leadership enabling (disabling) knowledge acquisition of self-managed teams: The consequences for performance. *Leadership & Organization Development Journal, 23,* 186-197. https://doi.org/10.1108/01437730210429052

Schmidt, L., & Pröpper, M. (2017). Transdisciplinarity as a real-world challenge: A case study on a North–South collaboration. *Sustainability Science, 12*(3), 365-379. https://doi.org/10.1007/s11625-017-0430-8

Schneider, M., & Somers, M. (2006). Organizations as complex adaptive systems: Implications of complexity theory for leadership research. *Leadership Quarterly, 17*(4), 351-365. https://doi.org/10.1016/j.leaqua.2006.04.006

Shrum, W., Genuth, J., & Chompalov, I. (2007). *Structures of scientific collaboration.* Cambridge, MA: The MIT Press.

Sonnenwald, D. H. (2007). Scientific collaboration. *Annual Review of Information Science and Technology, 41,* 643-681. https://doi.org/10.1002/aris.2007.1440410121

Srivastava, A., Bartol, K., & Locke, E. A. (2006). Empowering leadership in management teams: Effects on knowledge sharing, efficacy, and performance. *Academy of Management Journal, 49,* 1239-1251. https://doi.org/10.5465/amj.2006.23478718

Strauss, A. L., & Corbin, J. M. (1990). *Basic of qualitative research: Grounded theory procedures and techniques.* Newbury Park, CA: Sage.

Suldovsky, B., McGreavy, B., & Lindenfeld, L. (2018). Evaluating epistemic commitments and science communication practice in transdisciplinary research. *Science Communication, 40*(4), 499-523. https://doi.org/10.1177/1075547018786566

Taylor, A., & Helfat, C. E. (2009). Organizational linkages for surviving technological change: Complementary assets, middle management, and ambidexterity. *Organization Science, 20*(4), 718-739. https://doi.org/10.1287/orsc.1090.0429

Uhl-Bien, M. (2006). Relational leadership theory: Exploring the social processes of leadership and organizing. *Leadership Quarterly, 17*(6), 654-676. https://doi.org/10.1016/j.leaqua.2006.10.007

Uhl-Bien, M. & Arena, M. (2018). Leadership for organizational adaptability: A theoretical synthesis and integrative framework. *Leadership Quarterly, 29*(1), 89-104. https://doi.org/10.1016/j.leaqua.2017.12.009

Uhl-Bien, M. & Marion, R. (2009). Complexity leadership in bureaucratic forms of organizing: A meso model. *Leadership Quarterly, 20*, 631-650. https://doi.org/10.1016/j.leaqua.2009.04.007

Uhl-Bien, M., Marion, R., & McKelvey, B. (2007). Complexity leadership theory: Shifting leadership from the industrial age to the knowledge era. *Leadership Quarterly, 18*(4), 298-318. https://doi.org/10.1016/j.leaqua.2007.04.002

Ward, V., House, A., & Hamer, S. (2009). Knowledge brokering: The missing link in the evidence to action chain? *Evidence & Policy, 5*(3), 267-279. https://doi.org/10.1332/174426409X463811

Waring, J., Currie, G., Crompton, A., & Bishop, S. (2013). An exploratory study of knowledge brokering in hospital settings: Facilitating knowledge sharing and learning for patient safety? *Social Science & Medicine, 98*, 79-86. https://doi.org/10.1016/j.socscimed.2013.08.037

Yukl, G. A. (2005). *Leadership in organizations*, 6th edition. Englewood Cliffs, NJ: Prentice Hall.

Gaetano R. Lotrecchiano & Shalini Misra (Editors). 2020
Communication in Transdisciplinary Teams
Santa Rosa, CA: Informing Science Press

Chapter 5:
Facilitating Innovation in Interdisciplinary Teams: The Role of Leaders and Integrative Communication

Maritza R. Salazar
University of California Irvine, Irvine, CA, USA
smaritza@uci.edu

Theresa K. Lant
Pace University, Pleasantville, NY, USA
tlant@pace.edu

Chapter Objectives

1. To better understand the role of leaders in nascent interdisciplinary teams.

2. To identify the impact of work experience on leader effectiveness in interdisciplinary research teams.

3. To uncover the leader behaviors that positively impact effective collaboration in interdisciplinary teams.

4. To provide recommendations for a type of training that best prepares leaders for facilitating collaboration in diverse research teams.

5. To propose future directions for the investigation of scientific leaders involved in interdisciplinary research endeavors.

Introduction to the Chapter

The complexity of scientific problems has spurred the development of transdisciplinary science, in which knowledge experts and other stakeholders collaborate across disciplinary and practice boundaries to generate new theoretical frameworks that transcend disciplinary boundaries to address complex problems (Klein, Misra, & Lortrechiano, 2020). An important element of knowledge creation within transdisciplinary science is the use of interdisciplinary teams, whose members integrate diverse disciplinary expertise to the tackle intractable problems. These knowledge diverse teams can produce novel solutions, but they often fail to achieve their potential. Leaders have a crucial role to play in enabling effective collaboration among these diverse experts. We propose that a critical predictor of whether a newly formed interdisciplinary team will perform well is the leader's multidisciplinary breadth of experience, which we define as a leader's possession of significant experience in

An earlier version of this chapter was published as Salazar, M. R., & Lant, T. K. (2018). Facilitating innovation in interdisciplinary teams: The role of leaders and integrative communication. *Informing Science: the International Journal of an Emerging Transdiscipline, 21,* 157-178. https://doi.org/10.28945/4011

multiple areas of research and practice. We suggest that these leaders will have the capability to skillfully manage the interactions within the team. We test our prediction in a sample of 52 newly formed interdisciplinary medical research teams. We also observe and examine the communication patterns in a subset of these teams. There is a lack of systematic study of the impact leaders have on newly formed interdisciplinary science teams whose members have little or no prior collaborative experience with each other, possess specialized knowledge, and have limited overlapping expertise. This study combines quantitative and qualitative methods to examine the effect of leader multidisciplinary experience on team communication patterns and innovation. Our study finds that teams are more innovative when their leader has a moderate breadth of multidisciplinary expertise. Exploration of team communication patterns suggests that leaders with moderate multidisciplinary breadth of experience actively stimulated information sharing across expert domains by choosing cross-cutting topics and drew individuals' attention to the knowledge and approaches of others in the team.

Background

Major changes are underway in the organization and management of knowledge work, including the way in which science is conducted and translated into innovation. The complexity of scientific problems, coupled with a growing need for specialized expertise (Becker & Murphy, 1992; Jones, 2009), has spurred more transdisciplinary science, in which experts and other stakeholders come together to collaborate across disciplinary and practice boundaries to co-produce overarching frameworks that transcend disciplinary boundaries (Klein et al., 2020; Paruchuri, 2010; Wuchty, Jones, & Uzzi, 2007). The goal of bringing diverse perspectives to bear on a given problem is to provide the requisite variety of knowledge and breadth of expertise needed to tackle the most difficult scientific puzzles (Kerr & Tindale, 2004). These collaborations often involve nascent teams of experts without prior joint work experience and without training in team project management. These teams face the dual challenge of needing to bridge across knowledge boundaries to develop integrated innovations while lacking the skills and experience to manage such a difficult process. Thus, identifying the conditions that enable effective cross-boundary collaboration in newly formed teams is essential if this new design of scientific knowledge work is to be successful in generating innovation.

For generations, fundamental discipline-based science has been the pathway to scientific discoveries. Theory-driven basic research, fueled by the pursuit of attaining "knowledge deeper within the tree of information" (Fang & Casadevall, 2010, p. 564) has led to significant discoveries that have shaped fields such as medicine. Noteworthy examples are the work on telomeres that resulted in treatments for cancer and research on retroviruses led to therapies to treat HIV. Basic scientists typically do not begin their investigations with the practical implications of their work in mind; rather they are driven by a deep interest in understanding the natural world. The journey from fundamental scientific discovery to practical application is seldom straightforward. The road is long and circuitous (Garud & Rappa, 1994). This has led to frustration with the length, expense, and uncertain payoff from basic research. In medical science, funding agencies and policy makers alike have argued that therapies for a disease can be more readily identified by bringing basic scientists, clinical practitioners, and patient-oriented researchers together to collaborate in teams composed of experts from a variety of research disciplines and practice areas (Chen, Farh, Campbell-Bush, Wu, & Wu, 2013; Rip, 2004; Winter & Berente, 2012).

Despite the promise of teams that combine distinct theoretical and methodological perspectives to solve complex problems (Hessels & Van Lente, 2008), the presence of diverse expertise does not automatically produce desired outcomes (e.g., Homan, van Knippenberg, Van Kleef, & De Dreu, 2007; Simons, Pelled, & Smith, 1999). When the knowledge boundaries between team members are "thick" (e.g., pragmatic boundaries) compared to when boundaries are relatively thin (e.g., syntactic boundaries), they are so difficult to span due to differences in training, language, interpretation, and interests (Edmondson & Harvey, 2016) that the gaps in understanding can seem insurmountable (Carlile, 2004; Cronin & Weingart, 2007). To accomplish the aims of transdisciplinary science, utilizing knowledge resources effectively is essential. This requires the ability to coordinate team interactions in a way that facilitates the sharing, consideration, evaluation, and integration of relevant knowledge. Unfortunately, research to date has found that interdisciplinary teams often lack the effective coordination necessary to live up to their potential (Austin, 2003; Bunderson & Sutcliffe, 2002; Cummings & Kiesler, 2005).

Although enablers of interdisciplinary effectiveness such as a shared identity (Bunderson & Sutcliffe, 2002) and prior collaborative experience (Cummings & Kiesler, 2005) have been shown to support improved team functioning in teams with longer tenure, less is understood about the factors that support team effectiveness in newly formed interdisciplinary teams when a shared identity has not formed and members have little to no collaborative history. When experts first come together to work on an interdisciplinary team, we suggest that leaders have a crucial role to play in enabling effective collaboration among these diverse experts in order to facilitate common ground and to develop a shared direction. First, leaders can influence how team members respond to new perspectives and can regulate the interactions among individuals (C. L. Jackson & LePine, 2003; LePine & Van Dyne, 2001; Van Knippenberg, 2011). Indeed, the skillful facilitation of team processes by leaders has been shown to increase team effectiveness in general (Eisenbeiss, van Knippenberg, & Boerner, 2008; Mathieu, Maynard, Rapp & Gilson, 2008; Tansley & Newell, 2007; Zaccaro, Rittman & Marks, 2001) and innovation in particular (Mumford, Scott, Gaddis, & Strange, 2002). However, to date there have not been systematic studies of the impact of leaders on newly formed interdisciplinary science teams whose members have little or no prior collaborative experience with each other, possess specialized knowledge, and have limited overlapping expertise.

We propose that in these teams a critical predictor of whether a newly formed interdisciplinary team will perform well is the leader's *multidisciplinary breadth of experience*, which we define as a leader's possession of significant expertise in multiple areas of research and/or practice. Leaders of nascent interdisciplinary teams will need deep knowledge and experience in at least one domain to gain legitimacy. Yet, they will also need to understand both research and clinical aspects of a disease to facilitate communication and understanding among individuals in the team who have expertise ranging from basic research to patient care. As we explain in the following section, we hypothesize that a moderate degree of multidisciplinary breadth of experience will be most effective. We test our prediction in a sample of newly formed interdisciplinary medical research teams, each of which worked together to produce a research proposal, and plan to explore the cause, treatment, and cure for a complex medical disease. We also explore the communication patterns in a subset of teams to generate insights about how leaders with differing degrees of multidisciplinary breadth of experience manage the communication processes within their teams.

Effects of Leader Multidisciplinary Breadth of Experience on Team Innovation

The complex nature of scientific discovery often necessitates interdisciplinary collaboration among investigators from across scientific fields (Falk-Krzesinski et al., 2010). The move towards transdisciplinary science has increased the need for scientists and practitioners to engage in teamwork that requires them to not just collaborate, but to integrate distinct expertise across traditional disciplinary boundaries. The potential benefit is that the heterogeneity of expertise in these interdisciplinary teams can lead to increased consideration and use of all available knowledge resources (e.g., Watson, Kumar, & Michaelson, 1993), which can yield innovative solutions. However, team heterogeneity may also compromise performance, as it can trigger misunderstanding and conflict (S. E. Jackson & Joshi, 2011; van Knippenberg & Shippers, 2007). To illustrate this "double-edged sword" (van Knippenberg & van Ginkel, 2010), consider the success with which the Human Genome Project leveraged the varied, specialized expertise of its members (Collins, Morgan, & Patrinos, 2003), contrasted with the failure of the interdisciplinary effort responsible for the Challenger mission (Milliken, Lant, Bridwell-Mitchell, Starbuck, & Farjoun, 2005).

Research has suggested that mastery of domain relevant knowledge promotes *individual* creativity through improved ability to generate novel and appropriate solutions (Andrews & Smith, 1996; Mumford & Gustafson, 1988; Simonton, 1999). In interdisciplinary teams, individuals with specialized knowledge can contribute unique and valuable insight into a problem (Leahey, 2016). However, this specialization makes it difficult for individuals to share their contributions in a way that others understand and limits their ability to see how they could integrate their knowledge with their diverse team members. The lack of experience with problem-solving that incorporates multiple domains of knowledge may render the knowledge within the team incommensurate due to gaps in understanding (Cronin & Weingart, 2007). Moreover, the skills necessary to effectively negotiate contrasting perspectives and priorities among diverse experts (Long-Lingo & O'Mahony, 2010) are likely to be underdeveloped due to the prevalence of within-discipline training. Thus, teams composed of diverse specialists with little multidisciplinary experience will struggle to produce innovative approaches that incorporate integrated knowledge.

Because team leaders have a high-level view of a team's process, its task environment, and objectives (Morgeson, DeRue, & Karam, 2010) they are in a unique position to help minimize the adverse effects of diversity on team interactions. Currently there is limited research on how team leaders use their unique position to address the difficulty of integrating diverse expertise within a newly formed interdisciplinary team. Some studies have shown that transformational leadership, which emphasizes socioemotional support and recognition of the diverse needs and goals of team members, can foster improved creative performance of demographically or educationally diverse teams (Kearney & Gebert, 2009; Shin & Zhou, 2003). Other studies suggest that leaders with knowledge of different business functions are able to foster improved information sharing and unit performance (Bunderson & Sutcliffe, 2002). Baer (2010) demonstrates that when individuals possess expertise in a variety of domains they are better able to tap into and leverage the disparate ideas of others to generate new ideas. The breadth of a leader's task-relevant expertise has been shown to spur the creative performance of individual employees (Barnowe, 1975; Tierney, Farmer, & Graen, 1999). Taken together, prior research would suggest that the breadth of leader expertise, especially when it overlaps with areas of expertise within the team, enhances a leader's ability to facilitate collective creativity. It remains unclear, however, whether a leader's multidisciplinary breadth of experience is beneficial in the formative stages of an interdisciplinary team when individuals represent vastly different disciplinary perspectives and share no prior collaborative history.

Gaining expertise in numerous domains can require a great deal of time, energy, and effort for individual investigators. Technological uncertainty (Fleming, 2001), logistical challenges (Long-Lingo & O'Mahony, 2010) coordination costs (Cummings & Kiesler, 2005) and role strain (Boardman & Bozeman, 2007) associated with working across multiple boundaries can all contribute to lower scientific productivity (Leahey, Beckman, & Stanko, 2015). The consequence can be reduced mastery in any area (Kovács & Sharkey, 2014). Given the importance of technical expertise for leaders seeking influence among highly trained individuals (Mumford et al., 2002), leaders with a large breadth of multidisciplinary experience risk reduced scientific credibility to influence team members successfully if they have not produced high impact interdisciplinary work. Given that interdisciplinary, high impact work can be elusive to many (Leahey et al., 2015), the lack of legitimacy could hinder a leader's legitimacy and undermine their ability to facilitate innovation. Moreover, highly trained professionals often struggle to accommodate the concepts of multiple fields to produce category-spanning ideas (Lamont, Mallard, & Guetzkow, 2006), and leaders with high degree of multidisciplinary experience may lack the depth of expertise in the relevant knowledge arenas to support knowledge coordination and integration.

Thus, we suggest that a leader with moderate multidisciplinary breadth of experience will be most capable of facilitating innovation in interdisciplinary teams. They are likely to have depth of expertise in one area of work, while also having sufficient work experience in another to be able to identify interdependencies and complementarities between the two. Scientific contributions to a specialized domain will provide them with an acceptable amount of credibility to warrant the respect and followership of team members. Leaders will also have acquired various skills garnered from working across research and practice domains to foster collaboration across boundaries in a manner that an individual exposed to only one area would not. These arguments, therefore, suggest that relationship between leader multidisciplinary experience and team innovative performance will be positive up to a point and will begin to decline at high breadth of multidisciplinary experience, resulting in an inverted U-shaped pattern.

> *Hypothesis:* The relationship between leader multidisciplinary experience and team innovativeness will be curvilinear, such that innovation is highest when the level of multidisciplinary breadth of experience is moderate.

Methods

Research Site and Sample

The field study was set in a large medical center in the northeastern United States, referred to here as Metro Medical Center (MMC), which sought to reorganize the way it conducted medical research. The preparation for reorganization efforts began in August of 2007 with the appointment of a new Dean of Science who wanted to enhance interdisciplinary and translational research (Zerhouni, 2003) and funding for research at the institution. To accomplish this aim, the Vice Dean of Research formed a strategic science committee, composed of 13 expert faculty investigators from various academic departments, who would design and oversee an internal competition to identify interdisciplinary teams with cutting-edge research ideas that could attract funding to the University. All of these expert judges were full-time, tenured research faculty at MMC. Each judge had conducted scientific work that has had an international impact in their own fields. All of the judges had led at least one or more large, federally funded research grants. In October of 2007, an official announcement was made throughout MMC requesting proposals from newly formed inter-disciplinary teams. Sixty-one teams self-organized in response to the call for proposals. The teams worked together from early October through December 1, 2007, and each submitted a letter of intent and abbreviated proposal. In January 2008, the expert panel of faculty judges assessed each proposal based on the degree of innovativeness. To avoid potential bias or conflict of interest, no expert faculty judge evaluated a project if they were in any way affiliated with one of the teams. In the end, 18 teams were selected to submit a full research proposal by April 1, 2008. On April 6, 2008, six of the original 61 teams were designated as "Centers of Excellence."

The Dean of Research reached out to the University's business school in August 2007 for involvement in the kick-off and competition process, which is how our research team became involved. In October 2007, our research team began to collect data from several sources, including individual curriculum vitae, interviews, observation, documents, and the administration of a web-based survey to all people who were listed as members of the 61 newly formed interdisciplinary teams. None of the data collected from this research effort was provided for evaluation during the competition process. Due to limited CV data for some teams, 52 teams are included in the study, consisting of 394 full-time faculty members (64% male; 36% female). The dependent variable, team innovativeness, was measured based on scoring sheets provided to us by the strategic science committee after they evaluated team proposals. The teams in our sample have education and work area diversity on the two dimensions that characterize interdisciplinary translational science teams: disciplinary diversity (biochemistry, immunology, etc.) and area of practice diversity (basic research, clinical research, medical practitioner).

Measures

Innovativeness

Team innovativeness was measured using MMC's strategic science committee's rating of each team's research proposal. The expert faculty judges in the committee used a scoring sheet that included the following assessment criteria: (a) the proposed project makes distinct contributions to basic, translational, and clinical science, and (b) the proposed project benefits the MMC's clinical mission to provide world-class care to patients. These broadly accepted criteria are used by organizations such as the National Institutes of Health (http://www.niaid.nih.gov/researchfunding/grant/strategy/pages/5scoring.aspx#b). After considering these criteria, at least three expert committee members independently rated each team's proposal on a scale from 1 ("Not at All Innovative") to 6 ("Very Innovative"). These scores were then averaged to provide a final score. To avoid conflicts of interest, committee members did not serve as evaluators for teams on which they were also members. Interrater agreement was high, rwg = .92 (Bliese, 2000), permitting the creation of composite ratings of team innovativeness.

The assessment of innovation we used is related to the consensual assessment approach, which argues that the most valid assessment of the creativity of an idea is the collective judgment of recognized experts in the field (Amabile, 1982). Moreover, the use of expert, independent evaluators for the dependent variable (i.e., innovativeness) enables us to overcome common method bias (Podsakoff, MacKenzie, Lee, & Podsakoff, 2003). To further understand the specific components of innovation that our one-item measure captured, however, we also correlated it with additional data that we collected from committee members as they assessed the final phase of ratings. This scoring sheet asked them to assess the proposals in terms of novelty. Their assessment of innovativeness was found to be correlated significantly with novelty ($r = .74$).

Multidisciplinary Breadth of Leader Experience

Each team in our sample had a single leader and no leader led more than one team. To assess the influence of leader breadth of multidisciplinary experience on team innovativeness, we used CVs to code the degree of substantive experience in areas of research and practice. We developed a list of 16 work history indicators within the domains of either academic research or clinical medical practice based on interviews with faculty.

Coding Schema for Multidisciplinary Breadth of Experience

Using curriculum vitae, points are given for clinical and research experiences. After aggregating the number of clinical and research experiences in Tables 1 and 2, the totals from columns C and F are tallied to provide a final score.

Table 1. Tally of Clinical Experience

	A	B	C
	Clinical Experience	Example	Yes or No
1	MD	Degree in medicine	1 or 0
2	Intern & residency	In clinical area of practice	1 or 0
3	Clinical fellowship	In clinical area of practice	1 or 0
4	Licensure & certification	American boards, clinical license	1 or 0
5	5 years of practice	Time span from medical school to date	1 or 0
6	Professional clinical societies	American Board of Pain Medicine, Anesthesiology, or other clinical specialty	1 or 0
7	Awards–clinical	Top Doctor, Who's Who	1 or 0
8	Leadership in clinical centers	Director of cancer center, Parkinson's, geriatrics	1 or 0
			Total

Table 2. Tally of Research Experience

	D	E	F
	Research Experience Indicators	Example	Yes or No
9	PhD	Disciplinary Domain (biology, biochemistry, etc.)	1 or 0
10	Research fellow or postdoc	Participation in research in a lab or center	1 or 0
11	5 years of research experience	Time span from first to last publication	1 or 0
12	Participation in research-oriented boards	Institutional Review Board, NIH/NSF review committees	1 or 0
13	Peer reviewed publications	1st or 2nd authorship evident	1 or 0
14	Research awards	Albert Einstein Gold Medal, Outstanding Women in Science; Young Investigator Award, Career Scientist	1 or 0
15	Research support	PI or co-PI on Grants	1 or 0
16	Leadership in research lab	Director of their own research lab	1 or 0
			Total

Two independent coders counted the number of indicators of experience in the domains of academic research and clinical medical practice. Extensive experience as a researcher suggested years of cultivating skills related to conducting scientific studies and also being part of or leading research laboratories. Extensive experience in clinical medical practice involved years of apprenticeship, plus mastery as signaled by certification by boards or membership in clinical societies. Inter-rater agreement was above .80 (Cohen's kappa), so we calculated the average (across coders) count of types of experience for each leader (0 to 16). In our sample, this count ranged from 6 to 15; the mean being 9.6. Our check of counts for each leader confirms that those with scores of 6-7 had experience in only research or clinical practice, not both (low breadth). Leaders with scores of 13-15 had clear and substantial work area breadth that included both research and practice. Several individuals with scores of 8-10 had primary experience in one domain, and minimal experience in the other. The ordinal counts capture the essence of the distribution from low to high breadth of multidisciplinary experience.

Control Variables

Analyses controlled for a number of variables. In order to disentangle the impact of leader breadth of experience from that of team members, we also controlled for team *member* breadth of experience. Procedures used to measure breadth of experience for team members were the same as those for leaders. Drawing on data from each team member's CV, we also controlled for educational background diversity of the team, dominant work area diversity of the team, team size, gender diversity of the team, and tenure rank diversity of the team. The number of individuals listed as core team members in the team's letter of intent was used as the measure of team size. Teams in our sample were generally medium-sized ($M = 8.03$, $SD = 3.06$), and ranged in size from 4 to 17 members. Blau's (1977) formula was used to compute educational background diversity (48 specialized disciplinary departments), dominant work area diversity (basic research, clinical and population research, clinical practice, surgeon), tenure rank diversity (assistant, associate, full professor) and gender diversity. The Blau's (1977) index of heterogeneity, $1 - \sum (P_i)^2$, is calculated where P_i is the proportion of a team's members in the ith category (e.g., Wiersema & Bantel, 1992). This is the most common index for measuring diversity as variety (Harrison & Klein, 2007) and has a range of 0-1. For educational background diversity, the minimum and maximum levels of disciplinary heterogeneity in our sample were .32 and .90, respectively, and the average heterogeneity was .64. For team dominant work area diversity, the minimum and maximum indices were .00 and .81. The mean was .47. Finally, we also controlled for the leader's depth of expertise in the topic area by using the C.V. and calculating the proportion of the leader's publications in the team's focal topic area. We did so by counting the number of publications focused on the team's disease topic and dividing this number by the total number of publications they had published to date.

Results

Table 3 presents descriptive statistics and correlations for all variables. Table 4 presents the analyses used to test our hypothesis. The main effect of leader breadth of multidisciplinary experience is significant ($B = .12$, $p < .04$). Thus, scores for team innovation increased with the breadth of leader experience. The square term of leader breadth of experience ($B = -.04$, $p < .04$) is negative and significant, providing support for the inverted U shape effect predicted in Hypothesis 1. This curvilinear effect indicates that at very high levels of breadth of experience, the effect on team innovation begins to decline. Regarding control variables, we found a negative relationship between gender diversity and innovation ($B = -1.12$, $p = .05$). Team diversity is measured with two indicators – educational background diversity ($B = -0.02$, ns) and dominant work area diversity ($B = 1.90$, $p < .05$).

Table 3. Means, Standard Deviations, and Correlations

Variable	M (SD)	Min	Max								
1. Team Size	7.58 (3.45)		5								
2. Gender Diversity	.59 (.26)	11	.00	-.19							
3. Tenure Rank Diversity	.73 (.20)	13	.21	.03	16						
4. Team Education Background Diversity	.65 (.13)	.32	90	.02	.02	.04					
5. Team Dominant Work Area Diversity	.47 (.16)	00	81	.07	.04	.04	32*				
6. Team Member Breadth of Experience	8.25 (1.41)	.57	1.2	.14	02	.18	.04	.22			
7. Leader Breadth of Experience	9.63 (2.30)		5	05	.00	02	13	09	03		
8. Leader Topic Expertise Depth	.55 (.23)	04	.00	23	.11	.03	.11	04	.08	16	
9. Team Innovation	3.80 (.86)	.00	.60	11	.04	.30*	12	34*	02	33*	31*

Table 4. Effect of Leader Breadth of Experience on Team Innovation

		SE B	β
Team Size	.00	.03	.12
Gender Diversity	-1.12	.56	-.25*
Tenure Rank Diversity	17	40	05
Team Education Background Diversity	.10	84	.02
Team Dominant Work Area Diversity	.91	70	36*
Team Member Breadth of Experience	04	08	06
Leader Topic Expertise Depth	73	48	20
Leader Breadth of Experience	12	05	31*
Leader Breadth of Experience - Squared	.04	02	-.27*
Notes: R^2 = .29 (p < .05).			

Our quantitative analysis found that leaders with moderate levels of breadth of experience had the largest positive impact on team innovation. We predicted that this would be the case, arguing that leaders with both depth and breadth of experience would be more likely to foster cross-disciplinary collaboration and innovation. While there is general consensus that the generation of new ideas and solutions occurs through the dialectic integration of insights and perspectives (Hargadon & Bechky, 2006; Long-Lingo & O'Mahony, 2010; Okhuysen & Eisenhardt, 2000; Sawyer, 2003), it is unclear what approaches to communication these leaders used to manage interaction in their teams. In order to gain further insight into the behaviors and communication practices of leaders, we conducted a comparative case qualitative analysis of the observational and interview data we had collected concurrently with the quantitative data.

Comparative Case Analysis: Exploring Leader Communication Behaviors

Sample

We began the process of recruiting teams for observation in October 2007, soon after the initial call for proposals. Our aim was to obtain as much real-time interview and observational data as possible. Recruitment of teams involved first inviting leaders of the newly formed teams at MMC to take part in a qualitative study. Twelve team leaders responded to our solicitation and we began by conducting semi-structured interviews with each of them and observing their team meetings. In January 2008, a subset of the 61 teams in the competition was selected by the Strategic Science Committee to develop a full proposal. Six of the twelve teams we were observing were chosen for this last step in the competition. Thus, we continued interviews and observation of meetings with these six teams. All observational and interview data were collected before the selection of finalist teams.

For the supplemental study, proposals were once again evaluated by the strategic science committee at MMC. We were able to not only gather a rating of proposal idea novelty as we did in the primary study, but to also collect a one-item measure of knowledge integration. The integration of knowledge in a proposal was based on the following three criteria: 1) integration across projects; 2) integration between areas of practice (basic and clinical researchers) and 3) integration across disciplinary areas. The scores ranged from 1 (no knowledge integration) to 6 (great deal of knowledge integration). As with the rating of innovativeness, each team's rating of knowledge integration was based on the average score provided by at least three external ratings from expert members of the evaluation committee. Once again, no expert judge rated any proposal where he or she might be biased due to a potential conflict of interest.

Our assessment of the features of the six teams in the supplementary study made them appropriate for comparative case analysis (Yin, 2015). The teams had commonalities such as having a single leader, skill differentiation (variety of domain expertise), task type (developing a brief and full proposal), temporal stability (mid-January to April 1st) and the same organizational context (MMC). They also differed in key ways. Of theoretical interest to us was that the leaders in our study had variance in breadth of multidisciplinary experience (ranging from a low to a high), allowing for meaningful comparison of leader behaviors. The leaders were all mid-career, full professors, had organizational tenure of at least 7 years, and had obtained their own external funding. Of the six leaders, CVs indicated that three of them published over 60% of their work on the disease topic being explored by their team, while the remaining three had 40% or fewer of their publications in their team's focal area. Men led five of the six teams in the supplementary study, a proportion similar to that of the sample of 61 teams analyzed in the quantitative study. Using a Blau index, ranging from 0 to 1, the six teams had balanced gender diversity ($M = .54$, $SD = .23$) educational background diversity ($M = .67$, $SD = .09$), work area breadth ($M = .51$, $SD = .12$) and team size ($M = 8.43$, $SD = 4.11$).

Data Collection Procedures

Observations

One of the authors attended and observed team meetings from mid-January 2008 to the end of March 2008. The teams held an average of six meetings over this time. Each team was observed at least three times. Meetings were audio recorded and transcribed. Notes were taken during observations and further elaborated upon following each observation period (Emerson, Fretz, & Shaw, 1995). In total, we attended 30.5 hours of team meetings over a period of three months. All meetings took place at the research site, typically lasting from 60 to 90 minutes.

To uncover how leaders with varying levels of breadth of experience led team meetings we examined team interaction by studying statements made during meetings. The codes we used to analyze team communication during meetings closely aligned with the coding scheme developed by Kauffeld and Lehmann-Willock (2012). Their coding scheme builds upon the existing team process literature (e.g., Cooke & Szumal, 1994; Okhuysen & Eisenhardt, 2002; Wittenbaum, Hollingshead, & Botero, 2004). It covers four facets of verbal face-to-face meeting behavior including problem-focused, procedural, socioemotional, and action-oriented statement, as shown in Table 5.

Table 5. Coding Schema for Leader Communication in Team Meetings

Interaction Analysis Categories	Interaction Analysis Sub Codes and Definitions
Problem-focused Statements	**Cross-cutting problem construction.** Leaders present the research problem along a continuum from being narrow, discipline-specific aspect of the team's overall research project or on a broad, cross-cutting topic that integrates many interests.
Procedural Statements	**Cross-boundary team reflection.** Using descriptive statements to provide an overview of the expertise that team members possess and have access to.
Socioemotional Statements	**Encouraging cross-boundary participation**. The extent to which leaders increase awareness and use of heterogeneous knowledge of team members through introductions, referrals, and asking questions about diverse expertise.
Action-oriented Statements	**Interest in cross-disciplinary contribution.** Signalizing interest in ideas and options that bridge disciplinary and work areas of team members.

The problem-focused statements were directly related to differentiating the problem, finding appropriate solutions, and evaluating those solutions. Problem-focused codes we used included defining a problem, statements about who knows what, and asking questions about ideas. The procedural communication was aimed at structuring the meeting process (e.g., clarifying roles and goal orientation). Example codes used to analyze socioemotional communication included codes such as agreeing or cutting someone off. Similarly, action-oriented statements describe a team's willingness to improve their work (e.g., taking responsibility or action planning) or to not take action (e.g., no interest in taking charge or complaining). As we began to code team meeting transcripts, new codes also emerged from the data (Agar, 1980). For instance, when leaders described problems as intersecting various disciplines or practice areas, we coded this as describing a cross-cutting problem and when problems were framed for specialists, we coded it as domain-specific. Finally, axial coding was used to search for particular leader statements and convert them into higher order categories (e.g., problem construction and re-structuring interaction to be more cross-boundary). Two coders, who were research assistants, were blind to team identity and the final outcome scores. The coders were also provided the lead researcher's coding schema to analyze the transcripts. They coded independently and identified all second-order codes and obtained an acceptable level of interrater reliability (>80%). Disagreements were resolved through discussion.

Interviews

We conducted 46 semi-structured interviews (Wengraf, 2001) with both team members and leaders to aid in our understanding of the work the teams were doing, how they conducted the work, and their perceptions of the collaboration. One interview was conducted with each of the 46 individuals in our sample. Interviewees represented diverse disciplines, allowing the research team access to multiple perspectives and reducing the potential for bias (Krefting, 1991). Interviews occurred at different phases of the team collaboration and interviews were recorded, transcribed, and coded. We coded searching constantly for emergent themes (Rubin & Rubin, 2011) to better identify how members perceived the team leader, the impact of team leader communication and meeting facilitation, and their influence on team innovative performance. Often these interviews contained information about their perceptions of the team process (e.g., socioemotional statements) or their engagement with the team (e.g., action-oriented statements).

Comparative Case Analysis

We used a comparative case method to explore similarities and differences in the communication used by leaders with varying degrees of work area breadth to structure team interaction. This approach enables us to uncover why different processes and outcomes emerged across our sample, despite similarities across cases (Van de Ven & Poole, 1995). Although all leaders engaged in encouraging, socioemotional statements to motivate contributions from members, only leaders with moderate and high breadth of experience facilitated information sharing from a wide variety of team members; leaders with low breadth of experience sought engagement from only a subset of team members. Further, only leaders with moderate breadth of experience yielded synergistic cross-boundary interactions across departmental and specialist areas around a joint problem focus. By bringing together diverse experts around cross-cutting research problems, leaders with moderate breadth of experience were, therefore, able to foster more expertise integration and innovation.

Findings

Problem Construction to Foster Cross-boundary Integration

The process of identifying the problem is thought to be the first stage of the creative process (Amabile, 1996) and has the potential to shape not only the way that people respond to it, but the extent to which ideas produced are novel and useful (Berg, 2014). Research suggests that leaders tend to be primarily responsible for the problem construction process, even in self-managing teams (Nygren & Levine, 1996). The examination of team problem construction is critical to understanding interdisciplinary team effectiveness as it can affect perspective taking or team members' effort to understand the thoughts and motives of others (Hoever, van Knippenberg, van Ginkel & Barkema, 2012), and the social interaction among members. By constructing and framing the team's joint problem a particular way (Boland & Tensaki; 1995), leaders have the potential to influence whether team members discover new ways to integrate their heterogeneous inputs.

Drawing upon their experiences from different domains of work, all leaders in the sample valued pulling together distinct domains of expertise together in interdisciplinary teams. The influence of training across disciplinary fields and practice areas is well-reflected in the quote below by a leader with high multidisciplinary breadth of experience. One shared,

> *"I was a neurologist in a past life. I'm an MD/Ph.D. …lived in both worlds, and I thought, I should probably step up to the plate, but do it in a way, where it is not about me, it's about making the program work. Foster interactions so that people feel like everyone is getting something out of [the team]. The team, together, could be much better if we bring in all of these different elements. People will feel like it is worthwhile. That's the genesis."*

Despite valuing interdisciplinary collaboration, leaders with high breadth of expertise struggled to identify how to integrate members of their teams around joint projects or problems. The focus of team problems tended to be either oriented toward clinical or research interests, rather than both. For instance, the problem construction of one leader with high multidisciplinary breadth of experience, but more of a clinical background, focused their team on several clinically-oriented areas of inquiry, while the construction of more basic research projects was left to teammates who had more basic research expertise. As a result, separate clinical and basic projects were developed in isolation, without joint discussion of how they might influence one another. Links between projects in this team were largely limited to sharing of specimens from the clinic to be studied by researchers. Another leader with high multidisciplinary breadth of experience lamented that *bench to bedside* (from research project to clinical care) collaboration mostly involved using a "syringe and a FedEx package" to send specimens from the clinic to the lab for "that kind of research" to be done by others.

One leader with low multidisciplinary breadth of experience, a Ph.D. focused on fundamental aspects of the medical disease problem, also expressed enthusiasm about working with clinicians and more clinically-oriented researchers. He described himself as trying to "improve the basic research" related to the disease given the primarily clinical concentration of the university, with an emphasis on "balancing the efforts" between research and clinical care efforts because of the historic focus at the institution on clinically-oriented work. Problem construction, therefore, leaned heavily towards basic research at the exclusion of the input of more clinically-oriented team members. Group discussion tended to start with an overview of basic research – which often was well-aligned with the personal research interests of the team leader – and to rarely include branches to clinically oriented research or work. Team conversation involved basic scientists and rarely involved individuals from other work areas. A clinician team member shared that the team would have performed better, "if there were a component that related to clinical stuff."

Problem construction by a team leader with low breadth of experience and less topic area expertise focused almost exclusively on improving the clinical management of the disease. Perhaps unable to construct problems that meaningfully included more basic research on the disease topic, he did seek the contribution of more research-oriented investigators by asking them to suggest more fundamental research aims and objectives for the group. Members of these teams expressed that their leaders would frequently engage the team in overly general discussions, asking such questions as, "What are we—what do they want ...what's really going on here, and what should we do?" and that their team had failed to develop "fine-grained hypotheses." Generally, the clinical and research endeavors were largely kept separate. "I felt sad for him" shared one team member during a one-on-one interview, "knowing that he couldn't do the basic science – it's not in his background." One interviewee reported during an interview that their team's proposal reflected "individuals writing up their own vision" without "collectively coming together." Leaders with little multidisciplinary breadth of experience also tended to over-structure the team problem space, orienting it around sub-themes or smaller research aims that favored a single discipline rather than many. Such meetings were spent discussing the research of particular team members, and discussions were often dominated by individuals possessing the same disciplinary training as the presenter without acknowledgement of the value of alternative perspectives. Thus, the various efforts led by this team were disconnected, and the final product was characterized by individuals drafting sections independently.

Leaders with moderate breadth of experience more actively stimulated information sharing across expert domains by choosing cross-cutting topics. Cross-cutting problems focused on themes that the leader believed would appeal to the interest of a number of individuals within the team, even if each member might approach it drawing on different expertise and methodologies. We determined integrative problem construction occurred when topics were presented as requiring the contributions of diverse experts in the room and when coded dialogue of group discussion involved participation not only from a single discipline, but from numerous individuals in the team who represented clinical and research domains of expertise and various disciplinary perspectives. As an example, one of the leaders with moderate multidisciplinary breadth of experience focused the team discussion around the cross-cutting topic of impulsivity. This topic was presented as having behavioral, social, genetic, and cognitive aspects that would require insights from all group members. Team members, in turn, shared an appreciation of the narrowed scope, stating in interviews that this structure allowed for enhanced cross-boundary collaboration. One stated, "I think if you want to have an effective group, you have to set some form of – you have to impose some structure on it, otherwise people are just going to kind of drift apart." Moreover, interviewees noted that the confined problem space seemed to "set clear expectations of what the leader wanted over time. And so you kind of knew what you at least were expected to produce." Another team member commented in an interview that he could "easily see how other people think about [the] problem and how they could adjust their thinking and vice versa to inform each other."

Given the variety of ways that individuals from different work areas and disciplines thought about impulsivity and its relationship to their disease question of focus, discussion of the cross-cutting topic elicited novel perspectives and ideas. After discussion of the topic in his team, one member shared his impression. He stated during an interview:

> *"It's nice because you have a common language in a sense that we're all trying to look at how impulsivity might be related to [the disease]. But one thing that came out was the different kinds of definitions of [the disease] and different kinds of impulsivity."*

Another cross-cutting approach to problem construction was taken by a leader with moderate breadth of experience by encouraging her team to try to "characterize [the disease] phenotypically using many approaches including genetics, imaging, and blood." In this case, ideas and projects emerged drawing participation from individuals across specialties who had not worked together previously. Following the discussion involving several different specialists who had not interacted previously, the group decided to explore the use of a new imaging technique that had not been used to study this disease in this organ. One team member shared that exposure to this new approach ultimately led to a subset of pulmonologists to "look at things in a way that they haven't been used to before."

Socioemotional Communication and Cross-boundary Integration

Leaders with low breadth of experience struggled to foster interaction among the diverse experts in their team. Conversation during team meetings typically involved a subset of team members, consisting of a few highly-reputable team members who worked in the same work area as the team leader. During meetings, more peripheral members did attempt to join team discussions. In one exemplary instance, a clinician-surgeon seeking to contribute to a conversation dominated by researchers was cut off by the leader who quickly stating, "Ok, alright. Thanks for that" and returned to the original thread in the basic research conversation. Statements such as, "Great. Let's move on." were made without any request for further elaboration from the contributor. These negative socioemotional forms of communication signaled that their contributions were not as valuable as others. One teammate shared that although he did not feel that the leader was disrespectful toward his suggestions, his ideas were ultimately "dismissed" making him feel undervalued and less invested. Team members left meetings with the sentiment that "[clinical] input was not so valuable to them [basic scientists]" nor were basic science inputs viewed as "valuable to their [clinical] work, despite it being "interesting."

In contrast, leaders with high breadth of experience were inclusive of the multiple expert groups present within their team. Despite the time-pressure given the proposal deadline, these leaders regularly took meeting time to make the knowledge resources in the room visible to all team members. An example of this type of problem-orientated statement that helped to make the team's collective expertise visible is reflected in this quote below:

> *"...so this project is unique as it has got a very rich central clinical program and then it has got I think also the underpinnings of a lot of terrific science that interfaces well with this clinical work."*

Despite the clear expression of the value of the diverse expertise in the team by leaders with high breadth of experience, we witnessed few attempts to form bridges among expert groups represented within the team. For instance, one leader tended to spend the beginning of meetings focused on the interests of the basic researchers and the end of the meeting turn to topics of interest to the clinically oriented team members. During the basic research portion of the dialogue, he did actively "give hooks where other branches [of science] could fit into the discussion." In one conversation, for instance, this leader directed attention to a woman on the team in a different research field than himself, stating, "I thought Madelyn had an interesting project related to looking at sodium fluxes that may relate to what we're discussing here." When the conversation transitioned to a discussion of clinical research interests, the leader tried to link clinically-oriented team members together during the discussion, but was less unable to do so. The clinical conversation never opened up to involve research-oriented faculty. Ultimately, diverse experts interacted infrequently and worked on separate projects pertaining only to their own domain of expertise.

What distinguished leaders with moderate breadth of experience was that they did not keep the dialogue focused on any particular area of expertise, including their own. Rather, they actively drew individuals' attention to the knowledge and approaches of others in the team. In one meeting, for instance, a leader introduced a mathematician he had invited to the meeting and let him share, at length, his mathematical algorithm that could be applied to the team's work. Despite being from a completely different field, the leader encouraged the team to be open to how the mathematical approach could help with pressing group tasks, like "calculating organ fluctuation." Such knowledge management statements that involved asking questions of individuals from other areas of specialization to foster the team's collective consideration of alternative perspectives was how leaders with moderate breadth of experience structured integrative interaction among members. Another strategy to enhance individuals' engagement with the ideas of others in the team was to elicit expertise through inquiry. Leaders would ask questions such as, "Want to say a word about that? Nobody knows about your project," or "Do you want to take two minutes to tell everyone about your work?"

One leader described the process of actively moving the dialogue from one work area to the next in an interview, stating that it involved "turning the idea a bit and figuring out ways to relate it to some other perspective." To engage diverse experts with one another's ideas, questions to elicit divergent perspectives were common. For instance, in a conversation about a successful clinical drug, the leader probed "why the drug is having its effect at the cellular and pathology levels in the first place?" Peaking the interest of basic researchers, the conversation soon turned from being dominated by a small set of clinical researchers to also including basic scientists in the room. A synergistic dialogue ensued, and soon representatives from diverse work and disciplinary areas were collectively generating new hypotheses to test. Thus, we see leaders with moderate breadth of experience reconfiguring interaction away from working within disciplinary silos towards more cross-boundary collaboration.

The general pattern comparing breadth of multidisciplinary experience of the leader and team outcomes illustrates that teams with leaders possessing moderate breadth of experience ranked high on both innovativeness ($M= 4.59$) and integration $(M = 4.61)$. The average innovation and integration for teams with leaders possessing high transdisciplinary experience was 4.25 and 4.27, respectively. Finally, the worst performing teams in the qualitative sample were led by those with low work breadth of experience. These teams averaged an innovativeness score of 3.72 and an integration score of 3.8.

Discussion and Conclusion

The dominant narrative in existing research on scientific leadership is to focus deeply in a domain of expertise. This specialized, domain-specific knowledge is what is argued to enable a leader to effectively guide and direct scientific work. However, the complexity of the problems that interdisciplinary science teams are trying to solve make it difficult for a leader to rely solely on a single domain of specialized expertise. Our data supports the notion that some amount of breadth of experience and expertise is critical when leading interdisciplinary science teams – particularly when they are newly formed. Our conceptual argument is that leaders need a moderate mix of breadth and depth of experience that reflects the distribution of diverse disciplinary expertise represented within the team in order to facilitate the coordination and integration of these varied perspectives. These results contribute to a very nascent literature on creative leadership in science (Vessey, Barrett, Mumford, Johnson, & Litwiller, 2016). Our findings do not, however, control for other individual differences among leaders in our sample, such as leadership style (Jung & Avolio, 1999) or transdisciplinary orientation (Misra, Stokols, & Cheng, 2015), which could provide further insight into the kind of individuals who would be best equipped to lead interdisciplinary research teams. Future research should examine these other possible determinants of team effectiveness.

Our supplemental study provides insight into how leaders with multidisciplinary breadth of experience foster knowledge integration. Our comparative case analysis suggests that the leaders with expertise about a disease garnered from experience conducting substantial academic research and having had clinical experience working with populations or individuals suffering from the disease were more adept at helping their translational science teams use their deep-level knowledge resources. They did so through two key mechanisms. First, they construct a cross-cutting problem focus that intersects with the interests and expertise of the individual members and coordinate discussion around it. Second, they also engage in socio-emotional communication that demonstrates that they value and appreciate the contribution of all diverse experts in the team, regardless of their work experience or disciplinary background.

Even though leaders with high breadth of experience tried to involve team members with various types of expertise, they were less successful than leaders with moderate breadth of experience in facilitating synergies across domains of expertise. We view this as a by-product of the practical reality that too much breadth of experience is at odds with establishing a depth of expertise in at least one domain of practice. Without depth of knowledge, it is difficult to have sufficient perspective to meaningfully connect individual team members with one another's expertise. Least effective in facilitating innovation in interdisciplinary translational teams were those leaders who had expertise in either research or clinical work, but not both. Future research should explore whether there is a particular balance between breadth and depth that is critical for scientific leaders of interdisciplinary teams as it was beyond the scope of this project.

Limitations and Future Directions

Although this study makes a variety of contributions to the scientific understanding of the relationship between leader experience and the performance of newly formed interdisciplinary science teams, it has several limitations. First, this study was conducted in a single organization undergoing an intervention to foster the use of interdisciplinary collaboration to promote knowledge creation. Thus, the results are qualified by caveats typical of studies occurring within a single organization, including an idiosyncratic reward system, organizational culture, and motivation (e.g., interest in interdisciplinary collaboration). Features endemic to MMC's organizational context may limit generalizability.

Second, teams sampled in this study worked together for only a brief period and were engaged in a specific, yet complex task. The presence, consistency, and duration of the observed effects of team leaders may be inconsistent with those of other knowledge-creating teams with temporal stability (Hollenbeck, Beersma, & Schouten, 2012). Such inferences cannot be discerned from the current study. We do believe, however, that findings from this research generalize to many other project-based organizations where experts come together in teams to collaborate for a brief period of time (Edmondson & Nembhard, 2009; Huckman, Staats, & Upton, 2009). Moreover, we believe that the benefits of studying the predictors of innovation in real-world teams of scientific experts outweigh the inherent conceptual limitations of lab-based studies in which individuals do not typically possess and exchange deep expertise.

Finally, while our study does draw on interview and observational data to understand how a leader's multidisciplinary breadth of experience influences team process and performance, there remains the possibility that other individual-level leader differences could be important determinants as well. One possibility, for instance, is that leadership abilities or skills could have produced the differences that we observe rather than the breadth of prior multidisciplinary work experiences. Although we are doubtful of this possibility given that leaders in our sample had all led grant-funded teams in the past, future research should tease out these two drivers of influence to better understand the relative impact of a leader's work experiences and their skill as a leader.

Through the investigation into micro-processes that occur during social interaction of interdisciplinary science teams we elucidate a variety of communication strategies that leaders used to enhance the innovativeness of transdisciplinary science teams. This study highlights the strategies that effective team leaders can use even if they lack multidisciplinary experience. Further investigation into the underlying psychological states that these communication strategies elicit is needed.

In conclusion, this primary study illustrates that leaders' past work history affects interdisciplinary team performance. Specifically, we find a positive and significant relationship between teams led by leaders with moderate breadth of multidisciplinary experience and team innovativeness. Our supplementary analysis sheds light on effective leader strategies including 1) presenting interdisciplinary teams with research problems that cross-cut members varied domains of expertise and 2) communicating in a way that is inclusive and respectful to all members of the team. We hope that the insights garnered from this study can have practical implications regarding how to best to select and train leaders to facilitate cross-boundary collaboration in interdisciplinary science teams.

Questions to Further the Discourse

1. How might other psychological mediators such as knowledge consideration, the focusing of attention on determining the value of another's knowledge (Kane, 2010, p. 645), or perspective taking, considering the knowledge, ideas, and suggestions of another, (Hoever et al., 2012) affect team leader performance?

2. What other forms of leader experience or training could prepare leaders for fostering innovation in their interdisciplinary teams?

3. Can the behaviors identified in the current research be taught and provided to leaders who do not have work experience as both a researcher and physician?

4. Do the demands of leading an interdisciplinary team leadership change over a team's life cycle?

5. What kinds of training and development modalities will best prepare leaders for the challenging task of leading diverse interdisciplinary research teams?

Must Reads

Kearney, E., & Gebert, D. (2009). Managing diversity and enhancing team outcomes: The promise of transformational leadership. *Journal of Applied Psychology, 94*(1), 77-89. https://doi.org/10.1037/a0013077

Tierney, P., Farmer, S. M., & Graen, G. B. (1999). An examination of leadership and employee creativity: The relevance of traits and relationships. *Personnel Psychology, 52*(3), 591-620. https://doi.org/10.1111/j.1744-6570.1999.tb00173.x

Vessey, W. B., Barrett, J. D., Mumford, M. D., Johnson, G., & Litwiller, B. (2014). Leadership of highly creative people in highly creative fields: A historiometric study of scientific leaders. *The Leadership Quarterly, 25*(4), 672-691. https://doi.org/10.1016/j.leaqua.2014.03.001

References

Agar, M. (1980). *The professional stranger.* New York: Academic Press.

Amabile, T. M. (1982). A consensual assessment technique. *Journal of Personality and Social Psychology, 43*, 997-1013. https://doi.org/10.1037/002 2-3514.43.5.997

Amabile, T. M. (1996). *Creativity in context: Update to the social psychology of creativity.* Westview Press.

Andrews, J., & Smith, D. C. (1996). In search of the marketing imagination: Factors affecting the creativity of marketing programs for mature products. *Journal of Marketing Research, 33*(2), 174-187. https://doi.org/10.2307/3152145

Austin, J. R. (2003). Transactive memory in organizational groups: The effects of content, consensus, specialization, and accuracy on group performance. *Journal of Applied Psychology, 88*(5), 866. https://doi.org/10.1037/0021-9010.88.5.866

Baer, M. (2010). The strength-of-weak-ties perspective on creativity: A comprehensive examination and extension. *Journal of Applied Psychology, 95*(3), 592. https://doi.org/10.1037/a0018761

Barnowe, J. T. (1975). Leadership and performance outcomes in research organizations: The supervisor of scientists as a source of assistance. *Organizational Behavior and Human Performance, 14*(2), 264-280. https://doi.org/10.1016/0030-5073(75)90029-X

Becker, G. S., & Murphy, K. M. (1992). The division of labor, coordination costs, and knowledge. *The Quarterly Journal of Economics, 107*(4), 1137-1160. https://doi.org/10.2307/2118383

Berg, J. M. (2014). The primal mark: How the beginning shapes the end in the development of creative ideas. *Organizational Behavior and Human Decision Processes, 125*(1), 1-17. https://doi.org/10.1016/j.obhdp.2014.06.001

Blau, P. M. (1977). *Inequality and heterogeneity: A primitive theory of social structure* (Vol. 7). Free Press New York.

Bliese, P. D. (2000). Within-group agreement, non-independence, and reliability: Implications for data aggregation and analyses. In K. J. Klein & S. W. J. Kozlowski (Eds.), *Multilevel theory, research, and methods in organizations: Foundations, extensions, and new directions* (pp. 349-381). San Francisco: Jossey-Bass.

Boardman, C., & Bozeman, B. (2007). Role strain in university research centers. *Journal of Higher Education, 7*(4), 430-463. https://doi.org/10.1353/jhe.2007.0020

Boland, R. J., Jr., & Tenkasi, R. V. (1995). Perspective making and perspective taking in communities of knowing. *Organization Science, 6*(4), 350-372. https://doi.org/10.1287/orsc.6.4.350

Bunderson, J. S., & Sutcliffe, K. M. (2002). Comparing alternative conceptualizations of functional diversity in management teams: Process and performance effects. *Academy of Management Journal, 45*(5), 875-893. https://doi.org/10.2307/3069319

Carlile, P. R. (2004). Transferring, translating, and transforming: An integrative framework for managing knowledge across boundaries. *Organization Science, 15*(5), 555-568. https://doi.org/10.1287/orsc.1040.0094

Chen, G., Farh, J. L., Campbell-Bush, E. M., Wu, Z., & Wu, X. (2013). Teams as innovative systems: Multilevel motivational antecedents of innovation in R&D teams. *Journal of Applied Psychology, 98*(6), 1018-1027. https://doi.org/10.1037/a0032663

Collins, F. S., Morgan, M., & Patrinos, A. (2003). The human genome project: Lessons from large scale biology. *Science, 300*(5617), 286-290. https://doi.org/10.1126/science.1084564

Cooke, R. A., & Szumal, J. L. (1994). The impact of group interaction styles on problem-solving effectiveness. *The Journal of Applied Behavioral Science, 30*(4), 415-437. https://doi.org/10.1177/0021886394304005

Cronin, M. A., & Weingart, L. R. (2007). Representational gaps, information processing, and conflict in functionally diverse teams. *Academy of Management Review, 32*(3), 761-773. https://doi.org/10.5465/AMR.2007.25275511

Cummings, J. N., & Kiesler, S. (2005). Collaborative research across disciplinary and organizational boundaries. *Social Studies of Science, 35*(5), 703-722. https://doi.org/10.1177/0306312705055535

Edmondson, A. C., & Harvey, J. F. (2016). Unpacking team diversity: An integrative multi-level model of cross-boundary teaming. *Harvard Business School Technology & Operations Mgt. Unit Working Paper* (17-013).

Edmondson, A. C., & Nembhard, I. M. (2009). Product development and learning in project teams: The challenges are the benefits. *Journal of Product Innovation Management, 26*(2), 123-138. https://doi.org/10.1111/j.1540-5885.2009.00341.x

Eisenbeiss, S. A., van Knippenberg, D., & Boerner, S. (2008). Transformational leadership and team innovation: Integrating team climate principles. *Journal of Applied Psychology, 93*(6), 1438. https://doi.org/10.1037/a0012716

Emerson, R. M., Fretz, R. I., & Shaw, L. L. (2001). Participant observation and fieldnotes. In P. Atkinson, A. Coffey, S. Delamont, J. Lofland, & L. Lofland (Eds.), *Handbook of Ethnography* (pp. 352-368). Sage Publications. https://doi.org/10.4135/9781848608337.n24

Falk-Krzesinski, H. J., Börner, K., Contractor, N., Fiore, S. M., Hall, K. L., Keyton, J., & Uzzi, B. (2010). Advancing the science of team science. *Clinical and Translational Science, 3*(5), 263-266. https://doi.org/10.1111/j.1752-8062.2010.00223.x

Fang, F. C., & Casadevall, A. (2010). *Lost in translation—Basic science in the era of translational research.* Americal Society of Microbiology. https://doi.org/10.1128/IAI.01318-09

Fleming, L. (2001). Recombinant uncertainty in technological search. *Management Science, 47*(1), 117-132. https://doi.org/10.1287/mnsc.47.1.117.10671

Garud, R., & Rappa, M. A. (1994). A socio-cognitive model of technology evolution: The case of cochlear implants. *Organization Science, 5*(3), 344-362. https://doi.org/10.1287/orsc.5.3.344

Hargadon, A. B., & Bechky, B. A. (2006). When collections of creatives become creative collectives: A field study of problem solving at work. *Organization Science, 17*(4), 484-500. https://doi.org/10.1287/orsc.1060.0200

Harrison, D. A., & Klein, K. J. (2007). What's the difference? Diversity constructs as separation, variety, or disparity in organizations. *Academy of Management Review, 32*(4), 1199-1228. https://doi.org/10.5465/AMR.2007.26586096

Hessels, L. K., & Van Lente, H. (2008). Re-thinking new knowledge production: A literature review and a research agenda. *Research Policy, 37*(4), 740-760. https://doi.org/10.1016/j.respol.2008.01.008

Hoever, I. J., van Knippenberg, D., van Ginkel, W. P., & Barkema, H. G. (2012). Fostering team creativity: Perspective taking as key to unlocking diversity's potential. *Journal of Applied Psychology, 97*(5), 982-996. https://doi.org/10.1037/a0029159

Hollenbeck, J. R., Beersma, B., & Schouten, M. E. (2012). Beyond team types and taxonomies: A dimensional scaling conceptualization for team description. *Academy of Management Review, 37*(1), 82-106.

Homan, A. C., van Knippenberg, D., Van Kleef, G. A., & De Dreu, C. K. (2007). Interacting dimensions of diversity: Cross-categorization and the functioning of diverse work groups. *Group Dynamics: Theory, Research, and Practice, 11*(2), 79. https://doi.org/10.1037/1089-2699.11.2.79

Huckman, R. S., Staats, B. R., & Upton, D. M. (2009). Team familiarity, role experience, and performance: Evidence from Indian software services. *Management Science, 55*(1), 85-100. https://doi.org/10.1287/mnsc.1080.0921

Jackson, C. L., & LePine, J. A. (2003). Peer responses to a team's weakest link: A test and extension of LePine and Van Dyne's model. *Journal of Applied Psychology, 88*(3), 459. https://doi.org/10.1037/0021-9010.88.3.459

Jackson, S. E., & Joshi, A. (2011). Work team diversity. In S. Zedeck (Ed.), *APA handbooks in psychology. APA handbook of industrial and organizational psychology, Vol. 1. Building and developing the organization* (pp. 651-686). Washington, DC, US: American Psychological Association. http://dx.doi.org/10.1037/12169-020

Jones, B. F. (2009). The burden of knowledge and the "death of the renaissance man:" Is innovation getting harder? *The Review of Economic Studies, 76*(1), 283-317. https://doi.org/10.1111/j.1467-937X.2008.00531.x

Jung, D. I., & Avolio, B. J. (1999). Effects of leadership style and followers' cultural orientation on performance in group and individual task conditions. *Academy of Management Journal, 42*, 208-218. https://doi.org/10.2307/257093

Kane, A. A. (2010). Unlocking knowledge transfer potential: Knowledge demonstrability and superordinate social identity. *Organization Science, 21*(3), 643-660. https://doi.org/10.1287/orsc.1090.0469

Kauffeld, S. & Lehmann-Willenbrock, N. (2012). Meetings matter: Effects of team meetings on team and organizational success. *Small Group Research, 43*(2), 130-158. https://doi.org/10.1177/1046496411429599

Kearney, E., & Gebert, D. (2009). Managing diversity and enhancing team outcomes: The promise of transformational leadership. *Journal of Applied Psychology, 94*(1), 77-89. https://doi.org/10.1037/a0013077

Kerr, N. L., & Tindale, R. S. (2004). Group performance and decision making. In *Annual Review of Psychology, 55*, 623-655. https://doi.org/10.1146/annurev.psych.55.090902.142009

Klein, J. T., Misra, S., & Lortrechiano, G. R. (2020) Introduction: Communication in inter- and trans-disciplinary teams. In G. R. Lotrecchiano & S. Misra (Eds), *Communication in transdisciplinary teams* (pp. 1-17). Santa Rosa, CA: Informing Science Press.

Krefting, L. (1991). Rigor in qualitative research: The assessment of trustworthiness. *American Journal of Occupational Therapy, 45*(3), 214-222. https://doi.org/10.5014/ajot.45.3.214

Kovács, B., & Sharkey, A. J. (2014). The paradox of publicity: How awards can negatively affect the evaluation of quality. *Administrative Science Quarterly, 59*(1), 1-33.

Lamont, M., Mallard, G., & Guetzkow, J. (2006). Beyond blind faith: Overcoming the obstacles to interdisciplinary evaluation. *Research Evaluation, 15*(1), 43-55. https://doi.org/10.3152/147154406781776002

Leahey, E. (2016). From sole investigator to team scientist: Trends in the practice and study of research collaboration. *Annual Review of Sociology, 42*(1), 81-100. https://doi.org/10.1146/annurev-soc-081715-074219

Leahey, E., Beckman, C., & Stanko, T. (2015). Prominent but less productive: The impact of interdisciplinarity on scientists' research. *Administrative Science Quarterly, 62*(1), 105-139.

LePine, J. A., & Van Dyne, L. (2001). Voice and cooperative behavior as contrasting forms of contextual performance: Evidence of differential relationships with big five personality characteristics and cognitive ability. *Journal of Applied Psychology, 86*(2), 326. https://doi.org/10.1037/0021-9010.86.2.326

Long-Lingo, E. L., & O'Mahony, S. (2010). Nexus work: Brokerage on creative projects. *Administrative Science Quarterly, 55*(1), 47-81. https://doi.org/10.2189/asqu.2010.55.1.47

Mathieu, J., Maynard, M. T., Rapp, T., & Gilson, L. (2008). Team effectiveness 1997-2007: A review of recent advancements and a glimpse into the future. *Journal of Management, 34*(3), 410-476. https://doi.org/10.1177/0149206308316061

Milliken, F. J., Lant, T. K., Bridwell-Mitchell, E. N., Starbuck, W. H., & Farjoun, M. (2005). Barriers to the interpretation and diffusion of information about potential problems in organizations: Lessons from the space shuttle Columbia. In W. Starbuck & M. Farjoun (Eds.), *Organizations at the limit* (pp. 246-266). Wiley-Blackwell.

Misra, S., Stokols, D., & Cheng, L. (2015). The transdisciplinary orientation scale: Factor structure and relation to the integrative quality and scope of scientific publications. *Journal of Collaborative Healthcare and Translational Medicine, 3*(2), 1042.

Morgeson, F. P., DeRue, D. S., & Karam, E. P. (2010). Leadership in teams: A functional approach to understanding leadership structures and processes. *Journal of Management, 36*(1), 5-39. https://doi.org/10.1177/0149206309347376

Mumford, M. D., & Gustafson, S. B. (1988). Creativity syndrome: Integration, application, and innovation. *Psychological Bulletin, 103*(1), 27. https://doi.org/10.1037/0033-2909.103.1.27

Mumford, M. D., Scott, G. M., Gaddis, B., & Strange, J. M. (2002). Leading creative people: Orchestrating expertise and relationships. *The Leadership Quarterly, 13*(6), 705-750. https://doi.org/10.1016/S1048-9843(02)00158-3

Nygren, R., & Levine. (1996). Leadership of work teams: Factors influencing team outcomes. In M. M. Beyerlein, D. Johnson, & S. T. Beyerlein (Eds.), *Interdisciplinary studies of work teams* (Vol. 3, pp. 67-104). Greenwich, CT: JAI Press.

Okhuysen, G. A., & Eisenhardt, K. M. (2002). Integrating knowledge in groups: How formal interventions enable flexibility. *Organization Science, 13*(4), 370-386. https://doi.org/10.1287/orsc.13.4.370.2947

Paruchuri, S. (2010). Intraorganizational networks, interorganizational networks, and the impact of central inventors: A longitudinal study of pharmaceutical firms. *Organization Science, 21*(1), 63-80. https://doi.org/10.1287/orsc.1080.0414

Podsakoff, P. M., MacKenzie, S. B., Lee, J.-Y., & Podsakoff, N. P. (2003). Common method biases in behavioral research: A critical review of the literature and recommended remedies. *Journal of Applied Psychology, 88*(5), 879. https://doi.org/10.1037/0 021-9010.88.5.879

Rip, A. (2004). Strategic research, post-modern universities and research training. *Higher Education Policy, 17*(2), 153-166. https://doi.org/10.1057/palgrave.hep.8300048

Rubin, H. J., & Rubin, I. S. (2011). *Qualitative interviewing: The art of hearing data.* Sage.

Sawyer, K. (2003). Evaluative processes during group improvisational performance. In M. A. Runco (Ed.), *Critical creative processes* (pp. 303-327). Hampton Press.

Shin, S. J., & Zhou, J. (2003). Transformational leadership, conservation, and creativity: Evidence from Korea. *Academy of Management Journal, 46*(6), 703-714. https://doi.org/10.2307/30040662

Simons, T., Pelled, L. H., & Smith, K. A. (1999). Making use of difference: Diversity, debate, and decision comprehensiveness in top management teams. *Academy of Management Journal, 42*(6), 662-673. https://doi.org/10.2307/256987

Simonton, D. K. (1999). Significant samples: The psychological study of eminent individuals. *Psychological Methods, 4*(4), 425. https://doi.org/10.1037/1082-989X.4.4.425

Tansley, C., & Newell, S. (2007). Project social capital, leadership and trust: A study of human resource information systems development. *Journal of Managerial Psychology, 22*(4), 350-368. https://doi.org/10.1108/02683940710745932

Tierney, P., Farmer, S. M., & Graen, G. B. (1999). An examination of leadership and employee creativity: The relevance of traits and relationships. *Personnel Psychology, 52*(3), 591-620. https://doi.org/10.1111/j.1744-6570.1999.tb00173.x

van de Ven, A. H., & Poole, M. S. (1995). Explaining development and change in organizations. *Academy of Management Review, 20*(3), 510-540. https://doi.org/10.2307/258786

van Knippenberg, D. (2011). Embodying who we are: Leader group prototypicality and leadership effectiveness. *The Leadership Quarterly, 22*(6), 1078-1091. https://doi.org/10.1146/annurev.psych.58.110405.085546

van Knippenberg, D., & Schippers, M. C. (2007). Work group diversity. *Annual Review of Psychology, 58*, 515-541. https://doi.org/10.1146/annurev.psych.58.110405.085546

van Knippenberg, D., & van Ginkel, W. P. (2010). The categorization-elaboration model of work group diversity: Wielding the double-edged sword. In R. J. Crisp (Ed.), *The psychology of social and cultural diversity* (pp. 255-280). Wiley-Blackwell. https://doi.org/10.1002/9781444325447.ch11

Vessey, W. B., Barrett, J. D., Mumford, M. D., Johnson, G., & Litwiller, B. (2014). Leadership of highly creative people in highly creative fields: A historiometric study of scientific leaders. *The Leadership Quarterly, 25*(4), 672-691. https://doi.org/10.1016/j.leaqua.2014.03.001

Watson, W. E., Kumar, K., & Michaelsen, L. K. (1993). Cultural diversity's impact on interaction process and performance: Comparing homogeneous and diverse task groups. *Academy of Management Journal, 36*(3), 590-602. https://doi.org/10.2307/256593

Wengraf, T. (2001). *Qualitative research interviewing: Biographic narrative and semi-structured methods*: Sage. https://doi.org/10.4135/9781849209717

Wiersema, M. F., & Bantel, K. A. (1992). Top management team demography and corporate strategic change. *Academy of Management Journal, 35*(1), 91-121. https://doi.org/10.2307/256474

Winter, S. J., & Berente, N. (2012). A commentary on the pluralistic goals, logics of action, and institutional contexts of translational team science. *Translational Behavioral Medicine, 2*(4), 441-445. https://doi.org/10.1007/s13142-012-0165-0

Wittenbaum, G. M., Hollingshead, A. B., & Botero, I. C. (2004). From cooperative to motivated information sharing in groups: Moving beyond the hidden profile paradigm. *Communication Monographs, 71*(3), 286-310.

Wuchty, S., Jones, B. F., & Uzzi, B. (2007). The increasing dominance of teams in production of knowledge. *Science, 316*(5827), 1036-1039. https://doi.org/10.1126/science.1136099

Yin, R. K. (2015). *Qualitative research from start to finish*: Guilford Publications.

Zaccaro, S. J., Rittman, A. L., & Marks, M. A. (2001). Team leadership. *The Leadership Quarterly, 12*(4), 451-483.

Zerhouni, E. (2003). The NIH roadmap. *Science, 302*(5642), 63-64 + 72. http://www.jstor.org/stable/3835267?origin=JSTOR-pdf

Gaetano R. Lotrecchiano & Shalini Misra (Editors). 2020
Communication in Transdisciplinary Teams
Santa Rosa, CA: Informing Science Press

Chapter 6:
Knowledge Sharing in Teams:
Shifting Paradigms
in Information Flow

Megan Potterbusch
The George Washington University, Washington, DC, USA
mpotterbusch@gwu.edu

Gaetano R. Lotrecchiano
The George Washington University, Washington, DC, USA
glotrecc@gwu.edu

Chapter Objectives

- To expand exclusive conceptions of "publications" offered in journals and books. In many ways open science is a natural expansion of traditional forms of scientific communication.

- To facilitate research reproducibility and support the study of science team interactions by capturing the context as well as the research outputs, which could be especially valuable for understanding workflows and teaming behavior, through open workflow tools.

- To propose ways to engage with the pragmatic school of open science in order to ease the tension within teams when attitudes about ownership of knowledge differ amongst team members.

- To elaborate on the advancement and success of open science and its focus on trust and communication in order to foster research culture norms that value sharing and collaboration over individual primacy and singular authority.

- To promote team ownership and organization through the strategic application of open science centered communication technologies.

Introduction to the Chapter

This chapter considers the contributions of Open Science Theory (OST) to team science, and the opportunities and challenges associated with adopting open science principles in science team settings. The Open Science Framework (OSF), an online tool that facilitates open science, serves as an exemplar technology for illustrating the ways that OST can inform and expand cognitive and behavioral dynamics in teams at multiple levels in a single tool.

An earlier version of this chapter was published as Potterbusch, M., & Lotrecchiano, G. R. (2018). Shifting paradigms in information flow: An open science framework (OSF) for knowledge sharing teams. *Informing Science: the International Journal of an Emerging Transdiscipline, 21,* 179-199. https://doi.org/10.28945/4031

Team dynamics and characteristics affect human-machine assisted team-based interaction and the regulation between traditional and open science dissemination. Aspects such as workflow culture, attitudes about ownership of knowledge, readiness to share openly, shifts from group-driven to user-driven functionality and from group-organizing to self-organizing structures, and the development of trust within teams will be key in this regulation. This chapter aims to illuminate the shared goals between open science and the study of teams by focusing on science team activities and the products of those activities (data management, methods, algorithms, and outputs) as focal objects for further combined study. Materials and concepts have been sifted and curated to develop a synthesis of team science theories, current practice, and nascent literature on open science theory.

Background

In an effort to promote collaboration in research teams tackling complex problems, many new initiatives exist on local, regional, and national levels that aim to bring stakeholders together into cross-disciplinary teams so as to accelerate or diversify solutions. Many of these initiatives in the United States stem from responses to executive and federal mandates from agencies like the National Academies of Science (NAS), the National Institutes of Health (NIH), the National Science Foundation (NSF), and private funders as well as executive orders that have required greater collaboration within and across disciplines requiring more team-oriented scientific approaches (Bennet, Gadlin, & Levine-Finley, 2010; National Research Council, 2015; Obama, 2015). As a result, team-initiated projects have increased over the past decade (Jones, Wuchty, & Uzzi, 2008; Porter, Roessner, & Heberger, 2008; Ranwala et al., 2017) and outputs from these diverse teams have shown a noticeable increase across fields and sectors to value team efforts in science (Bahney et al., 2016; Hinnant et al., 2012). Success measures of these cross-disciplinary teams continue to be mainly attributed to published scholarly outputs in an attempt to justify and maintain that cross-disciplinary teaming effectiveness can be observed through publications impact and diversity of authorship (Bales et al., 2014; Rosas, Kagan, Schouten, Slack, & Trochim, 2011).

While efforts to justify increased impact of cross-disciplinary teams through bibliometric measurement methods like those mentioned above has provided insights into some of the advances made by team-initiated project teams, bibliometric analyses fall short in explaining the interactive dynamics of stakeholder involvement in scientific teams (Engwall & Blockmans, 2014; W. Klein & Bloom, 2005). A series of concerns about the measurement of contributions among scientific stakeholders emerges as sharing knowledge advances with our new and more open-centric technologies that defy the confines of traditional publishing avenues. These concerns include issues around recognition of author contribution; new forms of publishable research materials; ownership of knowledge; team contributions over the lifespan of a project; non-author contributions; and the impact that stakeholders have on the direction of research and scholarly projects. These along with other issues beg the question: *How do cross-disciplinary teams leverage technology in order to document, provide access to, and preserve scientific contributions?*

Embedded within the research and publication process is a complex array of interactions that, until the advent of communication and research management technologies, remained relegated to conversation, physical lab books, written notes, and even casual outings amongst colleagues. These forms of informal communication and physical research management do not facilitate bulk analysis and thus go largely unanalyzed or critiqued for their contributions to the process of science. With the rise of technologies that support, capture, and document much of the activity once veiled by these frequently inaccessible artifacts, the possibility emerges for much of the interactive material involved in scientific activity to be exposed and shared. This allows for scientific interactions and the 'process' of science to be part of the dissemination of scholarly activity. Thus, both products — such as data, methods, and algorithms — and the communication processes embedded in the act of doing research can become objects of study. The questions available for scientific inquiry multiply exponentially. Data could become part of a meta-study. Computational algorithms could be augmented in order to answer larger-scale questions. The communication processes of teams could be assessed to better understand the elements that go into team effectiveness and impact, which in turn would allow for the implementation of enhanced practices based on effective use of research assisting technology.

However, when it comes to making research results available to the public, the typical scholarly communication workflow remains very traditional, closely following an age old path, one that starts with the submission of an initial article draft to a publisher or editor, follows through private peer review, and frequently ends in a single form of final output: an article published in a scholarly journal. This process shapes the scholarly communication paradigm for information flow from scientists to communities of others scientists to the mainstream public knowledge base (Weimer & Andrew, 2013). The dissemination of scientific material that relies solely on this publication model neglects and loses out on the many other research products outlined above while simultaneously driving many of the behaviors of scientists wanting to attain the gold standard of publishable results – generally a citation, measured in bibliometric assessment. Several issues become easily apparent: from the reluctance to share openly about the complex processes and collaborator negotiations occurring in the course of research activity, to the lack of transparency and trust as it applies to scholarly recognition and credit, and to the still limited sharing of secondary research artifacts often not included in final publication outputs. All of these scientific teaming artifacts are veiled from the consumer of the science, thus, making the evaluation of *how successful teams work effectively* a mystery to science stakeholders and consumers. Many of these interactions, and others, that typically occur within science teams have the potential to provide rich data, which could greatly increase our understanding of team high-effectiveness processes.

By using tools and technologies that now exist and are a departure from the traditional flow of information, research teams can adapt to both the mandate and modern trends, which in turn can fundamentally inform interdisciplinary team science. This transition, in combination with increased transparency, would allow team science researchers to understand teaming processes and expand possible research about teams. Informal scientific contributions and communications are increasingly captured, because professionals now communicate and collaborate frequently through written virtual formats (Google Docs, Dropbox, emails, tweets, blogs, etc.) that generate digital artifacts of the interactions. Digital platforms bridge multiple stakeholders representing different disciplines, but more than that, they provide venues that facilitate learning and knowledge integration, which are critical to the advancement of cross-disciplinary team science initiatives (Pennington, 2011). These written digests and digital records of information serve as important data sources by which to map the interactions that humans have with one another as individuals while they collaborate especially in scientific teams. In an era when technological communications are increasingly freely available across scientific classes and the ability of individuals to access these technologies is only limited by one's freedom to explore them, further consideration and study of how communication technologies, especially in scientific sharing and collaborative activities, contribute to the advancement of science to achieve new levels of innovation is needed.

This chapter will explore how an understanding of human communication in cross-disciplinary teams might be enhanced through open science based technologies. In addition to reviewing the problems associated with cross-disciplinary communication through collaboration technologies, the authors will explore Open Science Theory (OST) as a framework to consider the potential of machine-assisted collaboration to enhance team knowledge mapping and interactions. As a case example, the Open Science Framework (OSF), a tool that supports collaborator controlled workflow transparency, will be introduced as a platform by which certain key issues associated with cross-disciplinary team engagement might be understood and improved.

Clarification of Concepts

Communication: Traditional forms of information exchange between individuals such as direct messages, peer review, and any other form of conversation (i.e., reciprocal communication) (Rollman, Krug, & Parente, 2004).

Interaction: Includes all forms of "communication" (verbal and behavioral), as well as newer forms of interaction such as reviewing workflow materials, exploring interactive visualizations, or copying and building off someone's idea (Parasuraman, Sheridan, & Wickens, 2000).

Team: Indicates collaborators that seek to solve a problem or work on a given research project or grant (Wuchty, Jones, & Uzzi, 2007).

Team science: The act of addressing scientific problems as a group dedicated to shared scholarly goals (Stokols, Hall, Taylor, & Moser, 2008).

Stakeholders: Invested members of the teams' scholarly community who may serve in the capacity of editorial reviewers or as participants in the team's professional network.

Consumers: Recipients of research products who do not typically communicate directly with the team and their **direct** stakeholders. This group may contribute in a very distant capacity, and in some cases they may also be stakeholders; however, generally they do not interact in a direct way with teams of scientists (Gibson, 2000).

Open science: A variety of activities and practices that support and/or promote transparency, accessibility, collaboration, and contribution in research by providing access to materials beyond formal publications such as data, lab-notes, open-source software, and methodology (FOSTER Plus, 2016; Suber, 2012). For a better understanding of the beliefs or motivations behind adopting, or not adopting, open science practices, one must look to the nascent field of Open Science Theory (OST).

What is Open Science Theory (OST)?

As outlined by Fecher and Friesike (2014), OST is best conceptualized in its entirety by highlighting the multiple perspectives or schools of thought, which motivate advocates, supporters, and practitioners of open science activities. One purpose of open science is the desire to democratize knowledge by lowering financial and other access barriers and reducing copyright restrictions to science in general and data or publications in particular (Fecher & Friesike, 2014). Similarly, some open science advocates and practitioners work to help make science more intellectually accessible and engaging to the public through more opportunities for general involvement in the process of science and through blogging/microblogging. Open science generally includes the importance of alternative forms of measurements (i.e., altmetrics, credit for peer review, etc.) and the infrastructure involved in supporting efficient, collaborative, and interoperable platforms and tools, because new forms of contribution require new forms of measurement in order to be acknowledged (Fecher & Friesike, 2014; Priem, Taraborelli, Groth, & Neylon, 2010). A pragmatic motivation drives many open science practitioners: the belief that "knowledge-creation could be more efficient if scientists worked together" and that this can be accomplished by "opening up the process of knowledge creation" (Fecher & Friesike, 2014, p. 20). Each perspective or motivation for open science can be viewed and explored somewhat independently of others, but the activities involved, such as sharing or re-using open data, overlap across these different schools of thought.

In order to focus on the impacts and implications of open science on team dynamics, the discussion of OST here focuses primarily on the pragmatic school, which includes transparency in the process of knowledge creation, and the infrastructure school, which pertains to open platforms, tools, and services (Fecher & Friesike, 2014). The goal behind this exploration of OST is to better understand the ways that it allows for new forms of interaction at all levels: from team communications, such as collaborative document writing, to stakeholder and consumer interactions, such as exploring published data using author/publisher provided visualization tools.

In many ways open science is a radical expansion of the historical forms of scientific dissemination (e.g., published articles, scientific conferences, and poster presentations). As opposed to only sharing final, published articles, open science allows researchers to provide more access points to their work. As such, in the context of this article, "publication" can refer to "any product (e.g., publications, datasets, experiments, software, web sites, blogs) resulting from a research activity, that is relevant to the interpretation, evaluation, and reuse of the activity or part of it" (Assante, Candela, Castelli, Manghi, & Pagano, 2015), which is accessible to the public. Accessibility in this case includes preservation and dissemination activities such as depositing the materials for publication into a repository that provides a Digital Object Identifier (DOI) or other form of persistent, interoperable, unique identifier (International DOI Foundation, n.d.).

Tools and Technology in Open Science and Team Science

Many modern tools and technologies that support research workflow and communications lie on a continuum from opaque, or "closed" to transparent or "open." Tools and technology for in-team communication include anything from email to conference-call software and from project management software to shared cloud storage. These communication tools can be designed for privacy or openness. In fact, many tools support either type of use. For example, a team can use Google Hangouts for a private meeting or choose to use Hangouts On Air which broadcasts live to YouTube.com in order to provide stakeholders with a window into the conversation. Teams can also choose to privately share documents using a cloud storage provider like Dropbox or publically share a link to a folder in order to promote stakeholder access to working documents and provide a view into the evolution of their research.

Similarly, tools and technology specifically designed for communicating with stakeholders and the general public can be more or less open. In this case, traditional publication is the most "closed" or limited-access communication system for the research process, because the only part of the research traditionally available is the completed manuscript. This process is becoming more aligned with open science principles through the increasing availability of preprints, open data sets, software, and supplementary materials. These tools and technologies can be visualized along an intersecting continuum (Figure 1). The point of intersection comes in the form of open workflow technology; in other words, tools designed for both the active work of research and the open publication of materials. At this time, few tools exist that wholly encompass both parts of this communication continuum, and only the Open Science Framework (OSF), created by the Center for Open Science and designed "to provide free and open source project management support for researchers across the entire research lifecycle" (Center for Open Science, n.d.-b), exemplifies many of the principles of open science outlined above.

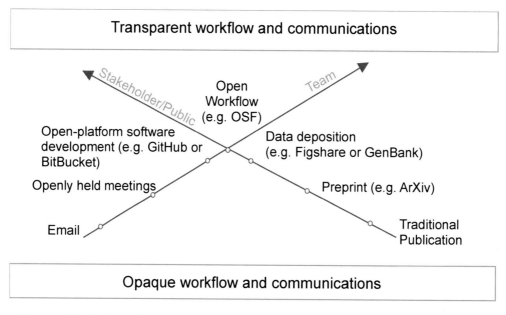

Figure 1. Technology Continuum: from Opaque to Transparent Communication within Teams and with Stakeholders

A published OSF project that has been used by a research team as an active workspace throughout a research project allows for transparency of both in-team research activities and public communication with stakeholders. This workspace would contain the version history, commentary, and other activities that contributors have carried out throughout the project while simultaneously providing access to the final dataset, code, and/or any other supplementary materials created in the course of normal research (e.g., codebooks and methodology). Publication of an OSF project can be achieved via making a project public and generating an indexed, permanent identifier (e.g., a Digital Object Identifier or DOI see http://www.doi.org/) or by generating a registration, which is a snapshot of a project at a particular moment in time (e.g., https://osf.io/aurjt/). These outputs and the activity feed generated over the course of normal OSF use create an opportunity to better understand the types of interactions occurring within team research activities. Coding of the individual, team, and even stakeholder interactions becomes possible when and if a project becomes public. This increases workflow transparency within and across teams with similar interests and with a stakeholder and consumer invested in the evolution of the science. It provides access to an otherwise untraceable exchange of knowledge and social relationship development in science, which is not only important to the study of teams but also important to maintaining both individual autonomy and team cohesion.

Other Options for Workflow Transparency:

- **Registered Reports**: a registration created before data are collected and that meets certain qualifications can be submitted to participating journals, peer-reviewed for sound methodology and published with an agreement to publish the final paper.

- **Electronic Lab Notebooks** (e.g., LabArchives): Sections of these digital research tools may be made public and issued DOIs and entire notebooks can be exported to PDF for publication, individual sharing, or preservation.

- **Online, Collaborative Version Control Tools** (e.g., GitHub): Primarily for software developing teams, these platforms can be used to track and manage entire research workflows and can be connected to preservation platforms such as Zenodo or FigShare.

If the suggested workflow is followed, certain registrations can even be published as Registered Reports in journals such as Nature Human Behaviour, which provides teams conducting research with an incentive and an opportunity to share their work at different stages ad in different ways (Center for Open Science, n.d.-a). Another form of workflow transparency can be achieved through the use and open sharing of Electronic Lab Notebooks; although these tools are not publishable in the same way, sections often can be issued DOIs and be made publically available and whole notebooks can be downloaded to PDF for publication, individual-sharing, and preservation (LabArchives, 2018). For teams that work primarily within software development, version control tools such as GitHub can also publish their entire workflows openly by connecting their repository (i.e., workspace) to a preservation platform that issues DOIs such as FigShare or Zenodo. Although not all communications or supplementary materials are likely to be attached to the software, this is still a way of publishing a workspace rich with team interactions.

Although open, transparent workflow – as a radically transparent approach to open science – promises the most disruption and the greatest variety of potential benefits from openness, it can also present great risks (Scheliga & Friesike, 2014), such as revealing personal file management habits via activity tracking and decreasing potential competitive advantage through shared datasets and software pipelines. Thus, there are other aspects and tools along this continuum to be addressed. Since the assumption underlying the infrastructure school of thought is that "efficient research depends on the available tools and applications" (Fecher & Friesike, 2014, p. 20), considering the various related technologies facilitates an understanding of the additional types and forms of interaction that have become possible in recent years. For example, open infrastructure technology for team communication includes such resources as Overleaf (https://www.overleaf.com/), a collaborative writing tool that facilitates publication through templates and publisher integrations while also supporting embedding data and code into images of figures, and GitLab (https://about.gitlab.com), an open source software development and code sharing resource. These and other collaboration-oriented technologies allow researchers to do more of their work openly or to facilitate lower barriers to making their research transparent in strategic ways.

As previously mentioned, many new forms of scholarly communication have arisen lately driven in part by the increasingly machine-mediated research process. These forms include sharing research building-blocks such as scientific algorithms, raw data, processed data, and pre-published articles. New funder and publisher requirements regarding sharing data associated with research and publications are responsible for some of the changes towards increased sharing of supplementary materials. Open data files may, but do not necessarily, include details describing collection and/or processing methodology or associated algorithms. Similarly, not all researchers who choose to share the code or algorithms that underpin their scientific discoveries choose to include their version history, associated data sets, or complete workspace with their shared software. Instead, algorithms may be shared as a single final output in one of the previously mentioned repositories, on personal websites, or through software papers. One website identifies and indexes software resources for the astronomy community is the Astronomy Source Code Library (http://ascl.net/). These are all pieces of software that have been cited in published articles and also made available via NASA ADS (https://ui.adsabs.harvard.edu/); thus, making the code discoverable in the same index as other scholarly resources – predominantly articles.

Data repositories, such as GenBank (https://www.ncbi.nlm.nih.gov/genbank), house data collected from many researchers and provided in highly specific formats with particular descriptions (metadata) that facilitate discovery of data sets from many entry points. By increasing distribution, sharing data in this way facilitates discovery and allows additional stakeholders to explore areas for novel research. In the case of GenBank, deposited data are exchanged on a daily basis across the "International Nucleotide Sequence Database Collaboration, which comprises the DNA DataBank of Japan (DDBJ), the European Nucleotide Archive (ENA), and GenBank at NCBI" (Johnson, 2017). Internationally broad distribution increases access for researchers, which means that data collected by a single research team can become even more impactful to the scientific community overall. Data repositories are not limited any particular scientific field, for example, "ICPSR [Inter-university Consortium for Political and Social Research] maintains a data archive of more than 250,000 files of research in the social and behavioral sciences" (Inter-university Consortium for Political and Social Research, n.d.) and FigShare provides a domain agnostic digital repository for researchers interested in preserving and receiving credit for all their research outputs (including data and software code). With both discovery and citation of data facilitated by the systems, authors and data collectors can receive additional scholarly credit for their contributions as well; thus, providing personal incentive to share beyond simply compliance with a government mandate (Alicea, 2016, Holdren, 2013) or the professional desire to increase the impact of the collected data.

Possible stakeholder communications have also become more open through such platforms as preprint servers and data repositories. Although ArXiv (https://arxiv.org/) has existed for decades, supporting the disciplines of physics, astronomy, and math, preprint servers like PsyArXiv (a preprint repository for psychology) and SocArXiv (a preprint repository for social sciences) are becoming increasingly popular places for scholars to make a pre-publication version of their soon-to-be-published articles available ("ArXives of Earth science," 2018; Fister, 2016). Allowing researchers to read and share cutting edge research early, preprint servers also facilitate public access to articles thus allowing for broader engagement with the material and increased visibility for the work and the research team (Berg et al., 2016). As much as these resources do disrupt the traditional scholarly communications landscape, it should be understood that they do not increase the openness or transparency of workflows or other interactions *within* a research team. Thus, preprints and open data resources provide expanded community access and consumption without necessarily impacting or highlighting team dynamics.

Visualization tools are not inherently part of open science. However, when they are used to create embedded interactive visualizations that allow consumers to better understand the published research and especially when they are nuanced or complex enough for consumers to make discoveries for themselves, the visualization then exemplifies the Public School of Open Science Theory as outlined by Fecher and Friesike (2014). In fact, it can be argued that good information visualization in general should facilitate user interaction and thus deeper meaning making on the part of consumers (Kosara, Hauser, & Gresh, 2003). Additionally, when code such as R (an open source coding language) is used to process data and generate figures, these figures can be published (by supporting platforms) with the data and code embedded and automatically generating the figure, which allows for increased scientific transparency. Inferring from open source software development communities, who rely on openness, this additional transparency allows for increased intellectual interaction between the information consumer and the research group who wrote the article, because the consumer can examine the process that went into creating the visualization, which in turn allows for a clearer understanding of the work (Dabbish, Stuart, Tsay, & Herbsleb, 2012).

Open Workflow Technology in Team Scholarship

Supporting the diverse needs, professional and interpersonal, of team members within open technology requires flexibility either within the technology itself or in how the teams apply the technology within their workflows. The OSF platform accommodates this need for flexibility by allowing for different levels of openness and customizable structure. Even teams desiring to implement a fully open workflow may still keep their project private until they are ready to share it. Conversely, teams not wishing to publish their workflow may still utilize the tool to provide open access to specific parts of their finished projects by uploading finalized files upon completion of their research. Researchers may also connect their preferred workflow tools, such as Google Drive or Dropbox, to the platform and allow their colleagues to engage in the OSF without them while still providing common team access to their materials. Adaptability of structure and terminology allow interdisciplinary teams to define the structural and descriptive vocabularies appropriate for their research needs and not be defined by a single discipline or by the platform of choice. Thus, teams are able organize their OSF projects to best suit specific team needs while also facilitating future public access to some or all of their work.

Consumers and stakeholders can build on the work of others without changing it and while maintaining attribution and provenance intrinsically within the OSF – through a process called forking. As potentially beneficial and timesaving as this functionality can be for the scientific ecosystem in general, concerns arise for many researchers about open sharing of materials (Scheliga & Friesike, 2014), and the possibility that information consumers could fork their research project to build out their own may increase this apprehension. To assure that intellectual credit remains with the original research group even when the project is public, the OSF provides citation guidance on every project that is created, and allows the administrators of the project to create DOIs, which are recognized throughout the publication system as a mark of a permanently available resource described with metadata, as previously mentioned. Researchers can further develop scholarship by making processes (e.g., workflow and previous versions of files) as well as products (i.e., data sets, software, or protocols) public, shareable, and citable. Increasing the social value for researchers sharing materials and for researchers studying or otherwise learning from openly shared materials is necessary for these functions to be valued and used (Alicea, 2016).

Naturally, different teams will need different tools and will be interested in different levels of openness. One example of a research group's use of the OSF is the Eleanor Roosevelt Papers Project. This is a historical documentation project centering on selection, transcription, and annotation of primary source materials (Brick & Regenhardt, n.d.). Seeking project management and communication technology, an editor and decision maker for this group reviewed their team needs as well as the functionality provided by the OSF. Requiring free storage, version control, automatic tracking of user activity, and different levels of access control, among other functions, the editor selected this tool for the project. The ability to make the platform public remains low on the research team's list of desires or motivations for adoption, because they have other methods for digital publication. However, now that the team's project is entirely in one location and organized, the editors are empowered to publish their workflow and work space within the OSF in the future with ease. Since their use of the technology is both novel and exemplary, their workspace could serve as an inspiration and template for other digital humanists or historians as well as being a potential object of study for team scientist interested in studying team dynamics or workflow behavior. External to the primary research, this team's implementation of the OSF has sparked curiosity from various stakeholders including fellow humanities researchers, librarians, and funders as demonstrated by numerous private and public speaking engagements on this novel implementation of the tool and on their visible and demonstrable workflow.

Another tangible example of a multi-level team working together and exploring judicious and appropriate use of open tools in a workflow is the University Seminar Creating a Culture of Collaboration at George Washington University (C3@GWU). Made up of "knowledge communities ("Think Tanks") [that] represent GWU, regional institutes, and federal government stakeholders" (https://blogs.gwu.edu/collaborativeculture/welcome-to-c3gwu/), C3@GWU engages stakeholders in trans-, inter-, and cross- disciplinary studies at different levels. This group uses fundamental technologies for communication such as email and teleconferencing services as well as a shared Google Drive for both administrative documentation and meeting notes, and a blog for external communication of activities and events performed or hosted by C3@GWU. By using the blog and making their work easily accessible to anyone, this group participates in open science in accordance with the "public school" of thinking. Through the comment feature, information consumers and stakeholders have a space to interact with the research team directly.

From an interest in exploring further opportunities for bi-directional non-team interactions and other aspects of open science in order to accomplish their own goals, C3@GWU reviewed their current abilities and what they wished to do, and found that there were additional levels of interaction available via Open Science Theory inspired tools and technology. Through the communication tools outlined above, this group centrally organizes around internally defined aims and goals; if they wanted to facilitate non-team member contributions or similar interactions in the future, they could explore open workflow tools like the OSF. These new forms of interaction could allow stakeholders to become agenda drivers and allow them to communicate in dialog with researchers within their team space instead of limiting communication to comments on blog posts written primarily for research consumers or to private emailing.

As is the hope of the Public School of Open Science Theory, the openness of the OSF platform (no pay subscription, discoverable through normal search engine searches) creates both opportunities for discovery by new consumers and additional space for interactions and engagement beyond one-way communication. Scholarship conducted publicly can lead to reservations on the part of researchers for many reasons, and, thus, selecting a single tool that facilitates both open (public) communication and private communication can help. In this case, the ability to provide public (seminar/stakeholder) and private (team-only) sections within a single workspace, such as the OSF provides, can help to mitigate the risks/challenges inherent in working entirely in the open.

Although exploring aspects of OST intrigues many team members of C3@GWU, overall the technologies currently in place generally meet the active needs of the team. Thus, most Think Tanks, smaller teams within the larger research group, have not adopted the OSF. The teams that have been using the tool did so when interest in exploring open science technology intersected with a need to communicate bi-directionally with stakeholders at a conference. Since this public use occurred within the initially developed project structure – currently private – future uses by other Think Tanks will be intellectually tied to this public component. This intellectual and technological connection will allow future consumers to understand the relationships between the Think Tanks without overall adoption of the tool happening simultaneously (or ever necessarily).

There are notable differences between working privately in a tool not designed for open science (e.g., email) and working privately in the OSF. By design, the OSF can be published along with all of the communications and interactions that took place in the course of research. With some notable exceptions (e.g., political figures), private email communications do not hold the same promise of future transparency or publication that working and communicating in a platform with built in publication capabilities; thus, the structural and content decisions must be carefully considered. Depending on decisions made by the team regarding how they would like to prepare their workspace for publication, their registration could even be published as a preprint (Assante et al., 2015). Projects that are published as registrations can continue to serve as active workspaces for the current team without impacting the contents of the registration. If the project is made public at the same time that the registration is created, even more possible interactions for consumers and stakeholders are generated. Suddenly there are two forms of available research (with different citations) that can be reviewed and understood. Stakeholders can even interact with research by duplicating or "forking" the public project in order to build on the research in a new direction without losing the record of the original creator/author/contributor/team's work (and thus a record of the original intellectual contribution is maintained for measuring impact and credit). Analytics for OSF projects include the number of times a project has been "forked" or used as a template along with more standard altmetrics (e.g., downloads, views, site visits, etc.) (Priem et al., 2010). This introduces a new form of contribution to the scholarly discourse, much like a teacher who molded a student's understanding of a concept or their way of shaping their research, building additional research off a project fork allows a consumer of the secondary researcher's work to clearly understand where they started from and who influenced them or provided them with the fundamental resources to build a new branch onto the original research.

However, in some cases, the ability to publish the workspace creates too much of a risk for the potential user – risks such as scooping or compromised intellectual property rights – which outweighs any current, tangible benefits to increased transparency (e.g., increased reproducibility and deeper consumer understanding). Such is the case with a Think Tank within C3@GWU. Without a strong enough need or perceived benefit to outweigh the researchers' concerns, this team choose not to adopt the OSF. Instead their communication needs are satisfied with the other technologies employed by the project as a whole, and the space remains available if they choose to create final products to share without impacting the other Think Tank's flexibility and autonomy within the platform.

Open Science Readiness in Teams and Their Stakeholder Communities

Open science generally serves as a framework for conceptualizing a new form of information sharing and collaborative effort that brings with it important shifts to a number of notable areas within scientific teaming. Joint scientific and scholarly collaborations, the integration of knowledge and the stakeholder communities that are impacted, when utilizing an open science approach, can serve as nodes of information sharing and scientific advancement with greater impact (as measured by citations) than more traditional venues might normally yield (Evans & Reimer, 2009; Gargouri et al., 2010). Thus far, we have focused on the technological tools and the techniques that these tools add to a culture of shared and integrated knowledge economies. Such fluid and collaboratively based economies, those found in transdisciplinary endeavors, even with their high-functioning potential for collaboration across networks still pose threats to individuals, their traditional communities of science and practice, and the teams that generate and disseminate knowledge. Many opportunities arise by utilizing machine-assisted communication, but challenges also exist that require cognitive and behavioral consideration (Scheliga & Friesike, 2014). Though these shifts are numerous and not yet fully considered, here we offer a few openings that are clearly apparent in the emerging open science culture suggesting a spectrum of change as collaborative technologies become more commonly utilized by teams and stakeholders within these knowledge economies (Hendriks, 1999).

Workflow Culture

As has been stated, the traditional workflow environment in knowledge generation, the development of products that can be disseminated through peer review, publication, and evaluation continues to evolve. In an age of communication and research technologies, parameters change so that in addition to increased speed and greater access to information, processes, and workflows also change, which require adjustments to otherwise time-tested processes of sharing and distributing information. Scientists and scholars are faced more than ever with challenges that test their decision making, behaviors, and strategies for maintaining individual, team, and stakeholder relationships in scientific projects. A culture that can embrace what open, machine-assistance has to offer in securing unhampered knowledge generation and dissemination across boundaries will require the cultivation of cultures that intentionally introduce, maintain, and nurture continual and practiced open science and communication (Nosek et al., 2015).

Workflows that assume linear processes of knowledge generation – the progression from problem identification, data acquisition, and experimentation leading to publication – are now being challenged by other workflows that are more complex and iterative (Spiegler, 2003), assuming and accommodating for different partners with their differing investments, styles, and motivations for accessing and sharing knowledge (Gravani, 2005). The demand for more intelligent and intuitive information technologies grows as disparate communities strive to flatten the divides of geographies, time zones, language, and class often found across networks of knowledge generators (Haythornthwaite, Lunsford, Bowker, & Bruce, 2006). However, technological advances that help to minimize these types of collaboration barriers are only part of the culture equation. Stakeholder and team member congruence, task interdependence, team commitment and participative decision-making need to be continually nurtured within a collaborative culture if open science is to be valued as a viable context in which to advance how knowledge is shared and disseminated in a new age of information fluidity (Lin, Shih, & Sher, 2007). This cultural shifting within science communities draws our attention to how open science, technologies, and the new relationships these contracts promote affect existing and emerging teams and stakeholder groups.

Knowledge producing scientific teams are similar to other types of organizations in that they ultimately strive to meet their pre-established goals. Ultimately, the goal of any science team is to generate knowledge around specified problems in order to inform the community and world that values the problem. Organizational culture, in this case team and stakeholder culture, plays an important and critical part in the achievement of these goals, as it has the ability to nurture or stifle processes that impact success. Numerous features inherent to team engagement can serve as challenges to maintaining a culture of high-functioning, sharing of knowledge. These can include high diversity of membership (Kozlowski, Watola, Jensen, Kim, & Botero, 2009), large team size (Tannenbaum, Mathieu, Salas, & Cohen, 2012), designing deep integration of knowledge (Drath et al., 2008), navigating goal misalignments (Salazar, Lant, Fiore, & Salas, 2012), permeating team and stakeholder boundaries (Hall et al., 2012), geographic dispersion, and securing high task interdependence (Burke et al., 2006).

Certain cultural behaviors are required to secure that information and workflow dynamics will foster integrated outcomes and counteract barriers to team science. These include (1) pairing the need for success with teaming procedures that complement these goals, (2) practicing the sharing of knowledge as a common team and stakeholder activity, (3) linking knowledge to identified and deeply shared values (for both teams and stakeholders) using the language of these values as a means to communicate results and impact, (4) constantly underscoring that information networks are human networks requiring a sensitivity about how these networks operate and need to be maintained, and (5) as in business corporate communities, recruiting scientific team members and stakeholders that already understand the value of openness and sharing so that team workflows can be reinforced through expansion and not hampered by each new addition to the network (McDermott & O'Dell, 2001). Such organizational culture dynamics and behaviors when utilized within scientific teams ideally should be embraced by all stakeholders; however, strong leadership that reinforces that these dynamics has been proven to result is greater and more successful collaborative outcomes (Lin et al., 2007; Srivastava, Bartol, & Locke, 2006).

Attitudes about Ownership of Knowledge

Maintaining cultures of collaboration and open sharing of knowledge depend greatly on individual attitudes so that team members and stakeholders can adequately contribute to the organizational culture that will breed constant and consistent sharing of information. That collaboration is increasingly a requirement of scientific teams often put forth by funders and other external factors is not enough to ensure that such priorities are met without resistance by individuals within teams and across stakeholder groups even when individuals desire to enhance collaborative relationships (Hower, 2012). Individual preoccupations about ownership of contributions and insecurities about how such shared knowledge will be integrated into team products, recognized within one's own community of practice or science or even their academic home, and shared with a road audience of consumers often hamper the sharing of knowledge (Bock et al., 2005). These internal conflicts can impede one's ability to adequately share information, trust a team or network, and even hamper the advancement of a science program especially if knowledge is withheld as a result of such insecurities (Lotrecchiano et al., 2016). Loss aversion (Fox & Faver, 1984; Georghiou, 1988; Sonnenwald, 2007), lack of recognition and reward (Dasgupta & David, 1994; Turpin & Garrett-Jones, 2010), concerns about achieving promotion and tenure (Carayol & Thi, 2005; Coleman, 1986; Harris, Lyon, & Clarke, 2009; Horlick-Jones & Sime, 2004; Maglaughlin & Sonnenwald, 2005; Rhoten & Parker, 2004; Zucker, 2012), and authorship embattlements (Barrett, Funk, & Macrina, 2005; Lewis, Ross, & Holden, 2012; Stokols et al., 2008) are just a few of the issues that can ensue from within a scientific team that struggles with diverse attitudes about knowledge sharing.

The challenges that can arise from inequitable attitudes about ownership of knowledge and more importantly the defining of what it means to share that which one also desires to own, concern teams that strive to advance science through collaborative effort. As teams grapple with these dynamics, team productivity and freedom to disseminate are not the only concerns. Rather as Rechberg and Syed (2013) have shown, these tensions can also impede the performance of individuals themselves within these networks as they grapple with moral and ethical dilemmas that are a part of negotiating what one might consider individual ownership and corporate ownership of contributions. In these instances, the authors recommend moving such issues to a level of moral consideration where agreements and contracts include ethical constructs and procedures that establish and increase trust, values, and fairness as knowledge management protocols (Rechberg & Syed, 2013). These types of 'pre-nuptial' agreements are commonplace in many team science arrangements that ensure that such considerations are dealt with early on in the teaming process (Bennet et al., 2010).

Readiness to Share Openly

Inviting participants to engage in scientific collaborations requires careful consideration of how team members and stakeholders will ultimately benefit from the efforts of a program of science. The invitation process may require leaders and teams to carefully weigh the scientific expertise of a potential collaborator along with the soft skills necessary for them to be an active and freely sharing member of a team. This is not always easy to negotiate, as it is not likely that all candidates with the appropriate *scientific* knowledge for a given research team will have the requisite soft skills needed to participate in a free sharing culture.

Readiness to collaborate in scientific teams is not a new concern to the science-of-team-science community who study team behaviors. Researchers developing measures of readiness have utilized many techniques to study multiple variables associated with this problem (Armstrong & Jackson-Smith, 2013; Lotrecchiano et al., 2016; Misra, Stokols, & Cheng, 2015; National Research Council, 2015; Olson & Olson, 2000). An individual's readiness to collaborate or one's collaborative orientation is often attributed to competency and leadership training that is (or should be) part of one's overall scientific training (Hall, Feng, Moser, Stokols, & Taylor, 2008; Hoffman et al., 2013; C. Klein, DeRouin, & Salas, 2006; Stokols, 2014) However, as is often more so the case, readiness to collaborate in teams is an iterative process that over time provides individuals opportunities and the vehicles by which to learn the necessary skills to adequately and successfully participate in the sharing of knowledge within teams. Research associated with technological readiness is also a factor. Technological readiness and, maybe more importantly, technological acceptance is particularly pivotal to issues of communication in these teams as each ultimately contributes to the degree to which scientific teams can more forward capitalizing on the benefits of machine assisted scholarship and communication tools that advance impact and dialogue with networks of scientists and stakeholders (Lin et al., 2007; Olson & Olson, 2000).

Within open science landscapes, this ability to operate at level participation and sharing depends greatly on the requisite skills and one might consider appropriate readiness to be successful. In fact, goal setting measures of success that include a team's ability to integrate and generate synthesized knowledge may require teams of relatively technologically skilled members that can consistently work within a high-sharing and transparent environment. Even in proprietary environments where sharing of knowledge with consumers before a product is fully developed is unlikely, teams and networks of contributors are expected to share internally and their behaviors to do so are part of the production equation (Hansen & Avital, 2005). Quality is also often measured by personalities (optimism, innovativeness, discomfort, and insecurity), which determine collaborative behaviors and in turn affect willingness and readiness to accept new and novel technological tools (Liljander, Gillberg, Gummerus, & van Riel, 2006; Walczuch, Lemmink, & Streukens, 2007). These personality traits can also be considered in the intrapersonal motivations a team member might have with regards to what drives their willingness to share knowledge (Andriessen, 2006; Mallinson et al., 2016; Swift, Balkin, & Matusik, 2010). Readiness in collaborative teams will require that individual members can adequately assess the breadth of tools available (Sarma, Redmiles, & Van der Hoek, 2010), adapt to new technologies as they become available (Majchrzak, Rice, Malhotra, King, & Ba, 2000), and grow in the understanding of sharing knowledge as a normative means by which to conduct open science. These issues will test the control/trust dynamic and decision-making capabilities of individuals in teams to navigate the sharing of their knowledge within the network.

Group-Driven to User-Driven Functionality and Organizing

It is not uncommon for team members and/or stakeholders to display variability or inequity in skill sets necessary for collaboration. In fact, the desire to access scientific skills that are not totally available to any one investigator or even a specific group motivates many teams and stakeholders to collaborate (Beaver & Rosen, 1979; Hara, Solomon, Kim, & Sonnenwald, 2003; Melin, 2000; Nash, 2008; Wray, 2006). These abilities having to do with disciplinary expertise, experience with specific methodologies, and even access to instrumentation, data or populations, as they relate to abilities to utilize and maximize the usefulness of technological tools, vary within groups. However, in addition to these scientific skills, a series of soft skills are also necessary for scientific success (Bennett, Maton, & Kervin, 2008; Gallagher et al., 2005; Mairesse, Greenan, & Topiol-Bensaid, 2001).

In open science systems, requisite abilities to utilize and master core technological functionality in machine-assisted work is a strong indicator of the impact technologies can have on the success of a team's contribution to open science. In order for technology to be applied productively, a user must be able to understand both its function and its relationships with other related technologies. In the case of open science technologies, quality of science and consumer's scientific understanding can be dependent on the capacity of users.

User-driven access control, or the freedom to decide to what degree and extent one might share one's work with the network, like functionalities available in the OSF, provides a dimension to requisite teaming skills. This is an opportunity for a departure from the confines of group-decision based knowledge sharing that can be the result of compromises or consensus about how knowledge is or should be integrated (Roesner et al., 2012). Dissemination of knowledge, even within the most collaborative teams, depends on decision-making processes that do not strive to meet all of the needs of individual team members. Publications, reports, or even co-authored electronic entities are subject to an internal polity that can lack a reflection of individual team members' particular or preferred contributions. This can leave individuals subject to decision-making technicalities that result in their work being blended and integrated with others' with more-or-less emphasis on each team member's needed recognition. Though usually an important and positive result of the collaborative process, many of the ownership and authorship challenges described already can serve as mechanisms by which individuals can feel underrepresented, thus, threatening their autonomy. These threats can affect an individual's own willingness to share and the quality of the team's work as a whole. User-driven access control, and a recorded activity feed or version control contributor record, allow for individual contributions to be identified within the context of group publication and scientific exchange. Such a record alleviates, at least in some cases, recognition concerns for individuals in teams who experience such threats to their contributions.

The shifting from group to user functionality in an open science network is similar to shifts between group-organizing to self-organizing. As with the previous dynamic, this shift may seem antithetical to the point of collaborative engagement. With similar challenges to those that impede an individual's ability to make decisions free from the group, as in user driven functionality when using communication technologies, here the emphasis is on individuals' ability to organize information based on their own decision processes independently yet congruently with the team working on similar problems (Leydesdorff, 2001). For example, any member of a team using the OSF, with read/write or administrative privileges, can alter the display order of contributor names on any project components with or without the consensus of the team. Thus, each member has self-organizing agency. Individuals must choose to work as a team instead of the tool's structure requiring and enforcing a hierarchical team structure.

Though we often think of shared communication spaces (the web, internet, shared drives, social media, etc.) as decentralized and freeform spaces in which users have ultimate autonomy, control, and decision-making authority, these spaces depend greatly on self-organization, the ability to navigate and maneuver amidst changing landscapes, as an important function of the collective knowledge that is integrated and presented as cumulative knowledge. Technologies that capitalize on the user-independence from the network and enhanced user-driven functionality positively impact network outcomes as communities of knowledge are more fluidly accessible to one another (Flake, Lawrence, Giles, & Coetzee, 2002). Such fluid exchanges permit both similar and divergent communities to interact in ways that would be unlikely using more traditional venues. This fluidity of interaction may increase the likelihood of advancing science while it is ongoing rather than only after it concludes This can allow for teams working on certain problems to interface with other teams working on adjacent problems and enter into dialogue that allows for various levels of knowledge sharing to be conducted simultaneously across different subunits in different phases of research.

Conclusion

This chapter intends to introduce a conversation about how team scholarship and the collaborative tools that are available to modern scholars shed light on a new era of knowledge generation and sharing. As is always the case, technology far out-paces the human capacity to fully utilize and master it. As this current information age progresses, humans will continue to be challenged as to how to harness the power that these constantly advancing technologies provide while evolving with it. Scientific teams, their stakeholders, and the consumers of the science they generate can be brought closer together through machine-mediated communication. In many cases this will accelerate science and its impact on society (Evans & Reimer, 2009; Gargouri et al., 2010). In some cases, the mere power of available technologies will hamper our willingness to become deeply sharing scholars; "sharing" being a paradigm that still has trouble taking root in our academic and scholarly communities.

The adoption of machine-assisted scholarly activity depends on tangible structures like access to useful technologies and the infrastructures necessary to support them. Over time, with the increased availability of tools and frameworks, adoption of open science infrastructure is becoming more normative. However, as the barriers to access diminish, time will tell if cultural barriers that are rooted in individual reluctance to share knowledge, concerns about receiving or distributing recognition and reward for new forms of scholarly contribution, and negative attitudes about transparency will diminish as well. The group behaviors that embrace open science need to be encouraged by team science leaders and exercised by team members and stakeholders so that the sharing of knowledge becomes paramount over some of the more secondary barriers found in the human condition that can stifle real scientific advancement.

Ultimately, the advancement of open science relies on trust and communication, which are far from new concerns. In fact, many organizational and psychological scientists would report that all effectiveness in teams is grounded in some form (functions and dysfunctions) of trust and the abilities of teams to communicate effectively. Here we provide a mediator of trust and communication found through the application of machine-assisted open science. The landscape of this emerging paradigm carries with it a means in which to advance science through multilevel and cross-sector communication. This in turn advances the collective abilities of scientific teams: their ability to remain in an intimate relationship with their stakeholders and to maximize their impact on the communities that their science hopes to improve. Future investigation into the cognitive and behavioral research conducted with teams that employ machine-assisted technologies in their workflows would offer researchers the opportunity to understand better the relationships between intelligent machines and science teams' impacts on their communities as well as the necessary paradigmatic shifts inherent when utilizing these technologies.

Questions to Further the Discourse

1. What situations or contexts lead to scientific teams choosing radically open in-team communication technology over more traditional communication methods that may be experienced as safer?

2. How might team trust influence members' confidence and technological readiness, knowledge creation, collaborative processes, and measurement aspects of open science?

3. How might the use of tools that provide new lenses into the work of research such as publishing electronic lab notebooks or sharing research data with interactive visualizations, increase stakeholder or consumer engagement with science teams?

4. How do team dynamics, particularly within interdisciplinary teams, shift with increased adoption of open science technologies, particularly open workflow technologies?

Must Reads

Fecher, B., & Friesike, S. (2014). Open science: One term, five schools of thought. In S. Bartling & S. Friesike (Eds.), *Opening science - The evolving guide on how the web is changing research* (pp. 17-47). Springer, Cham. https://doi.org/10.1007/978-3-319-00026-8_2

National Academies of Sciences, Engineering, and Medicine. (2018). *Open science by design: Realizing a vision for 21st Century research.* https://doi.org/10.17226/25116

Cho, S., Lee, H., & Yoo, Y. (2010). The impact of information technology and transactive memory systems on knowledge sharing, application, and team performance: A Field Study. *MIS Quarterly, 34*(4), 855-870. https://doi.org/10.2307/25750708

Chatenier, E. D., Verstegen, J. A. A. M., Biemans, H. J. A., Mulder, M., & Omta, O. (2009). The challenges of collaborative knowledge creation in open innovation teams. *Human Resource Development Review, 8*(3), 350–381. https://doi.org/10.1177/1534484309338265

References

Alicea, B. (2016). *Data reuse as a prisoner's dilemma: The social capital of open science.* BioRxiv. https://doi.org/10.1101/093518

Andriessen, J. (2006). To share or not to share, that is the question: Conditions for the willingness to share knowledge. *Delft Innovation System Papers, (IS - 2006-02).* Delft, The Netherlands.

Armstrong, A., & Jackson-Smith, D. (2013). Forms and levels of integration: Evaluation of an interdisciplinary team-building project. *Journal of Research Practice, 9*(1), M1.

ArXives of earth science. (2018). *Nature Geoscience, 11*(3), 149. https://doi.org/10.1038/s41561-018-0083-y

Assante, M., Candela, L., Castelli, D., Manghi, P., & Pagano, P. (2015). Science 2.0 repositories: Time for a change in scholarly communication. *D-Lib Magazine, 21*(1/2). https://doi.org/10.1045/january2015-assante

Bahney, C., Bruder, S., Cain, J., Keyak, J., Killian, M., Shapiro, I., & Jones, L. (2016). Accelerating the pace of discovery in orthopaedic research: A vision toward team science. *Journal of Orthopaedic Research, 34*(10), 1673-1679. https://doi.org/10.1002/jor.23307

Bales, M., Dine, D., Merrill, J. A., Johnson, S., Bakken, S., & Weng, C. (2014). Associating co-authorship patterns with publications in high-impact journals. *Journal of Biomedical Informatics, 52*, 311-318. https://doi.org/10.1016/j.jbi.2014.07.015

Barrett, K., Funk, C., & Macrina, F. (2005). Awareness of publication guidelines and the responsible conduct of research. *Accounting Research, 12*(3), 193-206. https://doi.org/10.1080/08989620500217321

Beaver, D., & Rosen, R. (1979). Studies in scientific collaboration Part III: Professionalism and the natural history of modern scientific co-authorship. *Scientometrics, 1*(3), 231-245. https://doi.org/10.1007/BF02016308

Bennet, L. M., Gadlin, H., & Levine-Finley, S. (2010). *Collaboration and team science: A field guide*. Bethesda, MD: National Institutes of Health.

Bennett, S., Maton, K. A., & Kervin, L. (2008). The 'digital natives' debate: A critical review of the evidence. *British Journal of Educational Technology, 39*(5), 775-786. https://doi.org/10.1111/j.1467-8535.2007.00793.x

Berg, J., Bhalla, N., Bourne, P., Chalfie, M., Drubin, D., Fraser, J., . . . Wolberger, C. (2016). Preprints for the life sciences. *Science, 352*(6288), 899-901. https://doi.org/10.1126/science.aaf9133

Bock, G-W, Zmud, R. W., Kim, Y-G, & Lee, J-N (2005) Behavioral intention formation in knowledge sharing: Examining the roles of extrinsic motivators, social-psychological forces, and organizational climate, *MIS Quarterly 29*(1), 87-111.

Brick, C., & Regenhardt, C. (n.d.). *About the Project, Eleanor Roosevelt Papers Project*.

Burke, C., Stagl, K., Klein, C., Goodwin, G., Salas, E., & Halpin, S. (2006). What type of leadership behaviors are functional in teams? A meta analysis. *Leadership Quarterly, 17*, 288-307. https://doi.org/10.1016/j.leaqua.2006.02.007

Carayol, N., & Thi, T. (2005). Why do academic scientists engage in interdisciplinary research? *Research Evaluation, 14*(1), 70-79. https://doi.org/10.3152/147154405781776355

Center for Open Science. (n.d.-a). *Registered reports*. Retrieved March 20, 2018, from https://cos.io/rr/

Center for Open Science. (n.d.-b). *The Open Science Framework*. Retrieved March 20, 2018, from https://cos.io/our-products/osf/

Coleman, J. (1986). Social theory, social research, and a theory of action. *The American Journal of Sociology, 91*(6), 1309-1335. https://doi.org/10.1086/228423

Dabbish, L., Stuart, C., Tsay, J., & Herbsleb, J. (2012). Social coding in GitHub: Transparency and collaboration in an open software repository. In *Proceedings of the ACM 2012 Conference on Computer Supported Cooperative Work* (pp. 1277–1286). New York, NY, USA: ACM. https://doi.org/10.1145/2145204.2145396

Dasgupta, P., & David, P. (1994). Toward a new economics of science. *Policy Research, 23*, 487-521. https://doi.org/10.1016/0048-7333(94)01002-1

Drath, W., McCauley, C., Palus, C., Van Velsor, E., O'Connor, P., & McGuire, J. (2008). Direction, alignment, commitment: Toward a more integrative ontology of leadership. *Leadership Quarterly, 19*(6), 635-653. https://doi.org/10.1016/j.leaqua.2008.09.003

Engwall, L., & Blockmans, W. (2014). *Bibliometrics: Use and abuse in the review of research performance*. London: Portland Press.

Evans, J. A., & Reimer, J. (2009). Open access and global participation in science. *Science, 323*(5917), 1025. https://doi.org/10.1126/science.1154562

Fecher, B., & Friesike, S. (2014). Open science: One term, five schools of thought. In S. Bartling & S. Friesike (Eds.), *Opening science - The evolving guide on how the web is changing research* (pp. 17-47). Springer, Cham. https://doi.org/10.1007/978-3-319-00026-8_2

Fister, B. (2016, August 18). *The acceleration of open access*. Retrieved March 8, 2018, from https://www.insidehighered.com/blogs/library-babel-fish/acceleration-open-access

Flake, G., Lawrence, S., Giles, C., & Coetzee, F. (2002). Self-organization and identification of web communities. *IEEE Computer Supported Cooperative Work, 35*(3), 66-71. https://doi.org/10.1109/2.989932

FOSTER Plus. (2016). *Open science definition*. Retrieved from https://www.fosteropenscience.eu/foster-taxonomy/open-science-definition

Fox, M., & Faver, C. (1984). Independence and cooperation in research: The motivations and costs of collaboration. *The Journal of Higher Education, 55*(3), 347-359. https://doi.org/10.1080/00221546.1984.11777069

Gallagher, A., Ritter, E., Champion, H., Higgins, G., Fried, M., Moses, G., . . . Satava, R. (2005). Virtual reality simulation for the operating room: Proficiency-based training as a paradigm shift in surgical skills training. *Annals of Surgery, 241*(2), 364–372. https://doi.org/10.1097/01.sla.0000151982.85062.80

Gargouri, Y., Hajjem, C., Larivière, V., Gingras, Y., Carr, L., Brody, T., & Harnad, S. (2010). Self-selected or mandated, open access increases citation impact for higher quality research. *PLOS ONE, 5*(10), e13636. https://doi.org/10.1371/journal.pone.0013636

Georghiou, L. (1988). Global cooperation in research. *Research Policy, 27*(6), 611-626. https://doi.org/10.1016/S0048-7333(98)00054-7

Gibson, K. (2000). The moral basis of stakeholder theory. *Journal of Business Ethics, 26*(3), 245-257. https://doi.org/10.1023/A:1006110106408

Gravani, M. (2005). *Academics and practitioners: partners in generating knowledge or citizens of two different worlds?* Paper presented at the European Conference on Educational Research, Dublin.

Hall, K. L., Feng, A., Moser, R., Stokols, D., & Taylor, B. (2008). Moving the science of team science forward: Collaboration and creativity. *American Journal of Community Psychology, 35*(supplement), S243-249. https://doi.org/10.1016/j.amepre.2008.05.007

Hall, K. L., Stokols, D., Stipelman, B. A., Vogel, A. L., Feng, A., Masimore, B., … Berrigan, D. (2012). Assessing the value of team science: A study comparing center- and investigator-initiated grants. *American Journal of Preventive Medicine, 42*(2), 157–163. https://doi.org/10.1016/j.amepre.2011.10.011

Hansen, S., & Avital, M. (2005). Share and share alike: The social and technological influences on knowledge sharing behavior. *Sprouts: Working Papers on Information Systems*, 5(13).

Hara, N., Solomon, P., Kim, S.-L., & Sonnenwald, D. (2003). An emerging view of scientific collaboration: Scientists' perspectives on collaboration and factors that impact collaboration. *Journal of the American Society for Information Science Technology, 54*(10), 952-965. https://doi.org/10.1002/asi.10291

Harris, F., Lyon, F., & Clarke, S. (2009). Doing interdisciplinarity: Motivation and collaboration in research for sustainable agriculture in the UK. *Area, 41*(4), 374-384. https://doi.org/10.1111/j.1475-4762.2008.00859.x

Haythornthwaite, C., Lunsford, K., Bowker, G., & Bruce, B. (2006). Challenges for research and practice in distributed, interdisciplinary collaboration. In C. Hine (Ed.), *New infrastructures for knowledge production: Understanding E-science* (pp. 143-166). https://doi.org/10.4018/978-1-59140-717-1.ch007

Hendriks, P. (1999). Why share knowledge. *Knowledge and Process Management, 6*(2), 91-100. https://doi.org/10.1002/(SICI)1099-1441(199906)6:2<91::AID-KPM54>3.0.CO;2-M

Hinnant, C., Stvilia, B., Wu, S., Worrall, A., Burnett, G., Burnett, K., . . . Marty, P. (2012). Author team diversity and the impact of scientific publications: Evidence from physics research at a national science lab. *Library & Information Science Research, 34*(4), 249-257. https://doi.org/10.1016/j.lisr.2012.03.001

Hoffman, R., Ward, P., Feltovich, P., DiBello, L., Fiore, S., & Andncyrews, D. (2013). *Accelerated expertise: Training for high proficiency in a complex world.* East Sussex: Psychology Press.

Holdren, J. (2013). *Increasing access to the results of federally funded scientific research.* Retrieved from https://obamawhitehouse.archives.gov/sites/default/files/microsites/ostp/ostp_public_access_memo_2013.pdf

Horlick-Jones, T., & Sime, J. (2004). Living on the border: Knowledge, risk and transdisciplinarity. *Futures, 36,* 441-456. https://doi.org/10.1016/j.futures.2003.10.006

Hower, M. (2012). Faculty work: Moving beyond the paradox of autonomy and collaboration. (PhD), Antioch University.

Inter-university Consortium for Political and Social Research. (n.d.). *About ICPSR.* Retrieved from https://www.icpsr.umich.edu/icpsrweb/content/about/

International DOI Foundation. (n.d.). *Factsheet. DOI system and the Handle System.* Retrieved from http://www.doi.org/factsheets/DOIHandle.html

Johnson, M. (2017, November 27). *GenBank overview.* Retrieved April 30, 2018, from https://www.ncbi.nlm.nih.gov/genbank/

Jones, B., Wuchty, S., & Uzzi, B. (2008). Multi-university research teams: Shifting impact, geography, and stratification in science. *Science, 322,* 1259-1262. https://doi.org/10.1126/science.1158357

Klein, C., DeRouin, R., & Salas, E. (2006). Uncovering workplace interpersonal skills: A review, framework, and research agenda. In G. Hodgkinson & J. Ford (Eds.), *International review of industrial and organizational psychology* (Vol. 21, pp. 80-126). New York: John Wiley and Sons. https://doi.org/10.1002/9780470696378.ch3

Klein, W., & Bloom, M. (2005). Bibliometrics: The best available information? *Journal Social Work in Health Care, 41*(3/4). https://doi.org/10.1300/J010v41n03_07

Kosara, R., Hauser, H., & Gresh, D. L. (2003). An interaction view on information visualization. *Proceedings of EUROGRAPHICS*, 123-137.

Kozlowski, S., Watola, D., Jensen, J., Kim, B., & Botero, I. (2009). Developing adaptive teams: A theory of dynamic team leadership. In E. Slas, G. Goodwin, & C. Burke (Eds.), *Team effectiveness in complex organizations: Cross disciplinary perspectives and approaches* (pp. 113-155). New York: Routledge.

LabArchives. (2018, March 15). 6.2 *Other ways to Share (URLs, DOIs)*. Retrieved March 20, 2018, from http://labarchives.kayako.com/Knowledgebase/Article/View/142/225/62-other-ways-to-share-urls-dois

Lewis, J., Ross, S., & Holden, T. (2012). The how and why of academic collaboration: Disciplinary differences and policy implications. *Higher Education, 64*(5), 693-708. https://doi.org/10.1007/s10734-012-9521-8

Leydesdorff, L. (2001). *A sociological theory of communication: The self-organization of the knowledge-based society.* Universal-Publishers

Liljander, V., Gillberg, F., Gummerus, J., & van Riel, A. (2006). Technology readiness and the evaluation and adoption of self-service technologies. *Journal of Retailing and Consumer Services, 13*, 177-191. https://doi.org/10.1016/j.jretconser.2005.08.004

Lin, C.-H., Shih, H.-U., & Sher, P. (2007). Integrating technology readiness into technology acceptance: The TRAM Model. *Psychology and Marketing, 24*(7), 641-657. https://doi.org/10.1002/mar.20177

Lotrecchiano, G. R., Mallinson, T., Leblanc-Beaudoin, T., Schwartz, L., Lazar, D., & Falk-Krzesinski, H. (2016). Motivation and threat indicators for collaboration readiness in knowledge generating teams (KPTs): A scoping review and domain analysis. *Heliyon, 2*(5), e00105. https://doi.org/10.1016/j.heliyon.2016.e00105

Maglaughlin, K., & Sonnenwald, D. (2005). *Factors that impact interdisciplinary natural science research collaboration in academia.* Paper presented at the International Society for Scientometrics and Informetrics (ISSI).

Mairesse, J., Greenan, N., & Topiol-Bensaid, A. (2001). *Information technology and research and development impacts on productivity and skills: Looking for correlations on French firm level data.* National Bureau of Economic Research Working Paper No. 8075. https://doi.org/10.3386/w8075

Majchrzak, A., Rice, R., Malhotra, A., King, N., & Ba, S. (2000). Technology adaptation: The case of a computer-supported inter-organizational virtual team. *MIS Quarterly, 24*(4), 569-600. https://doi.org/10.2307/3250948

Mallinson, T., Lotrecchiano, G. R., Furniss, J., Schwartz, L., Lazar, D., & Falk-Krzesinski, H. (2016). Rasch Analysis as a method for designing a readiness model for collaboration. *Journal of Investigative Medicine, 64*(7), 1186-1193. https://doi.org/10.1136/jim-2016-000173

McDermott, R., & O'Dell, C. (2001). Overcoming cultural barriers to sharing knowledge. *Journal of Knowledge Management, 5*(5), 76-85. https://doi.org/10.1108/13673270110384428

Melin, G. (2000). Pragmatism and self-organization: Research collaboration on the individual level. *Research Policy, 29*(1), 31-40. https://doi.org/10.1016/S0048-7333(99)00031-1

Misra, S., Stokols, D., & Cheng, L. (2015). The transdisciplinary orientation scale: Factor structure and relation to the integrative quality and scope of scientific publications. *Journal of Translational Medicine and Epidemiology, 3*(2), 1042.

Nash, J. (2008). Transdisciplinary training: Key components and prerequisites for success. *American Journal of Preventive Medicine, 35*(2S), 133-140. https://doi.org/10.1016/j.amepre.2008.05.004

National Research Council. (2015). *Enhancing the effectiveness of team science.* (N. J. Cooke & M. L. Hilton, Eds.). Washington, DC: The National Academies Press. https://doi.org/10.17226/19007

Nosek, B., Alter, G., Banks, G., Borsboom, D., Bowman, S., Breckler, S., . . . Yarkoni, T. (2015). Promoting an open research culture. *Science, 348*(6242), 1422-1425. https://doi.org/10.1126/science.aab2374

Obama, B. (2015). *Using behavioral science insights to better serve the American people* [Press release]. Retrieved from https://obamawhitehouse.archives.gov/the-press-office/2015/09/15/executive-order-using-behavioral-science-insights-better-serve-american

Olson, G. M., & Olson, J. S. (2000). Distance matters. *Human-Computer Interaction, 15*, 139-178. https://doi.org/10.1207/S15327051HCI1523_4

Parasuraman, R., Sheridan, T., & Wickens, C. (2000). A model for types and levels of human interaction with automation. *IEEE Transactions on Systems, Man, and Cybernetics, 30*(3), 286-297. https://doi.org/10.1109/3468.844354

Pennington, D. (2011). Bridging the disciplinary divide: Co-creating research ideas in eScience teams. *Computer Supported Cooperative Work, 20*(3), 165-196. https://doi.org/10.1007/s10606-011-9134-2

Porter, A., Roessner, J., & Heberger, A. (2008). How interdisciplinary is a given body of research? *Research Evaluation, 17*(4), 273-282. https://doi.org/10.3152/095820208X364553

Priem, J., Taraborelli, D., Groth, P., & Neylon, C. (2010). *Altmetrics: A manifesto* (v 1.01). Retrieved from http://altmetrics.org/manifesto/

Ranwala, D., Alberg, A., Brady, J., Obeid, J., Davis, R., & Halushka, P. (2017). Scientific retreats with 'speed dating': Networking to stimulate new interdisciplinary translational research collaborations and team science. *Journal of Investigative Medicine, 65*(2), 382-390. https://doi.org/10.1136/jim-2016-000261

Rechberg, I., & Syed, J. (2013). Ethical issues in knowledge management: Conflict of knowledge ownership. *Journal of Knowledge Management, 17*(6). https://doi.org/10.1108/JKM-06-2013-0232

Rhoten, D., & Parker, A. (2004). Education: Risks and rewards of an interdisciplinary research path. *Science, 306*, 2046. https://doi.org/10.1126/science.1103628

Roesner, F., Tadayoshi, K., Moshchuk, A., Parno, B., Wang, H., & Cowan, C. (2012). *User-driven access control: Rethinking permission granting in modern operating systems.* Paper presented at the Proceedings of the IEEE Symposium on Security and Privacy. https://doi.org/10.1109/SP.2012.24

Rollman, J., Krug, K., & Parente, F. (2004). The chat room phenomenon: Reciprocal communication in cyberspace. *CyberPsychology & Behavior, 3*(2), 161-166. https://doi.org/10.1089/109493100316003

Rosas, S., Kagan, J., Schouten, J., Slack, P., & Trochim, W. (2011). Evaluating research and impact: A bibliometric analysis of research by the NIH/NIAID HIV/AIDS clinical trials networks. *PLoS ONE, 6*(3), e17428. https://doi.org/10.1371/journal.pone.0017428

Salazar, M., Lant, T., Fiore, S., & Salas, E. (2012). Facilitating innovation in diverse science teams through integrative capacity. *Small Group Research, 43*(5), 527-558. https://doi.org/10.1177/1046496412453622

Sarma, A., Redmiles, D., & Van der Hoek, A. (2010). Categorizing the spectrum of coordination technology. *IEEE Computer Supported Cooperative Work, 43*(6), 61-67. https://doi.org/10.1109/MC.2010.163

Scheliga, K., & Friesike, S. (2014). Putting open science into practice: A social dilemma? *First Monday, 19*(9). https://doi.org/10.5210/fm.v19i9.5381

Sonnenwald, D. H. (2007). Scientific collaborations: A synthesis of challenges and strategies. In B. Cronin (Ed.), *Annual review of information sciences and technology* (Vol. 41). Medford, NJ: Information Today, Inc. https://doi.org/10.1002/aris.2007.1440410121

Spiegler, I. (2003). Technology and knowledge: Bridging a "generating" gap. *Information and Management, 40*(6), 533-539. https://doi.org/10.1016/S0378-7206(02)00069-1

Srivastava, A., Bartol, K., & Locke, E. (2006). Empowering leadership in management teams: Effects on knowledge sharing, efficacy, and performance. *The Academy of Management Review, 49*(6), 1239-1251. https://doi.org/10.5465/AMJ.2006.23478718

Stokols, D. (2014). Training the next generation of transdisciplinarians. In M. O'Rourke, S. Crowley, S. D. Eigenbrode, & J. D. Wulfhorst (Eds.), *Enhancing communication & collaboration in interdisciplinary research* (pp. 56-81). Los Angeles, CA: Sage Publication. https://doi.org/10.4135/9781483352947.n4

Stokols, D., Hall, K., Taylor, B., & Moser, R. (2008). The science of team science: Overview of the field and introduction to the supplement. *American Journal of Preventative Medicine, 35* (2 Supplement), S77-S89. https://doi.org/10.1016/j.amepre.2008.05.002

Suber, P. (2012). *MIT Press essential knowledge: Open access.* Cambridge, MA, United States: MIT Press. Retrieved from http://ebookcentral.proquest.com/lib/gwu/detail.action?docID=3339454

Swift, M., Balkin, D., & Matusik, S. (2010). Goal orientations and the motivation to share knowledge. *Journal of Knowledge Management, 14*(3), 378-393. https://doi.org/10.1108/13673271011050111

Tannenbaum, S., Mathieu, J., Salas, E., & Cohen, D. (2012). Teams are changing: Are research and practice evolving fast enough? *Industrial and Organizational Psychology, 5*(1), 2-24. https://doi.org/10.1111/j.1754-9434.2011.01396.x

Turpin, T., & Garrett-Jones, S. (2010). Reward, risk and response in Australian cooperative research centres. *International Journal of Technology Transfer and Commercialization, 9*(1-2), 77-93. https://doi.org/10.1504/IJTTC.2010.029426

Walczuch, R., Lemmink, J., & Streukens, S. (2007). The effect of service employees' technology readiness on technology acceptance. *Information and Management, 44*, 206-215. https://doi.org/10.1016/j.im.2006.12.005

Weimer, K., & Andrew, P. (2013). How we participate in the scholarly communication life cycle. *Journal of Map & Geography Libraries: Advances in Geospatial Information, Collections & Archives, 9*(3), 217-219. https://doi.org/10.1080/15420353.2013.824397

Wray, K. (2006). Scientific authorship in the age of collaborative research. *Studies in History and Philosophy of Science Part A, 37*(3), 505-514. https://doi.org/10.1016/j.shpsa.2005.07.011

Wuchty, S., Jones, B., & Uzzi, B. (2007). The increasing dominance of teams in production of knowledge. *Science, 316*, 1036-1038. https://doi.org/10.1126/science.1136099

Zucker, D. (2012). Developing your career in an age of team science. *Journal of Investigative Medicine, 60*(5), 779-784. https://doi.org/10.2310/JIM.0b013e3182508317

Gaetano R. Lotrecchiano & Shalini Misra (Editors). 2020
Communication in Transdisciplinary Teams
Santa Rosa, CA: Informing Science Press

Chapter 7:
A Social Machine for
Transdisciplinary Research

David G. Lebow
HyLighter LLC
David@Hylighter.com

Chapter Objectives

- To provide a clear description of a Transdisciplinary Social Machine (TDSM) for performing transdisciplinary literature reviews.

- To explain how TDSM assists team members in overcoming differences in language and meaning, information overload, and effects of cognitive bias.

- To describe how TDSM makes decision-making more transparent and evidence-based, facilitates the production of new knowledge, and promotes innovation.

- To discuss future applications of TDSM in preparing students for the 21st century information economy.

- To discuss the potential of TDSM as an instrument for investigating sensemaking, an environment for studying human and machine interactions, and a subject for further evaluation.

Introduction to the Chapter

A major challenge of the digital information age is how to tap into large volumes of online information and the collective intelligence of diverse groups to produce something of value. Social Machines represent a promising model for unifying machines and social processes to address this challenge. A development team led by the author is creating a Transdisciplinary Social Machine (TDSM) configured to the requirements and challenges of transdisciplinary literature reviews. TDSM enables new forms of interactions between humans, machines and online content that have the potential to (a) improve outcomes of sensemaking activities that involve combining information from large collections of online documents and the collective intelligence of diverse groups and (b) make machines more capable of assisting humans in such sensemaking efforts. Preliminary findings based on usability testing and formative evaluation suggest that TDSM promotes learning and the generation of new knowledge. Research is required to measure the effects of TDSM on cross-disciplinary communication, human and machine learning, and the outcomes of transdisciplinary research projects.

An earlier version of this chapter was published as Lebow, D. G. (2018). A social machine for transdisciplinary research. *Informing Science: the International Journal of an Emerging Transdiscipline, 21*, 201-217. https://doi.org/10.28945/4025

> **Social Machine**: A socio-technical construct where machines help humans to enhance creativity, facilitate collaboration, and increase global connectivity (Berners-Lee & Fischetti, 1999).
>
> **Epistemic machinery**: "…methodologies, techniques, tools and instruments used in our knowledge production and distribution" (Mørk, Aanestad, Hanseth, & Grisot, 2008, p15).
>
> **Epistemic cultures**: "Cultures that create and warrant knowledge" (Knorr-Cetina, 1999, p.1).

This paper introduces a Social Machine for transdisciplinary literature reviews (i.e., the exploration of various topics and publications through multiple disciplinary and theoretical lenses; Montuori, 2013) and for similar activities that require an individual or group to combine pieces of information from multiple sources for various purposes. Berners-Lee and Fischetti (1999) defined a Social Machine as a socio-technical construct where machines help humans to enhance creativity, facilitate collaboration, and increase global connectivity. At the time, they predicted that Social Machines would be central to the evolution of the Web and future relationships between humans and machines. Over the past two decades, Social Machines have become the focus of large-scale research programs (e.g., the SOCIAM initiative from EPSRC, the Laboratory for Social Machines at MIT) and many academic publications (Smart & Shadbolt, 2014). A common theme across diverse perspectives is that Social Machines represent a promising model for unifying machines and social processes (i.e., interactions between individuals and groups that influence attitudes, behaviors, and outcomes) for a wide range of purposes (Buregio, Meira, & Rosa, 2013).

Today, Social Machines are enabling new forms of social interaction and coordination through a variety of Web-based applications. These include, among others, Wikipedia—a collaborative editing site for democratically producing an encyclopedia, Facebook—a social networking system for allowing people to interact with other users, GalaxyZoo—a crowdsourcing approach for distributing the massive task of classifying galaxies and stars, and OpenRov—a distributed sensor network composed of underwater drones and their human handlers for exploring the ocean (Smart, Simperl, & Shadbolt, 2014). A Social Machine for supporting transdisciplinarity may help improve outcomes in such critical areas as sustainability and healthcare research.

As Knorr-Cetina (1999) wrote, science is not a unitary enterprise, but a market of independent epistemic monopolies producing vastly different products through different epistemic machinery (i.e., "methodologies, techniques, tools and instruments used in our knowledge production and distribution;" Mørket al., 2008, p.15). Extending this metaphor, integrative research (i.e., multi-, inter- and transdisciplinary) holds the promise of innovative products and solutions for teams of diverse members who are willing to relinquish their disciplinary monopolies.

Over the past fifty years, theorists have proposed various descriptions and definitions for distinguishing different approaches to integrative research (J. T. Klein, 2008a). The terms multidisciplinary, interdisciplinary, and transdisciplinary have frequently appeared in the literature but with varying and inconsistent definitions. For current purposes, multidisciplinarity takes into account knowledge from different disciplines but involves little interaction across boundaries. Interdisciplinarity involves interaction across boundaries with potential to affect the perspectives and research outputs of disciplinary members. Transdisciplinarity involves a creative synthesis where members of different disciplines transcend boundaries to form a new, integrated, and more holistic approach (Darbellay, 2014; J. T. Klein, 2008b; Rosenfield, 1992; Stock & Burton, 2011). In other words, multidisciplinary is additive, interdisciplinary is interactive, and transdisciplinary is holistic (Choi & Pak, 2006).

These distinctions aside, all approaches to integrated research face various barriers (e.g., institutional, compositional, contextual, and emotional) to productive cross-disciplinary collaboration (Salazar, Lant, Fiore, & Salas, 2012). Transdisciplinary research faces the additional challenge of reconciling differences in epistemic cultures (i.e., "cultures that create and warrant knowledge," Knorr-Cetina, 1999, p.1) to generate new and integrated knowledge. Succinctly stated, the main qualities of transdisciplinarity include (a) focus on socially relevant issues, (b) aim for a creative synthesis of disciplinary perspectives, (c) make research participatory and inclusive, and (d) pursue a unity of knowledge (Pohl, 2010). Consistent with this perspective, transdisciplinarity asserts that no one discipline sits in a privileged position for meeting the many problems and threats facing humanity (Vilsmaier, Brandner, & Engbers, 2017).

A development team led by the author has created a Transdisciplinary Social Machine (TDSM) to help address the challenges facing transdisciplinary research teams. TDSM enables machines as specially-abled teammates to assist humans in addressing three key obstacles commonly encountered in performing a transdisciplinary literature review. These are (a) overcoming differences in language and meaning between disciplines, (b) coping with information overload in attempting to synthesize information from multiple sources and disciplines, and (c) avoiding potentially negative effects of cognitive bias.

Three Problems in Performing a Transdisciplinary Literature Review

In a world facing numerous, intractable problems that refuse to fit neatly into disciplinary boxes, transdisciplinarity takes a holistic approach. However, teams of diverse stakeholders, including scientists from multiple disciplines and non-scientists face major stumbling blocks in their attempts to collaborate across epistemic boundaries. Keys to success include the ability of a team to develop integrative capacity and team effectiveness through quality of communication, ability to acquire and marshal relevant information, and attention to group process. Integrative capacity is an emergent property of social and cognitive processes that shape the ability of a team to overcome obstacles to effective collaboration and combine knowledge from diverse perspectives (Salazar et al., 2012). Team effectiveness is the capacity of a group of individuals to accomplish the goals of individual members and the goals shared by the group (Mathieu, Maynard, Rapp, & Gibson, 2008). From a related perspective, readiness for collaboration may influence outcomes for transdisciplinary research projects as determined by level of institutional support, prior experience of members with collaborative projects, and degree of epistemological and ontological incompatibilities, among other considerations (Hall et al., 2008).

Integrative capacity: An emergent property of social and cognitive processes that shape the ability of a team to overcome obstacles to effective collaboration and combine knowledge from diverse perspectives (Salazar, Lant, Fiore, & Salas, 2012).

Team effectiveness: The capacity of a group of individuals to accomplish the goals of individual members and the goals shared by the group (Mathieu, Maynard, Rapp, & Gibson, 2008).

Epistemic monitoring: A routine and continuously operating process in the evaluation of incoming information for internal consistency and plausibility (Richter & Maier, 2017).

Epistemological beliefs: Beliefs about the nature of knowledge and knowing.

Cognitive flexibility: Ability and willingness to adopt some arguments and reject others on rational grounds.

Epistemic elaboration: Effortful activity to critically evaluate information that conflicts with current beliefs (Richter, 2011).

Cognitive bias: An umbrella term covering a diverse typology of systematic errors in judgment and decision-making that are prevalent in all human beings (Kahneman, Slovic, & Tversky, 1992).

Frame: "An explanatory structure that defines entities by describing their relationships to other entities" (Klein, Phillips, Rall, & Peluso, 2007, p.118).

To illustrate the potential value of Social Machines for performing transdisciplinary literature reviews, we focus on three particularly challenging problems. These are (a) differences in language and meaning, (b) information overload, and (c) effects of cognitive bias.

Differences in Language and Meaning

Differences in terminology is a major barrier to transdisciplinarity, especially for teams with high diversity (Hall & Vogel, 2012). Practitioners within different disciplines use specialized terms or jargon, use different terms to talk about the same object, and use the same terms but attach different meanings. Teams that fail to develop a shared language are limited in their capacity to establish a shared mental model (i.e., an organized representation of knowledge or negotiated belief structure that is shared by team members; Mathieu et al., 2008; Walsh & Fahey, 1986) as a basis for participating in the integration of ideas from different disciplines.

To further complicate matters, transdisciplinary research inherently involves two simultaneous projects. One is to collaboratively define and address a problem, and the other is to reconfigure disciplinary boundaries to establish a new hybrid or "culture of emergence" (Cilliers, 1998; Robinson, 2008). From another perspective, establishing a new hybrid means fabricating new epistemic machinery to meet the requirements of the current context (i.e., by selectively integrating technology, methods, and ideas appropriated from different disciplines). To accomplish these interrelated projects, a team must develop a shared language for integrating multiple perspectives on the defined problem and defining what transdisciplinarity means within the current context.

Information Overload

Today, people are inundated with so much information, located in so many different places, that they frequently have trouble finding essential information and recognizing important associations between related pieces of information (Misra, Hall, Feng, Stipleman, & Stokols, 2011). The problem is compounded when organizational silos cut people off from expertise and information and projects require collaboration among people with diverse perspectives.

Transdisciplinary research teams commonly undertake literature reviews that cross multiple disciplinary boundaries. Considering that approximately 2.5 million research papers are published in over 28,100 journals annually (Boon, 2016), occupational hazards facing team members include feeling overwhelmed by the volume of available content scattered in different fields and worrying about what key ideas might be missing from the picture (i.e., unknown unknowns). Adding further to the challenges of transdisciplinarity, when researchers read literature outside of their own fields, they are at risk of having insufficient breadth of knowledge to know which pieces of information are relevant. Also, they are less likely to recognize non-obvious and meaningful associations across disciplinary literature—a key source of serendipitous discovery and innovation (Salazar et al., 2012).

Negative Effects of Cognitive Bias

Literature reviews frequently involve reconciling and resolving alternative views on the same or related issues. In transdisciplinary literature reviews, team members face the added challenge of achieving a creative synthesis of diverse views through interdisciplinary integration. This not only requires a high-level of coordination and trust but, also, a large measure of open-mindedness (i.e., receptiveness to new ideas, including ideas that conflict with current beliefs) among individuals who tend to see the world through different lenses (Shattuck & Miller, 2006).

According to Richter and Maier (2017), epistemic monitoring (i.e., a routine and continuously operating process in the evaluation of incoming information for internal consistency and plausibility) serves as a filtering device in reading comprehension. Information consistent with current beliefs acquires a processing advantage over inconsistent information in comprehension and memory. In other words, prior knowledge and beliefs of readers serve a gatekeeper function in processing information. In general, readers evaluate information in texts that is consistent with their beliefs as more plausible than information that is inconsistent with their beliefs (Richter, 2011). They also tend to value evidence that supports what they are motivated to believe and discredit evidence that contradicts what they believe (Golman, Hagmann, & Loewenstein, 2017).

Beliefs about the nature of knowledge and knowing, referred to as epistemological beliefs, among other terms (e.g., epistemic cognition, Greene, Azevedo, and Torney-Purta, 2008; personal epistemology, Hofer, 2004; and epistemic beliefs, Schraw, Bendixen, & Dunkle, 2002), influence cognitive flexibility (i.e., ability and willingness to adopt some arguments and reject others on rational grounds, Misra, Stokols, & Cheng, 2015; Stokols, 2014). Epistemological beliefs are relatively stable characteristics that appear to affect individual engagement in epistemic elaboration (i.e., effortful activity to critically evaluate information that conflicts with current beliefs (Richter, 2011). In the context of a literature review, epistemological beliefs of individual team members may inhibit cognitive flexibility.

Research on epistemic beliefs and epistemic monitoring is consistent with a growing body of literature in both psychology (e.g., Golman et al., 2017) and economics (e.g., Babcock, Loewenstein, Issacharoff, & Camerer, 1995) on the vulnerability of humans to various forms of cognitive bias (i.e., an umbrella term covering a diverse typology of systematic errors in judgment and decision-making that are prevalent in all human beings; Kahneman et al., 1992). Table 1 describes several forms of cognitive bias that researchers have identified and investigated.

Table 1. Examples of Cognitive Bias

Cognitive inflexibility	Individuals fail to flexibly adapt their thinking and actions to deal with changes in the environment. For example, (a) an individual insistently takes actions that were effective in a previous situation while in a new situation where they are ineffective and (b) an expert relies too heavily on automated performance routines and, as a result, is less able to judge the likelihood of a failure in a system (Canas, Fajardo, & Salmeron, 2006).
Text-belief consistency effect	Readers evaluate information in texts that is consistent with their beliefs as more plausible than information that is inconsistent with their beliefs (Richter & Maier, 2017).
Active and passive information avoidance	People use diverse tactics to avoid obtaining information, either intentionally or unintentionally (Golman et al., 2017).
Confirmation bias	People have a tendency to interpret new information in a way that confirms their preexisting beliefs or theories (Rabin & Schrag, 1999).
Bounded awareness	Individuals regularly fail to see and use information easily available to them, and groups ignore unique or unshared information held by group members while focusing on shared information (Chugh & Bazerman, 2007).
Focalism or focusing failure	People over-focus on selected information and ignore other easily available and pertinent information, resulting in ill-informed decisions (Chugh & Bazerman, 2007).
Completeness bias	Individuals select material for carrying out a literature review that is biased toward reaching specific conclusions (Lavallée, Robillard, & Mirsalari, 2014).

Ingroup favoritism	Group members demonstrate limited willingness to share knowledge with or value the contributions from individuals outside of their own discipline or community of practice (Lavallée et al., 2014).
Group think	Individuals adopt the prevailing opinion of a group as their own, at the expense of creativity and individual responsibility (Golman et al., 2017).

According to Schacter (2001), biases are not design flaws in human memory and thinking but are by-products of adaptive features. In other words, benefits inevitably come with trade-offs and disadvantages. For example, cognitive biases, viewed as information-processing shortcuts, may help the brain to quickly make sense of information and experiences (Fay & Montague, 2015). On the other hand, they may lead to systematic errors in judgment and decision-making (Kahneman, Slovic, & Tversky, 1982.

This notion seems consistent with the data-frame theory of sensemaking. As defined by G. Klein et al. (2007), a frame is "an explanatory structure that defines entities by describing their relationships to other entities" (p.118). (According to the authors, rather than trying to reconcile distinctions between frames, scripts, schemata, and mental models, they chose to use the term frame as a synthesis of these concepts). As data accumulates, the sensemaker will make decisions about whether to incorporate new information into the current frame or generate a new frame that better accounts for the new information. Consistent with Rumelhart and Norman (1978), updating an existing frame (i.e., accretion and tuning) requires less time and mental effort than re-framing or generating a new frame (i.e., restructuring).

Given that members of a discipline tend to narrow their focus to information within their own discipline, they may ignore information that does not fit within their disciplinary boundaries (Montuori, 2013). From this perspective, disciplinary literacy (i.e., approaches to reading, writing, thinking, and reasoning shared by members within academic fields, Shanahan & Shanahan, 2008) may inhibit cognitive flexibility (Mulane & Williams, 2013; Smith & Noble, 2014). In a sense, each discipline trains and enculturates its initiates in practices of *sanctioned cognitive biases*.

While many fields of knowledge are becoming increasing specialized, partly in response to the information tsunami of the digital age, transdisciplinarity points in a different direction. What sets transdisciplinarity apart from unidisciplinarity and other forms of integrative research (e.g., multi- and inter-disciplinarity) is its holistic perspective on the nature of knowledge and knowing. At its core, transdisciplinarity is about the creative synthesis of knowledge to address real-world problems through transcending ideological, scientific, religious, economic, political and philosophical boundaries (Shrivastava & Ivanaj, 2011). Ultimately, successful implementation requires teams to establish conditions that diminish disciplinary chauvinism and cognitive biases and favor transparency, self-reflection and willingness to question personal assumptions and beliefs (Stock & Burton, 2011).

Social Machine Components and Features

Sensemaking: The process of finding, organizing, and synthesizing high-value information from multiple documents and the collective intelligence of diverse group members to generate new knowledge and achieve other desirable outcomes.

HyLight: An annotation that includes a color-coded fragment and related meta-content such as author ID, comments, date/time stamps, tags, and a specific URL for the HyLight.

Session: An individual document that displays HyLights accessible to a given user for the selected document.

Mashup: A set of HyLights excerpted from multiple documents with links back to their exact locations within their sources.

Knowledge Trail: A set of HyLights that a user has filtered or distilled from multiple documents, arranged in a preferred order, and saved to a library for reuse and sharing.

Communication bus: A mechanism for efficiently managing streams of events within TDSM.

Breadboard: A mechanism for wiring machine components together that enables explicit connections between machine components, which allow for complex interactions among components.

Machine component plugins: Adapt machine behaviors to become available on the communication bus or breadboard for use within the TDSM ecosystem, especially to allow internal or external components to participate in TDSM through software adapters.

Entity extraction: Involves locating and collecting entity references within targeted documents. including key concepts and other types of entities of interest such as people, places, and organizations.

To assist teams in implementing a transdisciplinary literature review, we have designed and partially implemented a Transdisciplinary Social Machine (TDSM). The general function of the system is to support users in accomplishing activities that require individuals or groups to combine pieces of information from multiple online sources and file types for various purposes. The main theoretical framework underlying the design of the system draws on the learning sciences and, most centrally, the concept of sensemaking.

Theorists have offered a variety of definitions for sensemaking (also, sense-making and sense making) and descriptions of sensemaking behaviors (e.g., G. Klein, Moon, & Hoffman, 2006; Pirolli & Card, 2005; Slaney & Russell, 2005; Weick, Sutcliffe, & Obstfeld, 2005). Within TDSM and the context of performing a transdisciplinary literature review, we define sensemaking as: the process of finding, organizing, and synthesizing high-value information from multiple documents and the collective intelligence of diverse group members to generate new knowledge and achieve other desirable outcomes.

TDSM contains four main sensemaking components including (a) the graphical user interface (GUI), (b) the communication or message bus, (c) the breadboard or plugboard, and (d) machine component plugins. Table 2 describes these core sensemaking components.

Table 2. Main Components and Features for a Transdisciplinary Social Machine

COMPONENTS	FEATURES
1. TDSM Graphical User Interface (GUI) A Web-based environment for collaborative sensemaking activities that requires users to combine pieces of information from multiple online sources and file types for various purposes.	Provides a graphical user interface for managing and participating in sessions, mashups, and Knowledge Trails. • Session: an individual document that includes human and/or machine generated HyLights. • HyLight: a highlighted fragment of text or an area of an image and related meta-content or content about content (e.g., author ID, comments, date/time stamps, tags, links, and a HyLight ID with a specific URL). • Mashup: a set of HyLights excerpted from multiple sessions with links back to their exact locations within their sources. • Knowledge Trail: a set of HyLights that a user has selected from multiple documents (i.e., a type of mashup), arranged in a preferred order (e.g., a narrative structure) and saved to a library for reuse and sharing.
2. Communication Bus A mechanism for efficiently managing streams of events within the system.	Provides the system with a medium for internal and external components to publish and subscribe to messages about activities in the system.
3. Breadboard A mechanism for wiring machine components together.	Provides a wiring mechanism for establishing explicit connections between machine components that allow for complex interactions among components.
4. Machine Component Plugins A mechanism that adapts machine behaviors for use within TDSM.	Provides a set of interface definitions that allow internal or external components to participate in TDSM through software adapters.

The TDSM Sensemaking GUI

The design of the TDSM graphical user interface (GUI) is informed by user-experience design principles with the goal of enabling machines to assist non-technical people (and data scientists, too) in sensemaking activities. (An example of how a machine might participate in this process is described later below.) The GUI has provisions for importing a wide variety of document file types (e.g., PDFs, Office files, and most common image files). Upon import, the system creates high-fidelity copies of the original files as HTML. The converted files display in most browsers and allow for annotating user-selected fragments of text or areas of images.

The TDSM GUI enables users to add HyLights to documents, manage access and permissions to their sessions, and create mashups of HyLights from multiple documents. A HyLight is an annotation that includes a color-coded fragment and related meta-content (i.e., content about content) such as author ID, comments, date/time stamps, tags, links, and a HyLight ID with a specific URL. Figure 1 shows how HyLighter maps the distribution of highlighted fragments through a document for virtually any size group using a simple color-coding mechanism. An area highlighted by the logged in user but not by anyone else appears in yellow; areas not highlighted by the user, but marked by one or more contributors, appear in blue; and areas highlighted by the user and others appear in green.

A session is an individual document that displays HyLights accessible to a given user for the selected document. A mashup is a set of HyLights excerpted from multiple documents with links back to their exact locations within their sources (e.g., results of a search or user selections). TDSM stores HyLight information in a relational database. As requested, the system overlays color-coded highlighting on selected pages, displays HyLight information from the current document in the left session-margin, and displays HyLight information from multiple documents in the right mashup-margin.

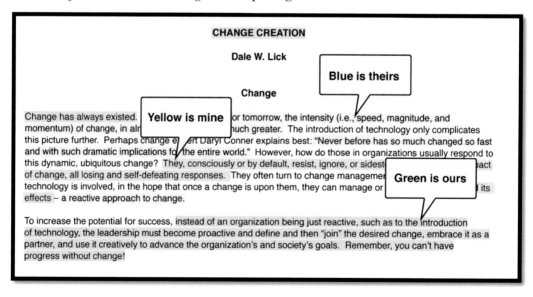

Figure 1. Color-coded annotations showing separation and overlap of highlighted fragments.

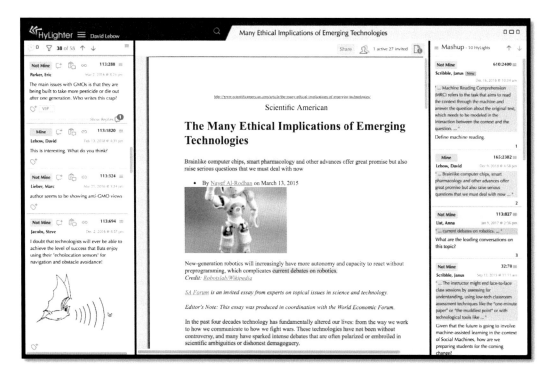

Figure 2. HyLighter screen shows the session document in the middle panel, comments linked to color-coded fragments on the left, and a Knowledge Trail on the right.

In addition to creating HyLights, users can (a) reply to an existing HyLight, (b) establish a link between two HyLights in different documents, (c) search and filter on HyLights and full document text, (d) add HyLights from a session to a mashup, and (e) create *Knowledge Trails*. A Knowledge Trail is a set of HyLights that a user (i.e., an individual, a group, a machine, or a combination of people and machines) has filtered or distilled from multiple documents (i.e., a type of mashup), arranged in a preferred order (e.g., a narrative structure or storyline), and saved to a library for reuse and sharing. To create a Knowledge Trail, a user (a) arranges selected HyLights displayed in the right mashup-margin into a preferred sequence (e.g., using cut & paste, among other features), (b) names and saves the results to a library for revisiting, repurposing, and sharing with others and, optionally, (c) exports or publishes the contents to an external application or file type (e.g., Word, Excel, Acrobat, or GoogleDocs). A key attribute of mashups, including Knowledge Trails, is that they provide nearly instantaneous navigation between HyLights. This capability enables rapid review of HyLights located in different documents, which may accelerate learning and increase serendipity (e.g., by helping users to make non-obvious associations between ideas that are distant from each other).

Connecting Machine Components to TDSM

In order to make the system easily extensible, TDSM provides two primary mechanisms for connecting new machine components to the system via implementation of a plugin interface:

1. The *communication bus* is a mechanism for efficiently managing streams of events within the system. The bus provides a medium for internal and external components to publish and subscribe to messages about activities in the system.

2. The *breadboard* is a mechanism for wiring machine components together. The breadboard enables explicit connections between machine components, which allows for complex interactions among components.

3. *Machine component plugins* adapt machine behaviors to become available on the bus or breadboard for use within the TDSM ecosystem. Machine component plugins provide sets of interface definitions that allow internal or external components to participate in TDSM through software adapters.

Both the bus and the breadboard represent modular, flexible approaches to connecting various applications and external data sources to TDSM. Such extensibility supports transdisciplinarity by allowing team members from different disciplines to connect their preferred applications to the system and/or select from an existing ecosystem of applications that may help to improve outcomes. To illustrate this point, the following scenario describes one of many possible scenarios where the addition of a text analytics application to TDSM can assist in the generation of new and integrated knowledge.

TDSM and Machine Analytics Scenario

In this example, machine assistants help team members to understand how members from different disciplines use key concepts to communicate important information.

1. The team leader of a transdisciplinary research project activates a machine analytics application on TDSM.

2. Team members, representing a number of different disciplines, collaborate on training the machine to recognize key vocabulary (i.e., concept terms and jargon that are not already in the machine lexicon).

3. Among a number of possible approaches, team members from each discipline compile representative collections of documents that are relevant to the project focus and feed each collection to the machine.

4. The machine uses various approaches to natural language processing to identify key terms from each collection and produce lists of the results by discipline.

5. Team members review the machine-generated lists and check off terms of interest.

6. The text analytics application adds the new vocabulary to its lexicon through a largely automated machine learning process.

7. The machine component is now capable of rapidly identifying key terms within large volumes of content (e.g., thousands of research articles in an online repository or Web-pages and files stored on servers around the world).

8. Given a source of online documents, the text analytics application engages in entity extraction. In brief, entity extraction involves locating and collecting entity references within targeted documents. This includes key terms from the training exer-

cise and, optionally, other types of entities of interest such as people, places, and organizations.

9. Based on results of the entity extraction process, team members select a manageable subset of high-value documents for import to TDSM.

10. On import, TDSM converts machine analytics to Machine HyLights. When users open documents, key vocabulary and other entities of interest are highlighted and related meta-content (e.g., category, attributes, and associations), ferreted out by the machine, is displayed in the left session-margin.

11. With Machine HyLights stored in TDSM, users have the option to create mashups of all or selected Machine HyLights located within the collection of documents.

12. By capitalizing on the high-speed navigation capability of the mashup-margin, users can rapidly inspect Machine HyLights in their exact locations within their source documents.

13. As users navigate from Machine HyLight to Machine HyLight and from document to document, they evaluate the surrounding context of each highlighted entity. When users find Machine HyLights within fragments of text that express information of value, they add new HyLights that encompass the fragments and include their comments.

14. As a layer of machine and human HyLights accumulates across the collection of documents, members of each discipline create Knowledge Trails. Members arrange selected HyLights within the mashup margin in a preferred order, name and save the results to the server, and invite other team members to follow their travels through the collection.

15. Subsequently, users may export Knowledge Trails to the text analytics application as feedback to improve performance of the machine in assisting users in their sensemaking efforts. For example, Knowledge Trails provide data that may help the machine to recognize non-obvious associations between key concepts.

This scenario describes one of many possible use cases involving TDSM and currently available machine components. Given its modular and extensible design, TDSM may accommodate machine components of the future with potentially transformative capabilities for transdisciplinary research.

The Conversation Model

From a system architecture perspective, the framework for TDSM is a simple conversation (D. Boyer, personal communication, February 22, 2016). In this context, a conversation is any set of HyLights, created by humans or machines, with the following attributes:

1. A conversation can have two types of users: people and machines.

2. A conversation has two types of roles: speakers with write permission and listeners with read only permission.

3. Users build conversations by (a) adding new HyLights to active conversations, (b) pulling in selected HyLights from existing conversations, and/or (c) combining existing conversations.

4. Users have the option to save conversations (e.g., Knowledge Trails) for reuse and sharing.

5. Conversations can be used to provide feedback to machines to improve their performance as sensemaking assistants.

6. In all instances, HyLights and conversations are preserved while related internal source documents and content remain immutable.

This combination of a simple model and indestructible history gives the system a 'Lego set' quality with HyLights serving as reusable building blocks, conversations as prefabricated assemblies and sub-assemblies, and workflows as instructions for defined sensemaking activities and their outputs. This simple architecture establishes the foundation for a highly scalable and adaptable Social Machine that is especially compatible with the goals and values of transdisciplinarity.

Three Examples of Machine-Assisted Sensemaking

The concept of extended cognition, as first proposed by Clark and Chalmers (1998) and revised by others since (Bartlett, 2016), extends the periphery of mind beyond the boundary of the body. Mind is not merely embedded within but extends into the environment of the organism. From this perspective, mind encompasses artifacts that capture and represent knowledge shared by team members and technologies that support the development and use of the artifacts (Fiore & Wiltshire, 2016). In the digital information age, extended cognition places intelligence into networks of interacting humans and machines (Ito, 2016). Arguably, this makes TDSM a type of external memory technology for representing the transactive memory system of a group through various boundary objects.

Extended cognition: Extends the periphery of mind beyond the boundary of the body - mind is not merely embedded within but extends into the environment of the organism (Clark & Chalmers,1998; Bartlett, 2016).

Transactive memory system: A mechanism for encoding, storing, and retrieving knowledge possessed by individual members of a team, including shared awareness of who holds what knowledge (Kotlarsky, den Hooff, & Houtman, 2015).

Boundary object: A tangible artifact that acts as a bridge for facilitating coordination and collaboration across disciplinary borders and maintaining shared representations of team knowledge (Fiore & Wiltshire, 2016).

Coactive: On-going and close interaction on shared tasks (Bradshaw, 2013).

Concordance: An alphabetical index of the principal words of a book with a reference to the passage in which each word occurs.

A transactive memory system is a mechanism for encoding, storing, and retrieving knowledge possessed by individual members of a team, including shared awareness of who holds what knowledge (Kotlarsky, den Hooff, & Houtman, 2015). A boundary object is a tangible artifact that acts as a bridge for facilitating coordination and collaboration across disciplinary borders and maintaining shared representations of team knowledge. Boundary objects are a technology-based form of transactive memory that emerges from the transactive memory system of a team (Fiore & Wiltshire, 2016).

TDSM provides three interacting mechanisms for producing various boundary objects to enhance sensemaking. These mechanisms, as described previously, include (a) a collaborative annotation system for pointing at high-value fragments, capturing related comments, and creating links between related annotations or HyLights, (b) a Knowledge Trail feature for producing preferred pathways through a document collection, and (c) a feedback loop that enables the coactive (i.e., on-going and close interaction on shared tasks, Bradshaw, 2013) emergence of human and machine intelligence. Among a number of potential benefits, TDSM may achieve its greatest impact by minimizing the time and effort required to navigate between related pieces of information located in the literature of different disciplines.

From the perspective of extended cognition (i.e., the idea that the physical apparatus of cognition encompasses both the individual organism and surrounding non-biological elements, Clark & Chalmers, 1998; Smart, 2017), the main objectives of TDSM are to augment human sensemaking capabilities and make machines more capable of assisting humans in their sensemaking efforts. TDSM attempts to achieve these objectives by facilitating purposeful interactions and collaborations between humans and machines when tapping into multiple sources of online content (Scaife & Rogers, 1996). To illustrate the potential of TDSM for supporting a transdisciplinary literature review, we describe how TDSM approaches each of the problems described previously (i.e., differences in language and meaning, information overload, and effects of cognitive bias).

An Electronic Transdisciplinary Concordance

To overcome differences between disciplines in such areas as epistemic dimensions, social dimensions, and knowledge production systems, effective collaboration requires the development of a shared language. TDSM addresses this problem through crowdsourcing of collaborative annotation activities to produce an electronic transdisciplinary concordance (ETC). A concordance is an alphabetical index of the principal words of a book with a reference to the passage in which each word occurs. Though similar to a standard concordance in some respects, ETC represents a new type of text in purpose, capabilities, production, and maintenance. Its main purpose is to assist members of transdisciplinary research teams in acquiring sufficient fluency in the terminology of multiple disciplines to participate effectively in the integration of ideas. In what follows, we briefly describe (a) how a reader may use ETC as a bridge across disciplinary literatures and (b) how ETC emerges from routine sensemaking activities enabled by TDSM.

ETC in use

While reading and marking up an article in TDSM, a user encounters an unfamiliar concept:

- The user selects the term within the article and opens ETC.

- Alternatively, the user opens ETC and enters the term in a search field or selects the term from an alphabetical index.

- ETC runs a search of accessible documents stored in TDSM (i.e., based on the security and permissions profile of the user) and displays the results as a Knowledge Trail.

- Each HyLight includes a tag indicating the disciplinary background of the author(s), a link to a full reference for the article, a link to the HyLight in its exact location within the source, and a list of terms that share the same or similar meaning.

Brown, Collins, and Duguid (1989) wrote that understanding the meaning of a concept means understanding its range of uses. ETC serves as a bridge across disciplinary literatures by situating selected terms within sets of exemplary HyLights to reveal multiple uses and shades of meaning.

ETC as an emergent product

ETC emerges as a product of the collective activity of TDSM users. Exemplary HyLights accumulate over time, as users annotate research literature across projects and departments at a single institution or on a larger, multi-institutional scale. While reading and marking up research articles in TDSM for a variety of purposes, a user will sometimes annotate a fragment that reveals the meaning of an important term through its context of use. The user who submitted the HyLight or anyone with privileges may add the HyLight to ETC:

- The user tags the HyLight with the targeted term and clicks a button to add exemplar status.

- The system automatically adds a discipline tag to the HyLight.

- TDSM has various administrative and analytic features for maintaining ETC as it grows.

In sum, ETC emerges through a crowdsourcing mechanism that captures the annotation activities of TDSM users. As long as TDSM is operating, users may continually add new terms and exemplars to the system.

Detection of Unknown Unknowns

Former Secretary of Defense, Donald Rumsfeld, speaking to the press in 2002, memorably used the phrase, "unknown unknowns," to refer to a problem that keeps analysts, researchers, and decision makers up at night:

> There are known knowns; there are things we know that we know. There are known unknowns; that is to say there are things that, we now know we don't know. But there are also unknown unknowns – there are things we do not know we don't know (U.S. Department of Defense, 2002)

In other words, a known unknown is a question that an analyst/researcher knows to ask and pursue further. An unknown unknown is a question that an analyst/researcher does not even know to ask. As an operational definition, within the context of TDSM, unknown unknowns are entities (e.g., key concept terms) in external sources that are strongly associated with entities of interest in a TDSM document collection or "conversation" but are not in the TDSM document collection and are unknown to participants in the conversation.

A Sufficiency Criterion for Transdisciplinary Literature Reviews

TDSM helps transdisciplinary research teams determine the sufficiency of their literature reviews through an enhanced search mechanism:

- Team members create a Knowledge Trail of high-value HyLights from within their existing document collection.

- The project manager feeds the Knowledge Trail to the TDSM text analytics application.

- The machine finds all entities in targeted external repositories that are strongly related to high-value entities in the document collection but do not appear in the collection (i.e., unknown unknowns, as operationally defined).

- The data that is returned to the researchers include (a) a list of entities in the external repository that have criterion-level relationships with entities in the TDSM collection and (b) a list of documents, ranked by likely value, that include the entities of interest.

- The researchers import files of interest to the TDSM collection and markup the new documents.

- The team repeats the process until satisfied with the sufficiency of their review.

TDSM makes high-speed text analytics compatible with deliberative, collaborative, human sensemaking practices. By adding a social component to machine analytics, TDSM establishes a feedback loop between machines and researchers that supports a systematic approach to the detection of unknown unknowns hidden in large volumes of content.

Moderating the Effects of Cognitive Biases

Cognitive biases appear to be a side-effect of the survival imperative to make our cognitive machinery capable of rapidly filtering information. Arguably, the network effects of social media have amplified cognitive biases and made them increasingly pervasive in human thought and communications (Chamorro-Premuzic, 2014). In the context of transdisciplinary research projects, cognitive bias can be a major obstacle to achieving desired outcomes. As a general strategy for mitigating this tendency of mind, transdisciplinarity promotes the values of transparency, dialogue, self-reflection, and building trust among team members (Montuori, 2013). TDSM may contribute to implementing this strategy by enabling interactions between humans and machines that support these core values. To illustrate this potential, we describe a number of TDSM capabilities that add transparency and opportunities for dialogue during collaborative sensemaking activities.

Every HyLight has its own address

As users markup documents in performing a literature review, TDSM assigns a unique URL to each user-generated HyLight. This endows HyLights with a number of key affordances that may contribute to transparency and related values:

- When HyLights move to external locations (e.g., to Word documents, Google-Docs, visualizations, and spreadsheets), each HyLight has a link or tether back to its exact location in its source. Accessing a HyLight in its source provides evidence for assessing the quality or provenance of the information. This includes information related to lineage—what is the origin of this information, and pedigree—how reliable is the source of this information.

- Users can create links between HyLights in different documents and describe the associations. Identifying non-obvious associations, especially between distantly related sources, creates opportunities for serendipity and the generation of new ideas. This record of links between HyLights located in different documents is available to machines for representing associations in node graphs and team members for review and dialogue.

Mapping the intellectual travels of a team through a document collection

TDSM enables teams to have discussions tied to fragments of text selected across collections of documents in a controlled, organized, efficient, and auditable manner. The system maintains an historical record for auditing past decisions, informing future actions, and as a source of analytics for assessing performance. TDSM manages accumulating and overlapping markup through various mechanisms:

- A color-coding feature for mapping the intellectual travels of team members through a document collection.

- The capacity to align commentary in the margin with related fragments in a document.

- The capacity to quickly navigate between related HyLights within and between documents (e.g., HyLights located in the literature of different disciplines).

- The capacity to organize and display HyLights in Knowledge Trails, graphic visualizations, and other representations.

By mapping the thinking of readers across document collections, enabling readers to share their HyLights, and providing a variety of options for displaying and navigating the terrain, TDSM supports rich feedback, self-reflection, transparency and other key enabling values for transdisciplinary research.

Conclusion

Transdisciplinary research teams face formidable challenges in adopting a holistic perspective on the nature of knowledge and knowing. Social Machines, as an approach to unifying machines and social processes, are a promising approach to enhancing transdisciplinarity as a research strategy. We have described how a Transdisciplinary Social Machine (TDSM), tuned to the requirements of a literature review, may assist team members in overcoming differences in language and meaning, information overload, and effects of cognitive bias.

TDSM helps non-technical users (and technical users, too) to find, organize, and synthesize high-value information from multiple sources. Among other desirable effects, it assists team members in creating new knowledge of value and maintains an historical record of conversations tied to important sections of documents for auditing past decisions and informing future actions. TDSM provides these benefits by assimilating machine analytics and other machine components into collaborative sensemaking networks. This approach redefines the human/machine division of labor to make machine-scale analytics more compatible with human-scale sensemaking practices. As a consequence of interacting with the system, users become more capable of thinking within a domain or problem space and machines become more capable of assisting users in their sensemaking efforts. In sum, the system establishes a feedback loop for the continuous improvement of human and machine intelligence.

In addition to supporting transdisciplinarity, TDSM may help to prepare students for the 21st century information economy and an uncertain future. As rapid technological change eliminates jobs in every sector and new types of work are emerging that require new and different skill sets, the curricula in schools remain largely out of sync with global economic reality (Soulé & Warrick, 2015). As an historical analogy, literacy in Western Europe until the fifteenth century was largely limited to wealthy elite, clergy, and scholars. With the arrival of Gutenberg's innovation and the availability of low-cost reading material, literacy spread widely, especially when newspapers appeared in the 1600s. By analogy, the Internet, smart machines, and related technologies are the movable type and printing press of today, and data scientists are the elite literate. Similarly, as the spread of literacy helped to fuel the growth of a merchant class and usher in the Renaissance period, the spread of Social Machines for collaborative sensemaking will help fuel a resurgence of the diminished middle-class and, potentially, contribute to a global transformation of society (Lanier, 2013).

Questions to Further the Discourse

Given the potential of TDSM for collaborative sensemaking in the context of transdisciplinary literature reviews, research is required to address the following 'how' and 'why' questions:

1. How and why does TDSM influence cross-disciplinary communication?

2. How and why does TDSM affect human and machine learning in the context of a transdisciplinary literature review?

3. How and why does TDSM affect outcomes of transdisciplinary research projects?

4. How and why does TDSM affect outcomes in blended and online classes?

Must Reads

Bradshaw, J. M. (2013). From knowledge science to symbiosis science. *International Journal of Human Computer Studies, 71*(2), 171-176.

Golman, R., Hagmann, D., & Loewenstein G. (2017). Information avoidance. *Journal of Economic Literature*, *55*(1), 96–135.

Hoffman, R. R., Klein, G., & Moon, B. M. (2006). Making sense of sensemaking 2: A macrocognitive model. *IEEE Intelligent Systems, 21*, 88-92.

Lanier, J. (2013). *Who owns the future?* New York, NY: Simon and Schuster.

References

Babcock, L., Loewenstein, L., Issacharoff, S., & Camerer C. (1995). Biased judgments of fairness in bargaining. *American Economic Review*, *85*, 128–141.

Bartlett, G. (2016). Extended cognition and the extended mind: Introduction. *Essays in Philosophy*, *17*(2), 1526-1569.

Berners-Lee, T., & Fischetti, M. (1999). *Weaving the Web: The original design and ultimate destiny of the World Wide Web*. San Francisco: Harper.

Bradshaw J. M. (2013). From knowledge science to symbiosis science. *International Journal of Human Computer Studies*, *71*(2), 171-176.

Boon, S. (2016, January 7). *21st century science overload* [Blog post]. Retrieved from http://www.cdnsciencepub.com/blog/21st-century-science-overload.aspx

Brown, J. S., Collins, A., & Duguid, P. (1989). Situated cognition and the culture of learning. *Educational Researcher*, *18*(1), 32-42.

Buregio, V., Meira, S. & Rosa, N. (2013). Social machines: A unified paradigm to describe social web-oriented systems. *WWW '13 Companion Proceedings of the 22nd International Conference on World Wide Web* (pp. 885-890).

Canas, J. J., Fajardo, I., & Salmeron, L. (2006). Cognitive flexibility. In W. Karwowski (Ed.), *International Encyclopedia of Ergonomics and Human Factors* (pp. 297-300).

Chamorro-Premuzic, T. (2014, May 13). *How the web distorts reality and impairs our judgement skills*. Retrieved from https://www.theguardian.com/media-network/media-network-blog/2014/may/13/internet-confirmation-bias

Choi, B. K., & Pak, A. P. (2006). Multidisciplinarity, interdisciplinarity, and transdisciplinarity in health research, services, education and policy: 1. Definitions, objectives, and evidence of effectiveness. *Clinical and Investigative Medicine*, *29*, 351-364.

Chugh, D., & Bazerman, M. H. (2007). Bounded awareness: What you fail to see can hurt you. *Mind & Society*, *6*, 1-18.

Cilliers, P. (1998). *Complexity and postmodernism. Understanding complex systems*. London: Routledge.

Clark, A., & Chalmers, D. (1998). The extended mind. *Analysis*, *58*(1), 7–19.

Darbellay, F. (2014). Rethinking inter- and transdisciplinarity: Undisciplined knowledge and the emergence of a new thought style. *Futures, 65*, 163-174.

Fay, R., & Montague, N. R. (2015). Witnessing your own cognitive bias: A compendium of classroom exercises. *Issues in Accounting Education, 30*(1), 12-26.

Fiore S. M., & Wiltshire T. J. (2016). Technology as teammate: Examining the role of external cognition in support of team cognitive processes. *Frontiers in Psychology, 7*(1531), 1-17. https://doi.org/10.3389/fpsyg.2016.01531

Golman, R., Hagmann, D., & Loewenstein G. (2017). Information avoidance. *Journal of Economic Literature, 55*(1), 96–135.

Greene, J., Azevedo, R., & Torney-Purta, J. (2008). Modeling epistemic and ontological cognition: Philosophical perspectives and methodological directions. *Educational Psychologist, 43*, 142–160.

Hall K. L., Stokols D., Moser R., Taylor B., Thornquist M., Nebeling L., & Jeffery R. W. (2008). The collaborative readiness of transdisciplinary research teams and centers: Findings from the National Cancer Institute's TREC year-one evaluation study. *American Journal of Preventive Medicine, 35*(2), 161–172. https://doi.org/10.1016/j.amepre.2008.03.035

Hall, K. L., & Vogel, A. L. (2012). A four-phase model of translational team-based research: Goals, team processes, and strategies. *Translational Behavioral Medicine, 2*, 415-430.

Hofer, B. (2004). Exploring the dimensions of personal epistemology in differing classroom contexts: Student interpretations during the first year of college. *Contemporary Educational Psychology, 29*, 129–16.

Ito, J. (2016, February 10). *Extended intelligence*. Retrieved from https://pubpub.ito.com/pub/extended-intelligence

Kahneman, D., Slovic, P., & Tversky, A. (1982). *Judgment under uncertainty: Heuristics and biases*. New York, NY: Cambridge University Press.

Klein, G., Moon, B., & Hoffman, R. R. (2006). Making sense of sensemaking 1: Alternative perspectives. *IEEE Intelligent Systems, 21*, 70-73.

Klein, G., Phillips, J. K., Rall, E. L., & Peluso, D. (2007). A data frame theory of sensemaking. In R. A. Hoffman (Ed.) *Expertise out of context: Proceedings of the sixth international conference on naturalistic decision making*, (pp. 113–153). New York, NY: Taylor & Francis Group.

Klein, J. T. (2008a). The rhetoric of interdisciplinarity. In A. Lunsford, K. Wilson & R. Ebeerly (Eds.), *The Sage handbook of rhetorical studies* (pp. 265-284). Thousand Oaks, CA: Sage

Klein, J. T. (2008b). Evaluation of interdisciplinary and transdisciplinary research: A literature review. *American Journal of Preventive Medicine, 35*, 116–123.

Knorr-Cetina, K. (1999). *Epistemic cultures: How science makes knowledge*. Cambridge, MA: Harvard University Press.

Kotlarsky, J., den Hooff, B., & Houtman, L. (2015). Are we on the same page? Knowledge boundaries and transactive memory system development in cross-functional teams. *Communication Research, 42*(3), 319-344.

Lavallée, M., Robillard, P. N., & Mirsalari, R. (2014). Performing systematic literature reviews with novices: An iterative approach. *IEEE Transactions on Education, 57*(3), 175-181.

Lanier, J. (2013). *Who owns the future?* New York, NY: Simon and Schuster.

Mathieu, J. E., Maynard, M. T., Rapp, T., & Gilson, L. (2008). Team effectiveness 1997-2007: A review of recent advancements and a glimpse into the future. *Journal of Management, 34*, 410-476.

Misra, S., Hall, K., Feng, A., Stipleman, B., and Stokols, D., (2011). Collaborative processes in transdisciplinary research. In M. Kirst, N. Schaefer-McDaniel, S. Hwang, & P. O'Campo, (Eds.), *Converging disciplines: A transdisciplinary research approach to urban health problems* (pp. 97-110). New York: Springer.

Misra, S., Stokols, D., & Cheng, L. (2015). The transdisciplinary orientation scale: Factor structure and relation to the integrative quality and scope of scientific publications. *Journal of Translational Medicine and Epidemiology, 3*(2), 1042.

Montuori, A. (2013). The complexity of transdisciplinary literature reviews. *Complicity: An International Journal of Complexity and Education, 10*(1-2), 45-55.

Mørk, B.E., Aanestad, M., Grisot, M., & Hanseth, O. (2008). Conflicting epistemic cultures and obstacles for learning across communities of practice. *Knowledge and Process Management, 15*(1), 12-23.

Mullane, K., & Williams, M. (2013). Bias in research: The rule rather than the exception? *Elsevier Editors' Update, 40*, 7-10. Retrieved from https://www.elsevier.com/editors-update/story/publishing-ethics/bias-in-research-the-rule-rather-than-the-exception

Pirolli, P., & Card, S. (2005). The sensemaking process and leverage points for analyst technology as identified through cognitive task analysis. *Proceedings of International Conference on Intelligence Analysis*, 2-4.

Pohl, C. (2010). From transdisciplinarity to transdisciplinary research. *Transdisciplinary Journal of Engineering & Science, 1*(1), 74-83.

Rabin, M., & Schrag, J. L. (1999). First impressions matter: A model of confirmatory bias. *Quarterly Journal of Economics 114*(1), 37-82.

Richter, T. (2011). Cognitive flexibility and epistemic validation in learning from multiple texts. In J. Elen, E. Stahl, R. Bromme, & G. Clarebout (Eds.), *Links between beliefs and cognitive flexibility* (pp. 125-140). Berlin: Springer.

Richter, T., & Maier, J. (2017). Comprehension of multiple documents with conflicting information: A two-step model of validation. *Educational Psychologist, 52*(3), 148-166.

Robinson, J. (2008). Being undisciplined: Transgressions and intersections in academia and beyond. *Futures, 40*, 70-86.

Rosenfield, P. L. (1992). The potential of transdisciplinary research for sustaining and extending linkages between the health and social sciences. *Social Science & Medicine*, 35, 1343-1357. https://doi.org/10.1016/0277-9536(92)90038-r

Rumelhart, D. E., & Norman, D. A. (1978). Accretion, tuning and restructuring: Three modes of learning. In J. W. Cotton & R. L. Klatzky (Eds.), *Semantic factors in cognition* (pp. 37-53). Hillsdale NJ: Erlbaum.

Salazar M. R., Lant T. K., Fiore S. M., & Salas E. (2012). Facilitating innovation in diverse science teams through integrative capacity. *Small Group Research, 43*, 527-558.

Scaife, M., & Rogers, Y. (1996). External cognition: How do graphical representations work? *International Journal of Human-Computer Studies, 45*, 185-213.

Schacter, D. L. (2001). *The seven sins of memory*. New York, NY: Houghton Mifflin.

Schraw, G. J., Bendixen, L. D., & Dunkle, M. E. (2002). Development and validation of the Epistemic Belief Inventory (EBI). In B. K. Hofer & P. R. Pintrich (Eds.), *Personal epistemology: The psychology of beliefs about knowledge and knowing* (pp. 261–275). Mahwah, NJ: Lawrence Erlbaum Associate.

Shanahan, T., & Shanahan, C. (2008). Teaching disciplinary literacy to adolescents: Rethinking content-area literacy. *Harvard Educational Review, 78*(1), 40-59.

Shattuck, L. G., & Miller, N. L. (2006). Extending naturalistic decision making to complex organizations: A dynamic model of situated cognition. *Organization Studies, 27*, 989-1009.

Shrivastava, P., & Ivanaj, S. (2011). Transdisciplinary art, technology, and management for sustainable enterprise. *Transdisciplinary Journal of Engineering and Science, 2*, 81-92.

Slaney, M., & Russell, D. M. (2005). Measuring information understanding in large document collections. *Proceedings of the 38th Annual Hawaii International Conference on System Sciences*, 105-114.

Smart, P. R., (2017). Situating machine intelligence within the cognitive ecology of the internet. *Minds & Machines, 27*, 357–380.

Smart, P. R., & Shadbolt, N. R. (2014) Social machines. In M. Khosrow-Pour (Ed.), *Encyclopedia of information science and technology* (pp. 6855-6862). Hershey, PA: IGI Global.

Smart, P. R., Simperl, E., & Shadbolt, N. (2014). A taxonomic framework for social machines. In D. Miorandi, V. Maltese, M. Rovatsos, A. Nijholt, & J. Stewart (Eds.), *Social collective intelligence: Combining the powers of humans and machines to build a smarter society* (pp. 51-85). Berlin: Springer.

Smith, J., & Noble, H. (2014). Bias in research. *Evidence-Based Nursing, 17*, 2–3.

Soulé, H. & Warrick, T. (2015). Defining 21st century readiness for all students: What we know and how to get there. *Psychology of Aesthetics, Creativity, and the Arts, 9*(2), 178-186.

Stock, P., & Burton, R. J. (2011). Defining terms for integrated (multi-inter-trans-disciplinary) sustainability research. *Sustainability, 3*(8), 1090–1113.

Stokols, D. (2014). Training the next generation of transdisciplinarians. In M. O'Rourke, S. Crowley, S. D. Eigenbrode, & J. D. Wulfhorst (Eds.), *Enhancing communication & collaboration in interdisciplinary research* (pp. 56-81). Los Angeles, CA: Sage Publications.

U.S. Department of Defense. (2002). *DoD News Briefing. Secretary Rumsfeld and General Myers.* Retrieved from https://archive.defense.gov/Transcripts/Transcript.aspx?TranscriptID=2636

Vilsmaier, U., Brandner, V., & Engbers, M. (2017). Research in-between: The constitutive role of cultural differences in transdisciplinarity. In H. Dieleman, B. Nicolescu, & A. Ertas (Eds.), *Transdisciplinary & interdisciplinary education and research* (pp. 89-102). USA: Atlas Publishing.

Walsh, J. P., & Fahey, L. (1986). The role of negotiated belief structures in strategy making. *Journal of Management, 12*(3), 325-338.

Weick, K., Sutcliffe, K. M., & Obstfeld, D. (2005), Organizing and the process of sensemaking. *Organization Science, 16*, 409-421.

Gaetano R. Lotrecchiano & Shalini Misra (Editors). 2020
Communication in Transdisciplinary Teams
Santa Rosa, CA: Informing Science Press

Chapter 8:
Challenges and Opportunities in Conducting Collaborative Transdisciplinary Research (TDR): A Case from a Small Academic Institution in Puerto Rico

Nilda G. Medina
Universidad Ana G. Méndez, Carolina Campus, Puerto Rico, USA
nmedina18@suagm.edu

Loggina S. Báez
Universidad Ana G. Méndez, Carolina Campus, Puerto Rico, USA
loggina.baez@gmail.com

Loyda B. Méndez
Universidad Ana G. Méndez, Carolina Campus, Puerto Rico, USA
lbmendez@suagm.edu

Chapter Objectives

- To identify and comprehend shared core aspects of CBPR, TDR and capacity building principles.

- To describe the implementation of a TDR/CBPR initiative in the context of a small academic institution.

- To support the need for developing multiple strategies for effective communication among stakeholders.

- To foster early and continuous capacity building efforts for the sustainability of TDR and CBPR research efforts and collaborations.

- To acknowledge the significance of community engagement for the successful implementation of TDR research efforts to address health disparities issues.

- To explore the challenges and benefits of TDR and CBPR research efforts in small institutions.

An earlier version of this chapter was published as Medina, N. G., Báez, L. S., & Méndez, L. B. (2018). Collaborative transdisciplinary research in a small institution: Challenges and opportunities. *Informing Science: the International Journal of an Emerging Transdiscipline, 21,* 235-253. https://doi.org/10.28945/4028

Introduction to the Chapter

Health disparities problems involve multiple factors that should be analyzed and evaluated from theoretical frameworks and research models that allow a broad view of these complex phenomena. Transdisciplinary Research (TDR) offers this opportunity through the intersection and integration of different disciplines for the creation of a common conceptual framework to tackle a problem (Lotrecchiano & Misra, 2018; Rosenfield, 1992). Using a TDR approach, investigators from different scientific disciplines, expertise, and cultural backgrounds interact to co-produce knowledge (Abrams, 2006). Community Based Participatory Research (CBPR) is a collaborative approach that begins with a research topic of importance to the community and combines knowledge with action, in order to achieve social change to improve health outcomes and eliminate health disparities (W.K. Kellogg Foundation Community Health Scholars Program, 2001). Therefore "Transdisciplinary, community-based, interactive, or participatory research approaches are often suggested as appropriate means to meet both the requirements posed by real-world problems as well as the goals of sustainability" (Lang et al., 2012, p. 25).

The implementation of both TDR and CBPR approaches requires a continuous capacity building effort. ESSENCE on Health Research (2014) defines research capacity building as any attempt to increase the ability of individuals and institutions to undertake high-quality research and to engage with the wider community of stakeholders. Most examples of the development and implementation of TDR and CBPR initiatives come from large-scale programs led by research-intensive institutions or centers with multiple resources to establish collaborations among experts from different disciplines (Cooper et. al. 2013; Emmons, Viswanath & Colditz, 2008; Stokols, Hall, Taylor & Moser, 2008). However, we know less about the process of establishing TDR and CBPR initiatives in small academic settings, which tend to focus more on teaching and have limited resources. Therefore, in this paper we outline how a TDR and a CBPR research initiative was conceptualized, developed, implemented, and sustained at a small academic institution with limited research infrastructure.

Key Terminology

Community Based Participatory Research (CBPR) is a collaborative research approach that equitably involves community members, practitioners, and academic researchers in all aspects of the process, enabling all partners to contribute their expertise and share responsibility and ownership (Israel et al., 1998). It begins with a research topic of importance to the community and combines knowledge with action, in order to achieve social change to improve health outcomes and eliminate health disparities (W.K. Kellogg Foundation Community Health Scholars Program, 2001).

Health Disparities are defined in the Center for Disease Control and Prevention (CDC) Health Disparities and Inequalities Report (2011) as "differences in health outcomes and their determinants between segments of the population, as defined by social, demographic, environmental, and geographic attributes".

Hispanic-Serving Institutions (HSIs) , are not-for-profit higher education institutions with a full-time equivalent undergraduate student enrollment that is at least 25% Hispanic as defined in Title V of the Higher Education Act (US Department of Education, n.d.).

Primarily Undergraduate Institutions (*PUIs*), also known as predominantly or undergraduate-focused institutions, are accredited colleges (including 2-yr community colleges) and universities in which undergraduate enrollment is greater than graduate enrollment and have awarded 20 or fewer PhD/D.Sc. degrees in all National Science Foundation (NSF) supported fields during the combined previous two academic years (National Science Foundation, n.d.).

Research Capacity Building is defined by ESSENCE on Health Research (2014) as any efforts to increase the ability of individuals and institutions to undertake high-quality research and to engage with the wider community of stakeholders.

Transdisciplinary Research (*TDR*) is an integrative process in which investigators from different disciplines work jointly to develop and use a shared conceptual framework that synthesizes and extends discipline-specific theories, concepts, methods, or all three to create new models and language to address a common research problem (Rosenfield, 1992)

Background

Universidad Ana G. Méndez (UAGM), Carolina Campus (formerly known as Universidad del Este) is a Primarily Undergraduate Institution (PUI) located in Puerto Rico, whose primary focus is teaching (see profile below). However, in 2001 UAGM-Carolina incorporated a research component into its mission and included it as a priority in the institutional strategic development plan, initially as a way to enhance science education and provide research experience to undergraduate students. The transition to a teaching-research institution required the implementation of holistic and sustainable strategies that could have a university-wide impact. Therefore, based on the definition of TD research, UAGM-Carolina embraced the use of this approach as a strategy to maximize the use of academic and financial resources.

Universidad Ana G. Mendez, Carolina Campus' Profile (2017)

Description: Universidad Ana G. Méndez (UAGM), Carolina Campus is a private non-profit small academic institution designated as a Hispanic-Serving Institution (HSI) and a Primarily Undergraduate Institution (PUI). It was originally established in 1949 as a 2-yr college, in 1992 it transitioned to a 4-yr college, and in 2001 into a university when it started offering master's degrees.

Enrollment at main campus: 5,231 (92% undergraduates)

Full-time faculty/teaching load: 189 (41% have doctoral degrees)/15 credits

Number of research faculty: 6

> *Research laboratory space:* 4,000 sq. ft.
>
> *Research & Development expenditure[1]:* 782,000 USD
>
> *Carnegie Basic/Enrollment Classification[2]:* Master's Colleges & Universities/High undergraduate

The aims of UAGM-Carolina's TD Research Efforts are to:

1. Strengthen institutional research infrastructure.

2. Promote TD research endeavors among its faculty, students and academic units.

3. Develop CBPR initiatives that focus on health disparities affecting the institution's surrounding communities.

To accomplish these aims, research capacity building is considered a priority to develop the necessary infrastructure to conduct research in health disparities using TD and CBPR approaches.

Conceptualization of a TD and CBPR Research Agenda

In 2008, UAGM Carolina was awarded a Research Infrastructure for Minority Institutions (RIMI) grant from the National Institutes of Minority Health and Health Disparities (NIMHD) to enhance research capacity in health disparity areas (P20MD003355). The overall goal of the NIMHD-RIMI grant was to enhance UAGM-Carolina's research capacity in health disparity research at the basic science, preventive health, socio-behavioral, and educational levels, as well as to increase student pursuit of advanced studies in these areas. This presupposed at minimum a multidisciplinary approach to tackle a problem of interest, as it involved the participation of faculty and students from different academic units (i.e., Science & Technology, Health, Social Sciences, and Education). The health disparities of interest were asthma and violence at elementary school settings in Puerto Rico. These were selected based on their prevalence in Puerto Rican population, and because they provided a wide context for collaboration among diverse disciplines. To address these issues, the VIAS Health Disparity Network was created with the goal of promoting TDR and CBPR approaches for the prevention of violence and asthma in UAGM-Carolina's surrounding communities (Lugo, Báez, Medina, & Santiago, 2011).

During the conceptualization phase of VIAS Health Disparity Network, careful attention was given to the *Transdisciplinary research design principles* (Table 1) to assemble the violence and asthma research teams. However, since the inclusion of the community in the research process requires a paradigm shift that not only replaces the community's position in re-

---

[1] For additional information on institutions with similar profiles see: NSF National Center for Science and Engineering Statistics (n.d.) Higher Education Research and Development Survey. Retrieved from https://www.nsf.gov/statistics/srvyherd/

[2] For Carnegie classification definitions see: The Carnegie Classification of Institutions of Higher Education (n.d.). About Carnegie Classification. Retrieved from http://carnegieclassifications.iu.edu/

search but also re-conceptualizes the role of the researcher, we incorporated the *CBPR guiding principles* described by Israel and others (Israel, Schulz, Parker, & Becker 1998, Israel et al., 2008) (Table 2) into the conceptual framework of our TD research initiative.

Table 1. Transdisciplinary research design principles (Lang et. al, 2012)

Principle	Description
Phase A: Design principles for collaborative problem framing and building a collaborative research team	
Build a collaborative research team	Identify researchers, collaborators and stakeholders with expertise in the research problem, and facilitate explicit team-building processes.
Create joint understanding and definition of the sustainability problem to be addressed	Define the sustainability problem and make sure all team members are involved in that process.
Collaboratively define the boundary/research object, research objectives as well as specific research questions, and success criteria	Formulate an overall research object in which all the partners agree on common success criteria.
Design a methodological framework for collaborative knowledge production and integration	The research team must agree upon a jointly developed methodological framework that defines how the research target will be pursued in the next phase and what settings will be employed.
Phase B: Design principles for co-creation of solution -oriented and transferable knowledge through collaborative research	
Assign and support appropriate roles for practitioners and researchers	In each research effort, the tasks, roles and responsibilities of the scientists and practitioners, must be clearly defined in a transparent process.
Apply and adjust integrative research methods and transdisciplinary settings for knowledge generation and integration	The research team employs a methodological framework to generate solutions to the research problem, as well as develop suitable settings for inter- and transdisciplinary cooperation and knowledge integration.
Phase C: Design principles for (re-)integrating and applying the created knowledge	
Realize two-dimensional integration	Review the research outcomes and evaluate if its implementation served to solve or mitigate the problem addressed.
Generate targeted product for both parties	The research products, such as publications, must be appropriate to both researchers and partners so they can use that information for real-world problem-solving, scientific progress and/or innovation.
Evaluate scientific and societal impact	Evaluate the project at different stages after completion.

Principle	Description
General Design Principles cutting across the three phases	
Facilitate continuous formative evaluation	Formative evaluation must involve experts related to the topical field and transdisciplinary research. This process should allow to review the progress and reshape the subsequent project steps and phases, if necessary.
Mitigate conflict constellations	The researchers and practitioners must prepare and anticipate conflict at the outset, as well as adapted agreements should accompany the transdisciplinary research process over the entire course of the project.
Enhance capabilities for and interest in participation	Pay adequate attention to the material and intellectual capabilities that are required for effective and sustained participation in the project over time.

Table 2. CBPR guiding principles (Israel et al., 1998; Israel et al., 2008)

Principle	Description
Recognizes community as a unit of identity.	Groups that have a common sense of identity involving emotional connection and/or identification with others.
Builds on strengths and resources within the community	Considers, includes and works with the skills, resources, support networks and social structures within the community.
Facilitates collaborative, equitable partnerships in all phases of the research.	Norms of partnerships include mutual respect, recognition of knowledge, expertise, resource capacities, and open communication.
Promotes co-learning and capacity building among all partners.	This process facilitates the reciprocal transfer of knowledge, skills, and capacity.
Integrates research and action for the mutual benefit of all partners.	Create a balance between the generation of scientific research and application of knowledge leading to social change.
Involves a long-term process and commitment.	The relationships and commitment of all partners go beyond the culmination of a specific project or funding period.
Involves systems development through a cyclical and iterative process.	The process should include partnership development, community assessment, problem definition, determination of action, and mechanisms for sustainability among others.
Emphasizes local relevance of public health problems attending multiple determinants of health.	It emphasizes an ecological approach that involves individuals, the immediate context in which they live, and the broader context in which they are embedded.

Principle	Description
Disseminates findings to all partners and involves them in the dissemination process.	Research results are interpreted and discussed by all parties involved, presented in ways that will be useful for the community, and disseminated among and beyond the partnership itself.

Development of TD and CBPR Research Infrastructure

A core aspect of the development of a TDR and CBPR research initiative is to promote capacity building among researchers and community partners, as well as enhance the collaborative readiness among them. According to ESSENCE's (2016) framework for research capacity strengthening, capacity building goes beyond training, involves shifts in power, elicits systematic changes, and is influenced by cultural aspects, among other factors (see Table 3). In the case of UAGM-Carolina, the NIMHD-RIMI grant contributed to direct on-going capacity-building efforts towards the development of the administrative, human, and physical infrastructure needed to promote a TDR institutional culture, a critical feature for the success of this type of initiative. During the five years of the grant, significant institutional and administrative changes were implemented, many of which remain, to continue supporting capacity-building efforts. Administrative changes included the creation of the Associate Vice Chancellor's Office of Research, an Institutional Program for the Advancement of Research (PIFI, *Spanish acronym*), and a Transdisciplinary Research Institute (TRI). The Associate Vice Chancellor's Office of Research was responsible for the promotion, coordination, administration, and dissemination of research activities and projects through a TD approach. PIFI provides seed money for pilot projects (up to $15K) to gather preliminary data and submit competitive research proposals for external funding. The TRI functions as a research support unit that collaborates in the coordination of activities related to faculty development, curricular assessment of research skills, development of research projects, and research compliance. In addition, full-time research positions (currently six) were created to allow faculty to spend all their time and effort on research endeavors. Moreover, physical infrastructure dedicated to research was increased to include 1,000 sq. ft. of office space for the TRI (including workstations with specialized software for qualitative and quantitative research and access to scientific databases), as well as 1,000 sq. ft. of laboratory space with specialized equipment in the School of Science and Technology.

Table 3. Research capacity building principles (ESSENCE on Health Research, 2014, 2016)

Principle	Description
Network, collaborate and communicate experiences	Involves collaboration and effective communication among stakeholders, provides the ability to become part of a research network.
Understand the local context and evaluate existing research capacity	Engage community representatives to promote research relevant to society. Perform needs assessment of research capacity efforts. Supports guidance and training in evaluation. Enable stakeholders to conduct independent evaluations.

Principle	Description
Ensure local ownership and secure active support	Engage academic, private and public sectors to identify gaps in research capacity. Consider local priorities in research development strategies. Involve stakeholders in the design, implementation and evaluation of research initiatives.
Build in monitoring, evaluation and learning	Incorporates a framework to evaluate and monitor capacity building efforts. Define quantitative and qualitative indicators of success. Provides periods for reflection.
Establish robust research governance and support structures, and promote effective leadership	Strengthen systems that enable high-level decision. Facilitate research support structures. Design sustainable capacity building strategies by harmonizing efforts and ensuring complementarity. Provides training in leadership and management skills to establish effective relations between research teams and stakeholders.
Embed strong support, supervision and mentorship structures	Foster support from supervisors and mentors to produce high-quality, timely and relevant research. Develop mentoring skills at all levels to promote sustainability efforts.
Think long-term, be flexible and plan for continuity	Develop a long-term systemic approach to reach a self-sustaining mass of research capacity. Place strong emphasis on developing fundraising and policy engagement skills to encourage long-term sustainable support for high-quality research.

Furthermore, the VIAS Health Disparity Network invited local, national, and international experts in TD, CBPR, and other research related areas to provide workshops and guidance to UAGM-Carolina's faculty and community partners, as well as to serve on the VIAS External Advisory Board. Among them were (a) a Senior Fellow in the Robert Wood Johnson Foundation Center for Health Policy and Professor of Early Childhood Multicultural Education at the University of New Mexico, (b) the Co-Director of the Resilience Research Centre and Adjunct Professor at the School of Social Work, Dalhousie University, Canada, (c) the Professor and Director of the Research, Evaluation, Measurement, and Statistics program at Texas Tech University (TTU), (d) an Associate Professor in Psychology (Affiliated with Latino and Latin American Studies) at the University of California, Santa Cruz, (e) a Professor of School of Public Health, University of Michigan, (f) an Assistant Professor of Department of Health Promotion, Education & Behavior, University of South Carolina, (g) Professors of School of Social and Human Sciences and School of Science and Technology, Universidad del Este, (h) the Associate Vice Chancellor's Office of Research, Universidad del Este, (i) the Director of Transdisciplinary Institute of Social Action Research and Associate Professor of University of Puerto Rico, Humacao Campus, (j) the Director, Office of Research Integrity at University of Kentucky, (k) an Associate Professor and Associate Director, Center for Community Health, Institute for Public Health and Medicine, Northwestern Feinberg School of Medicine, (l) the Director of the Department of Pediatrics, (m) an Associate Director for Community Engaged Research, Professor and Head of the Department of Community, and Behavioral Health and Director of Prevention Research Center for Rural Health, University of Iowa, and (n) the Professor of the Department of Pediatrics, University of Puerto Rico, Medical Sciences Campus, among others. The capacity-building activities were coordinated by the TRI, and were attended by faculty, administrators, students, researchers, as well as community stakeholders (see Table 4).

Table 4. Capacity-building activities and workshops

Category	Activities/Workshops	Audience
TD & CBPR	CBPR: Rationale, benefits, and challenges Setting the stage: The why, what, and how of interdisciplinary/transdisciplinary inquiry Open dialogue about TD research School violence prevention and CBPR: Strengths and challenges of community-university relations Challenges of school community engagement to prevent youth violence	Faculty
	Introduction to CBPR	Faculty & students
	CBPR & Health Disparities Summer Activities Engaging youth in participatory action research	Community
Health disparity issues	School needs assessment on violence and asthma Fundamentals of school violence Psychological aspects of school violence	Teachers
	Laws regarding self-administration of asthma rescue medications in schools Psychological Services Guide	Community
	Asthma as a multifactor illness: Research and service opportunities Particulate matter and asthma: Physiological, biochemical, and molecular mechanisms	Faculty
	Environmental factors & asthma Asthma management in children & adults	Faculty & community

Category	Activities/Workshops	Audience
Research development & methods	Grant writing and sponsored programs	Faculty
	Statistical Analysis: Theoretical Aspects	Faculty & students
	Quantitative research methods & software (i.e. SPSS)	
	Application of multivariate statistical models in the behavioral and social sciences	
	Qualitative research methods & software (i.e. NVivo)	
	Understanding the obscure and taken-for-granted: The use of visual methods	
	Photovoice	
	Strategies for Youth Violence Prevention	
Ethics	Responsible conduct of research	Faculty & students
	Responsible conduct of research & CBPR	Community
	Ethics in CBPR	IRB members
	Ethics in mentorship	Faculty & students
Mentorship	Monthly mentoring training series (Introduction to mentoring, Individual development plan, etc.) VIAS-RIMI Mentoring Guide	Faculty & students
	Writing effective letters of recommendation	Faculty

Hall et al. (2008) consider three categories in the evaluation of collaborative-readiness in TDR teams: the contextual-environmental conditions (e.g., institutional support, physical proximity of investigators), intrapersonal characteristics (e.g., research orientation, leadership, among others), and interpersonal factors (e.g., group size, diversity of disciplines represented, previous history of collaboration). In our case, the capacity-building activities helped address these factors by bringing researchers and community stakeholders together in a series of face-to-face meetings within an enabling environment that fostered collegiality and cultivated seeds for collaboration. As stated in Medina, Fernández, Cruz, Jordán, and Trenche (2016), these meetings "…helped create a productive environment in which all ideas were listened to and were integrated…" and fostered trust and respect among partners. In addition, it provided a common ground in which a shared language was developed, and teams were assembled to define the research questions and study design, as exemplified by the configuration of the VIAS Health Disparity Network teams (see Table 5).

Implementation of TD and CBPR Research Initiative

The VIAS Health Disparity Network consisted of two distinct TDR teams, one for Asthma Prevention and the other for Violence Prevention. Both teams had committees at each participating elementary school, whose members were researchers and undergraduate students from different disciplines and community stakeholders, which included parents, teachers, students, social workers, administrative staff, and other members of the community (see Table 5).

Table 5. VIAS Health Disparity Network Teams

TD Team	Disciplines represented		
	Researchers	Undergraduate students	Community members
Asthma prevention	Medicine Public Health Demography Environmental Toxicology Academic/Research Psychology	Biology Biotechnology Microbiology Nursing Social Work	Teachers Counselor Social workers Librarian Parents Students
Violence prevention	Clinical/Community Psychology School Psychology Academic/Research Psychology	Criminal Justice Education Psychology Social Work	Administrative Assistant School directors Leaders of community organizations Government officials

For effective communication among team members, face-to-face meetings at regular intervals (i.e., biweekly) were held to discuss the progress and challenges in the research activities, as well as ideas for new projects. A liaison was appointed to maintain an open line of communication between the community and the researchers. In addition, community engagement activities were frequently held to raise awareness of health disparity issues and to promote familiarity and social cohesiveness among team members and community stakeholders through both formal and informal settings (see Table 6).

Table 6. Community Engagement Activities

Category	Activities
Awareness	World Asthma Day Earth Day "No smoking" week Art Contests Health Fairs Movie Forums
Outreach	Mothers' SPA day School Open House Annual Turkey Run Christmas Lighting Field day Reading Week

Category	Activities
Service	Reforestation of school areas
	Vegetable garden
	Workshops for students, teachers, school staff
	Environmental health student club
	Fundraising for school activities

An example of one the projects that stemmed from these teams and committees was the development, validation, and implementation of a school violence observation instrument designed to gather information about the characteristics and behavioral patterns of school violence at each school community (Medina et al., 2016; Medina Santiago, Cruz Rivera, Trenche Rodríguez & Báez Ávila, 2017). In this study the principal investigator worked collaboratively with the school communities and VIAS' research team during the whole research process.

CBPR Approach to Develop a School Violence Observation Instrument
(Medina et al., 2016; Medina et al., 2017)

Objective: To engage school community members in the development, validation, and implementation of an observation instrument to identify characteristics of school violence in two Puerto Rican schools.

TD team: Composed of 12 to 15 members including academic researchers, undergraduate students and School Violence Prevention Committee (SVPC) members (i.e., school personnel, parents, and community leaders).

Capacity-building: Academic researchers and the university's institutional review board (IRB) members participated in workshops about ethical issues in CBPR and challenges in having community members as research partners. SVPC members took a one-day training on ethics, confidentiality and responsible conduct of research. The undergraduate students were trained on field observations, qualitative and quantitative research techniques.

Methods: The instrument was developed jointly between researchers and SVPC members to include particular violent behaviors previously identified by the school's community. The instrument was validated with input of student observers and external evaluators. Afterwards, the instrument was implemented during a 3-week period, in which the first week served for habituation and practice and the second and third weeks for data collection by undergraduate students. Data analysis was conducted by the principal investigator and undergraduate students, while it was interpreted with input from all members of the TD team.

Communication/Dissemination strategies: The TD team met on a monthly basis, with the project coordinator and school liaison follow-up all communication and between meetings. The SVPC kept the community informed through open letters, bulletin board announcements and during parent-teacher conferences. Results were disseminated through a final report presentation to parents and school personnel, a written report to school administrators and public education officials, as well as presentations and peer-reviewed publications to the academic community.

> *TD/CBPR* knowledge: This effort helped develop a better instrument tailored to the needs of the community and contributed to a better understanding of the phenomenon being researched.

In CBPR efforts, the dissemination of findings should be provided on an ongoing basis, using multiple strategies, so results can be used to guide the development of interventions and policy change (Israel et al., 2008). In this case, the results were discussed with community members and disseminated to the communities at large (e.g., school personnel and parents) through oral and written reports. Furthermore, action plans were developed at each school community to prevent and reduce school violence based on the results of the study. For instance, changes in school organization (e.g., lunch schedules, supervision duties) were implemented and parents were invited to participate in school activities as classroom assistants, lunch monitors, etc. In addition, dissemination of findings extended beyond the partnership itself, involving a community member (a school social worker) as co-author of publications and co-presenter at conferences and workshops.

Regarding this process of dissemination of results, CBPR recognizes the importance of the discussion and interpretation of the data obtained from the research by all parties involved. However, this information should be presented to the community in a clear and respectful language, and in ways which will be useful for decision-making and for developing action plans that will benefit the community (Balcazar, 2003). Thus, multiple strategies of dissemination were used to communicate the results on an ongoing basis to different audiences (see Table 7).

Table 7. Dissemination strategies

Strategy	Audience
VIAS biannual newsletter Brochures Teachers meeting Parents-teacher meetings Study Reports (Biannual)	School community members (students, parents, school personnel)
Faculty meetings Brown-bag series: "Almorzando y conversando" Seminar series: "Jornadas para la discusion de investigaciones y productos de labor creativa" Institutional magazine: UNEVISION (Medina, & Méndez, 2016)	Institutional personnel (administrators, faculty, staff, students)

Strategy	Audience
Documentary: López Román (2011); Radio broadcast: Medina (2010)	Community-at-large
Television broadcast: Lugo, Medina, & Santiago (2013); Medina (2014); Méndez & Medina (2016b)	
Web-based broadcast: Méndez & Medina (2016a)	

Sustainability of TD and CBPR Research Efforts

Sustainability is a core concept in TDR, CBPR, and capacity-building principles. Therefore, early and continuous capacity building efforts are necessary to sustain TDR and CBPR research efforts and collaborations. According to Hacker and colleagues (2012), "capacity building can be seen as both a determinant of sustainability and an outcome of it. Some have even referred to this as capacity sustainability" (p. 2). Referring to the conceptual model for the evaluation of collaborative initiatives described by Hall et al. (2008), the capacity building activities during the development and implementation of our TDR initiative, not only enhanced the collaborative readiness of the teams, but also their collaborative capacity which in turn translated into sustainable collaborative products.

For instance, the enabling institutional environment for cross-disciplinary collaborations, the development of research skills through capacity-building activities, and the convergence of investigators through formal and informal settings contributed to the submission in 2013 of a grant to the Environmental Protection Agency (EPA), aimed to determine the impact of urban environmental stressors in student health and achievement by means of a CBPR and TDR approach. For this grant submission, the research team was composed of investigators from both TDR teams of the VIAS Health Disparity Network working together towards a common goal. Even though the grant was not awarded, it received favorable comments from reviewers, but more importantly it set up the stage for future TDR collaborations in UAGM-Carolina. Thus, in 2015, two of the researchers involved in the submission of the EPA grant were awarded an Academic Research Enhancement Award (AREA-R15) from NIMHD (R15MD010201). The purpose of this research mechanism is to stimulate research in educational institutions that have not been major recipients of NIH support, and is intended to support small-scale research projects (National Institutes of Health [NIH], n.d.). As a small institution, being a recipient of this grant is an encouraging and positive outcome of fostering TDR collaborations, since it has been the first of its kind to be awarded to UAGM-Carolina and it had provided continuity to the collaboration with the surrounding school communities.

In addition, one of the guiding principles of CBPR is that it involves systems development through cyclical and iterative processes, including those for developing partnerships and establishing mechanisms of sustainability (Israel et al. 1998). This is also true for TDR and capacity building research efforts. Hall and colleagues (2012), proposed a four-phase model of TD team-based research in which a cyclical progression occurs through the phases (i.e., development, conceptualization, implementation, and translation) as well as recursive and iterative movements among them during the life cycle of a TD initiative. These movements may lead to new research directions and changes in the TDR team. Indeed, the evolution of the TDR team is a key process in the translation phase in which the development of new collaborations that provide additional expertise can aid in moving the TDR findings from one level of analysis to another and/or across the discovery–development–delivery continuum (Hall et al., 2012). In our case, the VIAS Health Disparity Network evolved into Project ECO-RED, through the awarded AREA-R15 grant. The main goal of this longitudinal project is to examine the relationships between exposure to traffic-related air pollution and the risk of developing respiratory and neurocognitive impairments in Puerto Rican children (Méndez Torres & Medina Santiago, 2019). The new research direction in our TDR initiative required the addition of an epidemiologist and a respiratory therapist to the previous research team of the environmental toxicologist, school psychologist, and academic research psychologist that participated in the VIAS teams. Although Project ECO-RED does not follow a CBPR approach, it still collaborates closely with participating schools as community engagement is a core element of any research involving communities. Community engagement can not only improve the ability of the community to address their own health needs and problems, but also represent an opportunity for researchers to understand community priorities (Ahmed & Palermo, 2010). Research in this area maintains that effective communication, trust, the development of a sense of belonging, the establishment of common agreements, shared leadership and social responsibility are indispensable factors to stimulate commitment and community participation (López-Bolaños, Campos Rivera & Villanueva-Borbolla, 2018) (See Figure 1).

This aspect was fundamental for the successful continuation and development of research projects, even in the aftermath of the devastating hurricanes Irma and Maria that ravaged Puerto Rico in 2017. The combined power of these two storms resulted in an island-wide power outage, which severely impaired telecommunications, healthcare facilities, etc. (Segarra Alméstica, 2018). In addition, 60% of the population had no access to drinking water and many areas became isolated due to severe road damages. This situation lasted weeks or months, for the most part, and contributed to an increase in PR's mortality rate during that period (Kishore et al., 2018; Santos-Burgoa et al., 2018). However due to our long-standing collaboration with school communities, we were able to participate in ongoing relief efforts, engage in activities that contributed to coping skills, and resume our research as soon as it was possible during the following semester. Moreover, community members have continued to participate in research dissemination efforts as recently published works can attest (Cordero et al., 2018).

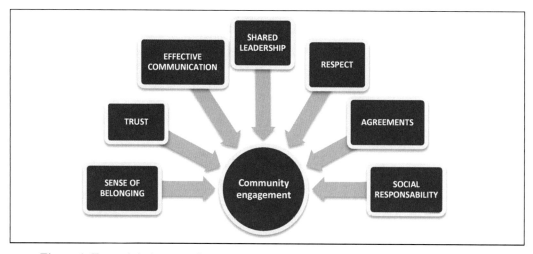

Figure 1. Essential elements for the development and strengthening of community engagement (López-Bolaños et al., 2018)

Challenges and Lessons Learned

Although we have been able to successfully implement and sustain a collaborative TDR and CBPR initiative we still face challenges (see Table 8) that have been reported in the literature on these topics (Kessel & Rosenfield, 2008; Stokols, Misra, Moser, Hall & Taylor, 2008; Vogel et al., 2014). For instance, there are institutional barriers, such as emphasis on academic-teaching tasks for faculty that does not have a research appointment. In our institution, most faculty are part-time and mostly hired for teaching. In addition, of the 186 full-time faculty members only 45.7% have a doctoral degree. These factors limit opportunities for collaboration within the institution. However, it has encouraged us to develop collaborations and partnerships with other institutions and organizations, which have enhanced our TDR and CBPR team.

The implementation of a research approach particularly focused on TD proved to be cost-effective to our institution as the investigators shared resources towards a same goal. However, as the research teams and projects keep expanding in disciplines and scope there is a need for additional research infrastructure and continuous capacity-building efforts to support the changing demands of the TD research. This element has been more difficult to sustain since, as a small institution with a primary focus on teaching, there are limited resources and opportunities for the development of areas designated for research activities. Also, in contrast with research-intensive institutions, UAGM-Carolina receives less than 530,000 USD a year in research grants and thus limited indirect costs. In addition, our institution does not have a critical mass of investigators to be able to successfully compete for major grants for construction, instrumentation, research centers, etc. This has created the need to identify other types of funding sources. For instance, UAGM-Carolina is one of the primarily undergraduate institutions served by the Puerto Rico IDeA Network for Biomedical Research Excellence (PR-INBRE, P20GM103475-14), which are funded by the National Institute of General Medical Sciences of the National Institutes of Health. Through PR-INBRE, UAGM-Carolina investigators have access to core instrumentation facilities, opportunities for collaboration with an island-wide network of researchers, career-development workshops, and research training. Furthermore, PR-INBRE has provided funds for alteration and renovation of laboratory spaces, research instrumentation, and pilot projects.

Table 8. CBPR, TDR and capacity building principles and challenges of sustainability

Principles	Challenges	Response to the challenges
CBPR Recognizes community as a unit of identity Facilitates collaborative, equitable partnerships in all phases of the research Integrates and achieves a balance between research and action for the mutual benefit of all partners *TDR* Collaborative problem framing and building a collaborative research team (Phase A) Co-creation of solution-oriented and transferable knowledge through collaborative research (Phase B) Mitigate conflict constellations *Capacity Building* Network, collaborate, communicate and share experiences Ensure local ownership and secure active support	Diversity in values and attitudes, as well as differences in terminology, methods and techniques among researchers across different disciplines and community members Requires more time Requires more faculty participation	Collaborations and partnerships with other institutions and organizations, which have enhanced our TD and CBPR research team Recruitment of a liaison to promote effective communication between researchers and community
CBPR Builds on strengths and resources within the community Involves a long-term process and commitment *Capacity Building* Understand the local context and accurately evaluate existing research capacity	Small institution with a primary focus on teaching Limited resources and opportunities for the development of areas designated for research activities. Lack of a critical mass of investigators to be able to successfully compete for major grants for construction, instrumentation, research centers, etc. (Most faculty is part-time and only 54% of faculty members have doctoral degree)	Investigators shared resources towards a same goal Need to identify other types of funding sources for investigators to have access to facilities, instrumentation, collaborations, career development, and research trainings (i.e. – PR-INBRE, UAGM-Carolina) Strengthening the capacity building component Peer mentoring

Principles	Challenges	Response to the challenges
CBPR Promotes co-learning and capacity building among all partners *TDR* Enhance capabilities for and interest in participation *Capacity Building* Establish robust research governance and support structures, and promote effective leadership	Difficulty to maintain activities aimed at capacity building when the funding period ends for programs that contribute to develop research infrastructure	Training of junior faculty Peer mentoring Develop modules and/or courses to provide formal TD training
CBPR Involves systems development through a cyclical and iterative process *TDR* Facilitate continuous formative evaluation *Capacity Building* Build in monitoring, evaluation and learning from the start	Limited human resources Lack of critical mass of investigators to compete for major grants	Institutional seed funds Collaboration between faculty with common research interests TD team-based research
CBPR Disseminates findings and knowledge gained to all partners and involves all partners in the dissemination process *TDR* (Re-)integrating and applying the created knowledge (Phase C)	Lack of experience in research work that involves community members as partners in the research process Institutional processes unrelated to this type of work	Institutional support to train researchers and community partners External collaborators with expertise in IRB process, writing of scientific articles, and presentations in professional forums, etc.

During the initial phases of the implementation of the TD and CBPR research initiative, a considerable time and effort was devoted to capacity-building activities focused on TD and CBPR training. This proved to be effective in stimulating collaborations among investigators and the community. Unfortunately, after the initial funding from the NIMHD-RIMI grant, these capacity-building activities have scaled-down, which has limited the participation of additional faculty in the TD research projects. We emphasize the need for training junior faculty since traditionally most investigators have not been involved in TD research and thus many lack the skills and dispositions to engage successfully in TD collaborative efforts. While others have focused on TD training for graduate students and postdoctoral fellows, as those described by Nash et al. (2003) and James, Gehlert, Bowen, and Colditz. (2015), as a small academic institution without doctoral programs, this may not be feasible. Thus, to sustain the institutional collaborative capacity, more emphasis should be made in developing modules and/or courses to provide formal TD training to faculty while encouraging researchers to interact and collaborate (Nash, 2008).

Diversity in values and attitudes, as well as differences in terminology, methods and techniques among researchers across different disciplines and community members are known barriers for TD and CBPR (Vogel et al., 2014). Thus, to promote effective communication between the researchers and the community, a liaison was appointed to facilitate the flow of information. Initially, the functions of the liaison were mainly structural tasks such as coordination and information exchange. However, throughout the tenure of VIAS Health Disparity Network, it became clear that the liaison was more than just an intermediary between parties, but a key player for the successful implementation of TD and CBPR initiative. As such, for Project ECO-RED, the liaison plays a central role (See Figure 2).

Gray (2008) states that brokers who function as representatives and liaisons are the most crucial in large TD teams as they are the only links connecting diverse groups. In our case, the liaison not only provided linkage, but also assumed a role of leadership due to the unique position of centrality within the TD teams. Thus, the liaison provides support to the principal investigators by facilitating team-based processes, maintaining frequent communication, and serving as translator to maintain a clear message and build trust among team members. As such, the liaison must be skilled in group processes, conflict resolution, and interpersonal communication. Since the role of the liaison takes a considerable amount of time and effort, in our TD and CBPR initiatives, an academic research psychologist has been exclusively tasked with this endeavor.

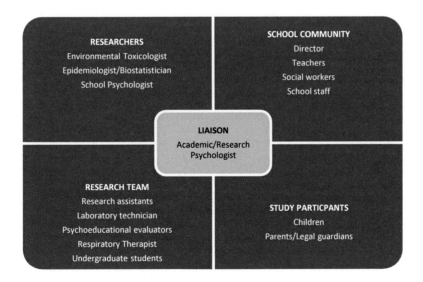

Figure 2. Liaison as a central key player in project ECO-RED

Conclusion

This chapter focuses on CBPR and TD approaches to the study of health disparities, paying attention to the capacity-building component as an important part of the process of achieving TD knowledge generation. As illustrated in Figure 3, capacity building shares core aspects with CBPR and TD efforts such as building and developing collaborations, supporting and sustaining research efforts, as well as evaluating and monitoring the research process.

Figure 3. Core concepts shared by TD, CBPR, and capacity building efforts

Capacity building sessions encouraged the convergence of researchers from different disciplines towards the same goals, providing a common ground to develop new ideas and projects to address health disparities in our communities. This became an opportunity to maximize limited research resources in our institution by expanding the scientific network of the researchers, increasing collaborations, and enhancing the translation of potential solutions to address the needs of community stakeholders. Even though capacity building can facilitate the implementation of TD and CBPR research, many challenges arise as an inherent result of community engagement and the integration of different disciplines. Thus, the need of continuous reflection to acknowledge them becomes critical for advancing TD and CBPR research efforts.

Questions to Further the Discourse

1. Compare and contrast the implementation of TD/CBPR initiatives in PUIs versus those developed in research-intensive institutions.

2. What other challenges could be encountered while integrating CBPR and TD research?

3. How can the lessons learned in this case study be applied to other contexts?

4. In what other innovative ways can CBPR and TD research be integrated?

5. How can this CBPR and TD research initiative be evaluated?

6.   Why is it critical to develop diverse strategies to enhance communication between CBPR and TD research team members?

7.   How can capacity building in TD and CBPR help researchers develop and sustain collaborative projects?

Acknowledgements

Participating communities, members of the VIAS Health Disparity Network, Dr. Carlos Santiago, Dr. Eduardo Lugo, Dr. Ivis Figueroa, Dr. Teresa Pedroso, members of Project ECO-RED, UAGM-Carolina's Transdisciplinary Research Institute (TRI), and Dr. Luis Iturralde, Associate Vice-Chancellor of Graduate Affairs and Research.

Funding

NIMHD-RIMI (P20MD003355), PR-INBRE (P20GM103475-14), NIMHD-NIH-R15 (R15MD010201), and UAGM-Carolina's Institutional Program for the Advancement of Research (PIFI, *Spanish acronym*).

Must Reads

ESSENCE on Health Research. (2014). Seven principles for strengthening research capacity in low- and middle-income countries: simple ideas in a complex world. *ESSENCE Good practice document series*. World Health Organization.

ESSENCE on Health Research. (2016). Planning, monitoring and evaluation framework for research capacity strengthening. *ESSENCE Good practice document series*. World Health Organization.

Israel, B. A., Schulz, A. J., Parker, E. A., Becker, A. B., Allen, A. J., & Guzman, R. (2008). Critical issues in developing and following CBPR principles. In M. Minkler & N. Wallerstein (Eds.), *Community based participatory research for health: From process to outcomes* (2nd ed.) (pp. 47-66). San Francisco, CA: Jossey-Bass.

Lang, D. J., Wiek, A., Bergmann, M., Stauffacher, M., Martens, P., Moll, P., Swilling, M., & Thomas, C. J. (2012). Transdisciplinary research in sustainability science: Practice, principles, and challenges. *Sustainability Science: Bridging the Gap between Science and Society*, 7, 25-43. https://doi.org/10.1007/s11625-011-0149-x

Minkler, M. & Wallerstein, N. (Eds.) (2008). *Community based participatory research for health: From process to outcomes* (2nd ed.). San Francisco, CA: Jossey-Bass.

References

Abrams, D. B. (2006). Applying transdisciplinary research strategies to understanding and eliminating health disparities. *Health Education & Behavior, 33*(4), 515–531. https://doi.org/10.1177/1090198106287732

Ahmed, S. M., & Palermo, A. G. (2010). Community engagement in research: Frameworks for education and peer review. *American Journal of Public Health, 100*(8), 1380-1387.

Balcazar, F. E. (2003). Investigación acción participativa (IAP): Aspectos conceptuales y dificultades de implementación [Participatory action research (PAR): Conceptual aspects and implementation difficulties]. *Fundamentos en Humanidades, I/II* (7/8).

Center for Disease Control and Prevention (CDC). (2011). CDC health disparities and inequalities report—United States, 2011. *Morbidity and Mortality Weekly Report 2011; 60* (Suppl; January 24, 2011).

Cooper, L. A., Boulware, L. E., Miller, E. R., Golden, S. H., Carson, K. A., Noronha, G., … Brancati, F. L. (2013). Creating a transdisciplinary research center to reduce cardiovascular health disparities in Baltimore, Maryland: Lessons learned. *American Journal of Public Health, 103*(11), e26–e38. https://doi.org/10.2105/AJPH.2013.301297

Cordero, G., Román, S., Jiménez, J., Fonseca, N., Colón, E., Fernández, G., & Medina, N. (2018). Creando espacios de colaboración multidisciplinaria en las escuelas: Retos y oportunidades. *Voces desde el Trabajo Social, 6*(1), 94-111. https://doi.org/10.31919/voces.v6i1.123

Emmons, K. M., Viswanath, K., & Colditz, G. A. (2008). The role of transdisciplinary collaboration in translating and disseminating health research: Lessons learned and exemplars of success. *American Journal of Preventive Medicine, 35*(2 Suppl), S204-S210. https://doi.org/10.1016/j.amepre.2008.05.009

ESSENCE on Health Research. (2014). Seven principles for strengthening research capacity in low- and middle-income countries: Simple ideas in a complex world. *ESSENCE Good practice document series*. World Health Organization.

ESSENCE on Health Research. (2016). Planning, monitoring and evaluation framework for research capacity strengthening. *ESSENCE Good practice document series*. World Health Organization.

Gray, B. (2008). Enhancing transdisciplinary research through collaborative leadership. *American Journal of Preventive Medicine, 35*(2 Suppl), S124-S132. https://doi.org/10.1016/j.amepre.2008.03.037

Hacker, K., Tendulkar, S. A., Rideout, C., Bhuiya, N., Trinh-Shevrin, C., Savage, C. P., & DiGirolamo, A. (2012). Community capacity building and sustainability: Outcomes of community-based participatory research. *Progress in Community Health Partnerships: Research, Education, and Action, 6*(3), 349-360. https://doi.org/10.1353/cpr.2012.0048

Hall, K. L., Stokols, D., Moser, R. P., Taylor, B. K., Thornquist, M. D., Nebeling, L. C., & Jeffery, R. W. (2008). The collaboration readiness of transdisciplinary research teams and centers findings from the National Cancer Institute's TREC Year-One evaluation study. *American Journal of Preventive Medicine, 35*(2 Suppl), S161-S172. https://doi.org/10.1016/j.amepre.2008.03.035

Hall, K. L., Vogel, A. L., Stipelman, B., Stokols, D., Morgan, G., & Gehlert, S. (2012). A four-phase model of transdisciplinary team-based research: Goals, team processes, and strategies. *Translational Behavioral Medicine, 2*(4), 415-430. https://doi.org/10.1007/s13142-012-0167-y

Israel, B. A., Schulz, A. J., Parker, E. A., & Becker, A. B. (1998). Review of community-based participatory research: Assessing partnership approaches to improve public health. *Annual Review of Public Health, 19*(1), 173-202. https://doi.org/10.1146/annurev.publhealth.19.1.173

Israel, B. A., Schulz, A. J., Parker, E. A., Becker, A. B., Allen, A. J., & Guzman, R. (2008). Critical issues in developing and following CBPR principles. In M. Minkler & N. Wallerstein (Eds.), *Community based participatory research for health: From process to outcomes* (2nd ed.) (pp. 47-66). San Francisco, CA: Jossey-Bass.

James, A. S., Gehlert, S., Bowen, D. J., & Colditz, G. A. (2015). A framework for training transdisciplinary scholars in cancer prevention and control. *Journal of Cancer Education, 30*(4), 664-669. https://doi.org/10.1007/s13187-014-0771-2

Kessel, F., & Rosenfield, P. L. (2008). Toward transdisciplinary research: Historical and contemporary perspectives. *American Journal of Preventive Medicine, 35*(2 Suppl), S225-S234. https://doi.org/10.1016/j.amepre.2008.05.005

Kishore, N., Marqués, D., Mahmud, A., Kiang, M. V., Rodriguez, I., Fuller, A., … Buckee, C. O. (2018). Mortality in Puerto Rico after Hurricane Maria. *New England Journal of Medicine, 379*(2), 162-170. doi: 10.1056/NEJMsa1803972.

Lang, D. J., Wiek, A., Bergmann, M., Stauffacher, M., Martens, P., Moll, P., Swilling, M., & Thomas, C. J. (2012). Transdisciplinary research in sustainability science: Practice, principles, and challenges. *Sustainability Science: Bridging the Gap between Science and Society, 7*, 25-43. https://doi.org/10.1007/s11625-011-0149-x

López-Bolaños, L. Compos-Rivera, M., & Villanueva-Borbolla, M. A. (2018). Compromiso y participación comunitaria en salud: aprendizajes desde la sistematización de experiencias sociales [Commitment and community participation towards health: knowledge creation from systematization of social experiences]. *Salud Pública en México, 60*(2), 192-201. https://doi.org/10.21149/8460

López Román, F. A. (Producer & director). (2011). *La investigación acción participativa y la violencia escolar* [Documentary]. Colección Jesús T. Piñero (LB 1028.25.P9 148 2011). Universidad del Este, Carolina, PR. Excerpt retrieved from https://vimeo.com/23142488/description

Lotrecchiano, G. R., & Misra, S. (2018). Transdisciplinary knowledge producing teams: Toward a complex systems perspective. *Informing Science: The International Journal of an Emerging Transdiscipline, 21*, 51-74. https://doi.org/10.28945/4086

Lugo, E., Báez, L., Medina, N., & Santiago, C. (2011). El proyecto VIAS: Acción y transformación para la prevención de la violencia escolar a través de la Investigación Basada en la Participación [Project VIAS: Action and transformation for school violence prevention through CBPR]. *Ámbitos de Encuentro, 4*(1), 125-153.

Lugo, E., Medina, N. G., & Santiago, C. (2013, October 6) *Prevention of school violence through research work of violence prevention component of VIAS-RIMI*. Interview by J. Rodríguez-Cancel. In UNEVISION [Television broadcast]. San Juan, PR: Sistema TV WMTJ

Medina, N., Fernández, G, Cruz, T., Jordán, N., & Trenche, M. (2016). Community participation in the development and validation of a school violence observation instrument. *Progress in Community Health Partnerships: Research, Education, and Action, 10*(2), 251-258. https://doi.org/10.1353/cpr.2016.0020

Medina, N. G. (2010, June 6). *School violence and bullying.* Interview in Comunidad Ley y Orden [Radio broadcast]. Ciudad, PR: Radio Vida 90.5 FM

Medina, N. G. (2014, April). *Effects of school violence in academic achievement.* Interview by David Reyes. In Noticias 24/7 [Television broadcast]. Ciudad, PR: Channel 6 WIPR

Medina, N. G., & Méndez, L. B. (2016, May). Se investiga la relación entre la contaminación atmosférica y las condiciones respiratorias en niños. *UNEVISION, 14,* 17. Retrieved from: http://www.suagm.edu/une/publicaciones/unevision/unevision_2016_mayo

Medina Santiago, N., Cruz Rivera, T., Trenche Rodríguez, M., & Báez Ávila, L. (2017). Estudio participativo para el desarrollo de un instrumento de observación de violencia escolar. [Participatory research to develop a school violence observation instrument]. *Ámbitos de Encuentro, 10*(2), 48-66.

Méndez, L. B., & Medina, N. G. (2016a, December 8) *Efectos de contaminantes atmosféricos en la salud respiratoria y cognición de niños puertorriqueños (Proyecto ECO-RED).* Interview by L. Gómez. In Utopística [Web-based broadcast]. Retrieved from: https://www.youtube.com/watch?v=XwD845VaBDU

Méndez, L. B., & Medina, N. G. (2016b, July 2). *Proyecto ECO-RED.* Interview by M. Carrasquillo. In Ruta U: Revista Pitirre [Television broadcast]. San Juan, PR: Sistema TV WMTJ

Méndez Torres, L.B., & Medina Santiago, N.G. (2019). Los efectos de la contaminación ambiental en el desarrollo neurocognitivo. [The effects of environmental pollution in cognitive development]. In: Pérez-Jiménez D, Rodríguez Acevedo A, Serrano-García I, Serrano Goytía J, & Pérez López S (Eds.), *Desarrollo humano: Travesía de oportunidades y retos* (pp. 19-30). Humacao, PR: Asociación de Psicología de Puerto Rico.

Nash, J. M. (2008). Transdisciplinary training: Key components and prerequisites for success. *American Journal of Preventive Medicine, 35*(2 Suppl), S133-S140. https://doi.org/10.1016/j.amepre.2008.05.004

Nash, J. M., Collins, B. N., Loughlin, S. E., Solbrig, M., Harvey, R., Krishnan-Sarin, S., & Spirito, A. (2003). Training the transdisciplinary scientist: A general framework applied to tobacco use behavior. *Nicotine & Tobacco Research, 5*(Suppl 1), S41-S53. https://doi.org/10.1080/14622200310001625528

National Institutes of Health (NIH). (n.d.). *Academic Research Enhancement Award.* Retrieved from: https://area.nih.gov/

National Science Foundation (NSF). (n.d.). *Facilitating research at primarily undergraduate institutions.* Retrieved from: https://www.nsf.gov/funding/pgm_summ.jsp?pims_id=5518

Rosenfield, P. L. (1992). The potential of transdisciplinary research for sustaining and extending linkages between the health and social sciences. *Social Science and Medicine, 35*, 1343-1357. https://doi.org/10.1016/0277-9536(92)90038-R

Santos-Burgoa, C., Sandberg, J., Suárez, E., Goldman-Hawes, A., Zeger, S., Garcia-Meza, A., … Goldman L. (2018). Differential and persistent risk of excess mortality from Hurricane Maria in Puerto Rico: A time-series analysis. *The Lancet Planetary Health, 2*(11), e478-e488. https://doi.org/10.1016/S2542-5196(18)30209-2

Segarra Alméstica, E. V. (2018). María y la vulnerabilidad en Puerto Rico. *Revista de Administración Pública, 49*, 13-38.

Stokols, D., Hall, K. L., Taylor, B. K., & Moser, R. P. (2008). The science of team science: Overview of the field and introduction to the supplement. *American Journal of Preventive Medicine, 35*(2 Suppl), S77-S89. https://doi.org/10.1016/j.amepre.2008.05.002

Stokols, D., Misra, S., Moser, R. P., Hall, K. L., & Taylor, B. K. (2008). The ecology of team science: Understanding contextual influences on transdisciplinary collaboration. *American Journal of Preventive Medicine, 35*(2 Suppl), S96-S115. https://doi.org/10.1016/j.amepre.2008.05.003

U.S. Department of Education. (n.d.). *Definition of Hispanic-service institutions*. Retrieved from: https://www2.ed.gov/print/programs/idueshsi/definition.html

Vogel, A. L., Stipelman, B. A., Hall, K. L., Nebeling, L., Stokols, D., & Spruijt-Metz, D. (2014). Pioneering the transdisciplinary team science approach: Lessons learned from National Cancer Institute grantees. *Journal of Translational Medicine and Epidemiology, 2*(2), 1027.

W.K. Kellogg Foundation Community Health Scholars Program. (2001). *Stories of impact* [Brochure]. Ann Arbor: University of Michigan, School of Public Health Scholars Program, National Program Office.

Gaetano R. Lotrecchiano & Shalini Misra (Editors). 2020
Communication in Transdisciplinary Teams
Santa Rosa, CA: Informing Science Press

Chapter 9:
Transdisciplinary Communication in Research Teams: Institutional Constructs and Practices from a Uruguayan Perspective

Bianca Vienni Baptista
Transdisciplinarity Lab, Swiss National Institute of Technology, Zurich, Switzerland
bianca.vienni@usys.ethz.ch

Maria Goñi Mazzitelli
Academic Department, Comisión Sectorial de Investigación Científica, Universidad de la República, Montevideo, Uruguay
mgoni@csic.edu.uy

Florencia Ferrigno Came
Extension and Outreach Unit, Facultad de Ciencias Sociales, Universidad de la República, Montevideo, Uruguay
mfferrigno@gmail.com

Chapter Objectives

- To define integrality in the context of a Uruguayan university and to provide relevant lessons for fostering transdisciplinary research and communication at other universities and contexts.

- To better understand how transdisciplinary research is being developed in Uruguay and how it relates to other research practices, such as integral activities, oriented towards the resolution of real world problems.

- To open new spaces for communication among researchers from different regions and countries as a way of reflecting not only on concepts, but also on research practices. The call for a theoretical-methodological discussion that promotes new formats of knowledge production, yet that also recognizes other formats of great academic validity that have been developed for more than thirty years in Latin American countries such as Uruguay.

- To value the legitimacy of non-traditional practices of doing science, which are often simplified as multi- or interdisciplinary, because they use those terms as a way to identify themselves.

Introduction to the Chapter

This chapter assesses developments in transdisciplinary communication in research teams in the Uruguayan academic context, specifically at the Universidad de la República (UdelaR). While we support the thesis that transdisciplinarity (TD) is still not mainstream and is rarely supported in different countries, this chapter examines the extent to which a Uruguayan university has embraced the concept of transdisciplinarity. We seek to contribute to the conceptual discussion on transdisciplinary research, taking UdelaR as our unit of analysis. We will focus our attention on the definition of transdisciplinarity, and discuss the nuances and distinctions in its understanding. We will also analyze contextual circumstances of transdisciplinarity, including larger structural factors and the different types of communicative formats developed by research teams.

Our guiding questions are the following: (i) How is transdisciplinarity conceptualized in these academic centres in the Uruguayan context? (ii) How are the communicative processes with diverse social actors defined and practiced in these four centres? (iii) What can we learn about transdisciplinary communicative processes in different cultural contexts?

We analyze four case studies that provide empirical data about the communicative processes developed between academia and diverse social actors aiming to address real-world or multidimensional problems (Bunders et al., 2010). We address how transdisciplinarity develops within a specific cultural context. We find evidence that research in Uruguay is achieving some elements of transdisciplinarity in research but these practices are termed differently as extension, outreach, or integral activities.

These characteristics shared by most Latin American universities guide the communicative processes among actors. We further expand the concept of transdisciplinarity and propose a revised definition that is better suited to this context. This definition should include the ways in which scientific knowledge is produced, who participates in its production, and who is authorized to state the objectives and research questions put in motion an interaction among different actors, types of knowledge and experiences.

The evidence suggests that transdisciplinarity in Uruguayan research is developing under other labels, and this fact does not necessarily impede the framing of research oriented towards societal issues. Our study also acknowledges that there is a growing capacity among interdisciplinary groups to evaluate the quality of transdisciplinary communicative processes and to learn from such evaluations. We aim to build bridges among researchers conducting transdisciplinary research in different countries and continents and show that there are practices and discourses that share a common understanding of this concept.

The empirical frame of reference is the experience gained in the construction and consolidation of four Interdisciplinary Centres (ICs) at UdelaR, between 2009 and 2017. The four Centres work on complex problems and address grand challenges, namely, (i) *Centro Interdisciplinario de Nanotecnología, Química y Física de los Materiales* (CINQUIFIMA; Interdisciplinary Centre for Nanotechnology, Chemistry, and Physical Analysis of Materials), (ii) *Centro Interdisciplinario de Manejo Costero Integrado del Cono Sur* (MCISur; Interdisciplinary Centre for Integrated Coastal Management of the Southern Cone), (iii) *Centro Interdisciplinario de Investigaciones Biomédicas* (CEINBIO; Interdisciplinary Centre for Biomedical Research), and (iv) *Centro Interdisciplinario de Envejecimiento* (CIEN; Interdisciplinary Centre on Aging).

This chapter is structured as follows. First, we describe the theoretical framework used to conceptualize transdisciplinarity. Second, we present the characteristics of UdelaR's model in the shared historical context of the Centres analysed in this research. Third, we describe the four case studies in detail and discuss each space by analyzing their similarities and differences. Fourth, we conceptualize our findings in light of the rationale introduced in the second section. Finally, we present conclusions regarding the lessons learned from the analysis of the four Centres and the future research challenges.

Background

Understanding the production of transdisciplinary knowledge implies a shared communicative process that gives meaning to a particular academic culture (Bunders et al., 2010). For transdisciplinary communication to be successful, many different processes and practices are integrated in order to address complex problems. This implies a different communicative framework that aligns with participatory and collaborative research approaches (Hoffmann, Pohl, & Hering, 2017a, 2017b).

Knowledge production processes are changing to respond to new demands from different social actors. It is in this context that transdisciplinarity has emerged and has positioned itself as an innovative response to the increasing complexity of our society. Its current ascendancy is characterized by an increased interest across academic, public and private sectors (Klein, 2014). The concept of transdisciplinarity has emerged due to the cooperation between different disciplines and social actors in the pursuit of solving social problems (Bergmann et al., 2012; Klein, 2010; Lang et al., 2012; Spoun & Kölzer 2014; Vilsmaier & Lang; 2015; Vilsmaier, Brandner & Engbers, 2017; to name a few). Transdisciplinarity has emerged as a solution to problems related to grand challenges, such as described in Lang et al. (2012) and Vilsmaier and Lang (2015). We acknowledge differing definitions of transdisciplinarity and we follow Klein's (2014) taxonomy, which characterizes the development of transdisciplinary research. Her research traces historical trends, rhetorical claims, and social formations that have helped to shape three major discourses of transdisciplinarity: (i) transcendence, (ii) problem-solving, and (iii) transgression.

Of these discourses, problem-solving is used as a framework to develop our study. This discourse is related to the increasing cooperation among different disciplines and social actors with the goal of addressing and solving social challenges and problems (Spoun & Kölzer, 2014). The premise of this discourse is that "real-world" problems constitute complex challenges and they become the focus of research questions and practices. Complexity, multidimensionality, and diversity play a central role in the process of knowledge production (Klein, 2014). From a methodological perspective, integration is critical to knowledge production, accompanied by iteration, revision, connection, reconnection, and recursivity (Bergmann et al., 2012).

The change in the processes of knowledge production has yet to fully permeate the institutions where such knowledge is produced (Weingart, 2014). This is necessary to consolidate a consequent and lasting transformation on the structures and practices in which knowledge is developed. In this context, different universities around the world have started to implement changes in their organizational structures with the aim of giving transdisciplinarity a space to branch out outside the traditional disciplinary space (Klein, 2010).

Some universities have introduced structural transformations, which institutionalize the concept of transdisciplinarity, mainly in the European (Frodeman, Klein, & Mitcham, 2010; Klein, 2010; Schneidewind, Singer-Brodowski, Augenstein, & Stelze, 2016; Spoun & Kölzer, 2014) and Australian (Fam, Palmer, Riedy, & Mitchell 2016) contexts. Moving towards transdisciplinary organizational structures in universities requires fundamental changes. According to Weingart (2014), there are obstacles which lie in the nature of disciplines as forms of knowledge production that are, at the same time, institutionalized in organizational structures that, like departments or faculties, cannot be easily changed. Disciplines, sub-disciplines, and —considered in a wider societal context— academia, are epistemic communities (Rist, Chiddambaranathan, Escobar, & Wiesmann, 2006) that vary according to their cultures of knowing and acting and serve as references for personal and professional identities. Transdisciplinary knowledge production, therefore, can be considered as an activity developed in an intercultural endeavour (Vilsmaier et al., 2017) that poses questions on how these cultural differences determine the way we understand science and its development.

In Latin America, transdisciplinary practices can be related to the activities named as extension, outreach, and integral activities. University extension represents the university getting closer to the disadvantaged sectors of society through activities that benefit the most vulnerable communities. The University's outreach is characterized by seeking collaboration among University actors and other social actors, based on inclusiveness of different perspectives, equality and open communication, with the aim of obtaining socially-valuable objectives and transforming reality (Consejo Directivo Central, 2010). Integrality articulates the processes of learning and teaching, researching and outreach. It implies a communicative and critical relationship between connected actors, based on an interdisciplinary multiprofessional take (Rodríguez & Tommasino, 2010)

The relationship between these practices is due to the historical context shared by almost all Latin American universities, which was influenced by the Córdoba Reform in 1918 (Vienni Baptista, Vasen, & Villa Soto, 2018). The reform was first initiated in the Universidad de Córdoba in Argentina and then influenced almost all universities in the continent. The Córdoba Reform cannot be analyzed without taking into account some transformations that were taking place in the Latin American political setting.

The Latin American student movement was historically committed to the need to rethink the relationship between university and society (Bralich, 2009). Students deployed postulates that sought to transform university education from the articulation between the political, social, and academic spheres. The most relevant demands were mainly focused on autonomy, co-governance, and outreach. University autonomy has been one the Reform's priorities. The objective of autonomy was to achieve greater independence for university activities and overcome barriers imposed by the Church and the government and social upper classes (Tünnermann Bernheim, 2008, as cited in Vienni Baptista et al., 2018). Since the Reform intended to reconsider the relationship between the university and society, autonomy was crucial to keeping a distance from the State and the Church in order to be able to perform social criticism. The concept of autonomy contemplated the possibility for the university community to select its own authorities and to choose its own professors and curricula, to make decisions on the budget, and – in the event of an authoritarian government – it included the protection of the building against law enforcement agencies.

Co-governance refers to the involvement of professors, students, and alumni in the governance of the institution. Professor participation is not unique to Latin America and can be traced back to the origin of universities conceived as self-regulated places for academic independence. Alumni participation reflects their intention to stay in touch with the institution they once studied in and to the community to which they belong. Student participation is the Reform´s fundamental contribution (Vienni Baptista et al., 2018). By doing this the university transforms itself into an institution bound to democratic guidelines with political representation based on election processes.

In Uruguay, the relationship between UdelaR and different social communities has a long history, and in the words of Baroldi, *"... the trilogy (research teaching extension) not only characterizes it and gives it a distinctive stamp but also constitutes the radical difference from any university institution … in the country, especially if it is private"* (2009, p.14). UdelaR's legacies are important aspects related to university autonomy, co-government, and the link of the University with social problems; that is developed by the aims of extension, outreach, and integral activities. The understanding of this third university mission, namely social service, is characteristic of the Latin American university, and would become an identity mark with impact on the relationship between universities and science in the region (Vienni Baptista et al., 2018).

Although the Reform did not make any explicit comments on interdisciplinarity or transdisciplinarity, we believe the implemented changes can be retrospectively associated with certain openness to interdisciplinary and transdisciplinary knowledge (Vienni Baptista et al., 2018). Firstly, the social commitment of the university community increased because of the Reform movement. Secondly, outreach and extension activities play a substantial role in the way research and teaching are practiced and performed in Latin American universities (Vienni Baptista et al., 2018). Some of the features called *integral* in Uruguay are shared with the definition of transdisciplinarity in the European context. Among them, there is the intention of transforming the social reality and the orientation of the university practices to the resolution of social problems with an interdisciplinary anchoring.

We analyze the differences and similarities between Integrality and Transdisciplinarity (TD) in the following section. In order to study these differences and the diversity of perspectives in interdisciplinary and transdisciplinary research and teaching, we have proposed a field within the Science, Technology and Society Studies (STS) named Studies on Interdisciplinarity and Transdisciplinarity (SoIT) (Vienni Baptista, 2016a, 2016c). There is currently renewed interest in interdisciplinarity and transdisciplinarity in some countries and universities in Latin America, evidenced by recent discussion of research methods and dissemination of results that critically engage theory and practice (Vienni Baptista, 2016b). The concept of regionalism that anchors these fields is aimed at building dialogue and systematizing lessons from Latin American initiatives (Vienni Baptista, 2016a).

Studies on Inter- and Transdisciplinarity (SoIT)

The field named Studies on Inter- and Transdisciplinarity (SoIT) constitutes a framework for systematic analysis of research practices and processes as well as perceptions of researchers and relationships within groups and institutions. The main objective is to create a theoretical and methodological framework for analyzing interdisciplinarity and transdisciplinarity in the Latin American context, while also studying aspects of interdisciplinarity and transdisciplinarity in scientific development (Vienni Baptista, 2016a). The relevance of this new field lies in theoretical contributions built from comprehensive analysis of practices and awareness of the increasing complexity of scientific knowledge (Frodeman et al., 2010).

These main features of transdisciplinarity are pivotal to the discussion on how this approach can be defined in different countries and institutions. They also constitute the pillars on which we can build common ground to understand the empirical data we have gathered in the Uruguayan academic context.

The Concept of Integrality in the Uruguayan University

Questions regarding the possibilities of the transformation of social reality based on knowledge production, and more specifically, the articulation of the University with its social context, has been highly debated by Latin American universities from the 19th century onwards.

The *Universidad de la República* was influenced by the Córdoba Reform, as mentioned before, which started in 1918 as a student protest against the on-going traditionalism and clericalism at universities. Between 2006 and 2014, a process of institutional transformation began in UdelaR, influenced by changes in the means of production and organization of knowledge on a global scale and permeated by the closest regional context. This process was based on the concept of development, seen as multidimensional, where knowledge production in UdelaR must aim towards the improvement of the Uruguayan inhabitants' life quality (Arocena, 2011). This process was called *Segunda Reforma Universitaria* (SRU; Second University Reform) and was guided by the Córdoba Reform principles and by the concept of *Universidad para el Desarrollo* (University for Development) (Arocena, 2014). The SRU calls for an institutional change based on UdelaR's social mission, namely extension and outreach, and its involvement in the studying and solving of national problems. This Reform allowed for dialogue between UdelaR and society, and its guiding principle was the democratization of knowledge (Arocena, 2011).

In accordance with the SRU, UdelaR must constantly find answers to problems that arise in its context. These transformations permeate the whole University's structure and the way in which it connects and relates with the social and productive contexts (Randall, 2009). Within this framework, UdelaR significantly progresses in the formalization and institutionalization of the extension and integrality, developing working methodologies alongside the community and integrating University actors to this type of work (Bralich, 2009).

Extension, outreach and integral activities apply participative methodologies for stimulating the participation of university and non-university actors in the educational or knowledge production processes. Thus, the participatory methodologies are applied to stimulate the active participation of the actors involved in the processes of knowledge construction. *"The interesting thing is that these participatory methodologies, in general, have been born precisely from social movements and with critical and transformative pretensions"* (Villasante, 2010). Extension, outreach and integral activities growth implies a significant deepening in the theoretical-epistemological and methodological development in the University-society relationship (Consejo Directivo Central, 2010).

Contributions from the Participatory Action Research (IAP) methodology, whose main representative is Orlando Fals Borda (Fals Borda, 2014; Fals Borda & Rodríguez, 1987), are applied in extension and integral activities. According to this author, other extra-academic knowledge for the production of knowledge is central in any process of knowledge production. The actors involved participate in the knowledge production process of a historical reality that is ultimately sought to be transformed. De Sousa Santos (2010) proposes a dialogical encounter of knowledge, an ecology of knowledge that combines thoughts and worldviews.

The SRU implied a deepening of the aforementioned methodological approaches together with an increasingly closer dialogue between the university and society, along with the democratization of knowledge as a guiding principle (Arocena, 2011). *"Extension can make an important contribution to the democratization of knowledge, by questioning the frequent notion that the power of knowledge can only be concentrated in some actors at the expense of others"* (Arocena, 2010, p. 15).

Although the development of the concept of extension in the UdelaR presumed a significant deepening in the theoretical-epistemological and methodological spheres in university-society relations, this deepening was not sufficient in itself. Thus, there was a need to reconfigure its articulation with the other functions of the university; namely teaching and research. The notion of Integrality in the university configures itself as one of the central axes of the so-called Second Reform.

Integrality "[…] *implies a specific type of articulation between the processes of learning and teaching, researching and outreach; it includes an interdisciplinary multi-professional take, and it implies a communicative and critical relationship between connected actors, where a communicative relationship between academic knowledge and general knowledge comes into play"* (Rodríguez & Tommasino, 2010).

"Combining teaching, research and extension in integral practices at the service of social development is an even more revolutionary proposal, which is at the heart of the Latin American University ideal" (Arocena, 2010: 7).

The approach to social problems is not a new fact within UdelaR's framework. As described previously, various policies seek to encourage the connection between social demands and knowledge production. What constitutes a new fact are the forms and characteristics these approaches acquire, and the broadening of the research agenda of academics, who integrate new problems, previously considered irrelevant or "out of context". The conceptual map outlined by some authors (Gibbons et al., 1994; Jasanoff, 2004; Ziman, 2003), related to the field of the Science, Technology and Society Studies (STS), accounts for the changes in the modes and characteristics of knowledge production processes. This also affects the approach to multidimensional or unstructured problems (Bunders et al., 2010), which demands collaborative research modes that cross disciplinary boundaries.

Integrality in the Uruguayan University

The concept of integrality developed at UdelaR, is characterized by (Rodríguez & Tommasino, 2010; Tommasino, Kaplún, & Etchebehere, 2015):

- The integration of the three university functions (*extension, research, teaching*).

- The interdisciplinary perspective is present at the epistemological level and in the intervention processes.

- The transformative intentionality of the intervention that conceives the social actors as central characters.

- The teaching and learning processes are interlinked, both in terms of their content and the methodologies that are applied.

- The territorial and intersectoral approach in intervention. This means that knowledge production processes are carried out with a local perspective and include different institutions and organizations.

In this sense, the UdelaR (Consejo Directivo Central, 2010) establishes the following constitutive aspects of integrality as a concept, which are synthesized in Table 1 and related to the main features of TD.

Table 1. Comparison between the constitutive aspects of the concept of Integrality and its relationship with the concept of Transdisciplinarity

Integrality's constitutive aspects	Description	TD related features
Integration of the three University missions	It refers to the articulation of teaching, research and extension to solve a real-world problem for the common good of a vulnerable community. This process implies different steps where different actors participate with diverse kinds of knowledge (Romano, 2014).	TD implies an integration process, which aims at improving the understanding of real-world problems by synthesizing relevant knowledge from diverse disciplines and stakeholders (McDonald, Bammer, & Deane, 2009; Pohl, Krütli, & Stauffacher, 2018). This process' goals are (i) to grasp the complexity of the problems, (ii) to link abstract and case specific knowledge; and (iii) to constitute knowledge with a focus on problem-solving or common good (Hirsch Hadorn et al., 2007).

Integrality's constitutive aspects	Description	TD related features
Interdisciplinarity	Integrality refers to the interdisciplinary integration in three senses: (1) Interdisciplinarity from an epistemological perspective: when trying to integrate aspects of the knowledge production process that are historically fragmented (De Sousa Santos, 2010). Interdisciplinarity is related to integrality as a possibility to approach phenomena by integrating different disciplinary perspectives when building the object of study / framing the problem, etc. (2) Problem framing: Related to the methodology applied to solve the problem under study. When intervening on a social problem, the aim is to articulate and integrate methodologies associated with different disciplines. (3) Constitution of groups: in integral processes, researchers try to always build an interdisciplinary group to approach the problem.	Relationship between ID and TD in knowledge processes. - TD implies an integration operation of establishing a novel connection between distinct epistemic, social-organizational, and communicative entities that make up the given problem context (Klein 2012 in Hoffmann et al, 2017a). - TD seeks to perform research that addresses societally relevant problems as drivers for posing scientific research questions. (Hoffmann et al, 2017a). TD seeks to grasp the complexity of the problem by involving a variety of scientific and societal actors and accounting for the diversity of perspectives on a problem (Hoffmann et al, 2017a). Transdisciplinary processes generate knowledge that is solution-oriented, socially robust and transferable to both scientific and societal practice (Hoffmann et al, 2017).
Transformational aim of the intervention (conceiving social actors as main actors)	Some authors refer to the possibility of building new knowledge from the articulation between academic knowledge and popular knowledge (Cetrulo, 2016). Integrality is based on common sense or popular knowledge to achieve an increasingly objective understanding of reality for its transformation (Torres, 1987 in Rodríguez & Tommasino, 2010). To do this, we take into account, for example, the perspective of Ecology of Knowledge (De Sousa Santos, 2010) and participatory research (Fals Borda & Rodríguez, 1987).	TD recognizes different types of knowledge that are at stake (Pohl, Krütli, & Stauffacher, 2017). For instance, systems, target and transformation knowledge.

Integrality's constitutive aspects	Description	TD related features
Comprehensive conception of teaching and learning processes both in their content and in their methodologies	It refers to the integral conception of the student and his education, of the teacher and of the object of knowledge (Romano, 2014).	Mutual learning process among the people who participate in the problem and help to pose the problem (Hoffmann et al, 2017a).
Territorial and intersectoral approach in the intervention	It refers to the need to intervene and / or produce knowledge both in the territory and in coordination with different institutions (Rodríguez & Tomassino, 2010).	Different types of involved actors and different levels of actor involvement (information, consultation, and collaboration) are also present in transdisciplinary processes (Hoffmann et al., 2017a, 2017b).
Participatory Methods	Participatory Action Research	Methods for transdisciplinary research (Hofmann et al., 2017b; McDonald et al., 2009; to name a few)

Integrality is materialized through specific policies for the development of extension in the university curriculum (Arocena, et al., 2013; Bralich, 2009; Berruti, Cabo, & Debezies, 2014; Cano, Cabo, & Debezies, 2011; Faldori, n.d.; Grabino & Carlos, 2013). The main policy was the implementation of "Espacios de Formación Integral" or Integral Training Spaces (EFIs, for their acronym in Spanish). *"The EFIs are areas for the promotion of integral practices in the University, favouring the articulation of teaching, extension and investigation in the formative process of the students, promoting the critical and proactive thought, and the autonomy of the subjects involved. Integral practices promote the initiation to group work from an interdisciplinary perspective, where different services and areas of knowledge can be linked, gathered by the same subject, a territory or problem"* (Arocena, 2010, p. 15).

The EFIs have increased both in number and in participatory theoretical and methodological perspectives since their creation. There were 92 EFIs in 2010 compared to 153 in 2013 (Red de Extensión, 2013). This meant that in 2013, 6,478 students and 686 teachers from across UdelaR were linked to these integral spaces.

The EFIs have in common the recognition of the need to stimulate work outside the classroom for the construction of relevant knowledge based on social problems. According to Antonio Romano:

> *"…then comes the idea that knowledge can be put into play in a learning space beyond the classroom and beyond professional practice to innovate in the most comprehensive teaching formats. That is, the classroom as a format, as "space", should not be the only place where knowledge is put into play."* (Romano, 2011, p. 91)

Methodology

Our study is based on data obtained by the research project entitled "The production of interdisciplinary knowledge in UdelaR: modalities, integration and evaluation processes", funded by the *Comisión Sectorial de Investigación Científica* (CSIC; Central Commission of Scientific Research) of UdelaR between 2017 and 2019. This research aims to answer three questions that guide the analysis of the Interdisciplinary Centres under study, namely, (i) How is transdisciplinarity conceptualized in these academic centres in the Uruguayan context? (ii) How are the communicative processes with diverse social actors defined and practiced in these four centres? (iii) What can we learn about transdisciplinary communicative processes in different cultural contexts?

Our research focuses on the study of four Interdisciplinary Centres financed for their development and consolidation by the *Espacio Interdisciplinario* of UdelaR. Since 2009, those Interdisciplinary Centres involve the consolidation of long-term teams (five years) for the study of a problem that is part of the Uruguayan political agenda. Their activities include teaching, research and extension activities, which seek to consolidate the integrality of functions according to the definitions provided in the previous sections. These teams and their members constitute our units of analysis (Table 2).

Table 2. The four interdisciplinary Centers under study. Source: the authors.

Interdisciplinary Center	Research problem	Disciplines
Centro Interdisciplinario de Nanotecnología, Química y Física de los Materiales (CINQUIFIMA; Interdisciplinary Centre for Nanotechnology, Chemistry, and Physical Analysis of Materials)	The problem addressed by this Centre is to develop Nanotechnology and Chemistry and Physics of Materials in Uruguay. This involves supramolecular chemistry, the synthesis of precursors, materials and nano-materials, their structural study and their physical characterization and the forecast of their properties. It is on this basis that the Centre also seeks to contribute to design applications, for example in health, in the production and generation of energy.	Chemistry, Physics, Engineering, Dentistry, and Biology

Interdisciplinary Center	Research problem	Disciplines
Centro Interdisciplinario de Manejo Costero Integrado del Cono Sur (MCISur; Interdisciplinary Centre for Integrated Coastal Management of the Southern Cone)	Its main goal is to consolidate the integration process of several action levels on the coast to agree on programs for the protection and sustainable development of coastal environments and their resources. This process is characterized by the resolution of conflicts among users, the reduction of cumulative impacts, and the participation of communities, on a local scale, as a fundamental managing component (Conde & Gómez, 2011).	Marine and coastal Biology, Coastal Ecology, Hydraulics, Sedimentology, Geomorphology, Coastal dynamics, Water quality, Urban planning, Environmental and territorial planning, Epistemology, Sociology, Social work, Environmental Sciences, Environmental Economics, Public and International Law, Public Policies, Culture and Coastal and Didactic Heritage.
Centro Interdisciplinario de Investigaciones Biomédicas (CEINBIO; Interdisciplinary Centre for Biomedical Research).	The Centre addresses the molecular and cellular processes linked to the development of human pathologies, focusing particularly on the study of cardiovascular, neurodegenerative, renal and inflammatory / infectious pathologies through studies in cell models, animals and humans. A major effort of CEINBIO has been to address in a rigorous and mechanistic molecular and cellular processes linked to human pathology and its translation to the physiopathological, pharmacological and clinical area, and in parallel to promote the development of new methodologies (immunochemical, bioanalytical, computational) that allow to advance in depth in the understanding of the problems posed (Centro de Investigaciones Biomédicas, 2015). Alongside with the training of highly qualified human resources, this Centre provides updated and operational research infrastructures to increase the understanding of health-disease processes, and as a tool to improve the quality of healthcare.	Chemistry, Biochemistry, Biophysics, Structural Biology, Molecular Biology, Cell Biology, Plant Biology, Biomedicine, Physiology, Nutrition, Pathophysiology, Pathology, Pharmacology, Clinical research.

Interdisciplinary Center	Research problem	Disciplines
Centro Interdisciplinario de Envejecimiento (CIEN; Interdisciplinary Centre on Aging).	The problem addressed by this Centre is the aging and the advanced age of the population studied from a psychosocial perspective, focusing on problems related to everyday life, social inclusion, rights and social construction of concrete modalities for the elder.	Psychology, Demography, Sociology, Medicine, Law, Industrial Design, Communication Sciences

The four Centres amount to a total of 107 researchers (17 members of CINQUIFIMA, 12 members of MCISUR, 65 members of CEINBIO and 13 of CIEN). The researcher distribution according to their gender shows that the number of women (52 in total, 48.5%) is slightly lower than that of men. In terms of age distribution, the age group most researchers belong to is between the ages of 46 and 55 (33.6%), followed by those between the ages of 36 and 45 (25.2%), and last, between the ages of 28 to 35 (23.4%). Eighty percent of researchers held a PhD, 17% have a master's degree, and there are few cases in which the researcher only had a bachelor's degree.

These Centres were analyzed as case studies (Yin, 1989). The purpose was to understand in depth actors' practices, meanings, beliefs, and representations. This required the use of specific data collection techniques. One of the distinctive elements of this type of research is its inductive and emerging character (Mendizábal, 2007). This way of exercising research is sought to create concepts from the data found before verifying theoretical hypotheses through empirical work (Mendizábal, 2007). The value of the selected cases does not lie in their specificity, in their intrinsic interest, but rather in what Stake (1998) calls an "instrumental case study". Thus, it is assumed that from the four selected cases it is possible to access a better understanding of the conceptualization of transdisciplinarity and how these processes are enacted and lived (Douglas, 1979).

The selection of the four Interdisciplinary Centres as case studies consisted of a detailed description and analysis of these unique social units (Yin, 1989, 2014). It can be assumed that, out of the selected cases, it is possible to have a better understanding of the development and characteristics of transdisciplinarity. *"The goal ... is to choose cases that can probably replicate or extend the emerging theory. ... The number of cases must be added until the saturation of the theory"* is achieved (Eisenhardt, 1989). Multiple cases are a powerful tool to theorize because they allow replication and the extension among individual cases (Eisenhardt, 1991).

For the selection of the cases, the following criteria were applied to the Centres: (i) disciplinary diversity in the way they are integrated; (ii) different problem areas as the focus of their work; (iii) strong orientation towards the application of research results; (iv) their linkage with actors outside the academic sphere; (v) participation of academics from UdelaR Schools that are not located in the capital of the country, but in the other departments; and (vi) strong connection to institutions outside UdelaR.

In order to address the questions posed, we conducted a combination of different data collection techniques. Yin (1989) recommends the use of multiple data sources and compliance with the principle of triangulation to ensure the internal validity of the research.

The following data-collection techniques were prioritized:

- Semi-structured interviews addressed to the members of the Interdisciplinary Centres: different interview guidelines were designed according to whether the interviewees were responsible for, or participants of the Centres. The interview guidelines were divided into four units in which we inquired about (i) the researchers' professional and academic trajectories, (ii) the Centre's research problem and projects, (iii) their working modalities and integration processes, and (iv) the linkage with social actors. Each unit contained a series of questions that allowed retrieving the data for the analysis of the selected dimensions. During the interviews, we worked with a set of concepts that emerged from the theoretical framework that were presented to the interviewees in a card. This step sought to reveal the interviewees' perception on different definitions and concepts. These concepts involved types of integration (methodological, theoretical and empirical), degrees of integration (narrow and broad), drivers of interdisciplinary and transdisciplinary research (problems at the border of different disciplines, solving problems, interest in the advancement of knowledge and interest academic). In total, 26 interviews were conducted (Table 3). The quotes extracted from the interviews were integrated into this text in quotation marks and italics.

- Participant observation in different activities promoted by the Interdisciplinary Centres: in total, 6 instances of observation took place, in meetings, seminars and plenary sessions, organized by the Centres under study. We developed the observation as outside researchers (Trowler, 2014), and we used a template designed for that purpose that included the dimensions of analysis. In total, we observed fifteen hours of work that were developed between 2017 and 2018. The data collected using this technique was limited to understanding the strategies of knowledge integration between disciplines and ways of linking researchers with non-academic actors. The information obtained through observation was an input with a more limited function in the study than the documentary analysis and the interviews (Table 3).

- Document analysis: the document analysis included three main types of documents: (i) internal reports and grey literature produced by each Centre. These reports cover the initial consolidation phase of each Centre, with its objectives and planned strategies, as well as the assessment reports produced at the middle of the funding period (three years); ii) internal documents of each Centre. These documents contain interdisciplinary and transdisciplinary reflections that have driven the Centres' working plans; and iii) scientific articles and chapters of books by the members of the four Centres. Three researchers of our team simultaneously analysed and systematized 27 documents that complement the set of data that has been collected throughout the project (Table 3).

Table 3. Techniques and features of the data collected for each case study.

Interdisciplinary Center	Techniques and types of data collected
Centro Interdisciplinario de Nanotecnología, Química y Física de los Materiales (CINQUIFIMA; Interdisciplinary Centre for Nanotechnology, Chemistry, and Physical Analysis of Materials)	Semi-structured interviews: Coordinator (1 male) and members (2 males and 1 female). Document analysis: Proposal for the creation of the interdisciplinary centre (2009-2014) and different products (reports, evaluations, articles in magazines, chapters of books and books).
Centro Interdisciplinario de Manejo Costero Integrado del Cono Sur (MCISur; Interdisciplinary Centre for Integrated Coastal Management of the Southern Cone)	Semi-structured interviews: Coordinator (1 male) and members (3 males and 3 females) Documentary analysis: Proposal for the creation of the interdisciplinary center (2009-2014) and products (reports, evaluations, articles in magazines, chapters of books and books)
Centro Interdisciplinario de Investigaciones Biomédicas (CEINBIO; Interdisciplinary Centre for Biomedical Research).	Semi-structured interviews: Coordinator (1 male) and members (5 males and 2 females). Document analysis: Proposal for the creation of the interdisciplinary centre (2015-2020) and products (reports, evaluations, articles in magazines, chapters of books and books) Participant observation (2 activities observed): (i) Center's general plenary session in which social actors also participated; and (ii) One-day seminar for theoretical discussion and the development of new research insights.
Centro Interdisciplinario de Envejecimiento (CIEN; Interdisciplinary Centre on Aging).	Semi-structured interviews: Coordinators (1 male and 1 female) and members (3 males and 2 females). Document analysis: Proposal for the creation of the interdisciplinary centre (2015-2020) and products (reports, evaluations, articles in magazines, chapters of books and books) Participant observation (4 activities observed): (i) Two Centre's general plenary sessions in which social actors also participated; (ii) One academic seminar with the participation of researchers from University and social actors; and (iii) One-day seminar for theoretical and conceptual discussion, in which researchers from the Centre participated.

The characterization and analysis of transdisciplinary communicative processes were performed according to a series of dimensions that were constructed for that purpose.

The dimensions that guided the data collection and the analysis arise from the systematization of the literature on interdisciplinarity and transdisciplinarity. We took into consideration the typologies developed by different authors who have studied inter- and transdisciplinary knowledge production and communicative processes (Aboelela et al., 2007, Huutoniemi, Klein, Henrik, & Hukkinen, 2009; Klein, 2010, 2014; Klein & Falk-Krzesinki, 2017; von Wehrden et al., 2017; Wagner et al., 2010).

The dimensions of analysis are a product of the theoretical input from the systematic literature review (Xiao & Watson, 2019) and its triangulation with the empirical data from fieldwork (Yin, 1989). We built the following analytical dimensions:

i.   Conceptualization of transdisciplinarity: this dimension seeks to systematize the way in which researchers define transdisciplinarity. Likewise, this is connected to the different characteristics, practices, and processes that they develop in their scientific work.

ii. Origins and impulses of communication among actors: this dimension identifies how communicative processes between academic and non-academic actors began, and it characterizes the reasons leading to their implementation.

iii. Characteristics of communicative processes: this dimension systematizes the features of communicative processes between the Interdisciplinary Centres and non-academic actors. These are the following: one-way communication (that begins from a single actor), bidirectional communication (dialogue between two or more actors), integral spaces (communication between actors that contributes to teaching, extension, and research and implies a learning process for all participants involved), co-construction (different actors, academic and non-academic who build knowledge together), and diffusion platforms (such as articles, seminars, workshops, etc. that constitute means of dissemination to different actors).

iv. Types of actors participating in communicative processes: this dimension seeks to recognize which non-academic actors participate in these communicative processes.

Table 4 details the dimensions applied. It is worth noting how these dimensions served as a guideline for each case study, without limiting the incorporation of new dimensions that emerged during the fieldwork process. This means that we have merged an inductive and deductive process of analysis throughout the study.

Table 4. Dimensions and categories of analysis applied in the study. Source: the authors.

Dimensions	Categories	Research Question
Conceptualization of transdisciplinarity	- Involving social actors - Integrality	How is transdisciplinarity conceptualized in the context of the four centers under study?

Dimensions	Categories	Research Question
Origins and impulses of communication among actors	- Endogenous: This is a product of demands that come from the academic system itself (Huutoniemi et al., 2009). - Exogenous: This is a product of exogenous demands that come from a broader social context.	How are these communicative processes with diverse social actors defined in the four case studies?
Types of actors participating in communicative processes	- Public sector: such as municipal and national governments, descentralized public bodies, among others. - Private sector: such as companies, cooperatives, etc. - Civil society: social and non-gubernamental organizations, civil associations, among others.	How are these communicative processes with diverse social actors defined in the four case studies?
Characteristics of communicative processes	- One-way communication: the communicative process begins from one actor. - Bidirectional communication: two or more actors actively engage in a communicative process. - Integral space: this process is cross-cut by teaching, research and outreach activities. It is a fundamental process for mutual learning. - Co-construction: different actors, academics and non-academics, exchange and build knowledge together. - Platforms for dissemination: articles, seminars, workshops, etc.- as means of diffusion in different settings and for different audiences.	Is there common ground among these practices among the four centres?

In order to analyze the set of data collected, the interpretative frameworks that the researchers provided in the interviews were used. Interpretive approaches assume a reality socially constructed by different actors that in their daily interaction gives meaning to their actions and that of their interlocutors and with it the world that surrounds them (Denzin & Lincoln, 1994). The interpretive analysis was oriented by the above mentioned dimensions and categories (Table 4). Our findings do not represent generalized patterns of behaviour or established transformations, but provide elements for a deeper knowledge of the ways in which transdisciplinary processes are carried out in Uruguay

Findings

Conceptualization of Transdisciplinarity

With these dimensions of analysis, we identified different meanings and understandings of TD that members of the four Centres put into practice. Under the premise of addressing and solving complex problems, we identified two different understandings and assumptions related to TD: (i) transdisciplinary research incorporates non-academic actors in the production of knowledge (Lang et al., 2012) and (ii) transdisciplinary research transcends the boundaries of disciplines (Nicolescu, 2008) building new fields of knowledge.

The conceptualizations of transdisciplinarity that influence the four Centres present some differences among them. On the one hand, there are researchers' conceptions of transdisciplinarity that focus their attention on the interaction with non-university actors, and on the other, we find researchers who focus their work on trying to transcend and overcome disciplinary boundaries. This difference is vital when considering the two ways in which the concept of transdisciplinarity has been defined in the scientific literature. The first definition considers transdisciplinarity as the process of working together with other social actors (Lang et al., 2012), with the aim of transforming reality and addressing complex problems. On the other hand, a second definition understands transdisciplinarity as a concept for the construction of a knowledge unity that transcends the boundaries among disciplines. This conceptualization of TD is associated with the work carried out by Basarab Nicolescu (2008).

In this sense, CIEN and the MCISur understand transdisciplinarity as the process of working with social actors. It should be clarified that CINQUIFIMA also approaches this definition of transdisciplinarity in a conceptual way; however, according to the interviews it is scarcely discussed and practiced.

Our data indicates that the MCISur believes that the field of study from where the research problems are defined, namely the Integrated Coastal Management, is strengthened from theoretical-conceptual development and from practice. These two spaces (theory development and practice), in parallel, contribute to the advancement and consolidation of the field. In such spaces, different actors play a role, coming from different fields, academic and non-academic. Based on this heterogeneity, researchers together with social actors frame and develop the problem and research questions. According to one interviewee: *"The coast is a complex problem, and it is a complex area, with complex problems due to the diversity of conflicts, actors, interests. ... There is no other way to approach it ... [other than using a] transdisciplinary [approach] because we work with actors."* (Interview 1, 2018, male). This interviewee also believed that: *"For us, transdisciplinarity is not so much about erasing the boundaries of disciplines, but about integrating non-academic actors, we belong to this school of thought. But there is always a part of erasing at least a piece of the boundaries to mix the Centre's members with something wider"* (Interview 1, 2018, male).

In this sense, interdisciplinarity and the integration of disciplines within the Centre is a necessary condition for the development of the transdisciplinary perspective, where non-university actors are also integrated.

The CIEN, on the other hand, develops transdisciplinarity in a more explicit manner. They develop multidisciplinary, interdisciplinary, and transdisciplinary research depending on the specific features of the problem under study. For example, when transdisciplinarity is present and it is applied to build the research problem, it is aligned with the definition developed by European authors (Lang et al., 2012; Hirsch Hadorn et al., 2008). One female senior researcher who was interviewed expressed that *"We have worked [together with social actors] on what we are going to ask, what the objectives are going to be.... We discuss what emerges or does not emerge.... In that sense we try to make [social actors] feel part of the investigation, sometimes we want to go one way and they want to go for another, so sometimes [it is necessary]...to renegotiate a bit the process, too."* (Interview, 12, 2008, female).

Transdisciplinarity is associated with the goal of transforming reality (Klein, 2014) by approaching social problems that need diverse knowledge for its resolution. The metaphor provided by a member of CIEN is relevant: *"A territory clearly denotes a delimitation of power relations, and a specific theoretical-practical delimitation which accounts for reality. One field refers to a level of force, a field of forces, that is articulated and built according to what is emerging, the semantics and meanings that the different aspects of this field take in certain socio-historical moment. While the territory leads to the disciplinary, the field leads to transdisciplinarity; yet there is a complementarity between them and not a closed territory"* (Interview 2, 2018).

In this way, CIEN and MCISUR share, in several aspects, the conception of transdisciplinarity considered under the problem-solving discourse defined by Klein (2014). One male interviewee considered that: *"I believe that we are closer, in some lines of work, to the transdisciplinary line, and in others, more to the interdisciplinary; and in some we go towards a disciplinary line. You can have all in the same line, you do not renounce that which is disciplinary"* (Interview 22, 2018).

CINQUIFIMA, in contrast, shows an incipient development of transdisciplinary research practices in comparison to CIEN and MCISur. Nonetheless, this Centre identifies non-academic actors as claimants of the knowledge produced and this has led to changes in their lines of research. Several interviewees recognized that some research streams emerged from the linkages between social and scientific actors. For instance, CINQUIFIMA had developed synthetic skin, with a very low cost of production. In Uruguay, there is a high incidence of severe skin lesions (burns) in vulnerable populations, due to the type of heating systems used and the type of housing. The cost of imported synthetic dermal segments available in the market is too high for these sectors of the population. The State cannot afford them massively and individuals cannot bear the cost in specific cases. This seriously compromises the likelihood of survival and subsequent quality of life for low-income people. The results achieved by CINQUIFIMA allowed the development of a synthetic skin prototype from soluble collagen of bovine tendon. One advantage that this type of skin has over others existing in the market is that, through the use of nanotechnology, scientists plan to encapsulate active products embedded in the skin. In this way, when synthetic skin begins to be degraded by the body, the product - whether antibiotics, anti-inflammatory drugs or analgesics - will be released gradually and topically, without the need to provide large doses.

In terms of how CEINBIO's members understand the concept of TD, one senior male researcher believes that *"Etymologically speaking, [the prefix] 'trans-' means 'on the other side'. Doing transdisciplinary research is exactly that, implies moving onto the other side, towards the other discipline. This entails taking from the other discipline the methods of study, the experimental strategies and even the ways of thinking that are aligned to the original discipline or problem under study"* (Interview 4, 2018). This definition of TD is related to an overarching aim of transcending disciplinary boundaries (Nicolescu, 2008).

Following this conception, this CEINBIO interviewee believed that the Center has yet not achieved this kind of TD. *"I would say that we did not arrive to that point. The nature of the work we do, … but we would need much more ambitious bets from the economic point of view."* (Interview 4, 2018).

This approach to the concept of transdisciplinarity raises differences that are reflected in the way in which communicative processes are elaborated with non-academic actors and decision makers.

Origins and Impulses of Communicative Processes

One factor that drives the communicative processes between actors is the possibility of jointly addressing the social problems that affect different sectors of the population (National Academy of Sciences, 2005). This can reduce the processes of exclusion and vulnerability suffered by some social groups and constitutes a characteristic for all the Centres analyzed here. In the words of one interviewee, the approach to social problems in the context of the Centre *"[is] part of the path we are in. I do not think it drives us, we have also transcended that"* (Interview 14, 2018).

According to the scientific literature we have systematized (Hoffmann et al., 2017a, 2017b) and based on some of the findings of our study, we consider that communicative processes between actors can be grouped under two broad categories: (i) as a product of endogenous demands that come from the academic system itself, and (ii) as a product of exogenous demands that come from a broader social context.

The first category refers to the strategies developed by each Centre individually to promote different modalities of multidisciplinary, interdisciplinary, and transdisciplinary research (Klein, 2010). The identification of social problems and the development of research, teaching, and extension activities constitute an important impulse for the development of collaborative practices within each Interdisciplinary Centre, but they originated in an academic context. Hoffmann et al. (2017a) consider that, in one-way forms of communication between actor groups, actors are informed about the research project through articles, newspapers, policy briefs, etc., but are afforded only limited power to influence the process and/or the outcome.

An example serves to illustrate this. The MCISur has reflected on these processes where it is recognized that the development of the various modalities —multi-, inter- and transdisciplinarity— constitute forms of work that seek to establish *"… a new paradigm in opposition to the fragmentation of the parts of the object"* (Conde et al., 2010, p. 53). The scientific production associated with the integrated management of the coastal area seeks to fill knowledge voids and build a new field, with a transdisciplinary approach, within UdelaR's framework.

The second category refers to those communicative processes between actors that arise from the broader social context and guide the Centres' working agendas. These communicative processes are related to consultation and collaboration processes (Hoffmann et al., 2017a). Actors are asked to comment on the project development and to bring their knowledge individually or in small groups (Hoffmann et al., 2017a). We called these processes as exogenous. For instance, in the case of CEINBIO, answers are given to help improve the problems associated with the health-disease processes of different groups. These problems are often raised by the users themselves, or by doctors, and they constitute the starting point to provide "... *knowledge for prevention, diagnosis and treatment*" (Centro Interdisciplinario de Investigaciones Biomédicas, 2015). In this process, the members of the Centre recognize that "*We learned to see clinical problems from the basic area and the importance of that, ... we have learned to access different sources of knowledge that one would not consult, because they were not directly related to clinics, and today we realize that they are worthwhile and of great value and importance*" (Interview 13, 2018).

The two types of demands generated by these communicative processes are related to each other. When there are overlaps between the identification of social problems and the possibilities of addressing them and how different knowledge is produced to reach their resolution, the communicative processes between actors acquire different characteristics that will be discussed later.

This has not been a simple or linear process for the Centre; on the contrary, it has been complex, but the strong territorial anchorage this team possesses has allowed it to transform the link with non-academic actors into a "natural" process. "*It is not always achieved, it is formulated and it is not put into practice, or sometimes it is not possible to formulate everything, but it is rare that a project does not have that degree of transdisciplinarity*" (Interview 1, 2018).

Based on the impulse and origin of communicative processes, we can identify the different actors that participate in them.

Types of Actors Participating in Communicative Processes

We identify different types of social actors who belong to different institutional/organizational structures and have diverse working objectives in comparison with academic actors, represented mostly by researchers.

Three types of social actors were identified: (i) public sector, (ii) private sector, and (iii) belonging to civil society. Figure 1 shows the social actors and the diversity of cases they represent within each Centre.

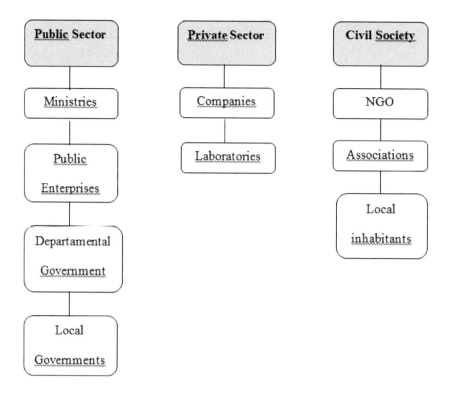

Figure 1. Social actors with whom communicative processes are established.

The communicative processes that take place between these sets of actors, academic and non-academic, are driven by different objectives, partly mediated by the problems addressed by each Centre and by the framework in which they carry out their extension activities, teaching, and research. In some cases, communicative processes between actors are linked to one of these three University functions; in other cases, these processes occur in the integrated development of the aforementioned process, which we call *integrality*.

These actors have different roles and objectives. In the case of public policy actors, communication is designed to sustain the development of policies, through the promotion of activities that allow building the empirical evidence for policies or by adding new approaches and perspectives to policy making. In the case of actors in the private sphere, their objectives are mainly seeking more knowledge for the development and / or application of new products.

Finally, civil society actors have objectives to directly address the problem in its context.

Establishing communication spaces with these different actors presupposes a commitment of the Centres to the broader social context. In turn, the establishment of communicative processes can mean expanding the research agendas of each Centre. It is worth mentioning how the actors who belong to the public sector, mainly represented in the Ministries, are present in instances of communication with all the Centres under study.

In the cases of the MCISur and CIEN, both Centres have developed an intense relationship with public actors and civilian actors.

Coastal Management as a Transdisciplinary Practice

The Interdisciplinary Centre for Integrated Coastal Management of the Southern Cone works from a transdisciplinary perspective, where researchers, decision makers, and managers of the coastal area face a cultural change in the way of constructing the concept of territory (Centro Interdisciplinario para el Manejo Costero Integrado del Cono Sur, 2011).

"The territory is valued as an environmental heritage and support for the population that forms it, thus acquiring a new and explicit cultural (socio-environmental) dimension in terms of its installed capacities and opportunities for the improvement of the quality of life of its people. [We seek to develop] a new way of thinking, which integrates knowledge and multiple capacities, an approach with a diversity of criteria and processes" (Conde et al., 2010).

This approach to the territory and coastal management as an area of research, *"... is something that escapes the academy"* and leads to *"... generate management inputs, work with the community at the most local possible level"* (Interview 11, 2018).

When it comes to communicative processes with public actors, CIEN develops various activities, namely, (i) formal agreements to carry out periodic activities based on jointly identified problems, (ii) advice and consultancy, and (iii) joint construction of regulations and social action plans. In this process, CIEN has established itself as the empirical support for the construction of the national legislation on advanced age and its ensuing issues. *"Today CIEN is recognized outside University, we have an impact, we have carried out research financed by the [Ministry], they have taken us into account in specific actions"* (Interview 12, 2018).

In the cases of CINQUIFIMA and CEINBIO, communicative processes are developed mainly with public and private actors.

According to the members, the process of CINQUIFIMA was transformed while it was being consolidated as an interdisciplinary academic space. *"We started with ultra-basic research, we would not leave the lab, and we were 'mice'. Then, we began to incorporate living things; we started asking for help outside ... As you grow up, you start leaving the lab, because your product starts coming out; ... it is the natural way. With a clarification, I am learning in that way ... the branching out of the lab has increased the knowledge of all the members, they call you from everywhere"* (Interview 4, 2018).

In the case of CEINBIO, the communicative processes with private-sector actors can occur through *"... technical consultancies and some projects with common interests"* (Interview 5, 2018). In these cases, for private actors, a male member of CEINBIO considers that *"it is better for them to call us, and work on a technical report about a product"* (Interview 5, 2018), since they do not have interdisciplinary units that can generate their own studies.

Characteristics of Communicative Processes

Some characteristics can be identified from the different communicative processes that are presented in the Interdisciplinary Centres, which contribute to making visible the heterogeneity of processes and the linkage with different actors. Figure 2 shows the five characteristics we have identified in the analyzed communicative processes and that allow their classification.

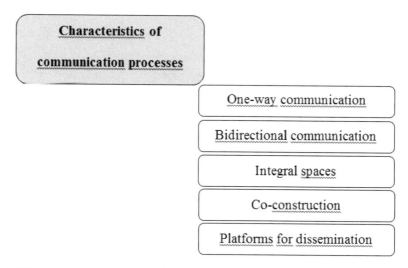

Figure 2. Characteristics of communicative processes between actors. Source: the authors.

One-way communication

When the communication occurs in one way, it links non-academic actors as sources of qualified information about a certain topic/problem that is addressed by the academic actor. In this case, information circulates in only one direction —that is, from non-academic actors to researchers— and constitutes an input for the researchers. The results obtained from this process have great legitimacy from an academic point of view because they constitute the traditional manner in which scientific knowledge is constituted, being translated unidirectionally to the social context.

Likewise, these processes can take the form of consultancies. For CINQUIFIMA, this is a common practice that has allowed the integration of research topics to the Centre that were previously absent in their agenda. This allowed for the generation of greater and better input for the counselling that the Centre provides to other institutions, and to respond to the demands of the exogenous context. CEINBIO shares this characteristic.

CEINBIO and CINQUIFIMA develop this type of communicative process, mainly based on the relationships they have with public policy actors and /or with the private sector. Their members consider these actors as experts who provide the necessary information in the knowledge production process that is carried out. Here, the main aim is to exchange information on a certain topic (Hoffmann et al., 2017a). According to the interviews and document analysis, the knowledge produced with this information, provided by the actors directly linked to the problem or as direct intermediaries of it, will be better applied as it was based on their knowledge (Centro de Investigaciones Biomédicas, 2015; Interview 3, 2018).

Bidirectional Communication

The communicative processes can be fostered in a bidirectional manner, that is, by establishing a back-and-forth dialogue between the participating actors. In this sense, communication can be established over time in order to improve the common understanding among different actors participating in this dialogue. Different circulating elements are identified, such as knowledge and practices. This form of communication promotes the development of active relationships between actors through the use of dialogue methods (McDonald et al., 2009) and trust building. Non-academic actors do not place themselves in a passive role, only providing information, but through this dialogue, the communicative process is improved, allows a greater understanding between the parties, and contributes to a joint construction of the problem to be addressed.

For CIEN, this process is common practice. There are demands that come from non-academic actors, so this active dialogue seeks to be built-in within the group and these actors. In the words of one interviewee: "*We have met and they have put forward concrete demands regarding the issue of household environment and public spaces accessibility. We seek to make a joint construction of problematic actions*" (Interview 6, 2018).

For the MCISur, aspects of governance, such as participative, transparent, responsive, equitable, and inclusive, are key to its integration in the research process. This is mainly due to the fact that the approach goal is related to the incidence and application of policy recommendations. These are elaborated from the integrated diagnosis of the coastal zone. This fact is acknowledged in one of the reports produced by this group: "*The guideline-design for a management plan for the wetlands implies, within the framework of sustainable development, the necessary participation of the different social sectors*" (Caporale et al., 2010, p. 200). It is in the framework of active participation, where social actors are linked to the problem and not only as actors that provide information, that MCISUR is able to develop relevant knowledge production processes.

Integral Spaces

As it was mentioned, integrality accounts for the articulation process between the three University functions and is a perspective developed by the four case study Centres. For some of them, the articulation of the three functions is part of the working strategy, and therefore, there is an active search to generate integral spaces.

The MCISur has experimented increased depth in this practice, achieving results of the utmost interest. For example, the Master program in Integrated Coastal Management of the Southern Cone, inaugurated in 2007 and ascribed to the Centre, is perceived by researchers and professors as a space for experimentation and implementation of integral processes, where research, teaching, and extension activities are jointly developed in a plural learning setting where scientific and social actors try to build a common understanding of the problem under study. The Master's program has acquired a particular profile, constituting a platform to promote synergies between different social actors; among them the decision makers of the coastal area of the Maldonado Department.

"The main objective [of the Master Program] is to train professionals who, beyond their previous training in a specific discipline, are specially qualified to approach coastal management from a critical, interdisciplinary and participatory perspective." (Álava, 2014, p. 66)

The Master's Degree is based on the conceptual field of integrated coastal management, which has been adapted to the conditions of the region and Uruguay. This is framed in the context of the continuous need to build new knowledge with an interdisciplinary base. Actors with practical experience on the ground engage in dialogue with the students and professors from different disciplines that participate in this space. As a result, practices of transdisciplinary research are being developed.

For CIEN, specific activities are proposed for each of the Centre's streams, seeking as a goal the development and implementation of a comprehensive interdisciplinary model. *"What is our ideal? A teacher who investigates, who produces, who is linked to the environment and who takes on the teaching starting from there. However, this ideal is in fact not a reality; in some cases more, and in others much less. We have it set as a horizon"* (Interview 2, 2018). This Centre's premise is that the development of transdisciplinary research affects all practices that develop university teachers. Teaching, and not only research, is permeated by the communicative processes between different actors within the research streams that the Centre develops.

The implementation of integral spaces is complex and is not always performed with the same intensity. The Universidad de la República has created some evaluation mechanisms for these spaces, but they still require a greater systematization of results (Martínez, Vienni, Cruz, & Repetto, 2015). The integration of the three university functions affects the communicative processes. The construction of a link among actors, who represent the different angles of the problem under study, is explicitly sought. This is related to the concept of University extension, which involves the political relationships with actors that generate demands on the knowledge production processes and that represent the social groups related to the problem under study.

We provide an example from the MCISUR. This is part of the practical work developed by students and social actors within the framework of the Master's Program in Integrated Coastal Management, already mentioned before. Students have to design and develop a concrete transdisciplinary project together with social actors that have identified the problem in their region. The resolution of social problems is a driving force for the development of transdisciplinary communicative processes in Maldonado, a department in the eastern region of Uruguay. These projects portray some forms of integration between teaching, research, and extension processes; that is, the integration of university functions or integrality.

> *"... part of the process implied important efforts to improve the group dynamics and to arrive at a common goal, which allowed to overcome the disciplinary limitations. For this, the alternating leadership of the different members throughout the work process was fundamental"* (Brum et al., 2010, p. 156).

Based on interdisciplinary integration (team of students and teachers) and integration with social actors, the cases sought to apply the MCI (Integrated Coastal Management Plan,

MCI for its acronym in Spanish) approach while taking into account the need for sustainability of the coast against different uses, both social and economic, that are carried out.

> *"The process was very challenging, and teamwork and knowledge construction hinted that acts of communication - speech, listening and silence - and the attitude of dialogue, respect and humility and make the difference of knowledge that is built."* (Goyos, Lagos, Verrastro, & de Álava, 2011, p. 246).

The main objective of one of the projects, entitled "Modalities of integration in the Integrated Coastal Management Plan of the stream Solís Chico Coast and the stream Solís Grande (Canelones)" (Conde et al., 2011), was to simulate a specific case of design and application of the Integrated Coastal Management Plan in the area between the Solís Chico and Solís Grande (Canelones, Uruguay) streams during the period from 2008-2009. The team was composed of students of the Master's program and regional actors. In relation to the articulation with the learning process, one of the team members mentioned that *"we had different subjects in which the different thematic products that we were asked to associate with the case study"* (Interview 6, 2018).

The group of researchers, who also participated in this project, inquired primarily about the information available from the area where the work was carried out, and then designed a diagnosis for the territory. The methodologies applied were participant observation, field trips, bibliographic review, analysis of secondary information, semi-structured interviews with local actors, and members of public and private institutions operating in the area.

An interesting aspect of this project is that the team assumes the action research as an inquiry format. The objective of the action research is not only the approach of a research problem, but simultaneously the intervention on the problem. Specifically, in this case, the action research allowed the generation of new knowledge to the research team. According to Hidalgo (2014), integrality —understood as the transcendence of a simple sum of the functions of teaching, extension, and research— fosters a profound change in the ways of focusing activities in the academic field.

Co-production: A Process of Transformation

The co-production of knowledge (Jasanoff, 2004), is considered as a way of hybridizing knowledge, values, and interests that are associated to achieve a more complete acquisition of the intended goals of research. The co-production of knowledge emphasizes the process of interaction between various actors in the framework of knowledge production. Science is not understood as a simple reflection of the truth about nature or as an epiphenomenon of social and political interest (Jasanoff, 2004). Recognizing the process of co-production involves accepting the interlinkage of social, economic, and cultural aspects in the political and the social spheres. This generates transformations in institutions, people (researchers and social actors outside the academic sphere), the language used and co-produced in that space, the collective discourse, and the applicability of the results / knowledge generated. According to Jasanoff (2004), co-production is much more a language than a theory. It constitutes a way of interpreting and accounting for complex phenomena to avoid the suppressions and strategic omissions of most other approaches in the social sciences. The co-production language emphasizes the intertwining of the cognitive, the material, the social, and the normative.

The processes among actors, where multiple exchanges are generated, presuppose a renewed commitment within a broader context. The different actors with whom interaction relationships are established, push the frontiers of science in new directions and challenge the identities and interests of both sides (Hess, Breyman, Campbell, & Martin, 2008). This implies an opening towards the need to expand the potential to answer new questions and/or solve problems that are beyond the capacity of a laboratory or a scientific discipline. This opening allows us to incorporate external knowledge and encourage the participation of heterogeneous experts, recognizing their own characteristics and revaluing them. In this way, the crossings can be diverse not only between researchers and other social actors, but also between different disciplines, being able to generate transdisciplinary processes.

The co-production of knowledge establishes specific communicative processes and shares with transdisciplinarity the goal of transgressing (Klein, 2004) the concept of traditional research and teaching (Vilsmaier et al., 2017). These types of practices are observed in CIEN and the MCISur, as part of their objectives and work methodology.

A member of CIEN details:

> *"In the retirement line ... we set up a teaching device that has one line of intervention and another of research....In the intervention, we are constantly negotiating with the NGO; therefore, we also put together a research-action proposal to understand how the retirement movement has been built.... In this sense, we try that [the elderly] get involved in the research"* (Interview 7, 2018).

To promote these co-production practices, different platforms are used: meetings, the setting up of workshops, and an elderly adults "voice" compilation. Regarding these practices, *"we have a tool we are seeing how to articulate, it is a conceptual tool: the life course paradigm, so as to be able to combine that macro social perspective with the micro social study"* (Interview 7, 2018).

In the case of the MCISur, the development of the co-production of knowledge is an essential part of the researchers' work, for they integrate the diverse knowledge that comes from different actors. This has a dual purpose. On the one hand, it seeks to promote a higher level of result appropriation by social actors, making knowledge useful to their needs. By result appropriation, we mean those situations where social actors make results their own and apply them in their everyday life.

On the other hand, integration leads to reverse paths in the knowledge production by developing theory from practice. One of the group members explains this process as defined by the MCISUR:

> *"[the participation of social actors] had two great entry points: One at the beginning, as qualified informants, ... where they were asked about concerns, problems and fears about climate change and natural events, that was like an input for methodology; ... the lexicon was adapted so they understood what was being discussed and could conceptualize what we wanted to ask; ... first they were asked what things were important in the lagoon, and what they thought were the problems. Then ... more concrete things that we refined or prioritized, partly in accordance with what they told us; we went to see what was of higher or lesser relevance to them; after that, a whole component about their life history that had to do with the vulnerability of these groups in the face of these changes"* (Interview 8, 2018).

In this case, MCISUR members were key actors in the process of developing a sustainable management plan for Laguna de Rocha in Maldonado (Uruguay). The project involved different local actors and authorities who have dichotomic visions on how to better improve the area and its conservation.

This dynamic presents a bidirectional process where not only information and knowledge circulate among actors, but they are integrated by producing knowledge as a whole. Co-production is proposed as a goal and is posed in the process a permanent interaction. As defined by one interviewee: *"It is difficult for us not to carry out an activity that is not for outside, everything is thought out for some user"* (Interview 17, 2018).

Platforms for Dissemination

Platforms for the dissemination of communicative processes between actors are divided into two broad categories: (i) under a traditional academic format (articles, books, or reports) and (ii) in a format geared towards a wider audience.

All the Centres register dissemination activities of their results and products under the traditional academic format, including articles, books, and chapters. It is interesting to observe how, despite the fact that the four Centres develop this type of diffusion, for CIEN and the MCISur these traditional platforms are not so useful for the communicative processes implemented and for the new fields of study they develop.

> *"We are rethinking this system because we need to have an impact on the academic world, one we are not having, and this is something that we have to guide in what is left of CIEN. It also has to do with the degree of academic development in the field of Gerontology and Aging"* (Interview 2, 2018).

The challenge for both Centres lies in how to legitimize themselves in the Uruguayan scientific system by testing transdisciplinary communicative processes, for the national scientific system has not yet reflected on these processes and does not legitimize them as valid in the traditional knowledge production system. On the other hand, knowledge diffusion in a broader sense – the set of practices that constitute the second category described here – can use different communication platforms, such as workshops to co-produce reports and articles together. When processes begin to actively incorporate non-academic actors, dissemination platforms are also produced together. For the MCISur and CIEN, dissemination strategies vary since the academic format is "translated" for this audience through training courses/workshops.

Discussion and Conclusions

Through the analysis of the four Centres we can account for different characteristics of communicative processes among actors that promote transdisciplinarity at different levels within each Centre. The communicative processes among different actors have broadened the base of knowledge production modes by the characteristics they acquire and the way they contribute to the diversification of the topics and questions addressed.

Table 1 has compared different features of the concept of TD with those that constitute the concept of integrality in Uruguay. We find that there is a correlation between the practices these Centres focus on and the concept of transdisciplinarity developed in other academic Centres. Integral practices aim at developing a mutual learning process to accomplish the transformation of reality and the resolution of complex problems that different social actors face. To achieve this goal, different participative methods are applied and social actors play an active role in the process of knowledge production. Transdisciplinarity shares these aims and features. It is defined as a functional-dynamic collaboration of disciplines and social actors to investigate and handle complex or real-world problems (Pohl et al., 2017). Some of the project examples we have provided here were developed as integral spaces but they also share the mission of shared-collaborative processes as in transdisciplinary knowledge production processes.

Table 5 summarizes the characteristics of communicative processes among actors and how they are presented in each of the Centres. Two possible types are translated from this table in the development of communicative processes between actors, and they define the different ways in which transdisciplinarity can be understood within the Uruguayan academic context.

Table 5. Summary of the analysis dimensions applied to the four Centres and their coincidence according to two periods (x- stands for less prominent presence o f this type of communicative process in the Centre's activities; x+ stands for high predominance of this type).

	2010 -2016		2015-2021	
	C-MCISur	**CINQUIFIMA**	**CIEN**	**CEINBIO**
Types of actors participating in communicative processes				
With the public sector	x	x	x	x
With the private sector		x		x
Civil society	x		x	
Characteristics of communicative processes				
One-way communication		x		x
Bidirectional communication	x	x-	x	x-
Integral spaces	x+		x	
Co-construction	x+		x	
Platforms for dissemination – Academic format	x	x+	x	x+
Platforms for dissemination – Wide format	x	x	x	x

In the Uruguayan case studied here, one communicative process between actors seeks to provide solutions to identified social problems, exogenously or endogenously, and affects certain populations. In this process, the interaction between actors acquires specific roles where each one identifies in a place, being the main objective of this process to revert these identified problems —or to at least contribute to their resolution— and to produce knowledge. Another communicative process is one that integrates, at different times, non-academic actors in different roles; not only as qualified informants, but also as knowledge producers. Both types account for differences in the ways in which transdisciplinary research can achieve integrality.

These characteristics are mostly shared in several Latin American universities (Vienni Baptista, Vasen, and Villa Soto; 2018) and expand the concept of transdisciplinarity that can be adapted to this context. Our study finds the need for dialogue between perspectives and the consolidation of a theoretical framework that allows the integration of extension practices as plausible initiatives to be considered as transdisciplinary. Future investigations are necessary to further delve into these findings.

Transdisciplinarity adds a new level of reflection to knowledge production processes, related to the resolution of multidimensional problems, and the development of research methods that can respond to them (Bergmann et al., 2012, Klein, 2014). Expanding the ways in which scientific knowledge is produced, rethinking who participates in its production, and who is authorized to state the objectives and research questions put in motion an interaction among different types of knowledge and experience and create challenges through which UdelaR is currently treading. It is in this framework of changes and impulses of new processes where the Centres analyzed here are located.

Integrality involves tensions, typical of the processes of change within *Universidad de la República* that seek to expand the ways in which knowledge is produced and put into practice processes that have been theoretically reflected upon. This aspect is of great relevance for the development of research at UdelaR, since it allows the consolidation of more democratic practices (Arocena, 2014) through integrality and even a new definition of what is traditionally named as research (Vilsmaier et al., 2017). Likewise, this new conceptualization of the links and processes of communication with actors imprints certain characteristics, which provide relevant lessons for other university contexts where inter- and transdisciplinarity are developed. For example, other Latin American universities and research centres can reflect on integral processes as a basis for the definition of transdisciplinarity and its development.

Our analysis found how, in the process of knowledge co-production, there are transformations which permeate the institutions, the relationships among actors, the collective discourse, and especially the individuals that experience them. The processes developed under the concept of "integrality" were part of a University Reform that seeks to build a more profound relationship between scientific and social actors. The Reform implied sweeping changes in the way teaching, research, and outreach are developed in Uruguay and also demanded institutional transformation to accompany those changes. This has also been studied for groups in North America (Lotrecchiano, 2014) and Europe (Vilsmaier et al., 2017).

Regarding the third element that Klein (2010) defines as a main feature in the definition of transdisciplinarity, namely the transgression of borders, the four cases analyzed here confirm that they have worked hard to move the edges of the disciplines to find a third space (Bhabha, 1994; Vilsmaier et al., 2017) where the knowledge production is carried out not only "for others", but also "with others". This space, in Uruguay named as EFI or integral space, is composed of practices that combine study programs, as in the case of the Master program in Integrated Coastal Management, and in different extension initiatives, as evidenced by the workshops developed by CIEN together with elderly adults. Also, our study has relieved the development of new research methods to consolidate transdisciplinary work and communicative processes with other actors that do not necessarily use academic vocabulary. This is related to the strong orientation to solving complex or multidimensional problems, a characteristic that Klein (2010) also elaborates to account for transdisciplinary discourses. In the Uruguayan context, this objective of resolving problems that cannot be solved from a single discipline entails the characteristic of integrality in the three university functions.

Returning to the question asked at the beginning of this chapter: what can we learn about communication and communicative processes in different cultural contexts? We consider that transdisciplinarity, as a concept and as a way of working, is a flexible and plural term that allows integrating practices that transgress the frontiers of research, and even the processes of linkage among actors. The evidence suggests that transdisciplinarity in Uruguayan research is being developed under other labels, and this fact does not necessarily impede the framing of research oriented towards societal issues. We conclude that communicative processes developed in inter- and transdisciplinary research are heterogeneous in terms of the actors and the contexts where they are developed. Nonetheless, these activities can be related to some features of the concept of TD, as we have shown in Table 1.

The systematized lessons of this study are two. On the one hand, there is an urgent need to open new spaces for communication among researchers from different regions and countries, as a way of reflecting not only on concepts, but also on practices. There is a call for a theoretical-methodological discussion that promotes new formats of knowledge production, yet that also recognizes other formats of great academic validity, which have been developed for more than thirty years in peripheral countries such as Uruguay. On the other hand, the second lesson learned from this analysis is to admit the legitimacy of non-traditional practices of doing science, which are often simplified as multi- or interdisciplinary, because they use those terms as a way to identify themselves. In order to analyze these practices and discourses in depth we have proposed the usefulness of a field named Studies on Interdisciplinarity and Transdisciplinarity (Vienni Baptista, 2016a, 2017b). This field may well pose some of the questions that remain open for future research as its own.

Questions to Further the Discourse

1. What is the impact of transdisciplinary research on processes of knowledge production in which different actors are invited to participate?

2. What is the relevance of transdisciplinary work for studies on development in Latin American countries such as Uruguay?

3. How can transdisciplinary communicative processes be taxonomized in an academic context? Are specific methodologies required for this?

Acknowledgements

The authors want to thank the four Interdisciplinary Centres of the *Universidad de la República*, that accepted to be part of this study, namely: (i) Centro Interdisciplinario de Nanotecnología, Química y Física de los Materiales (CINQUIFIMA; Interdisciplinary Centre for Nanotechnology, Chemistry, and Physical Analysis of Materials), (ii) Centro Interdisciplinario de Manejo Costero Integrado del Cono Sur (MCISur; Interdisciplinary Centre for Integrated Coastal Management of the Southern Cone), (iii) Centro Interdisciplinario de

Investigaciones Biomédicas (CEINBIO; Interdisciplinary Centre for Biomedical Research); and (iv) Centro Interdisciplinario de Envejecimiento (CIEN; Interdisciplinary Centre on Aging). We also thank their members, managers and administrative officials for supporting the project at all times, accepting to be interviewed and opening the doors to their work. Teachers and researchers belonging to these groups have provided valuable information and insights, as well as rich backgrounds for this research.

To the *Comisión Sectorial de Investigación Científica* and the *Comisión Central de Dedicación Total* (*Universidad de la República*, Uruguay) for providing the funding for the project "The production of interdisciplinary knowledge in the *Universidad de la República*: modalities, integration and evaluation processes" (2017 – 2019).

To the *Espacio Interdisciplinario* (*Universidad de la República*, Uruguay), for providing the necessary institutional framework for developing this research project.

To Prof. Dr. Franco Simini, for his support in the administrative continuity of the proposal and to Dr. Ismael Rafols (INGENIO, University of Valencia, Spain) for his academic counselling and support.

To the editors, for their valuable comments and suggestions on this chapter.

Must Reads

Arocena, R., Göransson, B., & Sutz, J. (2015). Knowledge policies and universities in developing countries: Inclusive development and the "developmental university." *Technology in Society, 41*, 10-20.

Arocena, R., & Sutz, J. (2016). Development studies as in interdisciplinary field: Research, teaching, and institutional building in Uruguay. *Issues in Interdisciplinary Studies, Association for Interdisciplinary Studies, 34*, 164-182.

Klein, J. T. (2016). Conclusion: Expanding international dialogue on interdisciplinarity. *Issues in Interdisciplinary Studies, Association for Interdisciplinary Studies, 34*, 200-207.

Vienni Baptista, B. (2016). Interdisciplinarity in Latin America: Building dialogue through regionalism. *Issues in Interdisciplinary Studies, Association for Interdisciplinary Studies, 34*, 109-121.

Vienni Baptista, B., Vasen, F., & Villa Soto, J. C. (2018). Interdisciplinary centers in Latin American universities: The challenges of institutionalization. *Higher Education Policy, 32*(3), 461-483. https://doi.org/10.1057/s41307-018-0092-x

References

Aboelela, S. W., Larson, E., Bakken, S., Carrasquillo, O., Formicola, A. J., Glied, S. A., Haas, J., & Gebbie K. M. (2017). Defining interdisciplinary research: Conclusions from a critical review of the literature. *Health Services Research. 330 HSR, 42*(1 Pt 1), 329-346.

Álava, A. (2014). La interacción interdisciplinaria en la Maestría en Manejo Costero Integrado. In *En_clave Inter 2014. Educación superior e interdisciplina*. Uruguay: Espacio Interdisciplinario de la Universidad de la República.

Arocena, R. (2010). *Hacia la reforma universitaria #10. La extensión en la renovación de la enseñanza: Espacios de Formación Integral.* Retrieved from http://www.extension.udelar.edu.uy/wp-content/uploads/2016/12/08_Hacia-la-reforma-universitaria_-la-extensio%CC%81n-en-la-renovacio%CC%81n-de-la-ensen%CC%83anza.pdf

Arocena, R. (2011). *Una perspectiva de la segunda reforma universitaria.* Manuscript, Montevideo, Uruguay.

Arocena, R. (2014). *Trabajando por una segunda reforma universitaria: La Universidad para el desarrollo.* Memorias de Rectorado (2006-2014). Uruguay: Udelar.

Arocena, R., Tommasino, H., Rodríguez, N., Sutz, J., Álvarez, E., & Romano, A. (2013). *Integralidad: tensiones y perspectivas.* Cuadernos de Extensión. Uruguay: Comisión Sectorial de Extensión y Actividades en el Medio (CSEAM). ISSN: 1688-8324.

Baroldi, E. (2009). *Aportes para pensar la Extensión Universitaria in Extensión en Obra.* Uruguay: Servicio Central de Extensión y Actividades en el Medio (SCEAM).

Bergmann M., Jahn, T., Knobloch, T., Wolfgang, K., Pohl, C., & Scharmm, E. (2012). *Methods for Transdisciplinary Research: A Primer for Practice.* Chicago: University of Chicago.

Berruti, L., Cabo, M., & Debezies, M. J. (2014). *Sistematización de experiencias de extensión.* In Cuadernos de Extensión. Uruguay: Comisión Sectorial de Extensión y Actividades en el Medio (CSEAM). ISSN 1688-8324

Bhabha, H. (1994). *The location of culture.* London: Routledge.

Bralich, J. (2009). *Una mirada histórica a la extensión universitaria,* pp. 53-61. In Extensión en Obra. Uruguay: Servicio Central de Extensión y Actividades en el Medio (SCEAM).

Brum, L., Cervetto, M., Chreties, C., Gorostiaga, J., Iriondo, L., Leicht, E., Roberto, C. & Rodríguez-Gallego, L. (2010). *Plan piloto de manejo costero integrado en el área de oportunidad Punta Colorada-Punta Negra, Maldonado.* In Manejo Costero Integrado en Uruguay: ocho ensayos interdisciplinarios. Uruguay: UDELAR/CIDA.

Bunder, J., Broese, J., Keil, F., Pohl C., Scholz, R., & Zwee-khorst, M. (2010). How can transdisciplinary research contribute to knowledge democracy? In Roeland J'int Veld (Ed.), *Knowledge democracy* (pp. 125-152.). Heidelberg: Springer.

Caporale, M., Lecuna, C., Gadea, L., Larrea, D., Medina M., & Rodríguez-Gallego L. (2010). *Hacia la construcción de un plan de manejo de la Cuenca Baja del Arroyo Maldonado.* In Manejo Costero Integrado en Uruguay: ocho ensayos interdisciplinarios. Uruguay: UDELAR/CIDA.

Cano, A., Cabo, M., & Debezies, R. (Eds.) (2011). *Apuntes para la acción. Sistematización de experiencias de extensión universitaria.* Uruguay: Comisión Sectorial de Extensión y Actividades en el Medio (CSEAM). ISBN 978-9974-0-0714-7

Centro Interdisciplinario para el Manejo Costero Integrado del Cono Sur. (2011). *Manejo Costero Integrado en Uruguay: ocho ensayos interdisciplinarios.* Uruguay: UDELAR/CIDA.

Centro Interdisciplinario de Investigaciones Biomédicas (2015). *Informe Centro Interdisciplinario, 2015.* Manuscript.

Cetrulo, R. (2016). *Desafíos de la integralidad en la universidad: metodología, teoría y epistemología.* En Producción de conocimiento en la integralidad: potencialidades y alcances en la Universidad de la República. Uruguay: Red de Extensión, Udelar.

Conde, D., Baliero, W., Biasco, E., Fossati, M., Lorenzo, E., Gorfinkiel, D., … Tejera, R. (2010). *Centro Interdisciplinario para el Manejo Costero Integrado del Cono Sur*, pp. 51-58. In En_clave Inter 2010. Reflexiones sobre la Interdisciplina en la Universidad de la República. Montevideo, Udelar.

Conde, D. & Gómez, M. (2011). *Scientific basis: Relevant knowledge and data for integrated coastal zone management.* In The sustainability of integrated management in the coastal zone of Uruguay. Montevideo: ECOPLATA/IDRC.

Consejo Directivo Central. (2010). *Hacia la Reforma Universitaria, N° 10.* La extensión en la renovación de la enseñanza: los Espacios de Formación Integral. Uruguay: Universidad de la República.

Denzin, N. K., & Lincoln, Y. S (Eds.). (1994). *Handbook of qualitative research.* Thousand Oaks, California: Sage.

De Sousa Santos, B. (2010). *Descolonizar el saber, reinventar el poder.* Uruguay: Ediciones Trilce-Extensión Universitaria, Udelar.

Douglas, M. (1979). How institutions think. *The Australian and New Zealand Journal of Sociology, 24*(3), 513-515

Eisenhardt, K (1989). Building theories from case study research. *The Academy of Management Review, 14*(4), 532-550.

Eisenhardt, K (1991). Better stories and better constructs: The case for rigor and comparative logic. *The Academy of Management Review, 16*(3), 620-662.

Faldori, G. (n.d.). *Metodología materialista para el análisis social. Cuadernos de Extensión.* Uruguay: Comisión Sectorial de Extensión y Actividades en el Medio (CSEAM). ISSN 1688-8324

Fals Borda, O. (2014). *Ciencia, compromiso y cambio social. Segunda Edición.* Uruguay: Comisión Sectorial de Extensión y Actividades en el Medio (CSEAM). ISBN: 978-9974-0-1125-0

Fals Borda, O., & Rodríguez, B. C. (1987). *Investigación participativa.* Montevideo: La Banda Oriental.

Fam, D., Palmer, J., Riedy, C., & Mitchell, C. (2016). *Transdisciplinary research and practice for sustainability outcomes.* London: Routledge Studies in Sustainability.

Frodeman, R., Klein, J. T., & Mitcham, C. (Eds.). (2010). *The Oxford handbook of interdisciplinarity.* New York: Oxford University Press.

Gibbons, M., Limoges, C., Nowotny, H., Schwartzman, S., Scott, P., & Trow, M. (1994). *The new production of knowledge. The dynamics of science and research in contemporary societies.* London: Sage Publications.

Goyos, F., Lagos, X., Verrastro, N., & de Álava, D. (2010). Goberanza para un sistema socioecológico: Construcción de agenda en MCI. In *Manejo Costero Integrado en Uruguay: ocho ensayos interdisciplinarios*. Uruguay: Universidad de la Repúlica/CIDA.

Grabino, V., & Carlos, S. (2013). *La integralidad como propuesta teórico-metodológica: Reflexiones a partir de la experiencia de la Universidad de la República*. Uruguay: Universidad de la República.

Hess, D., Breyman, S., Campbell, N., & Martin, B. (2008). Science, technology, and social movements. In O. Amsterdamska, E. J. Hackett, M. Lynch, & J. Wajcman (Eds), *The handbook of science and technology studies* (3rd ed.) (pp. 473-498). Cambridge, MA: MIT Press.

Hirsch Hadorn, G., Hoffmann-Riem, H., Biber-Klemm, S., Grossenbacher-Mansuy, W., Joye, D., Pohl, C., Wiesmann, U., & Zemp, E. (Eds.). (2007). *Handbook of transdisciplinary research*. Switzerland: Springer.

Hidalgo, C. (2014). La dinámica de coproducción de conocimiento. In *Producción de Conocimiento en la Integralidad: potencialidades y alcances en la Universidad de la República*, 63-88. Uruguay: Red de Extensión de la Universidad de la República.

Hoffmann, S., Pohl, C., & Hering, J. G. (2017a). Exploring transdisciplinary integration within a large research program: Empirical lessons from four thematic synthesis processes. *Research Policy, 46*(3), 678-692. https://doi.org/10.1016/j.respol.2017.01.004

Hoffmann, S., Pohl, C., & Hering, J. G. (2017b). Methods and procedures of transdisciplinary knowledge integration: Empirical insights from four thematic synthesis processes. *Ecology and Society, 22*(1), 27. https://doi.org/10.5751/es-08955-220127

Huutoniemi, K., Klein, J. T., Henrik, B., & Hukkinen, J. (2010). Analyzing interdisciplinarity: Typology and indicators. *Research Policy, 39*(1), 79-88.

Jasanoff, J. (Ed.). (2004). *States of knowledge. The co-production of science and the social order*. USA: Routledge.

Klein, J. T. (2010). Chapter 2: A taxonomy of interdisciplinarity. In R. Frodeman, J. T. Klein, & C. Mitcham, C. (Eds.), *The Oxford handbook of interdisciplinarity*. Oxford: Oxford University Press.

Klein, J. T. (2014). *Discourses of transdiciplinary: Looking back to the future*. Department of English, USA: Wayne State University.

Klein, J. T., & Falk-Krzeisinski, H. J. (2017). Interdisciplinary and collaborative work: Framing and tenure practices and policies. *Elsevier, 46*(6), 1055-1061.

Lang, D. J, Wiek, A., Bergmann, M., Stauffacher, M., Martens, P., Moll, P., Swilling, M. & Thomas, C. J. (2012). Transdisciplinary research in sustainability science: practice, principles, and challenges. *Sustainability Science, 7*(1), 25-43.

Lotrecchiano, G. R. (2014). Role and discipline relationships in a transdisciplinary biomedical team: Structuration, values override, and context scaffolding. *International Journal of Organisational Design and Engineering, 3*(3/4), 223-259.

McDonald, D., Bammer, G., & Deane, P. (2009). *Research integration using dialogue methods.* Canberra: Australian National University, ePress.

Martínez, C., Vienni Baptista, B., Cruz, P., & Repetto L. (2015). Saberes extendidos. Una mirada a la integralidad y la interdisciplina desde el Espacio Interdisciplinario de la Universidad de la República (Uruguay). *Interdisciplina, Revista del Centro de Investigaciones Interdisciplinarias en Ciencias y Humanidades, 5*(3). 223-240.

Mendizábal, N. (2007). Los componentes del diseño flexible en la investigación cualitativa (65-105). In I. Vasilachis de Gialdino (Ed.), *Estrategias de investigación cualitativa.* Buenos Aires: Gedisa.

National Academy of Sciences. (2005). *The drivers of interdisciplinary research in facilitating interdisciplinary research.* Washington, DC: The National Academies Press.

Nicolescu, B. (2008). *Transdisciplinarity and complexity: Levels of reality as source of indeterminacy.* Centre International de Recherches et Études transdisciplinaires.

Pohl, C., Krütli, P., & Stauffacher, M. (2017). Ten reflective steps for rendering research societally relevant. *GAIA - Ecological Perspectives for Science and Society, 26*(1), 43-51.

Pohl, C., Krütli, P., & Stauffacher, M. (2018). Teaching transdisciplinarity appropriately for students' education level. *GAIA - Ecological Perspectives for Science and Society, 27*(2), 250-252.

Randall, G (2009). La Reforma Universitaria en curso y la investigación. *Montevideo: Hacia la Reforma Universitaria, 5.*

Red de Extensión. (2013). *Estado de Situación y Propuestas para el Desarrollo de la Extensión y la Integralidad en la Universidad de la República.* Uruguay: Universidad de la República. Manuscript.

Rist, S., Chiddambaranathan, M., Escobar, C., & Wiesmann, U. (2006). "It was hard to come to mutual understanding..." - Multidimensionality of social learning processes in natural resource use in India, Africa and Latin America. *Systemic Practice and Action Research, 19*(3), 219-237.

Rodríguez, N., & Tommasino H., (2010). *Tres tesis básicas sobre extensión y prácticas integrales en la Universidad de la República,* pp. 19-43. In Cuaderno N°1 Integralidad. Uruguay: Comisión Sectorial de Extensión y Actividades en el Medio (CSEAM)

Romano, A. (2011). *Sobre los espacios de formación integral en la Universidad. Una perspectiva pedagógica.* In Integralidad: tensiones y perspectivas. Cuadernos de Extensión. SCEAM. Montevideo, Uruguay: Udelar.

Romano, A. (2014). *Evaluación de las políticas de extensión: La experiencia de los Espacios de Formación Integral (EFI).* Uruguay: Comisión Sectorial de Extensión y Actividades en el Medio, Universidad de la República.

Schneidewind, U., Singer-Brodowski, M., Augenstein, K., & Stelze, F. (2016). *Pledge for a transformative science. A conceptual framework.* Wuppertal Institute for Climate, Environment and Energy, Wuppertal. Retrieved from www.wupperinst.org

Spoun, S., & Kölzer, C. (2014). *A place apart: Opportunities in developing Leuphana University of Lüneburg.* University Experiments in Interdisciplinarity: Obstacles and Opportunities, 81-93. Bielesfeld: transcript Verlag für Kommunikation, Kultur und soziale Praxis.

Stake, R. E. (1998). *Investigación con estudio de caso.* Madrid: Morata.

Trowler, P. (2014). *Doing insider research in universities.* CreateSpace Independent Publishing Platform.

Tommasino, H., Kaplún, G., & Etchebehere, G. (2015). *Co-Producción de conocimiento en la integralidad.* Montevideo, Uruguay: Udelar.

Vienni Baptista, B. (2016a). Interdisciplinary in Latin America: Building dialogue through regionalism. *Issues in Interdisciplinary Studies, Association for Interdisciplinary Studies, 34,* 109-121.

Vienni Baptista, B. (2016b). Los Estudios sobre Interdisciplina: Construcción de un ámbito en el campo CTS. Redes. *Revista de Estudios Sociales de la Ciencia (Argentina), 21*(41), 141-175.

Vienni Baptista, B (2016c). Among institutions, spaces and networks: Inter- and transdisciplinary realms in the American continent. *Interdisciplina, Revista del Centro de Investigaciones Interdisciplinarias en Ciencias y Humanidades, 10,* 22-40.

Vienni Baptista, B., Vasen, F., & Villa Soto, J. C. (2018). Interdisciplinary centers in Latin American universities: The challenges of institutionalization. *Higher Education Policy, 32*(3), 461-483. https://doi.org/10.1057/s41307-018-0092-x

Villasante, T. R. (2010). *Historias y enfoques de una articulación metodológica participativa. Cuadernos CIMAS-Observatorio Internacional de Ciudadanía y Medio Ambiente Sostenible.* Retrieved from http://www.redcimas.org/wordpress/wp-content/uploads/2012/08/m_TVillasante_HISTORIAS.pdf

Vilsmaier, U., & Lang, D. J. (2015). Making a difference by marking the difference: Constituting in-between spaces for sustainability learning. *Current Opinion in Environmental Sustainability, 16,* 51-55.

Vilsmaier, U., Brandner, V, & Engbers, M. (2017). Research in-between: The constitutive role of cultural differences in transdisciplinarity. *Transdisciplinary Journal of Engineering and Science, 8,* 169-179.

Von Wehrden, H., Guimaraes, M. H., Bina, O., Varanda, M., Lang, D. J., Jhon, B., … Lawrance, R. J. (2018). *Intedisciplinary and transdisciplinary research: Finding the common ground of multi-faceted concepts.* 3rd INTREPID Report, COST Action TD1408.

Wagner, S. C., Roessner, J. D., Bobb, K., Klein, J. T., Boyack, K. W., Keyton, J., Rafols, I, & Börner, K. (2010). Approaches to understanding and measuring interdisciplinary scientific research (IDR): A review of the literature. *Journal of Informetrics, 5*(1), 14-26.

Weingart, P. (2014). Interdisciplinarity and the new governance of universities. In P. Weingart & B. Padberg (Eds.), *University experiments in interdisciplinarity obstacles and opportunities* (pp. 151- 174). Bielefeld: Transcript, Science Studies.

Xiao, Y., & Watson, M. (2019). Guidance on conducting a systematic literature review. *Journal of Planning Education and Research*, *39*(1), 93-112.

Yin, R. K. (1989). *Case study research: Design and Methods. Applied social research Methods Series.* Newbury Park CA: Sage.

Yin, R. K. (2014). *Case study research: Design and methods* (5th ed.). Los Angeles: SAGE.

Ziman, J. (2003). *What is science?* Cambridge: Cambridge University Press.

Gaetano R. Lotrecchiano & Shalini Misra (Editors). 2020
Communication in Transdisciplinary Teams
Santa Rosa, CA: Informing Science Press

Chapter 10:
A Multifaceted Discipline-Agnostic Approach to Training Transdisciplinary Teams in Communication

Sawsan Khuri
Collaborative Capacities. Exeter, UK
sawsan@collaborativecapacities.com

Chapter Objectives

- To train transdisciplinary teams in communication starting with an understanding of the diversity of professions and backgrounds of the teams involved, and the complexity of the project at hand.

- To describe core competencies for communication training in the academic, business, and nonprofit worlds.

- To propose a set of seven core competencies for training transdisciplinary teams in communication, based on research-based competencies developed for an introductory course in communication.

- To offer a flexible, customizable, and scalable curriculum based on these competencies. Comprised of three steps, 1) Setting the scene, 2) Living the project and 3) Telling the story, this curriculum uses tools from the business community and can be applied to any transdisciplinary setting.

Introduction to the Chapter

Training higher education students to work across disciplines, professions, and cultures has gathered momentum in recent years as global challenges have become more complex. Team work is a crucial element of transdisciplinary work, and is underpinned by the ability to communicate effectively across professions and disciplines. Formulating a set of core competencies for a training program in transdisciplinary collaboration therefore must contain a focus on communication. A close look at the core competencies and training practices for team communication, whether in a business, nonprofit or academic research context, highlights commonalities that are applicable to, but not necessarily specific to, transdisciplinary teams. This chapter highlights core competencies that were developed for an introductory course in communication that can be applied across many disciplines, i.e., is discipline-agnostic. A flexible, customizable, and scalable curriculum based on these core competencies is proposed, utilizing concepts from the business community, such as Tuckman's team dynamics (Tuckman & Jensen, 1977), as a teaching tool. Educators and facilitators running this curriculum can add materials and examples specific to their student base and setting.

This training curriculum is a contribution towards preparing the future workforce for impactful transdisciplinary work, regardless of their chosen professions.

Background

Ample evidence exists for the need to enhance team and communication competencies of professionals engaged in transdisciplinary work (Keck, Sloane, Liechty, Fiese, & Donovan, 2017; Lotrecchiano & Misra, 2018, 2020; Nash, 2008). Students in medicine, engineering, and the environmental sciences feel that their curricula inadequately prepare them for the broader collaborative stage of their professions (Brazile, Hostetter Shoop, McDonough, & Van Citters, 2018; Ekmekci, Lotrecchaino & Corcoran, 2014; Yu & Chiang, 2018). Similarly, scholars in multiple disciplines highlight communication skills as a key missing component in higher education (Akil et al., 2016; Besley & Tanner, 2011; Fung, 2017), and one that is a "wicked problem" to resolve (Johnson, Veitch, & Dewiyanti, 2015). Where explicit instruction in communication skills has been provided, it has met with success and highlighted the need for a more nuanced approach to such training in multiple settings (Fung, 2017; Hughes et al., 2016; McEwan, Ruissen, Eys, Zumbo, & Beauchamp, 2017; Razack et al., 2007).

The specific communication challenges that are encountered in transdisciplinary work are a reflection of the complexities of the teams involved (Lotrecchiano & Misra, 2018, 2020; Nash, 2008). Transdisciplinarity, defined as knowledge production at the intersection of professions and disciplines, typically involves a large diversity of stakeholders that may include academics, practitioners, nonprofits, government officials, and business leaders, and may be on a regional, national, or international scale (Stokols, 2006). Effective communication within these teams requires an understanding of the motivations, needs, and circumstances of the stakeholders even before the subject matter of the project begins to be discussed (James, Gehlert, Bowen, & Colditz, 2015; McEwan et al., 2017; Yu & Chiang, 2018, Lotrecchiano et al., 2016). A training curriculum for transdisciplinary communication would therefore reflect this and would necessarily be applicable across diverse disciplines, i.e., it will have to be discipline-agnostic. In addition, it should be possible to implement this curriculum in any research context and it should provide guidance on how information is exchanged, both within the team and between teams, external parties, and stakeholders.

This chapter describes a multifaceted approach to developing a training curriculum for communication competence in transdisciplinary teams, deliverable through a workshop model and scalable to potentially become a full-semester course (or module in the UK). To develop the curriculum, we used a process similar to that employed by Drago, McDonald, and Lotrecchiano (2018), which starts with a search of existing educational material for any type of team communication training in the peer-reviewed literature, on professional blog posts, and on institutional websites. Core competencies were identified and adapted to suit cross-disciplinary settings, where the team to be trained consisted of multiple professions, disciplines, and cultures. Finally, a curriculum was developed that mapped these competencies against a hypothetical program, allowing it to be integrated into existing programs at academic institutions interested in implementing transdisciplinary communication training.

Team Communication Training in Different Settings

This section provides an overview of the literature on key competencies and common practices for team work training in the business, nonprofit, and academic communities, with a focus on communication skills within diverse, if not necessarily transdisciplinary, teams. The themes are broad in order to be inclusive of diversity of scope, but did not include media, journalism, and marketing communication competencies. For literature searches, we used Google Scholar, Scopus, and PubMed literature databases and searched for phrases containing keywords such as team training, communication training, action research, and transdisciplinary communication. We focused our research within the last 5-7 years, and expanded to earlier original articles when needed.

Team Communication Competencies in the Business Community

Within the published material surveyed, team communication competencies are of paramount importance and are ubiquitously listed as one of the core competencies for successful teamwork. Seminal works by Belbin (1993) and Salas (2015) contain a wealth of information on effective communication skills in members and leaders of teams, and a recent handbook by Wallace and Becker (2018) discusses communication education and training pedagogies in business contexts. Organizations such as the Chartered Management Institute (CMI, 2014) and the Association of Chartered Certified Accountants, and large businesses such as KPMG and Pfizer have developed their own in-house communications training materials, available via their respective websites. Myriad business support companies exist that offer services and training programs in business communication and team building, often tailored to specific sectors and marketed through the Internet.

To supplement academic-focused scholarly articles, we searched the McKinsey Report and the Harvard Business Review for trending material on communication training, as well as TED talks and blog posts from business influencers such as Simon Sinek and Neil Patel. Perhaps unsurprisingly, here we found practical advice and pointers on how to structure communication (e.g., Sinek, Mead, & Docker, 2017), but not so much on pedagogical curriculum development that can be applied directly to transdisciplinary communication training.

The journal American Psychologist recently dedicated an issue to the science of teamwork (McDaniel & Salas, 2018), and communication skills were writ large in almost every article, with many highlighting significant and complex research on communication within and between individuals and teams in large complex settings such as the military and healthcare. To cite a few, Driskell, Salas, and Driskell (2018) reviewed the basis of the field and considered communication skills as inherent in all teamwork; Feitosa, Grossman, and Salazar (2018) explored the role of culture in practical team work applications; Shuffler and Carter, (2018) and Power, (2018) discussed multiteam systems where more than one team is involved in a project, which is a closely related concept to many transdisciplinary teams.

We distilled the information available to determine shared competencies between communication training in the business community and in transdisciplinary settings, and arrived at a set of high level competencies summarized in Table 1.

Table 1. A summary of communication competencies sought by the business community, and their overarching purpose (abstracted from various business sectors by the author).

Competency	Purpose
Interpersonal skills for a thorough understanding of who is around the table, what they bring, and why they are there.	More effective communication
Accurate, timely and relevant sharing of information between all parties	Better productivity
Building trust among all stakeholders and invoking trust in outside parties	Increased cooperation, efficacy and productivity
Identifying and resolving conflict early and with a win/win outlook	Increased cooperation and productivity
Enhancing leadership skills in the whole team	All the above

Communication Competencies in Nonprofits

Nonprofits, defined as charitable organizations dedicated to a social cause, generally work within communities and are often either on the funding, policy, or practical application ends of transdisciplinary research (Liu, 2012). The team training material we found within this sector focused on communication within the organizations, and on implementing change within their respective populations (e.g., Augustin, 2010; Giarratana, 2017; Liu, 2012; NCVO Knowhow, 2018). The team communication competencies of nonprofits were found to be very similar to those of the business community listed above, with additional emphasis on the specific target audiences. Our observations confirmed that the competencies summarized in Table 1 were equally applicable here, and that the closer a nonprofit is to the people on the ground, the higher the emphasis placed on empathy, culture, and language in its communication competencies. This expands the core competencies on interpersonal communication and building trust, and is highly relevant to transdisciplinary work.

Collaboration between academia and on-the-ground nonprofits usually takes place within what in different disciplines is called "action research" or "participatory research" (using the still-relevant definitions of Brown and Tandon, 1983, and expanded to participatory action research in MacDonald, 2012). These often have an international component, fall under transdisciplinarity, and therefore need to be taken into account when developing a training curriculum for transdisciplinary teams in communication.

Communication Training in Academic Practice

Team science, interdisciplinary and transdisciplinary training in academia is prevalent in the medical and the environmental sciences arena, where many institutions are implementing team science or transdisciplinary elements into their curricula. While each offering adheres to its own list of competencies and learning objectives, the underlying theme is to enhance effective communication within the specific setting of the training being provided. Structured whole-semester for-credit courses in team science (Khuri & Wuchty, 2015a, 2015b) and communication skills (Kaplan-Liss et al., 2018) proved valuable and helpful. Other institutions apply an integrated method that augments the program structure that trainees are enrolled in, either through small-group problem based sessions (e.g., Safavi et al., 2018), professional development workshops (Park & Park, 2018), or by making use of direct mentorship, journal clubs, and an individualized professional development plan for the trainees (James et al., 2015). Another method to integrate transdisciplinary learning within a traditional curriculum is by developing structured, assessed cross-professional or transdisciplinary internship programs where the trainees "learn on the job", and this serves the double purpose of also broadening their network and their worldview (Jeder, 2014; Kay, Kay, & Tuininga, 2018). Where resources or the scope for change are limited, trainees are at the very least exposed to transdisciplinary approaches in clinics, and whereas this is not ideal, it is still beneficial since trainees learn from veteran practitioners in their own professional and cultural contexts (Nandiwada & Dang-Vu, 2010).

Talking in general terms from an environmental sciences perspective, Pearce (2018) captured competence fields for transdisciplinary training and presented them as a set of interconnected, interdependent learning objectives. She framed them as communicating values, reflecting about self and others, applying concepts to the real world, framing complex problems with others, researching in and with the real world, and imagining solutions and their consequences. The first most striking observation about this list is how aligned it is with the competencies of participatory action research (MacDonald, 2012), and the second is that all these fields are underpinned by effective communication skills among the stakeholders. Communication training therefore must be a key component in research departments involved with transdisciplinary research, and the core competencies described above needed to be expanded accordingly.

Identifying the Core Competencies

Outside of specific medical or environmental science departmental efforts, there is a broad recognition that communication skills are increasingly sought after by a wide array of academic researchers. Most authors who have reported on transdisciplinary education and training conclude that a mixed approach would work best for training at all levels, and this matched our own experiences in team science training (Khuri & Wuchty, 2015b). In an attempt to address this gap in curricular development, communication faculty conducted an in-depth, three-year study and developed a core set of introductory communication competencies applicable across multiple disciplines (Engleberg et al., 2017). They identified seven core competencies that could be used to train students in introductory communication in a discipline-agnostic manner, and these are presented in Table 2 along with example behavior patterns that each competency is aimed at addressing.

Table 2. The seven core communication competencies for an introductory course in general communication and the behavioral patterns they correspond to
(adapted from Engleberg et al., 2017).

Introductory Communication Competency	Corresponding behavioral patterns
Monitoring and presenting yourself	How to enter the meeting, greet everyone, be aware of clothing and familiarity with and between the stakeholders, public speaking
Practicing communication ethics	Use influence wisely, be truthful, have knowledge of relevant ethics and laws, respect freedom of expression
Adapting to others	Understand, respect and be mindful of demographics, abilities, power play, attitudes and contexts of the group
Practicing effective listening	Listen more than talk, hear what the others are saying, make notes and mental associations if you have to in order to grasp the messages and issues at hand
Expressing messages	The spoken word is only part of communicating a message, non-verbal cues such as eye contact and body language are vital, as is the audio-visual or other medium you use to clearly and accurately relay your messages
Identifying and explaining fundamental communication processes	Focus on the desired outcome of a communication, apply appropriate leadership styles and guide the team towards the decisions being made
Creating and analyzing message strategies	Reflect on the messages being made and how they might be received, critical thinking is an essential part of a successful communication strategy

We used this set of core competencies and their descriptions as the backbone, and added elements to enhance their application to transdisciplinary teams (see the following text box). Taking lessons from the business and nonprofit communities, from our own work (e.g., Khuri & Wuchty, 2015a, 2015b) and from published reports of academic practice in team training, we framed our core competencies with this question:

What communication skills does a member of a transdisciplinary team need to have in order to work with other members to successfully and collaboratively achieve the integrative goal of the project at hand?

Core Competencies for Training Transdisciplinary Teams in Communication (expanded from Engleberg et al., 2017)

1) Monitoring and presenting your skill set in the context of your transdisciplinary team, ensuring relevance in your use of language and referenced examples.
2) Practicing communication ethics by being open about team and project values and recognizing each member's professional achievement needs early on in your discussions.
3) Adapting to others, in terms of their professional, demographic and ethnic cultures, and being willing to put effort and perhaps compromise to finding the inevitable win-win situation.
4) Practicing active and effective listening, of both verbal and non-verbal messages.
5) Expressing messages with clarity and kindness, unlocking the complexity of the transdisciplinary project at hand, and being aware of the professional, demographic and ethnic cultures of team members, and the interpretation of tonality and nonverbal cues in your team.
6) Identifying and explaining fundamental communication processes, to make it easier to recognize and respond to potential points of conflict within a transdisciplinary team.
7) Creating and analyzing message strategies to ensure that your transdisciplinary team continues to communicate effectively for the duration of the project.

A Multifaceted Approach

Using these core competencies, we formulated a multifaceted approach to communication training for transdisciplinary teams. We devised a scalable curriculum composed of three steps, each of which intersects with more than one of the core competencies, such that by the end of delivery the learning objectives implicit within the core competencies will have been achieved (Figure 1). This flexibility allows educators or facilitators implementing this curriculum to 1) formulate their own learning objectives particular to the project or program at hand, 2) expand the curriculum to include project- and/or stakeholder- specific material such as scientific, linguistic, cultural, geographic or other material, and 3) implement it either as a series of workshops or a full-semester course, depending on time and resources.

Step 1. Setting the Scene

The curriculum is briefly introduced and explained, engaging students in the journey and setting their expectations. Learning objectives are summarized and should include written, verbal, and non-verbal communication skills, plus any specialist (e.g., scientific, linguistic, cultural) learning objectives if applicable. This step addresses the core competencies of presenting oneself in the context of the project, adapting as necessary, establishing ground rules and understanding the ethics of the collaboration, and having a clearly defined yet flexible message strategy in place.

Tuckman's Stages of Team Dynamics

Forming: The team introduces themselves and begins to understand the project. Ground rules, expected outcomes, rewards and organizational infrastructure are all openly discussed and agreed upon.

Storming: Conflict arises within the group as human nature decrees that we try to find hierarchy in groups we enter into, and that we are wary of unknowns. The role of inter-team communication is crucial to making this stage short and relatively painless, and team leadership has a strong influence here. In best case scenarios most team members are unaware of this stage, and on the other end of that spectrum external facilitators or mentors are brought in to advise.

Norming: Cohesion is achieved, the team now is accustomed to how each member works and familiar with the overall objective and the resources available.

Performing: A task-oriented phase, here is where everyone is busy working productively and reporting back and forth among each other and the leadership.

Adjourning: Once the project is complete, team members meet to discuss the outcomes, find closure, and/or start planning the next project.

It is important to see these stages as iterative whenever a new person, resource or aim enters the project. It is also important to recognize that these stages are not linear in terms of time and energy, and that they do occur repeatedly and predictably in every team situation that they have been tested on since they were described (Bonebright, 2010).

At this point, the five sequential stages of team dynamics (Tuckman & Jensen, 1977) are described along with the communication tools needed to advance smoothly from one stage to the next. Figure 1 illustrates how Tuckman's team dynamics are connected to the different steps of the training and how they apply to the core competencies. By introducing them at the beginning of the training, participants are better able to anticipate and work with the evolving dynamics throughout the project. Examples relevant to the group are helpful here as team dynamics are used to explore the role of leadership, individual team members, and organizational structure in building trust and enhancing productivity. The disciplinary, professional, and ethnic cultures of team members are discussed and open communication is encouraged. It is important to alert participants that the Tuckman team dynamics do not conform to a linear progression, that some stages may last longer than others, and that this is dependent on several factors, including elements covered in the core competences such as active listening, expressing messages correctly, and being aware of team members' professional culture and reward mechanisms. While verbal and non-verbal communication skills are crucial in Step 1, written communication is also touched upon because here is when responsible and sensitive use of digital communication such as emails and social media is discussed. Educators and facilitators are encouraged to demonstrate how misunderstandings can easily occur with careless use of language, especially in texting or emails.

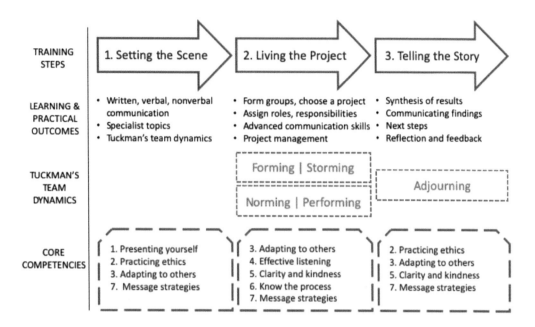

Figure 1. The relationship between the proposed steps of transdisciplinary communication training and the core competencies they address, with suggested learning outcomes and how Tuckman's team dynamics apply to the process.

Step 2. Living the Project

Even if the training is taking place within a specific center or department, students should be encouraged to search their own passions and interests to arrive at a project that they have an affinity towards. At this stage (and not before) they can form groups and tackle an issue that they share a concern about, such as one of the UN's Sustainable Development Goals, a healthcare challenge, or a local topic. That they can choose their own projects is important, it increases their engagement and enables them to focus wholeheartedly on the transdisciplinary communication training. Within their groups, they can assign the roles of different stakeholders, such that each group contains one or two academics, someone from a nonprofit, a business owner, and maybe a local civil servant or lay person who is interested in the outcomes. Each team member researches the motivations, resources, jargon, and professional culture of their role, and plays that role within the group project (Figure 2). If time is tight, the educational entity providing this training could potentially provide case studies from previous or ongoing research that the students could practice on, though it would still be important that students are allowed some creative scope at this step.

Once the groups have formed, students begin to experience the five stages of team dynamics firsthand. Students' interactions with each other in Step 2 is a managed mixture of prescribed exercises to inform the training and "on the job" training as they each have their roles to play to fulfill the project objectives. For example, exercises can be introduced for them to practice active listening (c.f., helpful practical tips by Zenger & Folkman, 2016), and they can be exposed to more specialized communications skills training techniques such as word associations or improvisation (Kaplan-Liss et al., 2018).

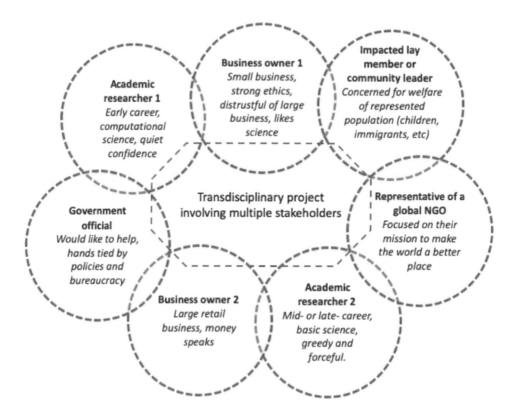

Figure 2. Hypothetical example of a discipline-agnostic project structure and how students can assign roles with specific personalities, motivations and cultures to explore transdisciplinary communication. These can be substituted by roles more suited to particular projects, such as medical doctors, teachers, entrepreneurs, larger/smaller NGOs (non-governmental organization), religious leaders and so on.

Step 2 feeds into several core competencies, starting around adapting to others, in terms of accepting and respecting input from each member of the team, which in turn requires active and effective listening to others, and being aware of the clarity and tone of one's own message. As a whole, Living the Project requires a solid knowledge of the process of communication and the careful design, analysis and potentially iteration of communication strategies (Figure 1) in order to move forward. Our suggestion is to build open discussion debriefing sessions into the last 10 or so minutes of each session during Step 2, giving participants the opportunity to provide feedback not only to each other, but to the educator or facilitator running the sessions as well. Acting on this feedback in the next iteration of this curriculum closes the educational learning loop and ensures the curriculum remains relevant and viable to the institution running it.

If time and budget allow, student projects can be scaled up to include real-world projects with community-based nonprofit or business partners, or even internships. If this training can only take place within a short 1-day workshop or series of workshops, then project examples from the literature can be found for students to "replicate" within the available time.

Step 3. Telling the Story

Roughly equivalent to Tuckman's adjourning stage, Step 3 is where students have completed their projects and are ready to deliver a presentation or a written report about their findings and achievements. As they consolidate their findings and synthesize the final messages of the collaboration, students revisit core competencies connected to communication ethics in how they analyze and deliver the new information, adapting to the needs of the other stakeholders in terms of cultural sensitivity and reward mechanisms, and ensuring that their final communication is presented clearly and accurately (Figure 1). This report should include a reflection on the communication training received, how the initial message strategy worked and whether the students modified it during the project, and how they will implement their learnings in future. Within a for-credit environment, this could be a short project report, which would allow the curriculum to include writing skills sessions and which are commensurate with common professional practice of most career choices. If time is limited, then this could simply be an informal oral presentation to celebrate team achievement.

With the completion of the three steps, and an open discussion and/or a report at the end, all core competencies will have been fulfilled, and the interconnectivity between them demonstrated (Figure 1). Students will have engaged with an unusual teaching style that merges didactic offerings with problem-based small group sessions and experiential learning activities, tied within the transdisciplinary framework of the project at hand. Further details on each step can be elaborated on and customized upon delivery, depending on the scope of the program in which the curriculum is being implemented.

Conclusions

There is nothing more important than effective communication in transdisciplinary collaborations, and this chapter offers a "how to" curriculum for training team members in the communication skills necessary to work in transdisciplinary settings. The curriculum is based on a set of core competencies (Text Box 1) that were adapted from generic communication competencies developed by Engleberg et al. (2017) and includes concepts and tools from the business and nonprofit communities (Figure 1).

A vital element is missing from this chapter, and that is the evaluation and assessment of the proposed curriculum. Since it has not yet been tested in this format, no hard data exists to evaluate its impact. Various early iterations of this curriculum have been offered at undergraduate and postgraduate level, and student feedback was largely highly positive and encouraging (Khuri & Wuchty, 2015b). Versions of it have been customized for specific projects or programs and have been offered as 1-day workshops to a range of different stakeholders at varying stages of their career. Feedback was positive on the interactive style of delivery that made it clear which competencies were being addressed when, and constructive on managing expectations about what can be achieved within the scope of the training, both of which informed further iterations (see examples in Khuri, 2019). A more thorough, systematic evaluation could follow the CATS method (Frankel, Gardner, Maynard, & Kelly, 2007) recommended for use in medical education (Havyer et al., 2016), or other evaluation methods reviewed in the context of climate change research by De-Lorme, Kidwell, Hagen, and Stephens (2016).

With significant changes taking place in the workplace, there have been many calls for a paradigm shift in how we educate and inform the next generation of our workforce (Jeder, 2014; Johnson et al., 2015; McDaniels & Skogsberg, 2017; Nash, 2008). A flexible, scalable curriculum for transdisciplinary training is a contribution in that direction. Employing a range of techniques that cover communication essentials, this basic curriculum design can be adapted to most research settings and to any number and variety of stakeholders. Educators with experience in working with transdisciplinary teams can insert their own examples, and draw upon the experience of participants. Transdisciplinarity is complex and multifactorial, and training teams in transdisciplinary communication practices merits a carefully layered strategy.

Questions to Further the Discourse

1. This curriculum is currently being implemented through a privately owned business. How might we implement it at a higher education institute where students can apply the learnings in real-world transdisciplinary research and educators can assess its adaptability, evaluate its success, and suggest improvements for future iterations?

2. In a transdisciplinary setting, it is as important for nonprofit and government collaborators to understand the motivational drivers within academia as it is for academia to be able to effectively communicate new concepts and findings to the public. Our research did not find guidelines for training nonprofit personnel in communicating with academic partners. How might we explore the training needs in this domain and what shape might such training take?

3. It would be valuable to have information on the long-term career paths of graduates with arts and sciences double majors, and of graduates from transdisciplinary doctoral programs. How have communication skills helped their journey and what specific skills do they feel might be missing from the communication training proposed here?

4. What parallel research on negotiation and the role of compromise in transdisciplinary settings might further inform the construct provided here?

Must Reads

Engleberg, I. N., Ward, S. M., Disbrow, L. M., Katt, J. A., Myers, S. A., & O'Keefe, P. (2017). The development of a set of core communication competencies for introductory communication courses. *Communication Education, 66*, 1-18.

Hughes, A. M., Gregory, M. E., Joseph, D. L., Sonesh, S. C., Marlow, S. L., Lacerenza, C. N., Benishek, L. E., King, H. B., & Salas, E. (2016). Saving lives: A meta-analysis of team training in healthcare. *Journal of Applied Psychology, 101*, 1266-1304.

Johnson, S., Veitch, S., & Dewiyanti, S. (2015). A framework to embed communication skills across the curriculum: A design-based research approach. *Journal of University*

Teaching and Learning Practice, 12. Retrieved from
http://ro.uow.edu.au/jutlp/vol12/iss4/6

McDaniels, M., & Skogsberg, E. (2017). The scholars we need: Preparing transdisciplinary professionals by leveraging the scholarship of practice. *New Directions for Higher Education, 178*, 71-83.

McEwan, D., Ruissen, G. R., Eys, M. A., Zumbo, B. D., & Beauchamp, M. R. (2017). The effectiveness of teamwork training on teamwork behaviors and team performance: A systematic review and meta-analysis of controlled interventions. *Public Library of Science ONE, 12*, e0169604. https://doi.org/10.1371/journal.pone.0169604

References

Akil, H., Balice-Gordon, R., Lopes Cardozo, D., Koroshetz, W., Posey Norris, S. M., Sherer, T., Sherman, S. M., & Thiels, E. (2016). Neuroscience training in the 21ˢᵗ century. *Neuron, 90*, 917-926.

Augustin, M. E. (2010) *Strengthening nonprofits: A capacity builder's resource library*. Retrieved from http://www.strengtheningnonprofits.org

Belbin, R. M. (1993). *Team roles at work*. Oxford: Butterworth Heinemann.

Besley, J. C., & Tanner, A. H. (2011). What science communication scholars think about training scientists to communicate. *Science Communication, 33*, 239-263.

Bonebright, D. A. (2010). 40 years of storming: A historical review of Tuckman's model of small group development. *Human Resource Development International, 13*, 111-120.

Brazile, T., Hostetter Shoop, G., McDonough, C. M., & Van Citters, D. W. (2018). Promoting innovation: Enhancing transdisciplinary opportunities for medical and engineering students. *Medical Teacher, Jan 30*, 1-11. https://doi.org/10.1080/0142159x.2018.1426841

Brown, L. D., & Tandon, R. (1983) Ideology and political economy in inquiry: Action research and participatory research. *The Journal of Applied Behavioural Science, 19*, 277-294.

CMI. (2014) *Effective verbal communication with groups, checklist 108*. Retrieved from https://www.managers.org.uk/~/media/Files/PDF/Civil%20Service/CHK-108.pdf

Drago, D., McDonald, P. L., & Lotrecchiano, G. R. (2018). Communication transdisciplinary characteristics in global regulatory affairs: An example from health professions education. *Informing Science: The International Journal of an Emerging Transdiscipline, 21*, 219-234. https://doi.org/10.28945/4030

DeLorme, D. E., Kidwell D., Hagen S.C., & Stephens S.H. (2016). Developing and managing transdisciplinary and transformative research on the coastal dynamics of sea level rise: Experiences and lessons learned. *Earth's Future, 4*, 194–209.

Driskell, J. E., Salas, E., & Driskell, T. (2018). Foundations of teamwork and collaboration. *American Psychologist, 73*, 334-348.

Ekmekci, O., Lotrecchiano, G. R., & Corcoran, M. (2014). The devil is in the (mis) alignment: Developing curriculum for clinical and translational science professionals. *Journal of Translational Medical Epidemiology, 2*, 1029.

Engleberg, I. N., Ward, S. M., Disbrow, L. M., Katt, J. A., Myers, S. A., & O'Keefe, P. (2017). The development of a set of core communication competencies for introductory communication courses. *Communication Education, 66*, 1-18.

Feitosa, J., Grossman, R., & Salazar, M. (2018) Debunking key assumptions about teams: The role of culture. *American Psychologist, 73*, 376-389.

Frankel, A., Gardner, R., Maynard, L., & Kelly, A. (2007). Using the communication and teamwork skills (CATS) assessment to measure health care team performance. *The Joint Commission Journal on Quality and Patient Safety, 33*, 549–558.

Fung, D. (2017). *A connected curriculum for higher education.* London: UCL Press.

Giarratana, C. (2017). *The top eight goals to consider for your nonprofit communication team.* Blog post from the Arizona State University Lodestar Center for Philanthropy and Nonprofit Innovation. Retrieved from https://lodestar.asu.edu/blog/2017/12/top-eight-goals-consider-your-nonprofit-communication-team

Havyer, R. D., Nelson, D. R., Wingo, M. T., Comfere, N. I., Halvorsen, A. J., McDonald, F. S., & Reed, D. A. (2016). Addressing the interprofessional collaboration competencies of the Association of American Medical Colleges: A systematic review of assessment instruments in undergraduate medical education. *Academic Medicine, 91*, 865-888.

Hughes, A. M., Gregory, M. E., Joseph, D. L., Sonesh, S. C., Marlow, S. L., Lacerenza, C. N., Benishek, L. E., King, H. B., & Salas, E. (2016). Saving lives: A meta-analysis of team training in healthcare. *Journal of Applied Psychology, 101*, 1266-1304.

James, A. S., Gehlert, S., Bowen, D. J., & Colditz, G.A. (2015). A framework for training transdisciplinary scholars in cancer prevention and control. *Journal of Cancer Education, 30*, 664-669.

Jeder, D. (2014). Transdisciplinarity – The advantage of a holistic approach to life. *Procedia – Social and Behavioral Sciences, 137*, 127-131.

Johnson, S., Veitch, S., & Dewiyanti, S. (2015). A framework to embed communication skills across the curriculum: A design-based research approach. *Journal of University Teaching and Learning Practice, 12*. Retrieved from http://ro.uow.edu.au/jutlp/vol12/iss4/6

Kaplan-Liss, E., Lantz-Gefroh, V., Bass, E., Killebrew, D., Ponzio, N. M., Savi, C., & O'Connell, C. (2018). Teaching medical students to communicate with empathy and clarity using improvisation. *Academic Medicine, 93*, 440-443.

Kay, M. J., Kay, S. A., & Tuininga, A. R. (2018). Green teams: A collaborative training model. *Journal of Cleaner Production, 176*, 909-919.

Keck, A. S., Sloane, S., Liechty, J. M., Fiese, B. H., & Donovan, S. M. (2017). Productivity, impact, and collaboration differences between transdisciplinary and traditionally trained doctoral students: A comparison of publication patterns. *PLoS ONE, 12*, e0189391.

Khuri, S. (2019, August 20). *Who we work with*. Retrieved from https://collaborativecapacities.com/category/case-studies/

Khuri, S., & Wuchty, S. (2015a). Core competencies in team science. *SciTS Conference Proceedings*, Bethesda, MD.

Khuri, S., & Wuchty, S. (2015b). Training undergraduates in cross-disciplinary team science. Iinvited blog on the *Science of Team Science Toolkit*, NIH, USA

Liu, B. F. (2012). Toward a better understanding of nonprofit communication management. *Journal of Communication Management, 16*, 388-404.

Lotrecchiano, G. R., Mallinson, T. R., Leblanc-Beaudoin, T., Schwartz, L. S., Lazar, D., & Falk-Krzesinski, H. J. (2016). Individual motivation and threat indicators of collaboration readiness in scientific knowledge producing teams: A scoping review and domain analysis. *Heliyon, 2*(5), e00105. https://doi.org/10.1016/j.heliyon.2016.e00105

Lotrecchiano, G. R., & Misra, S. (Eds.). (2018). Transcisciplinary communication. *Informing Science: The International Journal of an Emerging Transdiscipline Special Series, 21*, 41-253.

Lotrecchiano, G. R., & Misra, S. (2020). Transdisciplinary knowledge producing teams: Team processes, knowledge, skills, and competencies. In G. R. Lotrecchiano & S. Misra (Eds), *Communication in transdisciplinary teams* (pp. 19-54). Santa Rosa CA: Informing Science Press.

MacDonald, C. (2012). Understanding participatory action research: A qualitative research methodology option. *Canadian Journal of Action Research, 13*, 34-50.

McDaniel, S. H., & Salas, E. (2018). The science of teamwork: Introduction to the special issue. *American Psychologist, 73*, 305–307.

McDaniels, M., & Skogsberg, E. (2017). The scholars we need: Preparing transdisciplinary professionals by leveraging the scholarship of practice. *New Directions for Higher Education, 178*, 71-83.

McEwan, D., Ruissen, G. R., Eys, M. A., Zumbo, B. D., & Beauchamp, M. R. (2017). The effectiveness of teamwork training on teamwork behaviors and team performance: A systematic review and meta-analysis of controlled interventions. *Public Library of Science ONE, 12*, e0169604. https://doi.org/10.1371/journal.pone.0169604

Nandiwada, D. R., & Dang-Vu, C. (2010). Transdisciplinary health care education: Training team players. *Journal of Health Care for the Poor and Underserved, 21*, 26-34.

Nash, J. M. (2008). Transdisciplinary training: Key components and prerequisites for success. *American Journal of Preventive Medicine, 35*, S133-S140.

NCVO Knowhow. (2018). *Effective teams*. Retrieved from https://knowhow.ncvo.org.uk/your-team/people-management-skills/teams/effectiveteam/developing#good-communication

Park, K. H., & Park, S. G. (2018). The effect of communication training using standardized patients on nonverbal behaviors in medical students. *Korean Journal of Medical Education, 30,* 153-159.

Pearce, B. B. (2018) *Linking learning and research through transdisciplinary competences.* Blog post on the i2insights.org, please also see the comments section. Retrieved from https://i2insights.org/2018/07/10/transdisciplinary-competences/

Power, N. (2018). Extreme teams: Toward a greater understanding of multiagency teamwork during major emergencies and disasters. *American Psychologist, 73,* 478-490.

Razack, S., Meterissian, S., Morin, L., Snell, L., Steinert, Y., Tabatabai, D., & Maclellan, A. M. (2007). Coming of age as communicators: Differences in the implementation of common communications skills training in four residency programmes. *Medical Education, 41,* 441-449.

Safavi, A. H., Shi, Q., Ding, M., Kotait, M., Profetto, J., Mohialdin, V., & Shali, A. (2018). Structured, small-group hands-on teaching sessions improve pre-clerk knowledge and confidence in point-of-care ultrasound use and interpretation. *Cureus, 10,* e3484. https://doi.org/10.7759/cureus.3484

Salas, E. (2015). *Team training essentials.* New York: Routledge.

Shuffler, M. L., & Carter, D. R. (2018). Teamwork situated in multiteam systems: Key lessons learned and future opportunities. *American Psychologist, 73,* 390-406.

Sinek, S., Mead, D., & Docker, P. (2017). *Find your why: A practical guide for discovering purpose for you and your team.* Penguin.

Stokols, D. (2006). Towards a science of transdisciplinary action research. *American Journal of Community Psychology, 38,* 63–77.

Tuckman, B. W., & Jensen, M. A. (1977). Stages of small-group development revisited. *Group and Organization Studies, 2,* 419–427.

Wallace, J. D., & Becker, D. (Eds.). (2018). *The handbook of communication training: A best practices framework for assessing and developing competence.* Routledge.

Yu, C. Y., & Chiang, Y. C. (2018). Designing a climate-resilient environmental curriculum – A transdisciplinary challenge. *Sustainability, 10,* 77-92.

Zenger, J., & Folkman J. (2016). What great listeners actually do. *Harvard Business Review, July 14.* Retrieved from https://hbr.org/2016/07/what-great-listeners-actually-do

Gaetano R. Lotrecchiano & Shalini Misra (Editors). 2020
Communication in Transdisciplinary Teams
Santa Rosa, CA: Informing Science Press

Emerging Directions in the 'Science of Team Science': *An Interview with Professor Daniel Stokols*

Daniel Stokols
School of Social Ecology, University of California, Irvine, CA, USA
dstokols@uci.edu

Shalini Misra
School of Public and International Affairs, Virginia Tech, VA, USA
shalini@vt.edu

Gaetano R. Lotrecchiano
School of Medicine and Health Science, George Washington University, Washington, DC, USA
glotrecc@gwu.edu

Introduction

This volume provides a diverse yet incomplete survey of issues related to communication in transdisciplinary teams. While drawing attention to the theoretical, technical, applied, cultural, and research concerns, the volume only begins to introduce an agenda in need of further development and exploration.

In the epilogue of this volume, we (Misra & Lotrecchiano) chose to engage Professor Daniel Stokols in a dialogue about some of the themes in this volume to get his perspective on its contributions, gaps that remain, and new lines of research on communication in transdisciplinary contexts. Daniel Stokols is a pioneer and innovator in the 'Science of Team Science' (SciTS) field. Throughout his career he has worked toward conceptualizing *social ecology* --- an integrative, transdisciplinary conceptual mapping system, that provides a meta-theoretical framework for understanding and addressing complex societal challenges.

Among his most influential contributions is introducing the social ecological paradigm to health promotion research and evaluation and community problem-solving fields (Stokols, 1992, 1996, 2006, 2018). Stokols and colleagues have evaluated the collaborative processes, and the scientific and public policy outcomes of large scale team science initiatives such as the National Institute of Health's Transdisciplinary Tobacco Use Research Centers (Stokols et al., 2003; Stokols, Hall, Taylor, & Moser, 2008; Stokols, Harvey, Gress, Fuqua, & Phillips, 2005) and the National Cancer Institute's Transdisciplinary Research on Energetics and Cancer initiative (Hall et al., 2008). For over a decade, his theoretical and methodological contributions have shaped and advanced the SciTS research agenda. Engaging Professor Stokols in a dialogue was both confirming and thought provoking as we considered the value and impact of some of the themes emerging from the research reported in this volume.

We designed questions that encapsulated the major themes and findings of research presented in this volume and outlined linkages between the chapters. Over a video call in late September 2019, we discussed these topics with Professor Stokols. The interview presented below has been edited and condensed for clarity. In the final section of this chapter, we offer some reflections on the main conclusions of the research presented in the earlier chapters of this volume, outstanding questions, and a glimpse into the future to chart emerging directions of research on communication in transdisciplinary collaborative settings.

Interview

Q: Both Laursen (2020) and Trivedi and Misra's (2020) research emphasize "sensemaking" or "collective thinking" as a pathway to integrative knowledge creation and creative problem-solving in TD teams. Collective thinking or sensemaking is a form of cognitive shifting through which one's tacit knowledge, assumptions, or beliefs become explicit through dialogue and reflection. How might organizations create conditions for collective thinking to occur?

Laursen's (2020) and Trivedi and Misra's (2020) emphasis on the importance of collective sensemaking in teams addresses an important gap in the literature on team science. Prior studies of team science have focused extensively on evidence-based "best practices" for strengthening the interpersonal cohesion or *social integration* of cross-disciplinary teams—for instance, efforts to promote trust, effective communication, and collaboration planning--but have given considerably less attention to developing effective strategies for promoting idea generation and *intellectual integration* among team members. A major premise underpinning the formation of cross-disciplinary teams is that bringing together diverse perspectives on various research topics is a powerful strategy for generating novel ideas and scientific advances. However, many science teams and research centers, while taking steps to bolster social integration among their members, do not set aside sufficient time to promote intellectual synergy and integration.

Many interdisciplinary teams and centers get so bogged down with administrative bureaucratic routines, keeping the center funded, developing renewal funding proposals, and hiring staff, that they rarely have time for promoting intellectual synergy and sensemaking around the research topics they're investigating. It's important for teams to regularly schedule opportunities for their members to share, react to, and integrate disparate ideas. For instance, team retreats devoted to idea generation and integration can be scheduled periodically at a remote location that's free of the usual distractions and conducive to contemplation. Also, the initial portions of weekly or monthly team meetings can be reserved for the discussion of research ideas in an effort to sustain intellectual synergy.

There are many different strategies that can be used by teams to promote intellectual synergy and sensemaking. An excellent overview of these strategies is provided by Paul Pualus and Bernard Nijstad's (2019) *Oxford Handbook of Group Creativity and*

Innovation. One brainstorming tool that I've used in my graduate seminar on theory development at UC Irvine (and have implemented more recently with cross-disciplinary research teams) is the "idea tree" exercise (cf., Stokols, Salazar, Olson, & Olson, 2019), where groups of 6 to 8 members are seated at a table and each person is given a blank sheet of paper on which to write an initial idea (e.g., a research question, hypothesis, or theoretical idea). After all group members have written their ideas at the top of the page, they pass their pages to the persons seated next to them, who are then asked to react to or extend the idea written at the top of the page. This process is repeated several times until all group members have had a chance to respond to everyone else's ideas and the thread of group members' reactions to the initial prompt. At the end of the exercise, each individual receives a page of reactions to and elaborations of their initial idea. The group members then sift through the threads of ideas they've created to identify the most creative and interesting extensions of the initial prompts that warrant further refinement and investigation. Some research centers use this face-to-face brainstorming exercise to harvest novel ideas around which future research projects and grant proposals can be organized. The idea tree brainstorming exercise is designed to foster serendipitous connections between disparate perspectives that usually aren't brought together.

Interdisicplinary teams, of course, are typically situated within larger organizational and institutional contexts, such as academic departments, organized research units, and university campuses. Organizations and institutions can create intellectual climates that support (or sometimes hinder) intellectual synergy and innovation. For example, universities can incentivize faculty members to collaborate with academic colleagues and community partners by recognizing and rewarding their contributions to collaborative scholarship as an essential part of promotion and tenure reviews. At UC Irvine, team science scholars have worked with the Office of Academic Personnel to develop guidelines related to collaborative scholarship, that faculty members can refer to when preparing their reflective research statements for personnel reviews (UCI Office of Academic Personnel, 2019). Also, administrators of research organizations and universities can strengthen collaborative climates by developing curricula and training modules for faculty and graduate students that address team science "best practices" and strategies for enhancing cross-disciplinary innovation. Providing shared research space and online collaboration tools for members of cross-disciplinary teams are additional strategies that can help build institutional climates supportive of cross-disciplinary collaboration and sensemaking (cf., Stokols, Olson, Salazar, & Olson, 2019).

Q: Comparably, both Mäkinen (2020) and Trivedi and Misra (2020) highlight the importance of non-hierarchical or organic organizational structures to promote integrative knowledge production. Traditional universities are not designed to encourage the flow of information between individuals and units. How might university settings promote connectivity and interdependencies across units and individuals?

One organizational strategy for promoting inter-unit collaboration and exchange of ideas is to establish organized research centers that span multiple disciplines and advance knowledge integration (D. O. Gray, 2008). Many universities are striving to launch more and more cross-disciplinary research units, partly because they are competing for large center grants, many of which are funded and renewable over five-year cycles. The substantial funding associated with center grants is certainly desirable, but another important advantage of these collaborative projects is that they encourage people to get out of their disciplinary comfort zones and work with colleagues from diverse fields. Not all centers fulfill their initial aspirations of achieving intellectual synergy and innovation, so there's a strong incentive for the organizers of cross-disciplinary center proposals to ensure that scholars who are committed to long-term (and often laborious) collaboration are encouraged to join as Co-PIs (while those less strongly committed to collaborative goals are discouraged from joining). Also, some of the most successful research centers and teams develop detailed collaboration plans at the outset of their project and embed team science best-practices into their organizational routines, such as conducting regularly scheduled evaluative audits of communication and collaboration effectiveness and offering team science training modules for their members.

The collaborative success of cross-disciplinary centers depends heavily on the interpersonal skills and intellectual inclusiveness of their leaders (B. Gray, 2008; National Academies of Science Engineering and Medicine, 2015). Effective leaders set the right tone and are not heavy-handed or chauvinistic in pushing (or overvaluing) their own disciplinary perspective. Rather, they're open to ideas and methods drawn from fields that are different from their own area/s of expertise. They're also kind to others and receptive toward disparate ideas. Some leaders seem to be able to do those things well while others lack those skills and tend to over-emphasize their own fields of training in the research projects undertaken by center members. If you have the right kind of leader, it's easier to establish an organizational mission that facilitates teamwork, where everyone in the group, regardless of rank, has an equal opportunity to contribute. With regard to the gender composition and diversity of teams, it's important for team leaders and members to recognize that there's often a culturally-reinforced tendency--especially among junior female members of teams--to not say as much or to not be reinforced to participate actively in team discussions. Effective team leaders and members are sensitive to those tendencies, so they strive to promote demographic and intellectual diversity as they assemble teams and also establish collaborative norms that recognize the value of individuals of all ranks, genders, racial, and cultural backgrounds as a basis for promoting team cohesion and innovation.

At institutional levels, it's very important that credit for obtaining extramural funding for team-based research is equitably shared among co-investigators on the project. NIH for example now recognizes multiple principal investigators equally, rather than allowing for only one lead PI. At UC Irvine, our Vice Chancellor for Research has created a credit-sharing system where scholars listed on multi-investigator and inter-departmental grants are assigned equal credit for obtaining a collaborative grant rather than allocating all of the credit to the lead investigator and his or her department. So those are some additional strategies that can be implemented at organizational and institutional levels to reduce hierarchical circumstances that can sometimes hinder the effectiveness of cross-disciplinary initiatives.

Q: Two chapters in this volume find that certain leadership qualities are central to integrative communication and knowledge production. Mäkinen (2020) emphasizes the ability for leaders to "foster interdependencies" between team members, whereas Salazar and Lant (2020) emphasize the "multidisciplinary breadth of experience" of the leader as an antecedent to fostering interdependencies between team members and units. How might we advance such capacities in current and future leaders of transdisciplinary teams?

As noted above, the values and skills of team leaders have a profound impact on the collaborative dynamics and accomplishments of their teams. Some scholars are adept at leading mono-disciplinary teams and centers but are not as well suited to lead cross-disciplinary research initiatives. Not all scholars aspire to lead cross-disciplinary teams and should not be coaxed into serving as team leaders if they lack the motivation and experience to do so. Some of the interpersonal and intellectual qualities that enable scholars to lead cross-disciplinary teams well are that they bring an inclusive and receptive stance toward different disciplinary perspectives, an intellectual proclivity toward broad-gauged theorizing and research, and the ability to foster collaborative links among team members from diverse fields. So, it's important to recruit prospective leaders of cross-disciplinary teams and centers who possess those qualities, and avoid recruiting individuals for those roles who lack the requisite skills, motivation, and experience to lead their teams effectively.

But the question remains: *what are the best strategies for cultivating team leadership skills that are well matched to the needs of cross-disciplinary teams?* For those scholars who are committed to pursuing integrative, collaborative research, it's important that they have opportunities to gain as much experience as possible participating in academic and university-community partnerships. On-the-job experience as a member and leader of prior teams helps prepare scholars to lead subsequent teams even more effectively. For scholars who are motivated to lead cross-disciplinary teams but have not had extensive prior experience doing so, it's important that they familiarize themselves with the existing literature on team science and cross-disciplinary collaboration. This type of training is valuable at undergraduate, graduate, postdoctoral, and faculty levels. Many universities are beginning to include team science courses (e.g., "Team Science 101' workshops and training modules) within their undergraduate and graduate curricula. In our School of Social Ecology at UC Irvine, team science training is a vital component of the introductory core Graduate Seminar on Social Ecology taken by all first-year Ph.D. students admitted into our departmental degree programs. The *NIH Field Guide to Collaboration and Team Science* (Bennett, Gadlin, & Marchand, 2018), for example, is a required reading for all students taking that course, in which students work collaboratively in cross-departmental teams. Also, many government funding agencies and private foundations require that applicants for large cross-disciplinary projects submit a *collaboration plan* in addition to their research plan (Hall, Crowston, & Vogel, 2014). So, team science training is a crucial asset for aspiring cross-disciplinary team leaders, as well as for all students and faculty members who choose to engage in collaborative integrative research (National Academies of Science Engineering and Medicine, 2015). Scholars who are aware and up-to-speed on the team science literature (as well as management research on the "science of teams") tend to be better informed about how to participate in and lead cross-disciplinary collaborations.

With regard to encouraging cross-disciplinary partnerships among individuals trained in different fields, academic terminology and jargon can exert a strong and sometimes negative effect on collaborative success. The term *team science*, although widely recognized and accepted in academic circles, can be off-putting to scholars in the humanities and arts who do not categorize their scholarship as "scientific" *per se*. So, on our campus when we use the term team science, we add the proviso that we are referring more broadly to *collaborative scholarship* or *collaborative discovery and translation* in order to offset any implied, hierarchical evaluation of STEMM fields over non-STEMM disciplines.

Q: Developing teamwork skills and competencies among scientists are often points of controversy especially when viewed as "soft skills" compared to more discipline specific skills and competencies. Khuri's (2020) "discipline-agnostic approach" to competence in transdisciplinary communication includes monitoring and presenting yourself, practicing communication ethics, adapting to others, practicing effective listening, expressing messages, identifying and explaining fundamental communication processes, and creating and analyzing messages as core competencies that should be considered when developing training programs for transdisciplinary scientists and practitioners. Are these considerations robust enough when mentoring scientists who may not view such competencies as relatable to their own discipline? How might one bolster the importance of these communication competencies to compete with more discipline-specific priorities?

In at least some respects, scholarly teams are more fragile than non-academic teams (e.g., corporate and manufacturing, military, emergency response teams) because academic partnerships are intended to create and integrate new knowledge that leads to scientific advances (National Academies of Science Engineering and Medicine, 2015). The ideational products of scholarly teams are typically more difficult to measure and evaluate than those of non-academic teams whose outcomes can be more directly assessed (e.g., the number of widgets produced per unit of time on an assembly line; corporate profit and loss statements; or speed of response and lives saved by a medical team). Also, the organizational boundaries surrounding academic teams are more fluid or permeable than, say, for corporate departments. Scholars are free agents who often participate in multiple collaborative spheres simultaneously, sometimes extending the knowledge or insights developed by one of their teams to their other research projects. So, the intellectual products produced through academic collaborations are less proprietary or "owned" by a particular scientific team.

The fluidity of science team memberships and the relatively abstract nature of intellectual products make academic partnerships more vulnerable to collaborative uncertainties and tensions, and near-term dissolution, than non-academic teams whose boundaries and products are more clearly defined and vigilantly protected. These features of science teams suggest that scholars who participate in cross-disciplinary collaborations need to be just as adept in so-called "soft" interpersonal skills essential for collaborative effectiveness as they are in the discipline-specific (e.g., theoretical and methodological) competencies required for success in their respective fields. That's why "discipline-agnostic", basic training in team science skills adds tremendous value to cross-disciplinary research teams.

Earlier we discussed the sensemaking and knowledge creation competencies that go hand in hand with interpersonal skills in collaborative settings. The leaders and members of teams are certainly well-advised to nurture communication and empathic social skills needed for effective collaboration, but it's also important that they cultivate idea generation and integrative capacities so crucial for intellectual innovation. Science team members want to feel that they're actually coming up with new ideas. When a research team or center is stagnant and a kind of groupthink sets in, team members' drive for creativity is stifled. It's as if everyone on the team is complacently drinking the same intellectual "Kool Aid"—an experience that can be very enervating for the team as a whole and for its individual members. Scholars' ability to remain open to intellectual ideas from other fields that they may not be familiar with, and their commitment to integrate disparate ideas so that a field of knowledge or practice moves forward in some way – those are really important skills and values that should go hand in hand with the social competencies mentioned by Khuri (2020), especially among scientists engaged in or aspiring to conduct cross-disciplinary research.

There's a lot of emphasis these days on the benefits of "convergence science" (a term, by the way, which is highly overlapping with the notions of cross-disciplinary collaboration and integration) (National Academies of Science Engineering and Medicine, 2014, 2019). But there are certain costs to over-emphasizing convergence at the expense of divergence. Both *divergent thinking* as well as *convergent sensemaking* are needed to achieve scholarly advances bridging multiple fields (Guilford, 1950; Paletz & Schunn, 2010). Science team members should be encouraged to think "out of the box" and, at times, to resist the modal thinking and convergent sensemaking of their teammates. Teams should explicitly allot time for their members to come together to test out their ideas with each other and decide which ones they believe warrant further development. But there needs to be as much emphasis on divergence as there is on convergence – they are two sides of the intellectual innovation "coin". Otherwise, if convergent thinking is over-emphasized by a team, tendencies toward groupthink can arise where all members subscribe to the same model and think along the same lines. Excessive convergence in teams can lead to "conceptual ruts" that undermine intellectual synergy.

Q: What role might advanced digital technologies (e.g., AI, cyberinfrastructures) play in promoting or hindering integrative thinking? For example, Lebow's (2020)

"A Social Machine for Transdisciplinary Research" suggests that AI systems have the potential to promote collaborative sensemaking by offloading some of the cognitive effort needed for integrative thinking onto intelligent machines. At the same time, digital technologies also encourage a balkanization of knowledge, experiences, and worldviews and discourage the cognitive shifts required for integrative thinking and communication. Exposure to multiple realities, views, and experiences through digital technologies increasingly call into question the significance of the so-called "expert" voice. Misinformation, disinformation, and junk news proliferate in this environment. How do you view this tension?

In considering the value of advanced digital technologies such as artificial intelligence (AI) for cross-disciplinary research and collective sensemaking (Frankish & Ramsey, 2014), I would distinguish between at least two forms of AI: (1) *descriptive or diagnostic AI*, and (2) *predictive AI*. In the field of health informatics, for instance, the mining of very large databases and the development of algorithms based on those data are often used to identify and treat specific illnesses and injuries. Examples of these descriptive applications of AI are compiling thousands of patients' electronic health records, ultrasound images as well as CT, MRI, and PET scans to derive algorithmic criteria that can be used to provide faster and more precise diagnoses and treatment plans for future patients. Predictive AI, on the other hand, is sometimes used by epidemiologists and environmental scientists to forecast which sub-groups of a population are most likely to suffer the negative health consequences of future disruptions or other health risks. When attempting to develop reliable forecasts of these anticipated scenarios, various personal, sociodemographic, and geographic risk factors must be integrated in a novel fashion by the research team, whose members are likely to represent diverse fields. For example, in order to predict the future susceptibility of population sub-groups to health risks posed by climate change, disparate data bases related to group members' socioeconomic status, GPS coordinates of their residential locations, and other categories of Geographic Information Systems (GIS) data must be creatively combined.

Both descriptive and predictive forms of AI may involve close coordination among scholars and practitioners representing different fields. However, because descriptive AI involves the mapping of health conditions and diagnostic criteria as they currently exist, as compared to predictive AI which requires the envisioning of future scenarios, the latter is conceptually more challenging—it requires continual reflection and integrative dialogue among collaborators to a greater extent than the former. In a sense, descriptive AI can be most helpful in collaborative research for fast-tracking translational (e.g., diagnostic and therapeutic) solutions to existing, narrowly-targeted, disease-specific problems. Large data base mining and the development of AI algorithms also can contribute to cross-disciplinary predictive science, but they must be continually guided and tempered by the iterative reflections and conceptual insights of team members. So, in those respects, Lebow's (2020) proposed "social machine for transdisciplinary research" may be more directly applicable to descriptive and diagnostic situations, than to predictive modelling collaborations that draw on highly diverse data bases and are inherently more complex.

For both descriptive and predictive AI applications, the derived solutions are only as reliable and valid as the quality of the data on which the algorithms are based. To the extent that data are tainted by false information and unreliable methodology, the quality of the AI solutions based on them can be severely compromised. It's important that cross-disciplinary scholars inclined to use AI methods be aware of their limitations as well as potential for enhancing collective sensemaking about various public health, environmental, and social problems. It's also the case that many complex scientific and societal problems requiring cross-disciplinary analysis are not amenable to data base mining and AI solutions. Scholars must acquire the capacity to distinguish between research topics and settings that can benefit from AI applications and those where AI is more likely to constrain rather than advance innovative sensemaking about the phenomena under study.

Q: Potterbusch and Lotrecchiano (2020) proposed the "Open science framework" to democratize knowledge by lowering financial and other access barriers and reducing copyright restrictions to scientific data and publications. This assertion not only challenges many of the current trends in publication and knowledge translation, but also requires us to consider the broader implications of open access practices (e.g., information flow, accessibility, and the economic infrastructure of knowledge sharing). How might the open science framework contribute to the advancement of transdisciplinary research and collaboration? How might open science impact the way the way we study collaborations?

I do like the idea of open access because it makes knowledge more freely available to more people (c.f., Suber, 2012). Open access also enables a wider diversity of commentators and reactors to weigh in evaluatively on particular studies or reports that are published in scholarly outlets. When scientists' findings remain behind a paywall, many fellow scholars are not able to access them readily—so there's less opportunity to challenge the findings or to strengthen and affirm them by a diverse pool of evaluators. Open access facilitates input on published reports from scholars representing diverse fields and sociodemographic groups. Critical input on scientific findings, methods, and conclusions by diverse expert commentators can help hasten scholarly progress and avoid potentially invalid or unreliable interpretive claims that can arise from narrowly constrained and biased peer reviews.

Collaborative scholars should be encouraged to be as open to as many perspectives as possible. Cross-disciplinary research is inherently consistent with the principle of open access. When knowledge is segmented, siloed, and constrained by gatekeepers, there's a resistance to making that information available to others who may have a very different take on it. So, excessively restricted access to scientific information can certainly undermine the goals of cross-disciplinary research.

Q: Two chapters in this volume address Latin American perspectives on communication in transdisciplinary teams. Medina, Báez, & Méndez (2020) and Vienni Baptista, Goñi Mazzitelli and Ferrigno Came (2020) analyze cases of transdisciplinary collaboration and capacity building in Hispanic-Serving Institutions (HSIs). The former discusses community-based participatory research in Puerto Rico and the latter explores how transdisciplinary research is understood and operationalized in the Uruguayan context. How important is cultural context to the development of theory of communication in transdisciplinary teams? What might the Anglo-European academy learn from the insights of examples like these?

In my book, *Social Ecology in the Digital Age* (Stokols, 2018), I discuss the so-called "4T" competencies for 21st Century education and research: *transdisciplinary, team-based, translational*, and *transcultural* analytic skills. The transcultural aspect of collaborative research has become increasingly salient in recent decades as the Internet has enabled us to work with colleagues located in world regions and time zones that are distant from ours. Nurturing scholars' sensibilities about cultural differences in communication styles, core values, and political affiliations has always been valuable as a basis for enhancing collaboration among team members based in different locations. In the 21st Century Digital Age, cultivating scholars' competence in transcultural teamwork has become even more essential to the success of geographically dispersed teams whose members coordinate with each over the Internet using online multimedia software (Olson & Olson, 2014). Today, it is more important than ever to build transcultural communication training modules into team science curricula and research initiatives. The multicultural composition of a scholarly team can be an extremely valuable source of ideational diversity and, ultimately, a well-spring of collaborative innovation and success.

Q: According to Lotrecchiano and Misra (2020), TD learning has social, cognitive, emotional, and behavioral facets. It involves the process of understanding a question or problem through mental correspondence among group members and personal experience and reflection about objects and situations. What kinds of settings, practices, and systems (educational and institutional) could promote this type of learning? What might be some key characteristics of such settings, practices, and systems?

Cross-disciplinary scholars, especially those involved in translational research projects with community partners, often must traverse not only multiple disciplinary boundaries, but also a variety of non-academic knowledge cultures or epistemologies (Brown, Harris, & Russell, 2010). Examples of these non-academic knowledge cultures include the lived experience of lay citizens and the professional perspectives of government decision-makers, corporate leaders, and environmental practitioners. I refer to this kind of action research as not only cross-disciplinary, but also *trans-epistemic* (Stokols, Hall, & Vogel, 2013). Students of team science can be exposed in a preliminary way to non-academic perspectives through school-based curricula, but a deeper understanding of the differences between academic and non-academic knowledge cultures can best be gained through experiential learning opportunities such as internship placements of team scholars in community settings (e.g., government offices, neighborhood organizations, corporate and health care settings). The ability of team scholars to collaborate across academic and community settings with a diverse array of non-academic partners is widely recognized as an essential pre-requisite for engaging in community-based participatory research projects.

The *Patient Centered Outcomes Research Institute* (PCORI, 2013) in Washington DC exemplifies a trans-epistemic research center that effectively bridges academic and non-academic knowledge cultures by promoting close collaboration between medical patients and researchers in designing and implementing disease treatment and wellness programs. Team science training, ideally, should include experiential learning modules that encourage scholars to work with community partners toward integrating multi-disciplinary and non-academic perspectives on whatever research topics (e.g., public health, environmental design, sustainability science) they're investigating.

Q: Finally, we find ourselves in a world where increasingly unpredictable fluctuation marks every facet of life. Are contemporary modes of science, research, practice, and education responsive to these conditions of rapid and unpredictable socio-environmental and cultural change? What, according to you, would be the broad contours of a transdisciplinary framework for research and practice that could actively participate in creating a positive future?

Humanity today is facing major existential threats posed by climate change and destabilization of the earth system. Successive reports issued by the Intergovernmental Panel on Climate Change (IPCC) warn that we have barely more than 10 years to take actions to avoid the climatic tipping points that would trigger a "hothouse earth" scenario rendering much of the planet uninhabitable for humans and other species (IPCC, 2019; Ripple, Wolf, Newsome, Barnard, & Moomaw, 2019; Steffen et al., 2015; Steffen et al., 2018). The hazards and risks posed by global climate change—including the rapid melting of glacial ice sheets, sea rise, ocean acidification, biodiversity loss, extreme weather events, food insecurity, and violent conflicts over scare resources--are not only "wicked problems" (Rittel & Webber, 1973) due to their having multiple causes that are difficult to control by specific individuals or groups, but also "super wicked" dilemmas (Levin, Cashore, Bernstein, & Auld, 2012) in the sense that time is rapidly running out for finding solutions to them. These environmental dilemmas are exacerbating socioeconomic inequality in the world and the dangers of stumbling into intentional or unintentional nuclear war (Matthew, 2014).

At the same time, the foundations of liberal democracy seem to be eroding in many parts of the world and are being replaced by a populist embrace of authoritarian leaders, nationalism, nativistic, and anti-scientific world views, and violence directed toward ethnic minorities, immigrants, LGBTQ communities, and other vulnerable groups. Adding to those environmental and societal dilemmas, the rapid proliferation of digital technologies and the multifaceted cybersphere they comprise have injected additional chaos into human societies (Stokols, 2018), by providing online platforms for propagating false information and cybercrimes such as identify fraud, data theft, hate speech, incitements to violence, and cyberattacks on civil infrastructures (e.g., voting machines and urban power grids). The early

21st century is fraught with great anxiety and normlessness, driven by massive environmental and sociopolitical disruption (Clayton, Manning, Krygsman, & Speiser, 2017; Leiserowitz et al., 2018)—exemplifying what sociologist Emile Durkheim (1951) described as *anomie*—a condition of society in which people become unmoored from moral precepts and political norms. And, for the first time in human history, we're having to contemplate the very real prospect of our collective extinction, along with the loss of millions of other species comprising the earth's biosphere, on which our survival and well-being depend.

In the context of these enormous ecological and societal crises, cross-disciplinary collaboration among scholars and community partners is absolutely crucial. Multiscale ecological analyses of environmental and social problems are well-suited to addressing the complex wicked and super-wicked crises we're now confronting in the 21st Century. An inherent feature of social ecological frameworks for understanding and managing complex adaptive systems is broad-gauged cross-disciplinary research that draws on the analytic perspectives of multiple fields and non-academic knowledge bases as well (Stokols, 2018). Cross-disciplinary collaboration and comprehensive analyses of complex problems are essential for countering anti-scientific and nativist ideologies rampant in many countries today (for example, the derogation of climate science by the current U.S. Administration; and its repeal of life-saving and environmentally protective regulations such as the *U.S. Clean Air* and *Clean Water Acts* (US Environmental Protection Agency, 2011, 1997). Broad, inclusive, integrative research and evidence-based policies serve, in effect, as *antidotes* to narrow-minded, ideologically driven world views.

Consider, for example, the nationalistic trend in the U.S. and elsewhere toward excluding asylum seekers and immigrants from other countries. These nativistic tendencies are directly opposed to the value of diversity as a basis for societal innovation and progress. Yet, although diversity is devalued on ideological grounds by nationalistic governments, the adaptive benefits of diversity at individual, species, and ecosystem levels are empirically grounded. For individuals, the diversity of their knowledge, skills, and abilities broadens their capacity to adapt to rapidly changing environments. Also, the diversity of a species' gene pool increases the likelihood that the species will continue to survive and thrive in the face of sudden environmental perturbations. And at the ecosystem level, where multiple species share a common terrestrial or aquatic region, the resilience of each species is substantially diminished when one or a few other species sharing the environment can no longer survive. This is especially true for anchor species, such as phytoplankton in a marine ecosystem, whose demise (e.g., due to ocean acidification) can threaten the stability and survival of many other species inhabiting the region, all of whom are strongly dependent on each other for their mutual existence. So, the adaptive value of diversity at individual, species, and ecosystem levels is rooted in empirical facts and cannot be dismissed on ideological grounds for being politically incorrect (Stokols, 2019).

The fact that diversity, integrative thinking, and collaboration are core values of cross-disciplinary research underscores the tremendous value of team science as a basis for comprehending and ameliorating some of the most daunting dilemmas of the 21st Century. Only through broad-gauged thinking and inter-sectoral collaboration can we hope to understand and manage today's complex environmental and societal challenges. And, only by remediating those problems can we begin to re-stabilize the planet and ensure the survival of the biosphere. With those considerations in mind, a strong case can be made for the *moral imperative* of engaging in cross-disciplinary scholarship and community practice as a basis for reducing human pain, suffering, and planetary disruption caused by climate change, socioeconomic inequality, cyber chaos, and unmitigated violence and war.

Because the ecological and societal challenges we're facing are time-urgent and call for a variety of adaptive and mitigation strategies, many scholars are directing a greater proportion of their scholarly efforts toward *use-inspired* (or translational) research and away from purely *discovery-oriented* scholarship (Bush, 1945). There must always be room for basic discovery science as well as more applied forms of action-research. However, the time-urgency of solving or at least reducing contemporary existential crises is prompting more and more scholars to become involved in translational partnerships with fellow scholars and community stakeholders. So, we often must make normative decisions about which problems to study, and which to put aside for the time being. All this suggests that team science curricula and training modules should strive to nurture scholars' ethical decision-making and *normative competence*. As Arnim Wiek and colleagues (Wiek, Withycombe, & Redman, 2011) contend, normative competence is an essential facet of translational research and a prerequisite for training sustainability scientists who continually must grapple with moral decisions about which problems to study among many possible research foci; and how their findings can be most usefully applied toward the development of ameliorative interventions and policies. Explicit consideration of normative concerns (about issues of morality, ethics, and values) should be a central feature of cross-disciplinary team science and training.

Conclusions and Emerging Directions for Research on Communication in Cross-Disciplinary Teams

One promising line of research concerns the **design of contexts that promote convergent and divergent thinking in collaborative settings**. For example, at the group-level, what kinds of leadership styles, interpersonal and intellectual skills would be needed to encourage synergy and sensemaking along with 'out of the box thinking' that challenges the groupthink and conceptual ruts that teams sometimes are prone to? Further, what is the balance between these two types of thinking in collaborative knowledge producing teams? And, are particular reasoning and communication styles and processes better suited to certain stages of the collaborative initiative? For example, during the *initial stages of a collaboration*, one might benefit from divergent thinking when problems are scoped out, collaborative partners are identified, and ideas for future research directions are generated. At the *integrative and synthesis stages* of a project, there may be more value in finding points of overlap between divergent perspectives to generate common ground. What specific idea generation and synthesis tools can be used across collaborative contexts? At the organizational and institutional levels, what kinds of structures – physical, virtual or technological, organizational, and institutional – can support collaborative sensemaking, divergent thinking, and collective knowledge creation? We need large-scale, rigorous and systematic studies of the internal mechanisms to support cross-disciplinary collaboration, communication, and cross-fertilization of ideas to generate fundamental principles and policies that encourage transdisciplinary innovation.

Second and relatedly, *cultivating diversity* (cultural, racial, ethnic, religious, age, gender, sexual orientation, socio-economic status, and political orientation along with disciplinary and professional diversity) *and an inclusive climate are critical to convergent and divergent thinking.* Much of the present discourse on cross-disciplinary endeavors fails to include the different types of diversity that such climates demand. For instance, it is sometimes assumed that sociodemographic diversity of team composition is secondary to the more dominant disciplinary diversity of knowledge, skills, and abilities (KSA's) that dominate the literature. Relatively little attention has been paid to how collaborative projects can support and encourage diversity and inclusiveness. For example, *what organizational and institutional policies and norms are needed not only to build and sustain diverse teams but also ensure they are successful and effective over time*? Topics within this domain include addressing unconscious biases and increasing self-awareness among members of the dominant group through training programs and tutorials as well as meaningful interactions with diverse groups; specific requirements for diversity within collaborative initiatives mandated by funding agencies or institutions; and formalizing communication norms that engender an inclusive climate.

Third, it is widely recognized that *developing leadership and collaborative skills and competencies along with discipline-specific knowledge are critical to the success of transdisciplinary initiatives* and for fostering a culture of life long, adaptive learning. However, not much is known about the specific ways these skills and competencies can be nurtured within the constraints of educational settings, other curricular needs and requirements, and scientists' own biases about the value of these skills. Furthermore, we often view such learning interventions as critical in the developmental stages of scholars and scientists without considering what interventions need to continue to be employed over the lifecycle of collaborative projects. In addition, if we take seriously the contributions of more than those whose roles solely exist to create knowledge without also including the wide diversity of other stakeholders, the development of collaborators who embody the type of diversity we suggest here is reserved solely for scholars embedded in the scientific world, with little consideration of those whose contributions to science are as consumers, problem-bearers, and advocates. This volume and other work in this area have addressed questions concerning the particular intellectual, interpersonal, and behavioral competencies needed for cross-disciplinary collaborative work. But more nuanced studies are needed to understand the relative impacts of particular skills and competencies at different stages of one's scholarly career. For example, should general teamwork / collaborative skills be a required part of the K-12 curricula along with more traditional subjects like mathematics and science, thereby making it a fundamental part of basic education? Whereas general collaborative/teamwork skills are a part of many elementary and high school curricula in the US, students often do not receive systematic instruction on collaborative skills and competencies. Would this type of approach address some of the impediments to collaborative scholarship at the undergraduate and postgraduate levels? Another question to consider is the specific foci of collaborative skills and competencies at different educational/developmental stages. For example, how might educators balance the need for disciplinary knowledge with inter- and transdisciplinary integrative knowledge, competencies, and skills at different stages of a scholar or professional's career? Yet another question that would benefit from research is the particular pedagogic tools that would encourage trans-epistemic thinking and research. Could experiential learning in community and professional settings, exposure to meaningful cross-cultural experiences, and long-term cross-disciplinary and cross-cultural collaborative relationships over the course of one's undergraduate or postgraduate career enhance an individual's trans-epistemic orientation?

Finally, intelligent machines are likely to play a significant role in the collaborative ventures of the future. They already do in so many more ways than they did only ten years ago. Ethical and moral questions in this scenario are: *What role should AI technologies play in collaborative efforts? How might AI enhance or disable human interactions, and what dimensions of collaboration are solely and indelibly human and unable to be replicated through AI?* Considering there is widespread evidence that AI algorithms, facial recognition, machine learning, and other automated systems are susceptible to deep-seated biases that reflect and amplify societal inequalities (Devlin, 2017; Paul, 2019), scholars need to critically consider, evaluate and discern research topics that can benefit from AI. Education about *AI ethics, including ethical decision-making and normative competence,* should be a fundamental part of scientific and professional training.

As noted above, the prospects for our world are deeply troubling given the global environmental and political crises we are facing. More than ever before collaborative research that is firmly rooted in principles of diversity, inclusiveness, and ethical thinking and decision-making are needed to counter and reverse current global trends. The wicked problems we face at this time in the 21st century will require new and more advanced communications within the transdisciplinary teams that are striving to solve some of the dilemmas that challenge humans and the worlds we live in. We hope that this volume will spur creative and rigorous research on the topics outlined above and, further, contribute toward creating a more hopeful and positive future.

References

Bennett, L. M., Gadlin, H., & Marchand, C. (2018). *Collaboration and team science field guide* (2nd ed.). Bethesda, MD: National Cancer Institute. Available at https://www.cancer.gov/about-nci/organization/crs/research-initiatives/team-science-field-guide

Brown, V. A., Harris, J. A., & Russell, J. Y. (Eds.). (2010). *Tackling wicked problems through the transdisciplinary imagination*. London, UK: Earthscan.

Bush, V. (1945). Science, the endless frontier: A report to the President. US Government Printing Office. Available at https://www.nsf.gov/od/lpa/nsf50/vbush1945.htm

Clayton, S., Manning, C. M., Krygsman, K., & Speiser, M. (2017). *Mental health and our changing climate: Impacts, implications, and guidance*. Washington, DC: American Psychological Association and eco-America. Available at https://www.apa.org/images/mental-health-climate_tcm7-215704.pdf

Devlin, H. (2017, 13 April). AI programs exhibit racial and gender biases, research reveals. *The Guardian*. Retrieved from https://www.theguardian.com/technology/2017/apr/13/ai-programs-exhibit-racist-and-sexist-biases-research-reveals

Durkheim, E. (1951). *Suicide: A study in sociology*. New York: The Free Press.

Frankish, K., & Ramsey, W. M. (2014). *The Cambridge handbook of artificial intelligence*. Cambridge, UK: Cambridge University Press.

Gray, B. (2008). Enhancing transdisciplinary research through collaborative leadership. *American Journal of Preventive Medicine, 35*(2), S124-S132.

Gray, D. O. (2008). Making team science better: Applying improvement-oriented evaluation principles to evaluation of cooperative research centers. *New Directions for Evaluation, 118*, 73-87. https://doi.org/10.1002/ev.262

Guilford, J. P. (1950). Creativity. *American Psychologist, 5*, 444-454.

Hall, K. H., Crowston, K., & Vogel, A. (2014). *How to write a collaboration plan*. National Cancer Institute Team Science Toolkit. Available at https://www.teamsciencetoolkit.cancer.gov/Public/TSResourceBiblio.aspx?tid=3&rid=3119

Hall, K. L., Stokols, D., Moser, R. P., Taylor, B. K., Thornquist, M. D., Nebeling, L. C., . . . Berger, N. A. (2008). The collaboration readiness of transdisciplinary research teams and centers: Findings from the National Cancer Institute's TREC year-one evaluation study. *American Journal of Preventive Medicine, 35*(2), S161-S172.

IPCC. (2019). *IPCC special report on climate change and land*. Retrieved from Geneva, Switzerland: https://www.ipcc.ch/report/srccl/

Khuri, S. (2020). A multifaceted discipline-agnostic approach to training transdisciplinary teams in communication. In G. R. Lotrecchiano & S. Misra (Eds), *Communication in transdisciplinary teams* (pp. 293-308). Santa Rosa, CA: Informing Science Press.

Laursen, B. (2020). What is collaborative, interdisciplinary reasoning? The heart of interdisciplinary team research. In G. R. Lotrecchiano & S. Misra (Eds), *Communication in transdisciplinary teams* (pp. 55-89). Santa Rosa, CA: Informing Science Press.

Lebow, D. G. (2020). A social machine for transdisciplinary research. In G. R. Lotrecchiano & S. Misra (Eds), *Communication in transdisciplinary teams* (pp. 203-226). Santa Rosa, CA: Informing Science Press.

Leiserowitz, A., Maibach, E., Rosenthal, S., Kotcher, J., Ballew, M., Goldberg, M., & Gufstafson, A. (2018). *Climate change in the American mind: December 2018*. Yale Project on

Climate Change Communication (Yale University and George Mason University), New Haven, CT. Available at https://climatecommunication.yale.edu/wp-content/uploads/2019/01/Climate-Change-American-Mind-December-2018.pdf

Levin, K., Cashore, B., Bernstein, S., & Auld, G. (2012). Overcoming the tragedy of super wicked problems: Constraining our future selves to ameliorate global climate change. *Policy Sciences, 45*(2), 123-152.

Lotrecchiano, G. R., & Misra, S. (2020). Transdisciplinary knowledge producing teams: Team processes, knowledge, skills, and competencies. In G. R. Lotrecchiano & S. Misra (Eds), *Communication in transdisciplinary teams* (pp. 19-54). Santa Rosa CA: Informing Science Press.

Mäkinen, E. I. (2020). Complexity leadership theory and the leaders of transdisciplinary science. In G. R. Lotrecchiano & S. Misra (Eds), *Communication in transdisciplinary teams* (pp. 123-147). Santa Rosa,CA: Informing Science Press.

Matthew, R. A. (2014). Climate change and human security. In J. F. C. DiMento & P. Doughman (Eds.), *Climate change: What it means for us, our children, and our grandchildren* (pp. 257-294). Cambridge, MA: MIT Press.

Medina, N. G., Báez, L. S., & Mendez, L. B. (2020). Collaborative transdisciplinary research in a small institution: Challenges and opportunities. In G. R. Lotrecchiano & S. Misra (Eds), *Communication in transdisciplinary teams* (pp. 227-251). Santa Rosa, CA: Informing Science Press.

National Academies of Science Engineering and Medicine (Ed.). (2014). *Convergence - Facilitating transdisciplinary integration of life sciences, physical sciences, engineering, and beyond.* Washington, DC: National Academies Press. Available at https://ciret-transdisciplinarity.org/quoideneuf/NSF_Report_on_TD.pdf

National Academies of Science Engineering and Medicine (Ed.). (2015). *Enhancing the effectiveness of team science.* Washington, DC: National Academies Press. http://sites.nationalacademies.org/DBASSE/BBCSS/Enhancing_Effectiveness_of_Team_Science/index.htm.

National Academies of Science Engineering and Medicine (Ed.). (2019). *Fostering the culture of convergence in research: Proceedings of a workshop.* Washington, DC: National Academies Press. Available at https://www.nap.edu/catalog/25271/fostering-the-culture-of-convergence-in-research-proceedings-of-a

Olson, J. S., & Olson, G. M. (2014). *Working together apart: Collaboration over the Internet.* San Rafael, CA: Morgan & Claypool Publisher.

Paletz, S., & Schunn, C. D. (2010). A social-cognitive framework of multidisciplinary team innovation. *Topics in Cognitive Science, 2*(1), 73-95.

Paul, K. (2019, 16 April). 'Disastrous' lack of diversity in AI industry perpetuates bias, study finds. *The Guardian.* Retrieved from https://www.theguardian.com/technology/2019/apr/16/artificial-intelligence-lack-diversity-new-york-university-study

Paulus, P. B., & Nijstad, B. A. (2019). *The Oxford handbook of group creativity and innovation.* Oxford, UK: Oxford University Press.

PCORI. (2013). *Patient-Centered Outcomes Research Institute.* http://www.pcori.org/

Potterbusch, M., & Lotrecchiano, G. R. (2020). Shifting paradigms in information flow: An open science framework (OSF) for knowledge sharing teams. In G. R. Lotrecchiano & S. Misra (Eds), *Communication in transdisciplinary teams* (pp. 177-202). Santa Rosa, CA: Informing Science Press.

Ripple, W. J., Wolf, C., Newsome, T. M., Barnard, P., & Moomaw, W. R. (2019). World scientists' warming of a climate emergency. *Bioscience Magazine, 69.* https://doi.org/10.1093/biosci/biz088

Rittel, H. W. J., & Webber, M. M. (1973). Dilemmas in a general theory of planning. *Policy Sciences, 4*(2), 155-169.

Salazar, M. R., & Lant, T. K. (2020). Facilitating innovation in interdisciplinary teams: The role of leaders and integrative communication. In G. R. Lotrecchiano & S. Misra (Eds), *Communication in transdisciplinary teams* (pp. 149-175). Santa Rosa, CA: Informing Science Press.

Steffen, W., Richardson, K., Rockstrom, J., Cornell, S. E., Fetzer, I., Bennett, E. M., . . . Sorlin, S. (2015). Planetary boundaries: Guiding human development on a changing planet. *Science, 347*(6223), 1259855. https://doi.org/10.1126/science.1259855

Steffen, W., Rockström, J., Richardson, K., Lenton, T. M., Folke, C., Liverman, D., . . . Crucifix, M. (2018). Trajectories of the earth system in the anthropocene. *Proceedings of the National Academy of Sciences, 115*(33), 8252-8259.

Stokols, D. (1992). Establishing and maintaining healthy environments: Toward a social ecology of health promotion. *American Psychologist, 47*, 6-22.

Stokols, D. (1996). Translating social ecological theory into guidelines for community health promotion. *American Journal of Health Promotion, 10*, 282-298.

Stokols, D. (2006). Toward a science of transdisciplinary action research. *American Journal of Community Psychology, 38*(1), 63-77.

Stokols, D. (2018). *Social ecology in the digital age: Solving complex problems in a globalized world.* London, UK: Academic Press.

Stokols, D. (2019). *What matters to me and why: Interview on diversity and inclusive excellence.* University of California, Irvine. Available at https://www.youtube.com/watch?v=At3ig1lHGRU&feature=youtu.be ,

Stokols, D., Fuqua, J., Gress, J., Harvey, R., Phillips, K., Baezconde-Garbanati, L., . . . Trochim, W. (2003). Evaluating transdisciplinary science. *Nicotine & Tobacco Research, 5*(Suppl 1), S21-S39.

Stokols, D., Hall, K., & Vogel, A. (2013). Transdisciplinary public health: Core characteristics, definitions, and strategies for success. In D. Haire-Joshu & T. D. McBride (Eds.), *Transdisciplinary public health: Research, methods, and practice* (pp. 3-30). San Francisco, CA: Jossey-Bass Publishers.

Stokols, D., Hall, K. L., Taylor, B., & Moser, R. P. (2008). The science of team science: Overview of the field and introduction to the supplement. *American Journal of Preventive Medicine, 35*(2), S77-S89.

Stokols, D., Harvey, R., Gress, J., Fuqua, J., & Phillips, K. (2005). In vivo studies of transdisciplinary scientific collaboration: Lessons learned and implications for active living research. *American Journal of Preventive Medicine, 28*(2S2), 202-213.

Stokols, D., Olson, G. M., Salazar, M., & Olson, J. S. (2019). Strengthening the ecosystem for effective team science: A case study from the University of California, Irvine, USA. *Integration and Implentation Insights.* Available at https://i2insights.org/2019/02/19/team-science-ecosystem

Stokols, D., Salazar, M., Olson, G. M., & Olson, J. S. (2019). Idea tree: A tool for brainstorming ideas in cross-disciplinary teams. *Integration and Implentation Insights.* Available at https://i2insights.org/2019/03/12/idea-tree-brainstorming-tool/

Suber, P. (2012). *Open access.* Cambridge, MA: MIT Press. Available at https://cyber.harvard.edu/hoap/Open_Access_(the_book)

Trivedi, C., & Misra, S. (2020). Communicative processes in trans-sector transdisciplinary collaborations. In G. R. Lotrecchiano & S. Misra (Eds), *Communication in transdisciplinary teams* (pp. 91-121). Santa Rosa, CA: Informing Science Press.

UCI Office of Academic Personnel. (2019). *Identifying faculty contributions to collaborative scholarship.* Available at https://ap.uci.edu/faculty/guidance/CollaborativeScholarship/

US Environmental Protection Agency. (1997, October). *The benefits and costs of the Clean Air Act, 1970-1990.* Retrieved from Washington, DC:

US Environmental Protection Agency. (2011, March 1). *The benefits and costs of the Clean Air Act, 1990-2020, The second prospective study.* Retrieved from https://www.epa.gov/clean-air-act-overview/benefits-and-costs-clean-air-act-1990-2020-second-prospective-study

Vienni Baptista, B., Goñi Mazzitelli, M., & Ferrigno Came, F. (2020). Transdisciplinary communication in research teams: Institutional constructs and practices from a Uruguayan perspective. In G. R. Lotrecchiano & S. Misra (Eds), *Communication in transdisciplinary teams* (pp. 253-291). Santa Rosa, CA: Informing Science Press.

Wiek, A., Withycombe, L., & Redman, C. L. (2011). Key competencies in sustainability: A reference framework for academic program development. *Sustainability Science, 6,* 203-218.

Gaetano R. Lotrecchiano & Shalini Misra (Editors). 2020
Communication in Transdisciplinary Teams
Santa Rosa, CA: Informing Science Press

Editor Information

Gaetano R. Lotrecchiano in an associate professor at the George Washington University School of Medicine and Health Sciences, Washington, DC USA where he is the Associate Dean of Innovative and Colloborartive Pedagogy and Director of Doctoral Candidacy in the PhD in Translational Health Sciences Program. Dr. Lotrecchiano's work is grounded in the field of team science and transdisciplinary theory and education. He is the principal investigator of the Motivation Assessment for Team Readiness Integration and Collaboration (MATRICx). Professor Lotrecchiano is the founding Vice President of the International Society for Systems and Complexity Science for Health (2018-2019) and the President of the International Network for the Science of Team Science (2019-2020). He is the convener of the GW program entitled Creating a Culture of Collaboration at GWU. Dr. Lotrecchiano has a Ph.D in Ethnomusicology from the University of Maryland, College Park, an Ed.D. in Human and Organizational Learning from the George Washington University, an M.A. in Liturgical Studies from the Catholic University of America, Washington, DC, and B.S. in Music Education from West Chester University.

Shalini Misra is an Associate Professor in the School of Public and International Affairs at Virginia Tech. Her research focuses on the social, psychological, and cultural implications of the Internet and mobile communication technologies; and the study of the processes and outcomes of transdisciplinary collaborative scientific, training, and action research initiatives. Key themes in her research and writing include: cognitive and health consequences of information overload and multitasking; interpersonal relationships in ubiquitous computing environments; environmental orientations, identity and sense of community in the Digital Age; contextual influences on interdisciplinary collaboration; interdisciplinary education and curriculum development; and evaluation of team science initiatives. Her research has been supported by grants from NSF, NIH, Urban Communication Foundation, Intel Digital Cultures, and the National Academies Keck Futures Initiative. She serves on the Board of Directors of the International Network of the Science of Team Science (INSciTS). She has a Ph.D. in Planning, Policy, and Design from University of California Irvine, an M.S. in Sustainable Resource Management (Technical University of Munich, Germany) and a B.S. in Civil Engineering (Gujarat University, India).

Special Contributors

Julie Thompson Klein is Professor of Humanities Emerita in the English Department at Wayne State University and an Affiliate of the TdLab at the ETH-Zurich university for science and technology in Switzerland. Klein is past president of AIS and former editor of Issues in Interdisciplinary Studies. Her books include Interdisciplinarity (1990), Interdisciplinary Studies Today (co-edited 1994), Crossing Boundaries (1996), Transdisciplinarity (co-edited 2001), Interdisciplinary Education in K-12 and College (edited 2002), Mapping Interdisciplinary Studies (1999), Humanities, Culture, and Interdisciplinarity (2005), Creating Interdisciplinary Campus Cultures (2010), and Interdisciplining Digital Humanities (2015). She was also Associate Editor of The Oxford Handbook on Interdisciplinarity (2010, 2017). Klein has received numerous honors, including the Kenneth Boulding Award for outstanding scholarship on interdisciplinarity. Klein consults on interdisciplinary programs throughout North America. She has also served on task forces of the National Institutes of Health, National Science Foundation, and National Academies of Science, and is on board of the International Network for the Science of Team Science and HASTAC (Humanities, Arts, Science, and Technology Alliance and Collaboratory), Klein is active internationally as well. In 1978-79 she was Visiting Foreign Professor in Japan; in 1987, a Fulbright Lecturer in Nepal, and, in 1995, a Foundation Visitor at the University of Auckland.

Daniel Stokols is Research Professor and Chancellor's Professor Emeritus at the University of California, Irvine. His research focuses on people's transactions with their social and physical environments, and how those affect personal and public health, social behavior, and ecological sustainability. Professor Stokols' scholarship spans the fields of social ecology, environmental psychology, the science of team science, and transdisciplinary public health. He served as Director of the Social Ecology Program in 1988-92 and as Founding Dean of the School of Social Ecology at UCI from 1992-98. His faculty appointment at UCI is in Psychological Science and Urban Planning and Public Policy in the School of Social Ecology. He also holds an appointments in Public Health and UCI's Institute for Clinical and Translational Science in the College of Health Sciences. Professor Stokols co-authored *Behavior, Health, and Environmental Stress*, edited *Perspectives on Environment and Behavior*, and co-edited the *Handbook of Environmental Psychology, Environmental Simulation,* and *Promoting Human Wellness*. His most recent book, *Social Ecology in the Digital Age*, was published by Academic Press in 2018. Stokols has served as a team science consultant to the National Cancer Institute, Division of Cancer Control and Population Sciences and the National Academies Keck Futures Initiative (NAKFI). He is co-author of the National Academy of Sciences report on *Enhancing the Effectiveness of Team Science* (2015).

Author Information

Loggina S. Báez is the School Liaison of the Project *Effects of Air Pollutants in Respiratory Health and Cognition of Puerto Rican Children* (1R15MD01201-1) at Universidad Ana G. Méndez, Carolina Campus (formerly known as Universidad del Este). She has taught courses in the Graduate Program of Clinical Social Work at the same institution. Dr. Báez has a background in Academic-Research Psychology, with specific training in school contexts research, community work, Transdisciplinary and Community Based Participatory (CBPR). She has coordinated the VIAS Health Disparity Network (RIMI grant), Violence and Asthma Minority Research Network (*VIAS Project* - NIH-NIMHD) at UAGM, and also coordinated a NIMH R24 that offered support to faculty and advanced graduate students interested in mental health and HIV/AIDS at the University of Puerto Rico, Río Piedras Campus. She received a Ph.D. in Psychology from University of Puerto Rico, Río Piedras in 2010. Her research interests are: CBPR, Transdisciplinary Science, Cognitive Psychology, Sport Psychology and Neuropsychology.

Florencia Ferrigno Came was trained as a sociologist at the Universidad de la República (Uruguay). Currently, she is an Assistant at the Unidad de Extensión y Actividades en el Medio at the Facultad de Ciencias Sociales (Universidad de la República, Uruguay). Her main research interests include knowledge production processes and learning processes in "Integral Spaces". She is Co-Principal Investigator on the project entitled "The production of interdisciplinary knowledge in UdelaR: modalities, integration and evaluation processes", funded by the Comisión Sectorial de Investigación Científica (Central Commission of Scientific Research) of UdelaR between 2017 and 2019.

María Goñi Mazzitelli was trained as a sociologist at the Universidad de la República (Uruguay), where she obtained her Masters in Science, Technology and Society. Currently, she is an Assistant at the Comisión Sectorial de Investigación Científica (Universidad de la República, Uruguay). She is Co-PI on the project entitled "The production of interdisciplinary knowledge in UdelaR: modalities, integration and evaluation processes", funded by the Comisión Sectorial de Investigación Científica (Central Commission of Scientific Research) of UdelaR between 2017 and 2019.

Sawsan Khuri is a Lecturer in Biomedical Sciences at the University of Exeter College of Medicine and Health, with a focus on team science and science communication. She is also the executive director of Collaborative Capacities, a professional services company specialized in the design and facilitation of meetings and events that energize, enlighten and enable innovation through collaboration.

Theresa Lant is Professor of Management and Academic Director of Arts and Entertainment Management at Pace University. She received her Ph.D. from Stanford University in 1987. Dr. Lant is an internationally recognized scholar for her research on learning and adaptation in teams and organizations. Her current work explores cognition and learning processes in interdisciplinary teams, with a focus on team leadership and innovation in medical research. Dr. Lant's research has been recognized by a *National Science Foundation* grant to study and train interdisciplinary medical research teams. She has served in a variety of leadership roles in the Academy of Management and the INFORMS College on Organization Science. Her publications have appeared in *Clinical and Translational Science, Small Group Research, Group and Organization Management, Journal of Economic Behavior and Organization, Journal of Management, Management Science, Organization Science,* and *Strategic Management Journal.*

Bethany Laursen is an integration & implementation specialist, finishing an M.A. in Philosophy and a Ph.D. in Community Sustainability at Michigan State University. She previously received a B.S. in Biological Science with a minor in Chemistry from Biola University, and an M.S. in Environment & Resources and Forestry from UW-Madison. After practicing as an interdisciplinary environmental scholar and educator for 10 years, she switched fields to study theories of interdisciplinarity. She is particularly interested in tools that enhance interdisciplinary reasoning in sustainability studies. She also maintains an evaluation, data visualization, and leadership consultancy.

David Lebow is the inventor of HyLighter and CEO of HyLighter LLC. David received his Ph.D. in Instructional Systems Design from Florida State University in 1995 and has won several national awards for his work in the area of computer-enhanced collaborative learning environments.

Elina I. Mäkinen is an associate professor at Tampere University, Finland, in the Faculty of Management and Business and the New Social Research program. Her research focuses on collaboration among heterogeneous teams, academic entrepreneurship, and transdisciplinary and translational science in medicine and the life sciences. In her research, Dr. Mäkinen relies on qualitative methods and process research approaches. She received her Ph.D. at Stanford University's organization studies doctoral program.

Nilda G. Medina is an Associate Professor at the School of Social and Human Sciences of Universidad Ana G. Méndez (UAGM), Carolina Campus (formerly known as Universidad del Este) in Carolina, Puerto Rico. She holds a PhD in Academic-Research Psychology from the University of Puerto Rico, Rio Piedras Campus and a master's Degree in General Psychology from New York University. From 2011 to 2015 she was a Research Professor in UAGM's Project VIAS-RIMI and is currently Principal Investigator of several research projects, including Project ECO-RED (Effects of air pollutants on respiratory health and cognition of Puerto Rican children - R15MD010201), funded by the National Institute of Minority Health and Health Disparities (NIMHD) of the National Institutes of Health (NIH). Likewise, she has worked as a school psychologist in the public and private sector. Her research interests include neurocognitive development, language development, learning disabilities, school violence and school climate.

Loyda B. Méndez is an Associate Professor in the School of Science and Technology at Universidad Ana G. Méndez (UAGM), Carolina Campus (formerly known as Universidad del Este) in Carolina, Puerto Rico. After completing her Ph.D. in Environmental Toxicology at the University of California, Irvine in 2006, she completed postdoctoral studies in Biochemistry and Aerosol Dosimetry. From 2011 to 2013 she was the Associate Director and Research Specialist of the Air Pollution Health Effects Laboratory at the University of California, Irvine. In 2013, she joined the VIAS Health Disparity Network, which used Transdisciplinary (TD) and Community Based Participatory Research (CBPR) approaches for the Prevention of Asthma and Violence in local elementary schools. Currently, Dr. Méndez is a principal investigator of project ECO-RED, whose goal is to study the effects of traffic-related air pollutants in the respiratory and cognitive health of Puerto Rican children. Her main research interest is to understand the adverse health effects of inhaled toxicants in susceptible populations.

Megan Potterbusch is the data services librarian for George Washington University Libraries and Academic Innovation. She works with faculty and student researchers on data access and research data management and has a particular interest in the theory and practice of open science. Potterbusch received her masters of library and information science from Simmons College, and was a National Digital Stewardship Resident focused on implementing open science and digital stewardship principles through outreach and supporting researchers to explore new multi-function tools and technology. Correspondence concerning this chapter should be addressed to Megan Potterbusch.

Maritza Salazar is an Assistant Professor at the Paul Merage School of Business. She earned her PhD in Management from the Stern School of Business at New York University. Her research is focused on improving the collaboration processes and performance outcomes in knowledge-diverse and culturally diverse teams. Professor Salazar is the recipient of numerous research awards including several major multi-year grants from the National Science Foundation on team science in healthcare and the physical sciences. She has also consulted, advised, or spoken about her team science research at various academic institutions including the National Academies of Science and the National Institutes of Health.

Chitvan Trivedi is an Assistant Professor in Organization and Management Studies at Gettysburg College. He holds a Ph.D. in Social Ecology from the University of California, Irvine. Prior to joining Gettysburg College, he was a postdoctoral scholar at UCI. He also holds Masters degrees in Computer Networks and Business Administration. His research focuses on social entrepreneurship and its relationship to the creation and sustenance of societal change. Specifically, he is interested in the role of systems thinking and collaborative processes in addressing social problems. His research has been supported by the Newkirk Fellowship and the Heather Mills Graduate Fellowship in Human Security at UCI.

Bianca Vienni Baptista was trained as an Anthropologist (Universidad de la República, Uruguay) and obtained her Masters and PhD. at the Universidad de Granada (Spain). Currently, she is a postdoctoral researcher at Transdisciplinarity Lab at the Swiss Federal Institute of Technology (ETH Zurich, Switzerland). In the period 2016-2018, she worked at the Methodology Center at Leuphana University of Lüneburg (Germany). Between 2008 and 2017, she was an Associate Professor at the Academic Department at Espacio Interdisciplinario, Universidad de la República (Uruguay). Her main research interests include science, technology and higher education policy, and inter- and trans-disciplinary knowledge production and institutions. She coordinates and is the Principal Investigator (PI) of the project entitled "The production of interdisciplinary knowledge in UdelaR: modalities, integration and evaluation processes", funded by the Comisión Sectorial de Investigación Científica (Central Commission of Scientific Research) of UdelaR between 2017 and 2019.

Gaetano R. Lotrecchiano & Shalini Misra (Editors). 2020
Communication in Transdisciplinary Teams
Santa Rosa, CA: Informing Science Press

Index

Made in the USA
Middletown, DE
06 August 2021